LOCAL GOVERNMENT
IN CANADA

FOURTH EDITION

McGraw-Hill Ryerson Series in Canadian Politics

General Editor — Paul W. Fox

POLITICS: CANADA, Eighth Edition — Primis
   Paul W. Fox and Graham White
LOCAL GOVERNMENT IN CANADA, Fourth Edition
   C. Richard Tindal and Susan Nobes Tindal
POLITICAL PARTIES, LEADERS, AND IDEOLOGIES IN CANADA
   Colin Campbell and William Christian
THE REVISED CANADIAN CONSTITUTION: POLITICS AS LAW
   R. I. Cheffins and P. A. Johnson
FEDERAL CONDITIONS IN CANADA
   D. V. Smiley
THE JUDICIARY IN CANADA: THE THIRD BRANCH OF GOVERNMENT
   Peter H. Russell
POLITICS AND THE MEDIA IN CANADA, Second Edition
   Arthur Siegel

Also available

CANADIAN GOVERNMENT AND POLITICS: INSTITUTIONS
AND PROCESSES
   Michael S. Whittington and Richard J. Van Loon
POLITICAL IDEOLOGIES: TOWARDS THE TWENTY-FIRST CENTURY
   Roger Gibbins and Loleen Youngman

LOCAL GOVERNMENT
IN CANADA

FOURTH EDITION

C. RICHARD TINDAL

SUSAN NOBES TINDAL

McGRAW-HILL RYERSON LIMITED

Toronto Montreal New York Auckland Bogotá
Caracas Lisbon London Madrid Mexico Milan
New Delhi Paris San Juan Singapore Sydney Tokyo

LOCAL GOVERNMENT IN CANADA
Fourth Edition

ISBN: 0-07-551874-0

2 3 4 5 6 7 8 9 10 BBM 4 3 2 1 0 9 8 7 6 5

Printed and bound in Canada

Sponsoring Editor: Anne Louise Currie
Supervising Editor: Margaret Henderson
Developmental Editor: Norma Christensen
Production Editor: Kate Forster
Production Coordinator: Nicla Dattolico
Cover Design: Dianna Little
Cover Photo: V.Wilkinson/VALAN PHOTOS

Canadian Cataloguing in Publication Data

Tindal, C. R., date—
    Local government in Canada

(McGraw-Hill Ryerson series in Canadian politics)
4th ed.
Includes bibliographical references and index.
ISBN 0-07-551874-0

1. Municipal government – Canada. I. Tindal, S. Nobes, date—   . II. Title. III. Series.

JS1708.T55 1995   352.071   C95-930150-X

About the Authors

Richard (Dick) Tindal has been teaching, researching and writing about local government for more than 25 years. He is Head of the Centre for Government Education & Training at St. Lawrence College, Kingston, responsible for the administration and delivery of a wide range of professional training programs in local government. He is also a Visiting Professor in the School of Policy Studies at Queen's University.

Dick is also President of Tindal Consulting Limited, a firm established in the early 1970s. Its projects have included local government restructuring studies in several areas of Ontario, developing professional training courses and manuals, designing and delivering training seminars across Canada, and facilitating strategic planning exercises.

Susan Tindal is a lawyer and alternate dispute resolution practitioner. She has taught courses in local government and municipal law for two decades and has been involved in a number of the projects of Tindal Consulting Limited. Susan has served on the executive of a number of community organizations and is past chair of the Kingston Local Architectural Advisory Committee and current chair of the Kingston, Frontenac and Lennox & Addington District Health Council.

Table of Contents

Editor's Foreword

It is a pleasure to welcome the fourth edition of *Local Government in Canada*. The Tindals' book has proved to be both a very successful text for students and a valuable information source for general readers.

Each successive edition has built on the strength of its predecessor and extended the book's scope. In this fourth edition the Tindals have not only updated their work and substantially rewritten, rearranged, and supplemented many portions of it but they have given much greater attention to the normative aspect of their subject. While they still describe comprehensively the history, structure, and functioning of local government, they are now much more concerned with its potential and future as a democratic instrument. In their opinions the services side of local government has been overemphasized at the expense of its political nature. By political they do not mean sordid wheeling and dealing. They are referring instead to the opportunity of citizens in a democracy to participate actively in the conduct of their public affairs.

The authors contend that from the beginning municipal governments were created to satisfy two key purposes — to deliver administrative services, such as the provision of roads, water, and sewerage, and to extend democratic aims by enabling citizens to govern themselves more fully. Unfortunately, in their view, the first function has overwhelmed the second, for several compelling reasons. Provincial governments have been eager to unload their service responsibilities — and the taxes that go with them — to municipalities, and local residents were not always eager to pick up the mantle of government if it meant paying more money for the privilege. The British aristocratic tradition, moreover, which was carried over into the colonies and reflected in the power of the elitist courts of quarter sessions, was inimical to the extension of self-government to a myriad of parochial councils. Local governments also lacked a firm, independent, prestigious, legal base since their existence was never enshrined in the constitution the way the provincial and federal regimes were. Judicial interpretation also reduced the power of municipalities, keeping them in tutelage to their provincial masters. When additional responsibilities at the local level were acknowledged, they were often hived off to special purpose boards or commissions. Finally, turn-of-the-century reformers gave local politics a bad name, identifying it with corruption, patronage, inefficiency, and scandal.

Little wonder then that local government has been derided as inferior, or blatantly disregarded, Yet, obviously, this is an important sector of government activity. It provides many of the services that touch people xiv

most intimately and more and more individuals are affected as urbanization increases apace.

This is the nub of the Tindals' argument. If the significance of local government is growing, it is all the more essential that its democratic elements be strengthened. They strongly believe that municipalities can play a major role in redeeming the function of government in our troubled and critical age. They assert that local government should be "reinvented" — meaning rehabilitated — so that it fulfils both its primary roles of providing services and promoting self-government, and they make no bones that in their opinion the latter is more important than the former.

> The service delivery role is (or at least should be) subservient to the political role; services [should be] provided in accordance with the needs and wishes of the local inhabitants.

To achieve this end, they believe that:

> ... a different conception of municipal government is needed, one which sees the municipality as an extension of the community, as the community governing itself.

Municipalities should be given the power of general competence, such as is enjoyed by many West European cities, "the right to take any action on behalf of its local community, that is not specifically barred to it." They also should be accorded some form of constitutional recognition, perhaps by provinces in their fundamental documents. The cities themselves should be more assertive in their actions, in strategic planning, for instance, or in becoming more entrepreneurial, rather than passively accepting the role of merely supplying services. In short, they should be "steering not rowing." But above all, they must be more concerned with involving the community in its own governance.

This is a very brief and inadequate summary of the extensive and lively discussion in which the Tindals engage in their final chapter. It is wideranging, knowledgeable, creative, and stimulating — a fitting conclusion to the authors' informative description of local government that they have provided in the earlier chapters.

By voicing their views on what should be done to improve local government while retaining a thorough explanation of how the institution functions throughout Canada, the Tindals have improved the fourth edition immensely.

Victoria College
University of Toronto
October, 1994

Paul W. Fox
General Editor

Preface to the Fourth Edition

This edition retains an examination of the evolving structure of local government in Canada and the political process through which that structure operates. A major addition is the presentation of a series of suggestions for reinventing municipal government to face the challenges of the 21st century. The ingredients in this new turn of the century reform movement are drawn from the lessons of history and from numerous present-day examples of actions being taken by progressive municipalities.

For reviewing all or parts of this manuscript and for offering suggestions for its improvement, we are grateful to David Cameron of Dalhousie University, Terrence Downey of the University of Waterloo, Paul Kellogg of Ryerson Polytechnic University, Christopher Leo of the University of Winnipeg, Warren Magnusson of the University of Victoria, Paul Tennant of the University of British Columbia, and especially Jon Caulfield of York University. As with all previous editions, Paul Fox read the entire manuscript and provided guidance and encouragement.

Helpful information was provided by many others including George Betts of the University of New Brunswick (retired), Lowell Boyle of the New Brunswick Department of Municipalities, Culture & Housing, Anna Burtnyk of the Alberta Ministry of Municipal Affairs, Martin Corbett of the Maritime Municipal Training & Development Board, Lisa Doyle-MacBain, Executive Director of the Federation of Prince Edward Island Municipalities, Shingai Nyajeka of the Department of Municipal Affairs in Nova Scotia, Andrew Sancton of the University of Western Ontario, and Ken Simpson, Executive Director of the Union of Nova Scotia Municipalities.

We are indebted to the staff at McGraw-Hill Ryerson Limited, including Susan Calvert, Norma Christensen, Margaret Henderson and, most especially, Anne Louise Currie, for their cooperation and support.

When the second edition of this text was published in 1984, it was typeset from diskettes produced on our computer — a first for the publisher at that time. This edition has been prepared from a "camera-ready" copy which we supplied to the publisher. The big advantage of this approach is the much faster turnaround between completion of the writing and publication of the text. Because of this approach, however, we must accept responsibility not only for any deficiencies in the content of this text but also for any shortcomings in its layout and physical appearance.

Richard and Susan Tindal,
Inverary, Ontario
December, 1994

CHAPTER 1

Introduction and Overview

OBJECTIVES:

1. To introduce the local government system in Canada, distinguishing between municipalities and other local governing bodies.

2. To examine the roles of municipal governments, with particular reference to their unfulfilled political role.

3. To preview the case for the reinvention of municipal government to meet the challenges of the 21st century.

4. To outline the approach and organization of the text.

Canada's local governments offer a rich field of study, and one filled with paradoxes. They count among them our oldest governing institutions, with many municipalities incorporated well before Confederation brought us our provincial and national government, and they also include our newest, as the result of restructuring and reform initiatives. They are the level of government closest to the people, and yet some of their indirectly elected and appointed upper tier governing units may be the most remote level. They are hailed as the foundation of democracy and also dismissed as nothing more than the servants of the property industry. They offer a mechanism through which local citizens can debate and resolve issues affecting their community, even while many continue to exhort that "politics has no place in local government." Municipalities are indicted as contributing to a pattern of urbanization which has very adverse economic, environmental and social consequences, even as they are cited as the level of government most responsible for the physical planning decisions which can shape our urban environment for the better.

What Is Local Government?

Matters don't become much simpler when one attempts a definition of Canada's local governments. There are well over 4 000 incorporated municipalities in Canada, approximately half of these found in Ontario and Quebec. The specific classifications include cities, towns, villages, rural municipalities (also categorized as townships, parishes, and rural districts), counties (both single and upper tier), and regional and metropolitan municipalities. In addition, there are various other local special purpose bodies that defy classification or even precise numbering. In Ontario alone, where the use of such local bodies has been most prevalent, it is estimated that there are at least 2 000 of these bodies of 70 different types. Common examples include police commissions, health units, conservation authorities, public utilities commissions, parks boards, and school boards.

Are all of these bodies local governments? Yes, they are, as we tend to use that term. For the purpose of this text, local government is defined broadly to embrace both municipalities and local boards. Most of the discussion which follows relates to the operations of municipalities. However, the other local governing bodies — the local boards — are also quite important players on the local scene. Indeed, in many provinces, school boards rival municipalities, at least in terms of the amount of the local tax dollar which they claim. They also share with municipalities the distinction of being governed by elected bodies (school trustees, rather than municipal councillors), and they usually surpass municipalities in the low voting turnouts which they attract. As local government operations come under increasing scrutiny, the activities of the various local boards — and particularly the degree of cooperation among these boards and between boards and municipalities — are receiving greater attention.

What Do Local Governments Do?

The most obvious answer to this question (but a dangerously limited one) is that local governments provide a very wide range of services, programs, facilities and regulations which largely shape our day to day lives. Jack Layton, an academic and experienced municipal politician, offers the following categories of local government responsibility:[1] protective services (police and fire), transportation services (roads and public transit), environmental services (sewers, garbage disposal and water supply), social and health services (welfare administration, day care, homes for the aged,

---

[1] Jack Layton, "City Politics in Canada," in Michael S. Whittington and Glen Williams (eds.), *Canadian Politics in the 1990s*, Third Edition, Scarborough, Nelson Canada, 1990, pp. 405-408.

and public health programs), recreation and cultural services and land use planning. A recent monograph by Sancton offers a quite similar list of local government responsibilities, but adds the provision of public education.[2]

What is striking about both lists is that most of the responsibilities can be characterized as services to property. This is true even of such services as education. As Sancton points out, the quality of a local school system can be a major factor in attracting new residential growth and, sometimes, new businesses as well.[3] Many municipalities have also experienced the fact that the location of a new school, or the closing of an existing school, can have a significant effect on the growth and development in the surrounding area. As will be discussed throughout this text, since local governments provide such an extensive range of services to property and also raise much of the money to pay for these services from a tax on property, it is not surprising that their role has long been seen primarily in terms of serving the needs of property owners.

Valuable as all of these services may be, they are not the only reason — or the most important reason — for local governments to exist. More specifically, they are not the main reason why *municipal governments* exist. That reason is to provide a mechanism for inhabitants of defined local areas to express, debate and resolve local issues and concerns. In other words, municipal governments perform a political role. They provide local citizens with the opportunity to choose representatives who will make decisions which reflect the views and concerns of those local citizens.

It follows then that municipal governments exist to serve two primary purposes:

1. To act as a political mechanism through which a local community can express its collective objectives; and
2. To provide a variety of services and programs to local residents.

These two separate purposes of municipal government are evident when one examines the origins of Canada's municipal government system. From the early years of settlement of the then colony of Canada, local services were provided. As the need for local services increased, more local government responsibilities were assigned to the existing form of local administration — the Courts of Quarter Sessions and their Justices of the Peace. These arrangements resulted in services being provided

---

[2]Andrew Sancton, *Governing Canada's City Regions: Adapting Form to Function*, Montreal, Institute for Research on Public Policy, 1994, p. 11.

[3]*Ibid.*, p. 12.

locally, but local residents had no say in what was done. This situation proved particularly unacceptable to the United Empire Loyalists, many of whom had experienced a form of elected municipal government in the New England colonies from whence they came. The result, as will be described, was constant agitation from the Loyalists which, along with other factors, ultimately led to the provision for elected municipal governments which took over the responsibility for local services from the Courts of Quarter Sessions.

Of these two purposes of municipal government, the first purpose should have been paramount, and perhaps it was that in the minds of the local settlers of the time. This first purpose essentially sees the municipality as an extension of the community, as the community governing itself.[4] It emphasizes the role of municipal governments as representing the views and concerns of their local communities, and taking actions to deal with these concerns. The service delivery role is subservient to this political role; services are provided *in accordance with* the needs and wishes of the local inhabitants.

Viewed in this manner, municipal government can be seen as offering a number of benefits or potential benefits.[5] It diffuses the power of government and involves many decision makers in many different localities. This "localness" of municipal government makes possible greater local knowledge of the situations about which decisions are being made. This arrangement offers the possibility that there will be diverse responses to varying needs of particular localities, thereby allowing the provision of services that better fit local conditions and circumstances than would be the case under more distant decision makers. The experimentation which arises may also lead to improved and more efficient approaches than would be possible if only one central standard were to be accepted. This network of municipal governments also greatly broadens the opportunities for citizen participation. Local governments are more accessible and more exposed to the possibility of public influence.

Notice that the virtues outlined above are presented as *possibilities*, as *potential benefits* derived from a system of municipal government. They

---

[4]For a more complete examination of this concept, see various writings by John Stewart including "A Future for Local Authorities as Community Government," in John Stewart and Gerry Stoker, *The Future of Local Government*, London, Macmillan Education Ltd., 1989, and Michael Clarke and John Stewart, *The Choices for Local Government*, Harlow, Longman, 1991.

[5]The arguments which follow are partly based on B. Jones and J. Stewart, *The Case for Local Government*, London, George Allen & Unwin, 1985.

may not arise; indeed, they clearly do not arise in all instances. However, they can never arise, even partially or sporadically, if municipal governments are allowed to decline into nothing more than vehicles for delivering services, largely at the behest of the senior levels of government. Yet, it will be argued, this has largely been the fate of municipal governments in Canada.

Politics Denied and Decried:
The Narrowed Scope of Canadian Municipal Governments

As will become clear in subsequent chapters, municipal governments in Canada never really had an opportunity to develop as an extension of the community, as a political mechanism which allows local citizens to decide what services they want and need (and are willing to pay for with their taxes).

Authority from the Province, Not the People

The first blow to any such hopes came with the total lack of any constitutional recognition of municipal governments within the British North America Act which created the country of Canada in 1867. Isin[6] points out that Canada's first incorporated city (Saint John, in 1785) was established by a Royal Charter drafted and confirmed by the Privy Council in Whitehall, but that later incorporations such as those of Montreal and Quebec City in 1832 and Toronto in 1834 were carried out through acts of the colonial legislatures. The result, he argues, is that by the 1830s colonial legislatures were attaining powers to create municipal corporations which were not prescribed in their constitutions. This was to have lasting effects, according to Isin,[7] because during the pre-confederation debates of the 1850s provincial governments were considered to have natural and inalienable rights over municipal governments.

The 1867 British North America Act (now subsumed within the Constitution Act of 1982) enshrined this concept of municipal governments as "creatures" of the Provincial Governments which incorporated them. This meant, according to Isin, that the modern municipal corporation would have two essential characteristics:

---

[6]Engin F. Isin, *Cities without Citizens*, Montreal, Black Rose Books, 1992, pp. 142-144.

[7]*Ibid.*, p. 144.

1. It is created at the pleasure of the legislature, and need not require the consent of the people of the affected locality. The act of incorporation is not a contract between the legislature and the local inhabitants; and
2. The authority conferred on the corporation is not local in nature but derives from the Provincial Government.[8]

Such an arrangement is obviously not compatible with the concept of municipal government as an extension of the community, of the community governing itself. Instead, the constitutional arrangements defined municipal governments in terms of the specific classifications they were given which, in turn, determined the powers which they could exercise. As a result, municipal governments have operated since Confederation within a constitutional and legal framework, reinforced by ample case law, which limits their scope to matters specifically delegated to them by the Provincial Governments which have established them.

Political Role Discredited

The second major setback for municipal governments occurred one hundred years ago during the turn of the century reform movement. Advocating more efficient administration and the removal of all corruption, reformers called for the exclusion of politics from local government. Decisions should be made on objective, rational grounds. Municipal administrators should be free to provide municipal services without political interference from the elected representatives. In their misguided zeal, the reformers substantially undermined the very system of municipal government which the Loyalists and others had fought so hard to obtain only half a century earlier! From the reform era came a number of structural changes designed to reduce the influence of the politician and to elevate the role of the appointed expert. An even more significant legacy of this era has been the lingering notion that politics has no place in local government.

In attempting to eradicate the excesses of patronage and the pork barrel, the reformers were making a positive contribution. But in denying any political role for municipal government, the reformers were misguided and harmful. The fact is that politics exists inevitably in every society because humans have wants and needs that must be satisfied from resources that are scarce and insufficient. As a result, competition and conflict arise, and the central purpose of governments is to resolve these

---

[8]*Ibid.*, p. 2.

disputes by deciding who gets what resources and how equitably they are distributed. Governments possess legal authority which provides the foundation for their allocative decisions.

It follows that politics is an integral part of local government operations. It is no less true at this level that decisions must be made about the allocation of scarce resources. Competition and conflict are equally prevalent. Divisions arise on such questions as urban and rural interests, city and suburb, haves and have-nots, pro and anti-development, and ethnic and racial issues.

"Politics, like sex, cannot be abolished. It can sometimes be repressed by denying people the opportunity to practice it, but it cannot be done away with because it is in the nature of man to disagree and to contend."[9]

The fact that politics is denied and decried at the local level has led to a harmful narrowing of the perceived scope of municipal operations. If municipal governments don't have a political role — without which they obviously cannot operate as an extension of the community — then they are left with only that other role of service delivery. But what services, and on what basis? Without a political role based on the local community, the answer is whatever services Provincial Governments see fit to authorize or mandate.

Impact of Industrialization and Urbanization

The political role of municipal government has been further constrained by the impact of industrialization and urbanization and, even more, by the municipal adaptations which have resulted. Much of the rapid urbanization following World War Two was stimulated by policies of the federal and provincial governments, which saw urban development as a key economic stimulus for the postwar economy. The primary role for municipal governments within this economic strategy was to provide the physical services needed to support growth and development.

Some observers like Fowler and Jacobs have been very critical of the results of urbanization in terms of the sprawl, and the lack of physical diversity in the built environment of our cities.[10] They find that the physical characteristics of the postwar urban environment have an ad-

---

[9]Edward Banfield and James Q. Wilson, *City Politics*, New York, Random House, 1963, pp 20-21.

[10]Edmund P. Fowler, *Building Cities That Work*, Kingston, McGill-Queen's University Press, 1992, and Jane Jacobs in such works as *The Death and Life of Great American Cities*, New York, Random House, 1961.

verse impact on our social behaviour, including our political activities. Lowi goes so far as to contend that suburbs represent "a failure of citizenship" in the way they allow people to remove themselves from the responsibilities of civic participation.[11]

It must be acknowledged that political activity noticeably increased at the local level during this postwar period. In particular, many citizens objected to the rapid growth and development which was underway, to federal government urban renewal schemes which seemed to involve a crude bulldozing of the inner city, and to the changes being made in the urban environment to facilitate the movement of the automobile. Citizens and citizen groups increasingly questioned the actions of municipal councils and demanded a more open, consultative decision making process.

Sadly, the increase in political activity on the part of local groups did not enhance the political role of municipal governments. To the contrary, the political activism mainly served to highlight deficiencies within the municipal government system as it had been evolving and adapting. Enforcing accountability for action (or inaction) proved difficult for citizens when pertinent responsibilities were divided among several municipalities within an urban area, or between municipalities and various separate boards. Even within any one municipal council, the absence of a recognizable governing group made accountability elusive. Further probing often revealed that the municipal council had very little power or discretion to respond as citizens might wish. Over the first half of the 20th century, the municipal government system had adapted by shifting responsibilities outward to boards or upward to higher levels of government and by obtaining increased financial assistance from provincial governments, mainly in the form of conditional grants. By the mid-20th century — 100 years after the establishment of the first system, in Ontario, under the 1849 Baldwin Act — the sad reality was that municipal councils had less and less freedom to operate as an extension of their communities no matter how much they might have wished to do so.

Misplaced Emphasis of Local Government Reform

Matters did not improve with the municipal government restructuring initiatives introduced in a number of Provinces in the 1960s and 1970s. For the most part, these were preoccupied with improving the service

---

[11]Theodore Lowi, *The End of Liberalism*, 2nd Edition, New York, W. W. Norton, 1979, p. 267.

delivery role of local government and most of the reforms introduced paid very little attention to the even more important political role. The end result was new municipal government structures which were often perceived as more bureaucratic and less accountable, and yet structures which were still not noticeably stronger or more autonomous in their capacity to provide needed services.

This result was probably inevitable given the insights provided by Stewart after comparing the British experience with that of a number of European countries.[12] He notes that municipal government reform in Britain (and the same is true of Canada) has been preoccupied with issues of structure, and that changes have always been in the direction of larger municipalities — perceived to be necessary to meet the increased service demands effectively. But, argues Stewart, this pattern unfolds because municipalities are being defined by the services they provide. If they were defined, as in many other parts of Europe, by the community they serve, much smaller municipal units would emerge. These smaller municipalities still meet their servicing needs. They enter into partnerships with other municipalities or even other organizations, making whatever arrangements best allow them to serve their communities.

Sancton makes a similar point when he states that:

> When municipalities are seen primarily as service arrangers rather than as producers, then the problem of ensuring that their boundaries are optimal for the production of their mix of assigned functions becomes much less problematic. Municipal boundaries can then be used to delineate real communities, and optimal boundaries for service production can be worked out by other agencies and even by the private sector.[13]

That notion, that municipalities don't have to be totally responsible for the provision of a service, but could instead act as a broker to ensure that the service gets provided by some organization or organizations, is gaining increasing acceptance in North America. As it does, it may help to spark a revival of the political role of municipal government.

Possible Revival of Political Role?

The past decade has been particularly difficult for municipal governments, but out of this adversity may come a fundamental redefinition of what municipal governments are and what they do.

---

[12]Stewart and Stoker, *op. cit.*, pp. 236-240.

[13]Sancton, *op. cit.*, pp. 42-43.

Underlying these developments, of course, has been the "pass the buck" mentality infecting Canadian federalism as the senior levels of government grapple with their debt loads. The Federal Government has been cutting transfer payments to the Provincial Governments which, in turn, have reduced their transfers to municipalities and local boards. Provinces have also engaged in a process of "downloading" in which they have shifted responsibilities (and costs) to the local level, but without necessarily providing compensating financial resources. The new financial reality for Canadian municipal governments includes the prospect of a permanent reduction in transfer payments from the senior levels to a very modest scale.

Underlying the financial belt-tightening on the part of the senior levels of government have been some very fundamental economic and political shifts affecting Canadian society. An increasingly globalized economy, and the development of a North American free trade area, have unleashed competitive forces that are still causing painful adjustments in the Canadian economy. We have moved into a post-industrial era, or what a number of British authors term "post-fordism," to reflect the movement beyond the manufacturing assembly line first popularized by Henry Ford.[14] Information technology is the driving force of this new post-industrial era, and new, more flexible forms of production geared not for the masses but for filling specialized needs and market niches.

The 1980s saw a pronounced swing to the right in political thinking, manifested in such regimes as that of Ronald Reagan in the United States, Margaret Thatcher in Britain and Brian Mulroney in Canada. As part of the right wing agenda, downsizing, privatizing, opening government up to competitive forces, and putting government operations on a business footing — all have received attention and debate.

Municipal governments, of course, must function within this broader economic and political environment. They face a rather dramatic shift from the traditional concern with roads to navigating the "information superhighway." They are being challenged to demonstrate "business-like" efficiency in their operations, but must remember the central importance of their political role as well, and the fact that they are much more than a business operation measured by a profit and loss statement.

A number of adjustments are already underway within municipal government circles. Municipalities have been forced to finance an increasing

---

[14]See, for example, Stewart and Stoker, *op. cit.* and Allan Cochrane, *Whatever Happened to Local Government?*, Buckingham, Open University Press, 1993.

portion of their expenditures from the real property tax and from miscellaneous local revenues — both sources of revenue which are under the control of municipalities. Thus, while it may seem little more than "making a virtue of necessity," municipalities have been gaining greater financial autonomy through this difficult adjustment process.

Another result of these developments is that municipalities have been forced to rethink "what kind of business they are in," what services they can realistically provide, and what new and different arrangements they can make to fulfill their obligations with reduced resources. Gone are the days of simply increasing expenditures (and taxes) to deal with whatever problems arise. We are past the stage when governments could do "more with more." We are even past the stage when governments can do "more with less" — an expression frequently heard in recent decades to signify governments' new found commitment to greater efficiency. The new reality is that governments must learn to do "less with less."

In perhaps another example of "necessity being the mother of invention," we are now seeing many exciting and progressive new initiatives on the part of municipal government. Central to these changes has been a growing acceptance on the part of municipalities that they cannot, acting alone, provide all of the services and programs needed by their inhabitants. Nor, it is increasingly appreciated, need that be their role. Instead, municipal councils can define problems and then act as a broker or catalyst to ensure that resources are brought to bear to deal with these problems. This concept which separates policy decisions from service delivery has been popularized as the difference between steering and rowing.[15] It is also reminiscent of the earlier comments from both Stewart and Sancton about defining the municipality in terms of the community it serves rather than the services it provides.

If Canadian municipalities continue to define themselves only in relation to how many services they can afford to provide directly on their own for their inhabitants, they are facing a bleak future of permanent financial constraint. If, however, they can recast themselves as governing bodies whose primary role is to help their communities give expression to collective feelings and concerns and then to reach out and seek partnerships which will generate the resources which can address these community concerns, their future may only be limited by their imaginations and cooperative spirit.

---

[15]Notably in David Osborne and Ted Gaebler, *Reinventing Government*, New York, Penguin Books, 1993.

Organization of the Text

This admittedly brief overview has presented municipal governments in terms of unfulfilled potential. There has been insufficient recognition of their political role, and a dangerously narrow focus on service delivery. But ferment and change are in the air, and one hundred years after a turn of the century reform movement which contributed greatly to the weakening of municipal government there is an opportunity for a new turn of the century reform movement — one that will reinvent municipal government to face the challenges of the 21st century.

The organization of the remainder of the text essentially traces the themes highlighted in this introductory overview. The early chapters retain a traditional approach of tracing the historical evolution of the local government institutions. As will be demonstrated, however, a number of important insights are gained from an historical perspective. It provides an awareness of the relevance and influence of urbanization from the very earliest beginnings of local government. Also prevalent from the beginning has been controversy and confusion about the political role of municipal government and its appropriateness. Moreover, the organizational structure and governmental machinery found in most municipalities today still reflect historical developments. Many boundaries have not changed since their original delineation. Such internal governmental arrangements as the use of executive committees and chief administrative officers also derive from an earlier period. If one is to understand the present institutions of municipal government, therefore, it is necessary to appreciate how and why they arose and evolved.

An historical perspective is also helpful in any assessment of municipal government relationships with the senior levels of government. While the constitutional division of responsibilities merits much of the emphasis it receives, it is important to remind ourselves that many municipalities were incorporated before Confederation and had already experienced a period of considerable operating independence before becoming "creatures of the provinces." In addition to the formal, legal arrangements, therefore, a number of other political and practical considerations have shaped the relationships which evolved between municipalities and the provincial level. These latter considerations are also evident in the development, in spite of the constitutional provisions, of federal-local and tri-level relationships.

The historical evolution described in this text is by no means confined to the development of municipal government institutions. Much of the discussion relates to the changes which have been occurring in the external environment and the interaction between that environment and the evolving municipal government system. Particular attention is given to the impact of urbanization, not just the new service demands and costs that arose but also the new patterns of social and economic development and their effect on municipal government operations.

Finally, the historical perspective of this text provides a wealth of fascinating parallels between past and present, reminding us of the enduring nature of certain issues and themes, and also offering opportunties to learn and benefit from what has gone before. Consider the following four examples:

1. A later chapter discusses servicing difficulties faced by councils because of problems with assessment, provincial control and scarce finances, and notes the harmful effect on the country of the resistance to increases in the property tax. These comments certainly apply to most municipalities today, and the problems they face with deteriorating infrastructures. However, the comments relate to the operation of district councils in Upper Canada in the 1840s.

2. In recent years, there has been increased recognition of the limits of growth, of the need to balance growth with the protection of our environment — an objective which is often referred to as "sustainable development." While this concern is commendable, the recognition that industrialiation was consuming natural resources at an alarming rate and creating waste and pollution had led to a Federal Commission on the Conservation of Natural Resources in 1909!

3. Canada's large cities have experienced a substantial influx of immigrants, who have been encouraged to maintain their distinctive heritage and culture through the federal government's policy of multiculturalism. City governments face racial tensions and servicing challenges but, here again, the situation is not new. A later chapter describes conditions in Winnipeg at the turn of the century, when rapid immigration and problems with assimilation produced what has been described as a "Divided City."

4. The conservative ideology of recent years has championed the virtues of the marketplace, of privatization, and of "running city hall more like a business." That slogan, as will be discussed, was also a central theme of the turn of the century reform movement of 100 years ago.

Looking more specifically at the organization of the text, the historical foundations of local government are traced in **Chapter 2**, and **Chapter 3** examines the turn of the century reform era and its contribution to the machinery and operating philosophy of local government. **Chapter 4** continues the chronological evolution through the 20th century and gives particular attention to the impact of post-war urbanization. The various local government restructuring and reform programs introduced in response to the pressures of growth and change are examined in **Chapter 5**, which concludes with a summary of the present municipal government system and its predominant features. These same pressures also affected the internal governing structures, and **Chapter 6** outlines the basic municipal machinery — including such reformed structures as C.A.O. and Executive Committee systems — and assesses their adequacy. No examination of the local government system would be complete without some consideration of the senior levels of government with which municipalities have become increasingly intertwined. Therefore, **Chapter 7** examines both provincial-local and federal-local and tri-level relations. In addition to illustrating the intergovernmental context within which local governments must operate, the chapter attempts to demonstrate the importance of local government for the senior levels, and the interdependent nature of the present relationships among our levels of government.

The remainder of the text is more focused on the *process* of government. Having traced the evolution of municipal governments in earlier chapters, we now want to examine how they are being used, for what purposes, and with what effectiveness. Accordingly, the emphasis in the remaining chapters is on the political process within which municipalities operate and, more specifically, the way in which policy decisions are made and resources allocated.

Chapter 8 explores the local political process and the environment within which it operates. The dynamics of this process are illustrated by examples of activities of citizens' groups and political parties at the local level, and of the links between municipal government and the property development industry. Key players in the local political process are discussed, including councillors and staff, interest groups, political parties and the media. **Chapter 9** explores the municipal policy-making process and examines the validity of several theories or models which attempt to explain how policy decisions are made. The concluding chapter of the text, **Chapter 10** attempts to build on the insights gained from the preceding chapters and offers suggestions for the key ingredients in a new turn of the century reform movement which will prepare municipalities to enter the 21st century.

CHAPTER 2

The Foundations of Local Government

OBJECTIVES:

1. To trace the historical evolution of the municipal government system in the provinces and territories of Canada.

2. To identify the dominant influences in shaping the particular structures which evolved.

3. To describe the main features of the municipal systems originally established.

Introduction

How did our municipal governments evolve, and why in the particular form which we find in Canada? One answer — which is correct as far as it goes — is that they were shaped by decisions made by the provincial governments to which they owe their very existence (and by the federal government in the case of municipalities in the Yukon and Northwest Territories).

This explanation is based on the constitutional, legal arrangements provided by the British North America Act (now the Constitution Act). While both the national and provincial levels of government were given separately defined spheres of operation within which each would act relatively autonomously, municipal governments were accorded no such status. Instead, municipal governments were only mentioned in the British North America Act as one of the responsibilities allocated to the provinces. It follows, therefore, that from a strict legal perspective, municipal governments only exist to the extent that the provincial governments have seen fit to provide for them. The types of municipality and their boundaries, responsibilities and finances must be authorized through provincial legislation. But since provincial governments are responsible to their legislatures and their electorates, they are unlikely to create municipal institutions which are too out of step with public views and attitudes concerning local government. In any event, the basic features of Canadian

15

local government evolved before Confederation and the new provincial governments established in 1867 inherited existing municipal institutions and/or operating philosophies of how local governments ought to operate. It is necessary, therefore, to look beyond the legal explanation, important though it is.

The earliest municipal governments in Canada evolved in response to the settlement of the country. As the population increased, and particularly as it became concentrated in the limited urban centres of the early years, it was necessary to administer a growing variety of programs and regulations. With pockets of population scattered in a vast area, and with very rudimentary forms of transportation and communication, the responsibilities could not be handled directly by a centralized colonial government.

While some form of local administration was inevitable for quite practical reasons, therefore, the particular form which did evolve was strongly influenced by the political values and traditions of the settlers of this country and the beliefs which they held or developed about municipal government. In this connection, the extent to which this country was settled through immigration was a significant factor, especially because of the belief in local self-government held by many of the United Empire Loyalists who entered this country in the years during and after the American War of Independence.

These and other influences will be evident throughout this chapter as we trace the historical evolution of municipal government in each of the provinces. No standard time frame is employed; rather, developments in each province are described up to the point where the basic municipal structure was established. Chronological considerations are evident, however, in the sequence of provinces. We begin with Central Canada because a comprehensive system of municipal government was first established there — in Upper Canada (Ontario) — and this system influenced the municipal institutions subsequently created in a number of other provinces. The chapter then examines developments in the Atlantic Provinces, the Western Provinces and, finally, the Northern Territories.

Central Canada

Local government made its first, although somewhat brief, appearance in Canada under the French regime in the settlements of Montreal, Quebec and Trois Rivières. As early as 1647 a mayor, councillors, and syndics d'habitations (who made representations on behalf of local residents to the provincial authorities) were elected in Quebec. This practice was strongly discouraged by the very authoritarian and centralized home government in France, which felt that it was a dangerous innovation, and in 1663 the mayor and aldermen of Quebec resigned. The whole issue of local self-government was allowed to lapse until 1760 and the advent of British rule.

After the British conquest all government was vested in the military and subsequently in a Governor and an appointed council. In 1763 a proclamation was issued which promised to introduce English law and the English system of freehold land grants in Quebec, in order to encourage English settlement. In the following year the Governor-General did establish the ancient English system of local justices of the peace meeting in the Courts of Quarter Sessions for the three districts around Montreal, Quebec, and Trois-Rivières for the trial of unimportant matters.

Despite the rule by British Governors and the promise of the benefits of English law, little occurred to interrupt the traditional running of the affairs of Quebec. There was little interference with the Roman Catholic Church, the Court of Common Pleas continued to administer French civil law, and land was still granted through the feudal French system, "en fief et seigneurie." The Quebec Act, which was passed in 1774, formally recognized this situation and also extended the Quebec boundaries west to the Great Lakes and Mississippi River and north to Labrador.

The American Revolution broke out soon after and precipitated a flow of United Empire Loyalists to Nova Scotia and the western part of Quebec. The peak years of this immigration were 1782-1783, when about 10 000 arrived in the Saint John area of the Bay of Fundy, 25 000 arrived in Nova Scotia (doubling its previous population), and 20 000 arrived in the unsettled areas around Lake Ontario, particularly around Kingston, Toronto, and Niagara.[1]

These immigrants came chiefly from New York and the New England colonies, where they had enjoyed a certain measure of local self-government. They brought with them the tradition of municipal government through the town meeting. Under this system, selectmen (councillors) were elected at the annual town meeting by the inhabitants residing within one-half mile of the meeting house. These selectmen were to oversee the affairs of the town between meetings. In theory their appointment and actions were to be approved by the Governor but in practice they operated independently of the central authorities.

---

[1]K. G. Crawford, *Canadian Municipal Government*, Toronto, University of Toronto Press, 1954, p. 21.

Upper Canada (Ontario)

Needless to say, these Loyalists were unhappy under French civil law, especially the system of land grants under the seigneurial system, and the limited local autonomy. There soon were numerous petitions from the Loyalists around Lake Ontario for some form of local courts and administration, English civil law, and separation from that area of Quebec which was east of Montreal. Because of population growth pressures, but much against their better judgment, the British acquiesced and in 1787 passed an ordinance which divided the western settlements, previously a part of the District of Montreal, into four new districts with various appointed officials including justices of the peace who constituted the Courts of Quarter Sessions. The Quarter Sessions assumed judicial, legislative, and administrative responsibilities including maintaining the peace, regulating domestic animals running at large, the conduct of licensed taverns, the appointment of minor officials, and the superintending of highways.[2] As new problems arose, the Quarter Sessions, which were the only official agency dealing with local matters, were simply given more powers to deal with them.

However, this new system proved to be unworkable under the French feudal laws and institutions which had been established with the Quebec Act and pressure continued for a separate province with English civil law and an English system of land tenure. This continuing pressure finally culminated in the Constitutional Act of 1791 (also referred to as the Canada Act).

The main provisions of the act were:

1. The creation, from the province of Quebec, of the provinces of Upper and Lower Canada, with the Ottawa River roughly as the dividing line.
2. The provision of a government for each province consisting of a British Lieutenant-Governor, an appointed executive council, an appointed legislative council, and an elected legislative assembly.
3. The use of English law and land tenure in Upper Canada.
4. The allotment of land as clergy reserves for the support of the Protestant clergy.

Lord Dorchester, then Governor-General, was reluctant to approve the Constitutional Act because he felt that the Loyalists would be safer under French than British law since, in his view, too free an indulgence in British political institutions had led to the American Revolution. There-

---

[2]*Ibid.*, p. 23.

fore the Act contained certain precautions against the rise of democratic institutions such as the establishment of an hereditary political aristocracy (through the appointed councils) and the establishment of an episcopal state church (clergy reserves).

Both Lord Dorchester and also J. G. Simcoe, the first Lieutenant-Governor of Upper Canada, strongly discouraged any form of local government. To this end surveys were to be of royal seigniories and not townships, and they were to be numbered and not named as was customary, to discourage any strong attachment to a particular place. However, the Loyalists had already set up town meetings and designated their settlements townships named after King George and his family, even before the Constitutional Act was passed.

In 1792 Simcoe divided Upper Canada into counties for militia purposes and for the election of representatives to the newly created assembly. He was very keen to develop an aristocracy in an effort to reproduce the highly classed society found in England. From this privileged class he planned to appoint his executive council to oversee the actions of the assembly. He therefore promoted half-pay army officers as candidates in the first provincial election, most of whom were rejected by the voters in favour of men of lower classes. Instead of heeding this indication of popular thought and giving up his plans, Simcoe redoubled his efforts to eradicate all democratic tendencies and in time an aristocracy known as the Family Compact became organized around the executive branch of the provincial government. This group had developed both family and economic ties throughout the province.[3] Its members felt it was their duty to "guard the body politic from the corrupting influences of republicanism" and fought all efforts at establishing any kind of responsible government at any level.[4]

On the other hand, the Loyalists, who constituted most of the population of the province, felt that they had proven their loyalty to the Crown by fleeing the rebellious colonies and therefore deserved to have local self-rule. Perhaps it is not surprising then that the first bill introduced in the first session of the legislative assembly of Upper Canada was "to authorize town meetings for the purpose of appointing divers parish offi-

---

[3]In Lower Canada the Family Compact had a counterpart known as the Chateau Clique with whom it also had family and economic ties. An elite group surrounding the Lieutenant-Governor, such as the Family Compact and Chateau Clique, was found in most of the provinces.

[4]Adam Shortt, *Municipal Government in Ontario, An Historical Sketch*, University of Toronto studies, History and Economics, Vol. II, No. 2, p. 8.

cers." Although not passed in that session, it was passed in 1793 as the Parish and Town Officers Act. The Act permitted annual town meetings[5] to appoint a town clerk, assessors, a tax collector, road overseers and fence viewers, a poundkeeper, and town wardens. The town wardens were to represent the inhabitants in the Quarter Sessions of the District in which the town(ship) was located. The only legislative authority the town meeting had was to fix the height of fences and to regulate animals running at large. An assessment act was also passed in 1793 to provide for raising money to pay for the costs of court and jail houses, paying officers' fees, and building roads.

By the turn of the century, urban concerns of sanitation, streets, education, welfare, and local police were becoming sufficiently pressing that the powers of the justices of the peace had to be extended.

A severe fire in Kingston in 1812 persuaded central authorities that some action was needed and in 1816 an act to regulate the police[6] was passed for Kingston. This act gave the magistrates the power to make and publish rules and regulations for the safety and convenience of the inhabitants and to finance local improvements through a special tax. By the end of the year, Kingston had fourteen rules which covered such areas as streets, slaughterhouses, weights and measures, and animals running at large.

Another potentially important event in 1816 was the passage of the first public school act. This act enabled local residents to meet together to elect three trustees who were to hire a teacher and authorize school textbooks. This was the first example of true local self-government, whereby local people could elect representatives to administer a local need. Unfortunately, this was not a successful attempt at local government because of the lack of funds and experienced trustees.

The end of the War of 1812 in North America and the Napoleonic Wars in Europe saw the beginning of a new wave of immigration from the British Isles. Between 1815 and 1850 approximately 800 000 came to British North America, the great bulk of whom settled in Upper Canada. This population growth magnified the already existing urban problems and petitioning continued for some form of municipal government. In 1828 Belleville applied to be incorporated as a town. The Legislative Council rejected this application, saying that:

---

[5]In Ontario, town meetings were actually township meetings.

[6]Use of police in this sense meant regulation, discipline and control of a community.

Since men do not like to be forced, they are pretty certain to elect only
such persons as will not make effective rules or adequately enforce
them; hence in the interest of efficient administration, such innovations
must be discouraged.[7]

Despite this setback for Belleville, in 1832 the Legislature capitulated
and created a distinct corporate body in the President and Board of Police of the town of Brockville. This body was, in essence, the first form
of elected municipal council and it assumed responsibility for all of the
local government functions previously undertaken by the Quarter Sessions, with the justices of the peace retaining only their judicial functions
within Brockville. This movement to representative local government
proved to be popular. In 1834 York was created the self-governing city of
Toronto and by 1838 there were eight police towns and two cities.

One should not overstate the significance of this development, however.[8] Only the members of the boards of police were incorporated, not
the town inhabitants. The qualifications to be a member of the board
required that a town inhabitant be a freeholder or a householder paying
a certain amount of rent per annum for his dwelling. A governing elite
was formed whose obligation was to govern the town. The qualification
to be a voter in the election required that the town inhabitant be a male
householder, a subject of the King, and possessing a freehold estate.
"These qualifications for board membership and voting demonstrate the
calculated restrictions that were put upon participation in town politics."[9]
Moreover, the terms of incorporation for these boards suggest that the
Upper Canada legislature was very cautious in conferring corporate capacities on towns.

> The boards of police had more duties and obligations than rights and
> liberties. Or, stated another way, these bodies politic were constituted
> so as to make them accept the delegated powers of the State; and, by
> empowering a qualified elite to govern through taxation, these commu-
> nities also relieved the State of the costs of governance.[10]

While the urban areas of Upper Canada were gaining more local self-
government, the rural areas were still functioning under the Parish and

---

[7]Shortt, *op. cit.*, p. 19.

[8]See Engin F. Isin, *Cities without Citizens*, Montreal, Black Rose Books, 1992,
pp. 112-114, on which this discussion is based.

[9]*Ibid.*, p. 113.

[10]*Ibid.*, p. 114.

Town Officers Act with the magistrates of the Quarter Sessions in almost total control of local affairs. Reform newspapers of the time charged that many magistrates were unfit, intemperate, and ready to stir up the mob against reformers.[11] The magistrates decided which local works were to be carried out, often ignoring areas in which they had no personal interest, and how much tax revenue was to be raised. In 1835 the assembly came under the control of a reform group which produced a report stating that magistrates were half-pay officers and strangers who often became members of the Family Compact.[12] Similar conditions existed in the other provinces, with the unrest culminating in the Rebellion of 1837 in Upper and Lower Canada.

After the Rebellion, the Earl of Durham was appointed to investigate the insurrection particularly and the general state of government in all of the provinces. Durham produced a comprehensive report dealing with the conditions in British North America, and of particular importance for our purposes are his recommendations dealing with local government. He wrote that "municipal institutions of local self-government ... are the foundations of Anglo-Saxon freedom and civilization."[13] Further he stated: "The latter want of municipal institutions giving the people any control over their local affairs, may indeed be considered as one of the main causes of the failure of representative government and of the bad administration of the country."[14] Durham recommended that the two Canadas be reunited and that local matters should be looked after by municipal bodies of a much smaller size than the province.

Governor-General Sydenham, who replaced Durham in 1840, recognized the importance of the recommendations in Durham's report and he wrote to the Colonial Secretary:[15]

> Since I have been in these Provinces I have become more and more satisfied that the capital cause of the misgovernment of them is to be

---

[11]Fred Landon, *Western Ontario and the American Frontier*, Toronto, McClelland and Stewart Limited, 1967, p. 223.

[12]John M. McEvoy, *The Ontario Township*, University of Toronto studies, Politics, 1st series, No. 1, 1889, p. 22.

[13]Gerald M. Craig (ed.), *Lord Durham's Report*, Toronto, McClelland and Stewart Limited, 1963, p. 60.

[14]*Ibid.*, p. 67.

[15]Landon, *op. cit.*, p. 223.

found in the absence of Local Government, and the consequent exercise by the assembly of powers wholly inappropriate to its functions.

Sydenham also sent the Colonial Secretary a draft bill for union of the Canadas which incorporated Durham's recommendations. Unfortunately at this time Durham had fallen into personal unpopularity and the Colonial Office considered the Family Compact and the Chateau Clique as the loyal heart of the country.[16] The principle of responsible government and the clauses on local government were dropped from the Union Act introduced and passed by the English Parliament. One cannot overstate the importance of this omission. Had the Union Act contained clauses providing for a system of municipal government, then such a separate and distinct provision might well have been reproduced in the British North America Act which brought Canada into existence. Instead, while a number of specific municipalities were incorporated before Confederation, municipal government received no formal recognition or legal status in the constitution of Canada.

In any event, Lord Sydenham persisted in spite of his initial setback. In 1841 he persuaded the new Canadian legislature to pass an act which established an elected district council to take over the administrative authority formerly exercised by the Courts of Quarter Sessions in rural areas. There were no drastic changes in the general way that local government was carried on; the annual town meeting still elected various officers and passed town laws. But it also elected one or two district councillors from each township. The head of the district council, the warden, was appointed by the Governor-General although subsequently the councils were given the right to choose their own warden. The councils were given responsibility for roads, municipal officers, taxing, justice, education, and welfare. Their expenses could be met by tolls or taxes on real or personal property or both. The Governor-General could disallow any by-laws and could dissolve any or all of the district councils.

The District Councils Act is perhaps even more important than any succeeding act because it was the first real break with the system of local government by Courts of Quarter Sessions and preceded by almost 50 years the abandonment of this system in England.[17] While it was too radical for conservative elements in the legislature and not radical enough for the reformers, it did provide for a transition period in the rural areas

---

[16]Thomas H. Raddall, *The Path of Destiny*, Toronto, Doubleday and Company, Inc., 1957, p. 31.

[17]Crawford, *op. cit.*, p. 31.

between no local self-government and full local self-government. The central authorities retained much power because it was genuinely felt that local people would not be able to manage their own affairs.

Despite initial fears, the first district councillors were apparently fairly capable people who were able to stimulate the development of their townships because of their knowledge of local needs. By far the most important functions were the construction and repair of roads and bridges and the laying out and creating of school districts. The councils were hampered, however, by problems with assessment, provincial control and scarce finances; problems which persist to this day. It has been written of the revenues available to district councils that:

> These were paltry sums for the needs of large districts, and it is quite certain that the very light direct taxation on which Canadians long prided themselves was a rather important factor in the backward condition of the country for so many years.[18]

[In a rather fascinating parallel, one could argue that the backward and dangerously deteriorated condition of the infrastructure of many municipalities today is at least partly a result of the modest levels of property tax demanded by local citizens.]

In 1843 the Baldwin or Municipal Act was introduced, although because of a rupture with the Governor-General it was not passed until 1849. A primary function of the act was the consolidation of all municipal legislation under one measure. It built upon the District Councils Act while extending certain powers. The Baldwin Act differed *in two major respects*:

1. the county rather than the district became the upper tier of municipal government, and
2. for the first time townships were recognized as a rural unit of municipal government.

As well, the act established villages, towns, and cities as urban municipal units. Cities and separated towns were not a part of the county for municipal government purposes. This municipal system established in 1849 has endured to the present in many areas of Ontario. Moreover, as will be discussed in Chapter 5, even the reformed structures introduced in recent decades (the controversial regional governments) are essentially modified county systems.

---

[18]Adam Shortt and Arthur G. Doughty (gen. eds.), *Canada and its Provinces, A History of the Canadian People and Their Institutions*, Toronto, Glasgow, Brook and Company, 1914, Vol. XVIII, p. 437.

Lower Canada (Quebec)

It will be recalled that under the French regime the province of Quebec enjoyed little or no autonomy and the first attempts at local government were strongly discouraged. This was undoubtedly because of the extent of local control by central authorities and the lack of a French tradition of local self-rule. The British conquest and takeover in the 1760s made little impact on this situation, although by 1764 the Quebec grand jury petitioned for regulations regarding markets, schools, and poor houses. In 1777 an ordinance was passed to "empower the Commissioners of the Peace to regulate the Police of the Towns of Quebec and Montreal for a limited time."[19] But this must have proven inadequate since both Quebec and Montreal petitioned for incorporation because of the bad conditions existing in the towns. In 1799 districts were established under justices of the peace to supervise roads and bridges and by 1807 a market was established in Montreal under the magistrates.

In Lower Canada, as in Upper Canada, government by the magistrates grew to be very unpopular. A citizen meeting in Montreal in 1828 expressed the need for an improved local administration

> ... to cope with police and financial problems of the prosperous town, the long neglected harbour, the insanitary conditions of surrounding swamps, and the lack of a general and effectually prosecuted plan of improvements.[20]

It was not until 1832 that Quebec and Montreal were granted charters which enabled the citizens to elect a mayor and two aldermen per ward. According to Isin,[21] the long delay since the 1785 incorporation of Saint John as the first city incorporated city in British North America, reflected the caution and hesitancy of colonial and British authorities about the use of this legal device. Indeed, the incorporations were limited to a four year term. When the provisions expired in 1836, they were not renewed until after 1840 because of the political turmoil caused by the 1837 Rebellion.

Although Lower Canada was subject to almost the same urban pressures as Upper Canada, the first 80 years of British rule saw little progress in the establishment of local government. Lord Durham made the following observation on Lower Canada in 1839:

---

[19]*Ibid.*, Vol. XV, p. 301.

[20]*Ibid.*, p. 304.

[21]Isin, *op. cit.*, p. 142.

In fact, beyond the walls of Quebec all regular administration of the country appeared to cease; and there literally was hardly a single public officer in the civil government except in Montreal and Three Rivers, to whom any order could be directed.[22]

Thus the need for some system of municipal government was apparent and in 1840, under the guidance of Lord Sydenham, an ordinance was passed which provided for a system of local government that in many respects resembled the district councils established soon after in Upper Canada. Lower Canada was divided into districts which were to be governed by an elected council and an appointed warden. Another ordinance passed at the same time provided for the election of a clerk, assessors, tax collector, surveyors, overseers of roads and the poor, fence viewers, drain inspectors and poundkeepers. Townships and parishes with sufficient population were constituted corporate bodies and elected two councillors each to the district councils. Although the district councils were given the power of taxation, much of the real power remained with the Governor.

Both of the 1840 ordinances proved to be unpopular in Lower Canada. The execution and deportation of rebels of the 1837 Rebellion caused resentment and mistrust and the people were especially wary of Lord Sydenham and his motives. The Union Act itself was unpopular and local government was seen as another means of oppression. But perhaps the most unpalatable measure was the power of taxation which, except for customs duties, had previously been unknown in Lower Canada. Therefore, it is not surprising that in 1845 an act was passed which repealed both ordinances and constituted each township or parish a body corporate with an elected council with most of the duties of the district councils.

In 1847 a county system roughly based on the district councils was established. This system lasted until 1855 when the Lower Canada Municipal and Road Act was passed which became the foundation of Quebec municipal institutions. This act established parishes, townships, towns, and villages, while retaining the county level as an upper tier unit. The heads of the local councils sat on the county council and chose their own warden. Each level could appoint the officers it felt were necessary and could levy taxes. Cities continued to be provided for by special charters rather than being incorporated under the provisions of the general act. This system remained in effect with minor changes until the turn of the century.

---

[22]Shortt and Doughty, *op. cit.*, p. 290.

TABLE 1
Historical Highlights: Central Canada

ONTARIO

1763	British rule of Quebec begins
1774	Quebec Act
1782-83	United Empire Loyalists immigrate
1791	Constitutional Act
1793	Parish & Town Officers Act
1816	Public School Act
	Police regulations in Kingston
1832	Board of Police (Council) in Brockville
1837	Rebellion, followed by Durham's Report
1840-41	District Council's Act
1849	Baldwin (Municipal) Act

QUEBEC

1777	Ordinance regulating police of Quebec & Montreal
1832-36	Quebec City & Montreal granted charters
1840	System similar to District Councils
1845	Townships and parishes incorporated
1847	Townships and parishes abolished, in favour of county government
1855	Lower Canada Municipal and Road Act

Atlantic Provinces

The development of municipal institutions in the Atlantic provinces initially paralleled that in Ontario. In the early 1700s the area known as Acadia was ceded by France to Britain. The area soon became known as Nova Scotia and gradually people from New England spread north and settled in the new province. These settlers brought with them a tradition of local government through the town meeting, although officially local government was to be carried on by the Courts of Quarter Sessions and a grand jury.

After the American Revolution, a wave of Loyalists migrated to the area, this time less from New England than from New York, New Jersey, Pennsylvania, and the South. The Southern Loyalists brought with them a different tradition of local government based on the classed society of the American South in which the Courts of Quarter Sessions discharged local government functions and the Governor appointed local officials. Because of anti-American feelings caused by the Revolution, the New England Loyalists were unsuccessful in promoting local self-rule. Despite dissatisfaction with corrupt practices of certain magistrates, the system of the Courts of Quarter Sessions was to prevail for over 100 years.

At this point, developments in the Atlantic provinces proceeded on a different course from those in Ontario. Far from fighting for local municipal institutions, many Loyalists actively discouraged their development. Many reasons have been suggested for this attitude. They include the feeling that the town meeting had contributed to the revolutionary tendencies of the Americans, a fear of increased taxation, a concern that local officials would lose patronage, and public apathy. In addition, the compactness of the area and the availability of cheap water transportation rendered road construction, one of the major municipal functions, less important. The developments in each province will now be briefly examined.

Nova Scotia

Early local government in Nova Scotia was provided by Courts of Quarter Sessions established by the British authorities around 1750. A wave of immigration from New England at the beginning of the 1760s brought settlers accustomed to the town meeting form of local government. The colonial authorities were unwilling to consider such a democratic approach, especially after the American War of Independence. It wasn't until 1841 that the first municipal incorporation occurred, with the granting of a charter to Halifax.

After the introduction of responsible government in 1848 the authorities showed more willingness to allow local government. Legislation permitting the incorporation of counties was enacted in 1855, and the following year the incorporation of townships was authorized. Ironically, now that the right to local government was finally granted, Nova Scotians did not exercise it. According to Higgins, the early enthusiasm waned with the realization that incorporation would bring with it higher taxation.[23] However, the provincial government was determined to shift some of the financial burden for local services on to local residents

[23]Donald J. H. Higgins, *Local and Urban Politics in Canada*, Toronto, Gage, 1986, pp. 39-40.

The result was the 1879 County Incorporation Act.

That Act was conceived in secrecy at the provincial level and it was the direct offspring of the financial difficulties of the provincial government. The then Attorney General, J.S.D. Thompson, who later became Prime Minister of Canada, frankly stated that the main object of the Act was "to compel Counties to tax themselves directly to keep up their roads and bridges."[24]

Under the Act, the rural areas of the province were incorporated as counties or districts, single tier municipalities governed by a warden and an elected council. Urban areas were dealt with in the Towns Incorporation Act of 1888. It stipulated geographic and population requirements which would enable a town to apply for a charter of incorporation. (Eight such towns had already been incorporated by charter prior to the passage of the statute.) These provisions for separate rural and urban municipalities have remained the basis for the Nova Scotia system to this day.

Prince Edward Island

In 1769 Prince Edward Island separated from Nova Scotia. Two years earlier the island had been divided into counties, parishes, and townships for judicial purposes and for the election of representatives to the provincial legislature, but these areas were never used as municipal units. Indeed, there wasn't any obvious need for municipal government, or even for a decentralization of the colonial administration, given the small size and tiny population of Prince Edward Island.

The first municipal government appeared in 1855 with the incorporation of Charlottetown as a city. In 1870 an act was passed which enabled the resident householders of a town or village to petition the provincial authorities to allow the election of three or more wardens who could appoint local officers and pass by-laws with regard to finance and police matters. Summerside was incorporated as a town in 1875 but, presumably because of the very small population of most settlements, only six more towns had been incorporated by the time the procedure fell into disuse, in 1919. It was abolished in 1950. That same year, the Village Services Act was passed, but the villages established under this statute were not municipalities. Instead of elected councillors, they were governed by commissioners appointed by the provincial government. These villages

---

[24]A. William Cox, Q.C., in a 1989 paper "Development of Municipal-Provincial Relations," quoted in *Task Force on Local Government*, Report to the Government of Nova Scotia, April 1992, Briefing Book, p. 13.

are now known as communities, of which there are presently 80. The main difference between towns and communities is that the town councils adopt their own budgets whereas communities must get their budgets approved at an annual meeting of residents.[25] Half of the province's area and forty per cent of its population is still not municipally organized, with the province continuing to provide many of the usual local government services.

New Brunswick

Fifteen years after Prince Edward Island separated from Nova Scotia, New Brunswick followed suit — the break being precipitated by an influx of United Empire Loyalists. The following year, 1785, Saint John was incorporated as a city, preceding by almost fifty years the creation of cities in the rest of Canada. Elsewhere in the colony, however, local government was carried on by the Courts of Quarter Sessions and a grand jury. The local citizenry, according to Higgins, seems to have been largely indifferent to the idea of local self-government.[26] This attitude has been partly attributed to the smaller population of Loyalists who came from New England and had thus experienced local government. Whalen, however, rejects this viewpoint, contending that only about 7% of the Loyalists came from the Southern Colonies with their system of Quarter Sessions and that, in any event, even the Loyalists from New England made little demand for more democracy at the local level.[27] Certainly the substantial French population of the province, with their tradition of centralism, did not push for local government.

Interestingly, much of the impetus for the incorporation of municipalities came from the central authorities who were concerned about "reducing the time consumed on endless debates and squabbles over parish and county issues in the legislature" and anxious to shift a growing expenditure burden.[28] Finally, in 1851 an act was passed for the incorporation of

---

[25]Allan O'Brien, *Municipal Consolidation in Canada and its Alternatives*, Toronto, Intergovernmental Committee on Urban and Regional Research, May 1993, p. 27.

[26]*Ibid.*, p. 40.

[27]H. J. Whalen, *The Development of Local Government in New Brunswick*, Fredericton, 1963, Chapter Two.

[28]*Ibid.*, p. 20.

counties, but its provisions were permissive and only six counties were established over the next three decades. However, the Municipalities Act of 1877 made county incorporation mandatory, thus bringing the entire population and area of the province under municipal government. The county system was two-tiered like that in Ontario, but differed in that councillors from the rural areas were directly elected to county council while all urban areas, except Fredericton, were represented at the county level, usually by ex-officio members.

During this period a number of urban communities sought corporate status. Fredericton had received its charter in 1848, over 60 years after the first urban incorporation in Saint John. By 1896 nine towns had been established by separate charter. In that year the Town Incorporation Act was passed providing for a uniform system for the creation of towns with an elected council consisting of a mayor and aldermen.

The basic municipal system of New Brunswick was established in this 1896 statute and the 1877 Counties Act. Cities each have their own separate charters of incorporation and a 1920 act provided for the incorporation of villages. As discussed in Chapter 5, however, a major reorganization of local government in New Brunswick begun in 1967 resulted in the abolition of county governments and a number of other major changes.

Newfoundland

The development of municipal institutions in Newfoundland has been a slow and arduous process, attributed to several factors.[29] The settlements which developed in the early years were numerous but geographically isolated from each other, generally quite limited in population, and financially unable to support any form of local government. Moreover, since Newfoundlanders only gained the right to own property in 1824, they jealously guarded this right against the taxation which would inevitably come with local government.

Newfoundland, because of its geographic isolation, was not influenced by the development of municipal government elsewhere; nor did its early settlers have prior experience with such a system. In any event, there was little apparent need for municipal government in much of the province. Transportation needs were partly served by water and the central government provided services such as roads that were provided at the local level in other provinces.

---

[29]Higgins, *op. cit.*, pp. 33-34.

TABLE 2
Historical Highlights: Atlantic Provinces

PRINCE EDWARD ISLAND

1769	P.E.I. separated from Nova Scotia
1855	1st municipal government, city of Charlottetown
1875	Summerside incorporated as a town

NEW BRUNSWICK

1784	New Brunswick separated from Nova Scotia
1785	Saint John incorporated as a city
1877	Municipalities Act
1896	Town Incorporation Act

NOVA SCOTIA

1841	Halifax received charter
1879	General Municipal Act
1888	Town Incorporation Act

NEWFOUNDLAND

1888	St. John's created a town
1949	Province joined Confederation
	General local government act passed

After some unsuccessful attempts, St. John's was created a town in 1888, but once again the impetus was not the demand for local democracy but the desire of the colonial authorities to shift some of their expenditure burden. As Higgins explains, municipal status for St. John's was imposed partly to facilitate costly improvements to the sewerage and street systems and partly to be a mechanism whereby the privately owned and heavily in debt St. John's Water Company would become the financial responsibility of the City — a Water Company in which the Premier of Newfoundland and other prominent government supporters and business people were shareholders![30]

---

[30]*Ibid.*, pp. 34-35.

No other municipalities were formed for fifty years. Acts were passed in 1933 and again in 1937 providing for the incorporation of municipalities. However, no community requested incorporation and the central authorities did not use their authority to impose such incorporations. Instead, a new approach was attempted which offered subsidies and provided a special act giving a municipality any taxation form it desired if it would incorporate. By 1948 twenty municipalities had been incorporated by special charter and only five of these imposed the real property tax.[31]

After Newfoundland joined Confederation in 1949, the provincial legislature passed a general local government act which bestowed municipal status by proclamation for areas with a population of at least one thousand, and also provided for rural districts. Since that time the number of municipalities has grown steadily as have such quasi-municipalities as local improvement districts and local government communities. Chapter 5 describes Newfoundland's prolonged efforts to bring about restructuring in the St. John's area as well as its ambitious municipal consolidation program.

Western Provinces

The provinces of Manitoba, Saskatchewan, and Alberta were part of the original Hudson's Bay Company land grant and later of the Northwest Territories. For most of their early history these provinces were governed by the Company, which had complete judicial, legislative, and administrative authority. In 1869 the Company's rights in Rupert's Land and the Northwest Territories were acquired by the newly created Dominion of Canada. It was not until late in the nineteenth century that a substantial amount of settlement occurred in the Prairie provinces. When population growth pressures finally necessitated the provision of local services and subsequently a local government system, it was only logical for these provinces to look to their nearest eastern neighbour, Ontario, for a model upon which to base their systems. Because of the different physical characteristics of the West, the Ontario model was somewhat modified to suit local needs.

Manitoba

In 1870 Manitoba was created a province separate from the Northwest Territories. The first provincial legislature provided for a system of local government by a grand jury and Courts of Sessions which were to admin-

---

[31]Crawford, *op. cit.*, p. 41.

ister a County Assessment Act and a Parish Assessment Act. As well, the judges of the Sessions selected local officers such as treasurers, assessors, highway surveyors, poundkeepers, and constables from lists presented by the grand jury.

The first municipality was established in 1873 with the incorporation of Winnipeg as a city — although not without a struggle. Apparently the Hudson's Bay Company and four other property owners, who together owned well over half of the assessable property in Winnipeg, had opposed the incorporation and the resultant taxation of that property.[32] In that same year, general municipal legislation was also passed which provided for the establishment of local municipalities upon petition of the freeholders within a district. Only six areas became incorporated during the decade that this act was in force.

This permissive approach was dropped in 1883 when the Manitoba Government decided to introduce a municipal system for the whole province modelled on the two tier county system of Ontario. The new act established twenty-six counties with councils composed of the heads of both rural and urban local (lower tier) municipal councils. The county council elected a warden from among its own members. This Ontario county system proved to be ineffective, however, because of the large areas covered, the often sparse and scattered population, and the local objections to a two tier system. It was abandoned after only three years and the province was divided into smaller rural municipalities.

In 1902 a general act established cities, towns, villages and rural municipalities as the basic units of local government, although Winnipeg was given its own special charter. This system has continued to the present, except for major changes in the structure of government for the Winnipeg area as discussed in Chapter 5.

Saskatchewan

Like Manitoba, Saskatchewan had been part of the lands granted to the Hudson's Bay Company. It was taken over by the Canadian Government in 1870 and administered essentially as a colony until it gained provincial status in 1905. The territorial council first provided for municipal government in 1883 by enacting a municipal ordinance which was patterned on the previously cited Manitoba legislation of that year which, in turn, had been modelled on the 1849 Municipal Act of Ontario. The ordinance provided for either rural municipalities or towns depending on area and pop-

---

[32]Higgins, *op. cit.*, pp. 50-51.

ulation and on whether local citizens petitioned for municipal status. Regina received town status that very year and four rural municipalities were organized in 1884, but little initiative was evident thereafter. By 1897 only one additional town had been created and two rural municipalities had dropped their municipal status. One major problem was the vast area and small, scattered population which made it difficult to generate the financial base needed to support municipal government.

However, since some form of local organization was necessary to provide roads and protection against prairie and forest fires, an ordinance was passed allowing the creation of "statute labour and fire districts" in areas not organized as rural municipalities. By 1896 these local improvement districts, as they were now called, were made mandatory and the following year legislation was passed which allowed for elected committees to administer the districts. In 1903 the districts were reorganized into larger units made up of four of the former districts, each with one elected councillor on a municipal district council. Meanwhile, a revision and consolidation of municipal ordinances in 1894 provided for the incorporation of cities, towns and rural municipalities.

Throughout this period the federal government was strongly encouraging Western settlement and large numbers of settlers arrived from Europe and from Eastern Canada, the latter bringing previous experience with municipal government. The impetus which these developments gave to the creation of municipal institutions is evident from the fact that when Saskatchewan became a province in 1905 there were already four cities, 43 towns, 97 villages, two rural municipalities and 359 of the local improvement districts.[33]

The new province appointed a Commission to carry on with a study previously started by the assembly of the Northwest Territories, which was to consider all aspects of municipal government. In 1908 Saskatchewan adopted the Commission's recommendation that a system of municipal units be established with a separate act covering each type of unit. Accordingly, the City Act, Town Act, and Village Act were passed in 1908 and the Rural Municipalities Act in the following year. One result was a very rapid increase in rural municipalities — to 200 by 1912. However, many rural residents opposed municipal organization, mainly because of a fear of increased taxes,[34] and the provincial government had to force

---

[33]Horace L. Brittain, *Local Government in Canada*, Toronto, Ryerson Press, 1951, p. 179.

[34]Higgins, *op. cit.*, p. 53.

remaining local improvement districts to become rural municipalities. This municipal structure has remained basically unchanged through to the present.

Alberta

Since Alberta was also part of the federally administered Northwest Territories from 1870 until 1905, its municipal background resembles that of Saskatchewan. The first municipal government was introduced in Calgary, which was incorporated as a town in 1884 under the previously described municipal ordinance of 1883. In what has by now become a familiar pattern, incorporation efforts were initially thwarted by large landowners, among them the CPR, opposed to the prospect of property taxes.[35] Two more urban municipalities were created over the next decade (Lethbridge and Edmonton in 1891 and 1892 respectively), but because of the very sparse, scattered rural population, there were no petitions for the creation of rural municipalities under the ordinance. As in the area which later became Saskatchewan, the main form of local government was the statute labour and fire district or local improvement district.

Toward the end of the century, however, the large influx of settlers began to stimulate the creation of local governments. When Alberta became a province in 1905 its population was about 170 000 (compared to 18 000 in 1881) and it had two cities, fifteen towns and thirty villages. By 1912 a new municipal system was established with cities, towns, villages and local improvement districts. The latter could be erected into rural municipalities upon reaching a specified population, but here again few incorporations were requested because of local fears about tax increases.

The organization of municipal government in rural Alberta has undergone considerable change over the years.[36] Beginning in 1942 the provincial government began to reduce the number of local improvement districts (by now called municipal districts) through amalgamation. A much more radical change was introduced in 1950 with the creation of single tier county governments in the rural areas handling virtually all local government functions including education. As discussed in Chapter 5, the main structural changes since have involved annexations around Calgary and Edmonton.

---

[35]*Ibid.*, p. 54.

[36]See Eric J. Hanson, *Local Government in Alberta*, Toronto, McClelland and Stewart Limited, 1956 and Jack Masson, *Alberta's Local Governments and Their Politics*, Edmonton, University of Alberta Press, 1985, Chapter Four.

British Columbia

The area of what is now British Columbia was also under the jurisdiction of the Hudson's Bay Company during its early years of settlement. In 1849 the British assumed responsibility for Vancouver Island. By this time there was a general movement of population to the west side of the continent because of the discovery of gold in California (in 1848). A significant influx of population to the mainland of British Columbia occurred with the discovery of gold on the Fraser River in 1858, and that year the British also assumed control of the mainland from the Hudson's Bay Company. The mainland and Vancouver Island were administered as two separate colonies until 1866.

The physical characteristics of British Columbia played a significant role in the development of municipal institutions in the province. Because of the mountainous terrain, early settlements were scattered and isolated. New Westminster, the capital of the mainland colony, became a municipality in 1860, and two years later Victoria, the capital of the Vancouver Island colony, was incorporated as a town. Shortly after gaining provincial status in 1871, British Columbia enacted the Consolidated Municipal Act providing for local petitions for municipal incorporation, but by the end of 1874 there were still only five municipalities in the province.

In 1892 the Municipal Clauses Act was passed, governing all new municipalities formed and providing for a system similar to that in Ontario, but without a county level. Municipalities were either cities with a mayor and council or rural districts with a reeve and council. By 1900 there were some 52 of these municipalities. In 1920 a Village Municipalities Act was passed allowing for smaller urban areas to incorporate with limited powers.

It is noteworthy that most of the larger towns established in the period from the 1870s to the 1920s were incorporated under their own "charters," statutes that were drafted locally by the applicant citizens and dealt with by the legislature as private bills. These arrangements contributed to the strong tradition of local autonomy that continues to characterize municipal government in British Columbia.

Even with these incorporations, however, the vast majority of the area of the province remained unorganized territory. The British Columbia Government was directly responsible for the provision of all necessary services.[37] Under this centralized administration, a government agent received local revenues and supervised public expenditures, and often was

---

[37]Shortt and Doughty, *op. cit.*, Vol. XXII, p. 355.

stipendiary magistrate, gold commissioner, mining recorder, water commissioner, issuer of marriage licenses, assessor, tax collector, and
policeman. As described in Chapter 5, a municipal response to the
governing of the vast rural areas was introduced beginning in 1965 with
the creation of regional districts. These have proven to be among the
most flexible of the various structural reforms introduced in the various
provinces in recent decades.

TABLE 3
Historical Highlights: Western Provinces

MANITOBA

1870 Created a province
1873 City of Winnipeg incorporated as first municipality
1873 General Municipal Act
1883 Municipal Act based on Baldwin Act of Ontario
      26 counties established
1902 General legislation for cities, towns, villages and rural units

SASKATCHEWAN & ALBERTA

1872 Surveyed into townships
1883 Ordinance for creating municipal units
1897 Won right of responsible government
1905 Separate provinces created
1908 Saskatchewan passed City, Town & Village Acts
      Established first Municipal Affairs Department
1909 Saskatchewan passed Rural Municipalities Act
1912 Alberta appointed Municipal Affairs Minister
      Established general local government system

BRITISH COLUMBIA

1871 Became a province
1872 Permissive municipal legislation
1886 Vancouver incorporated
1892 Municipal Clauses Act
      System similar to Ontario, but without a county level

Northern Territories

The area of the Yukon and Northwest Territories was controlled by the Hudson's Bay Company until acquired by the federal government in 1870.[38] Its territory was reduced that year by the establishment of Manitoba as a separate province, and further reductions occurred in 1905 when Alberta and Saskatchewan became provinces and in 1912 when the northern boundaries of Ontario, Quebec and Manitoba were extended north to their present positions. The discovery of gold in the Klondike in 1896 sparked a rapid increase in the population of the Yukon and in 1898 it was established as a separate territory.

Dawson City was incorporated as the first municipality in 1901, but its charter was revoked in 1904 and the provision of local services reverted to the territorial administration for a number of years. Also in 1901, a provision was made for the establishment of unincorporated towns upon petition. These units were not full municipal governments, however, since residents could only elect one official and only a very limited range of services could be provided. In any event, the one unincorporated town created was disbanded when its population subsequently declined.

This often temporary nature of northern settlements has added to the problems caused by the extremely small, scattered population. Therefore, while both the Yukon and Northwest Territories have municipal ordinances authorizing the establishment of municipal governments, relatively few units were created until the past couple of decades. As late as 1964 there were only three incorporated municipalities — the towns of Yellowknife and Hay Bay and the village of Fort Smith.

Prior to 1960, virtually all real government within the Northern Territories came from Ottawa. With the re-location of the Territorial Council from Ottawa to Yellowknife in 1967, however, new municipal structures were introduced which allowed for more decision making at the local level.[39] The category of city was introduced in 1969, with Yellowknife becoming the first city.

There has been increasing emphasis on the passing of authority down from the Territorial Government to local governments, along with an attempt to strengthen the political role of the municipalities. One gov-

---

[38]The description in this section is partly based on Higgins, *op. cit.*, pp. 59-60.

[39]This discussion is based on Government of the Northwest Territories in conjunction with the Association of Municipal Clerks and Treasurers of Ontario, *Municipal Administration Program*, 1984, Unit 1, Lesson Two.

ernment study claimed that "[In] the NWT the importance of the local level of government is of particular magnitude because of the cultural diversity and the vast distances between communities."[40]

While only a very small portion of the vast area of the Northern Territories is organized municipally, the organized portion contains three-quarters of the population. The few cities, towns and villages, which contain the bulk of the population, are basically modelled upon the structure of municipal government found in Southern Ontario. In addition to these tax-based municipalities, there are some 40 non-tax-based municipalities (mostly hamlets) with more limited powers. Of particular interest is a relatively new form of municipal unit called the charter community, whose specific features depend on what is spelled out in the charter establishing it. This flexibility is especially useful in areas where band councils have provided the traditional leadership in the community. Natives have tended to view municipalities as "foreign" structures. The charter community approach allows the creation of a new governing arrangement which can incorporate elements of the band council structure and that of municipalities.

In addition to these municipal structures, a very large number of local boards and special purpose committees are found in the Northern Territories.[41] Many of these bodies were established to obtain feedback from the local communities, to compensate for the fact that there were few elected members of the territorial council (now the Legislative Assembly) and few elected municipal councils. Even though municipal councils are now more widespread, these special purpose bodies have proven difficult to eradicate — a problem also experienced in Southern Canada.

Further changes and boundary adjustments are inevitable as a result of reviews which will be carried out in response to the several aboriginal land claim settlements which are changing jurisdictions in the north. Particularly dramatic is the Nunavut land claim of the Eastern Arctic which will lead to territorial division before the end of this century. The Nunavut Political Accord signed in October 1992 sets out guidelines establishing a new region to be carved out of the Northwest Territories by 1999, essentially cutting it in half.[42]

---

[40]*Constitutional Development in the Northwest Territories, Report of the Special Representative* (Drury Report), Ottawa, 1980, quoted in *ibid.*, p. 33.

[41]See Report of the Project to Review the Operations and Structure of Northern Government, *Strength at Two Levels*, November 1991.

[42]*Canada Year Book 1994*, Ottawa, Statistics Canada, p. 288.

Summary

By the beginning of the twentieth century, most provinces had in place, or were about to establish, a system of municipalities. The one major exception is the Northern Territories where the development of municipal institutions was much slower because of the very small, scattered and largely migratory population and the concentration of government power in Ottawa until the mid-20th century.

All of the systems were fairly similar, in large part because of the influence of the Ontario model established in 1849. The systems generally consisted of cities, towns, and villages as urban units, a rural unit variously known as a township, municipal district, or rural municipality, and in some cases an upper tier county unit. Councils were for the most part directly elected, with the notable exception of the county level in Ontario, Quebec, and to some degree New Brunswick. Generally, an Assessment Act was also passed which provided municipalities with their main source of revenue.

These municipal systems were quite appropriate for the conditions of the time. They were generally based on a distinction between urban and rural classifications of municipality, on an expectation that municipalities would provide a quite limited range of services, primarily services to property, and on an assumption that the property tax would be both appropriate and adequate to finance the cost of these limited services. However, the primarily agricultural and rural nature of the economy and society in which these municipal systems were established was to undergo a fundamental change over the next fifty to one hundred years. As Chapter 4 makes clear, this change rendered the traditional municipal systems increasingly inadequate.

But, what of the circumstances surrounding the introduction of municipal institutions in each province, and the expectations held out for the new level of government? Over the years a romantic notion has developed concerning the long, bitter struggle waged by our ancestors to wrest local self-government from an unsympathetic and paternalistic regime both in the colonies and in Britain. This vision is used to defend the status quo whenever change threatens "historic" boundaries.

Yet the true record is considerably less stirring. While something approaching this chain of events did take place in Ontario, municipal government was less warmly received in Quebec where it was viewed as simply another means of oppression because of the power of taxation. In the Atlantic provinces, this fear of the property tax prompted strong opposition to the introduction of municipal government. An editorial in the *New Brunswick Courier* in 1843 about a proposed municipal bill stated that had the bill been passed, "it would have cut loose that many-headed monster, Direct Taxation and its Myrmidon, the Tax-Gatherer, into the happy home of every poor man throughout the land."[43] Indeed, the history of municipal government in Newfoundland, far from being a tale of local agitation and central government resistance, was instead a case of central government overtures complete with financial incentives, all of which were largely ignored by the local people.

It is also noteworthy that where the provincial authorities did encourage or ultimately impose municipal governments on their populace, it was not because of any apparent belief in the values of local democracy — rather it was motivated by a desire on the part of the provincial administrations to shift at least some of the growing burden of expenditures to the local level. This pattern is evident in the historical developments in a number of the Atlantic and Western provinces — and there are some fascinating parallels with developments today.

Because of the later settlement of the west, however, there was fairly general acceptance of the logic and desirability of having municipal government. Usually one of the first actions of the new Western provincial governments was to establish a municipal system. This was due in part to the fact that many of the settlers arriving in the new provinces had come from areas where they had enjoyed municipal government, and in part to the fact that, with the greatly increased population, it was more efficient to provide certain services at the local level.

From the historical developments in the various provinces it is clear that municipal governments were mainly established in response to population growth and consequent service demands. Even in Ontario where pressure for local self-government was most pronounced, an important factor in the creation of municipal institutions was the inability of the Courts of Quarter Sessions to deal with growing urban problems. The preoccupation with local government as a provider of services has remained a central feature of the system to the present day.

Kaplan suggests that there were a number of conflicting views and motivations influencing the establishment of our original municipal institutions and that these contradictions continue to affect local governments.[44] He notes that while reformers pushed for the democratic virtues

---

[43]Quoted in Whelan, *op. cit.*, pp. 20-21.

[44]Harold Kaplan, *Reform, Planning and City Politics: Montreal, Winnipeg, Toronto*, Toronto, University of Toronto Press, 1982.

of local government, the image of local officials as magistrates — arising from the operation of the justices of the peace and the Courts of Quarter Sessions — was too firmly established to be completely erased. Landowners liked this latter image which appeared to provide some assurance that the new municipal institutions wouldn't embark on costly local improvements. "Rather than seek out local problems and needs and then devise suitable governmental solutions, the municipal officials would wait until individual complaints were brought before them and then would resolve only the case at hand."[45]

In addition to these perspectives, a third view saw local government as a public corporation, drawing its life from a Crown-issued charter, and exercising only those powers assigned to it in the charter. These three premises were obviously inconsistent. As Kaplan points out:

> One cannot model local government on both a judicial tribunal and a business corporation. Local government cannot be both an experiment in mass participatory democracy and a corporation created by and for property owners.[46]

The democratic image emphasized that local government was another level of government but "far more democratic and more intimately linked to the average citizen than were the remote senior levels." According to the other two images, local government was "an arbiter of individual complaints or a dispenser of limited assistance to property owners but not ... a general purpose government."[47]

Further confusion about the appropriate role of local government occurred during the turn of the century reform era with its strong emphasis on removing politics from the local level. These developments, whose influence on both operating philosophy and governmental machinery is still felt today, are examined in the next chapter.

---

[45]*Ibid.*, p. 61.

[46]*Ibid.*, p. 63.

[47]*Ibid.*

CHAPTER 3

Turn of the Century Reform Era

OBJECTIVES:

1. To describe the forces and influences which formed part of the turn of the century reform movement in Canada and the U.S.

2. To describe the main changes in municipal machinery which were introduced as part of the reform movement.

3. To assess the influence of the reform movement on the structure and operating philosophy of municipal government today.

4. To demonstrate the narrowing of the political role of municipal government resulting from developments during this reform movement.

Introduction

With the onset of the twentieth century Canada was at the end of twenty-five years of industrialization and in the midst of large-scale immigration. During this period of unprecedented economic and population growth, Canadians developed a "boom" mentality and municipal councils were no exception. They began to compete with each other for the location of industry, population growth, and new residential and commercial construction. An indication of the extent of this growth is the fact that the number of real estate agents in Halifax, Saint John, Montreal, Ottawa, Toronto, London, Winnipeg, Regina, Calgary, Edmonton, Vancouver, and Victoria increased from 506 in 1901 to 4 250 in 1913.[1] This surge of development brought with it not only prosperity but also new servicing demands and problems. As discussed in Chapter 4, the physical nature of this development changed the urban environment and the human

---

[1]John C. Weaver, *Shaping the Canadian City: Essays on Urban Politics and Policy 1890-1920*, Toronto, Institute of Public Administration, Monographs on Canadian Urban Government, No. 1, 1977, p. 12. This monograph offers an excellent insight into the reform era and is a partial basis for this chapter.

interaction taking place there. In this chapter we will examine the impact that this growth had on Canadian municipal institutions and on the operating philosophy of municipal government.

Urban Problems Develop

Between 1901 and 1911 Canada led the Western world in population growth. Much of this growth was due to immigration, with the foreign-born population of Canada increasing by over 2 000 000. While many of these immigrants were in Canada as temporary labour, a significant number were permanent arrivals seeking employment in urban centres. For example, Calgary and Edmonton multiplied their populations forty times and changed almost overnight from villages to cluttered cities. Winnipeg, which had already shown an impressive increase in population from 1800 to 40 000 between 1874 and 1899, surged to 150 000 by 1913. The bulk of this increase came from immigration, and by 1911 no other city in Canada had as high a proportion of European-born residents. The problems of assimilation which resulted led to what Artibise called a "Divided City."[2]

Even without these ethnic and cultural strains, however, the sheer numbers involved generated greatly increased service demands. The years 1900-1913 saw a tremendous jump in urban land values which was accompanied by extensive land speculation. In 1913 an English traveller wrote of the Victoria land boom that in two and one half years values increased 900 per cent.[3] The increase in land values precipitated a change in downtown land use from that of a mix of small businesses and residential housing to high rise office towers. This change in land use and higher real estate prices also served to push the working class out to the suburbs. These new settlement patterns continued to unfold throughout the 20th century, with disturbing results which are discussed in the next chapter. Despite a building boom accompanied by large scale land assemblies and suburban development, the supply of housing could not keep up with the demand. Soon all major Canadian cities were faced with a serious housing shortage and the subsequent development of ghettos and slums.

---

[2]Alan F. Artibise, "Divided City: The Immigrant in Winnipeg Society, 1874-1921," in Gilbert A. Stelter and Alan F. Artibise (eds.), *The Canadian City: Essays in Urban History*, Toronto, McClelland and Stewart, 1977.

[3]John Bensely Thornhill, *British Columbia in the Making*, London, Constable and Company, 1913, pp. 126-127, as quoted in Weaver, *op. cit.*, p. 13.

Besides a scarcity of housing, Canadian cities were confronted with other new servicing problems. In order to accommodate immigrant workers, inferior housing units were hastily built, often without sanitary conveniences. Families frequently shared accommodation and overcrowding became a strain on already overworked municipal water and sewer systems. In 1910 in Canada, 57 systems of inland water were receiving raw sewage from 159 municipalities, and 111 water supply systems were obtaining their water from bodies of water into which raw sewage had been discharged. The combination of these factors produced a serious health hazard which became only too apparent in the early 1900s with an alarming increase in the number of epidemics. During this period, one of every three deaths was caused by tuberculosis, and typhoid and flu epidemics produced more casualties than World War One.[4]

Other major problem areas were transportation and the provision of utilities. The overcrowding of the downtown district plus the increased numbers commuting from the suburbs created the need for new modes of transportation or, at the very least, the construction of more roads and sidewalks. By 1913 most cities had electrified streetcar systems, which were often privately owned monopolies, and at the same time municipalities were being pressured into providing municipal electric power plants. The mayor of Medicine Hat proclaimed "The municipal ownership town is in a better position to deal with industrial institutions.... Municipal ownership (of utilities) and industrial progress go hand in hand."[5]

These new and expanded services in turn meant increased costs and therefore higher municipal taxes. Morley Wickett, an academic, businessman, and Toronto alderman, pointed out in 1907 that:

> The annual expenditure of Winnipeg clearly exceeds that of Manitoba; Montreal's that of the province of Quebec; and until the present year Toronto's that of the province of Ontario.[6]

---

[4]The above figures on the pollution and health problems are from Alan H. Armstrong, "Thomas Adams and the Commission on Conservation," in L. A. Gertler (ed.), *Planning the Canadian Environment*, Montreal, Harvest House, 1968, pp. 20-22.

[5]Mayor Foster, "Development of Natural Resources Under Municipal Ownership," *Canadian Municipal Journal*, II, April 1906, p. 133, as quoted in Weaver, *op. cit.*, p. 38. See Weaver's monograph, pp. 37-39 for a detailed discussion of public ownership of utilities.

[6]As quoted in Paul Rutherford, "Tomorrow's Metropolis: The Urban Reform Movement in Canada, 1880-1920," in Stelter and Artibise, *op. cit.*, p. 376.

These growth pressures resulted in the development of various reform movements throughout Canadian society which were also part of a larger international movement common to most industrialized nations. At this time groups such as the Women's Christian Temperance Union, YMCA, YWCA, Salvation Army, and White Cross Army were founded to help stamp out crime, vice, and poverty, evils associated with the emergence of the wicked city. In response to the servicing and financial pressures facing municipal governments, groups were formed such as the Civic Art Guild of Toronto, City Improvement League of Montreal, Union of Canadian Municipalities, Good Roads Association, and the Civic Improvement League of Canada. The goals of these various groups included social justice, a healthy and beautiful city, regulation of utilities and the restructuring of municipal government. Two movements which had a significant impact on local government were those that encouraged municipal planning and the reform of municipal government.

Development of Municipal Planning

There were three main forces which affected the development of municipal planning. The first to emerge was the civic enhancement or "city beautiful" movement which was often embraced by civic boosters. While city beautiful had supporters who wanted to improve the city for its own sake, councillors and businessmen frequently regarded it as simply another means of attracting industry and growth. The central belief of the boosters was the desirability of growth and the importance of material success.[7] Their views were very influential, partly because not to be a booster was portrayed as lacking both community spirit and business sense. "Good citizenship and boosterism were synonymous."[8]

The city beautiful movement was embraced by Canadian architects, engineers and surveyors unhappy with the squalor and the ugly environment developing in Canadian communities with the rapid urbanization of the time. Their objective was the achievement of civic grandeur through the development of civic centres featuring monumental public buildings grouped around a public square and a broad tree-lined avenue leading to

---

[7]Alan J. Artibise, "In Pursuit of Growth: Municipal Boosterism and Urban Development in the Canadian Prairie West, 1871-1913," in Gilbert Stelter and Alan Artibise (eds.), *Shaping the Urban Landscape: Aspects of the Canadian City-Building Process*, Ottawa, Carleton University Press, 1982, p. 124.

[8]*Ibid.*, p. 125.

it.[9] The grand designs provoked criticism of the city beautiful movement as "mere adornment" and extravagence, which failed to address the "real problems" of city housing and sanitation.[10]

A second force which influenced planning resulted from the deteriorating health conditions in urban areas. For example, Fort William tripled its population between 1896 and 1905 as the result of railroad expansion. In the winter of 1905-1906 a sewer which emptied into the city's water supply caused approximately 800 cases of typhoid.[11] This and other similar situations gave rise to the "healthy city" movement, with public health advocates pressing for better public water supplies and sewer systems and for the eradication of slums.[12]

People became convinced that housing conditions were related to public health. Toronto's Medical Officer of Health described slums as "cancerous sores on the body politic, sources of bacteria spreading disease, crime, and discontent throughout the city."[13] The middle and upper classes were continually warned that disease did not respect social standing and they pressed for measures which expanded the powers of health and building inspectors and legislated housing standards. J.J. Kelso, an Ontario lobbyist for children's aid, advocated a form of urban renewal:

> Rear houses and those built in the notorious alleys and lanes of the city should be pulled down. There should be a by-law that every dwelling must front on a forty or sixty foot street and that only one dwelling should be created to each 20 by 100 foot lot.[14]

Unfortunately, because many dwellings were subsequently condemned, these measures only served to make the existing housing shortage worse.

The early public health movement was to have a very significant effect on the development of municipal government. The prevention of illness called for municipal action on a wide range of matters. Municipal public

---

[9]Gerald Hodge, *Planning Canadian Communities*, Scarborough, Nelson Canada, p. 53.

[10]*Ibid.*, p. 56.

[11]Weaver, *op. cit.*, p. 28.

[12]Hodge, *op. cit.*, p. 83.

[13]Rutherford, *op. cit.*, p. 375.

[14]*Labour Gazette*, July 1910, p. 128, as quoted in Weaver, *op. cit.*, p. 33.

works departments grew out of the public health movement, and so did urban planning, parks, housing and social service functions.[15] As the 20th century advanced, however, advances in medicine shifted the emphasis of health from prevention to the treatment of sickness and from municipal government preventive programs to massive expenditures on hospitals and doctors. It is only recently, through the revival of a "healthy communities" movement that we are rediscovering the vital links between municipal government services and the maintenance of a healthy population.

The two reform themes we have been discussing, those of city beautiful and city healthy, were brought together with the creation in 1909 of a federal Commission for the Conservation of Natural Resources. The impetus for its establishment was a recognition that "industrial processes were consuming natural resources at an alarming rate, often leaving in their wake waste and pollution."[16]

Dr. Charles Hodgetts, in summing up the purpose of the Commission, stated that housing and town planning involved two important factors, the physical and the vital:

> The former relates to the protecting of our land, our forests, our minerals, our water, our sunlight, our fresh air; the latter, to the prevention of diseases, to health, and the prolongation of life.[17]

Thomas Adams was appointed Advisor on Town Planning to the Commission in 1914. Adams, a native of Scotland, had studied law and then been attracted to the Garden City Movement, which aimed to disperse the population and industry of a large city into smaller concentrations and to create more amenable living conditions in what we would now call "new towns" or "satellite towns."[18] He had served on the board which administered the British Town Planning and Housing Act and when he arrived in Canada he already had a reputation as "an eloquent author and speaker on the Garden City Movement, on agricultural land use and on town planning and housing as aspects of local government." Adams proceeded to draft local plans and model provincial town planning acts

---

[15]Trevor Hancock, Bernard Pouliot and Pierre Duplessis, "Public Health," in Richard Lareto and Trevor Price (eds.), *Urban Policy Issues: Canadian Perspectives*, Toronto, McClelland and Stewart, 1990, p. 192.

[16]Hodge, *op. cit.*, p. 86.

[17]Armstrong, *op. cit.*, p. 21.

[18]Hodge, *op. cit.*, p. 50.

based on the British Act and by 1916 only British Columbia and Prince Edward Island did not have a planning statute of Adams' making in force. His model created a separate honorary planning board, influenced by American prototypes, with the mayor as the only elected representative. Adams also assisted many Canadian municipalities in the preliminary stages of local planning and promoted the creation of provincial departments of municipal affairs in Ontario and Quebec.

A third force, and one which also influenced municipal structural reforms, was the "city efficient" movement. In this movement the goals of city beautiful and city healthy — that is beauty, order, convenience, and health — were interpreted as economy and efficiency. Planning became a rational scientific process in which experts would provide technical solutions. As one spokesman explained, "if all the facts can be collected ... then a solution of any town planning problem becomes comparatively simple."[19] This point of view was consistent with, and reinforced by, the new ideas of "scientific management" which were becoming popular at this time. Disciples of scientific management advanced the claim that there was only "one best way" to run any organization, to be discovered by rational inquiry.

Athough most reformers claimed that they were working to improve the plight of the slum dwellers, a certain amount of self-interest can be detected in reforms actually implemented. Zoning by-laws were often passed to protect middle and upper-class property values and neighbourhoods since, according to one of the supporters of the Manitoba Tenement Act of 1909, tenement houses "may ... to a large extent spoil the appearance of a neighbourhood."[20]

Development of Municipal Reform Movement

By 1900 urban reformers were advocating changes in the structure of local government as a means of eliminating corruption and improving efficiency. Structural reforms had first been popularized by newspapers covering the corruption of the Tammany Society in New York City (and other American political machines) and subsequent American efforts at

---

[19]Gilbert Stelter and Alan Artibise, "Urban History Comes of Age: A Review of Current Research," *City Magazine*, vol. 3 no. 1, September/October 1977, p. 31.

[20]John C. Weaver, "Tomorrow's Metropolis Revisited: A Critical Assessment of Urban Reform in Canada, 1890-1920," in Gilbert A. Stelter and Alan F. J. Artibise (eds.), *The Canadian City: Essays in Urban History*, p. 407.

municipal reform. In fact, much as American immigrants had influenced the original developments of Canadian municipal government, Americans also exerted a strong influence on Canadian reforms at the turn of the century. But while the corruption of municipal government had reached crisis proportions in the United States, the situation in Canada was somewhat less severe.

This is not to say that Canadian municipal politicians were immune to the opportunities presented by the sudden urban growth and get-rich mentality of the times. In Toronto, corporations bidding on contracts and franchises complained that aldermen were "shaking them down" and precipitated an inquiry in which only a few were found guilty but the whole council was tarnished by association. It was also soon after discovered that the Montreal Police Commission was running a protection racket, the Toronto zoo keeper was stocking his own kitchen with food meant for the animals, and Regina city councillors were being given unusually low assessments and utility bills.[21] These revelations and others left the public with a rather low opinion of municipal government and calls for some kind of action were soon heard.

In the forefront of the municipal reform movement were middle-class merchants and businessmen. Many of these businessmen had little sympathy for the democratic aspects of local government. They were mainly concerned with expanding local services in order to attract more growth (often on land they owned) which in turn would expand the local tax base to help pay for new services. To these business people, most of whom were part of the boosterism discussed above, local government was just a tool to serve personal and community prosperity. "It was merely a device to be used for the benefit of the people who managed to gain political power or influence."[22] It was business people, of course, who gained control very early and used it for their ends.

As the labour movement developed, working people tried to exert influence as a counterbalance to the strength of business interests. The Industrial Workers of the World (I.W.W.), later known as the One Big Union (O.B.U.), was a force to be taken in earnest in the second decade of the 20th century — pledged to the overthrow of the capitalist system.[23] By the end of World War One, it had begun to attract allies in other

---

[21]Weaver, *Shaping the Canadian City, op. cit.*, pp. 56-59.

[22]Artibise, *Shaping the Urban Landscape, op. cit.*, p. 128.

[23]The description which follows is based on Ralph Allen, *Ordeal By Fire*, Toronto, Doubleday, 1961, p. 175.

countries, including Canada. With the end of the war, returning soldiers swelled the labour force, jobs were scarce and many workers were dissatisfied with their wages and their hours. On May 13th, 1919, the growing labour unrest in Canada exploded in a general strike in Winnipeg, leaving Canada's third largest city half paralyzed. Sympathy strikes broke out in a dozen other cities, including Toronto, Vancouver, Edmonton and Calgary, but not with the same intensity or impact. Gradually, the civilian authorities began to reassert their authority and, more than a month after it began, the strike was ended with the arrest of its alleged leaders. This polarization of business and labour contributed to continuing clashes between business and labour for control of municipal councils in Canada's major cities, as discussed in Chapter 8.

Businessmen were not prepared to accept any responsibility for the problems caused by urban expansion since this growth was perceived as only allowing nature to follow its own course. Instead they blamed corrupt local politicians and inefficient municipal governments for the situation. While the initial purpose of municipal reforms was to eliminate corruption, a second important purpose was to improve efficiency. The obvious solution, to the business community at any rate, was to take the politics out of municipal government and to run it on business principles. In Hamilton, reform mayor Captain McLaren ran on the slogan that "civic business is not politics."[24]

The business community was not alone in its perception of municipal government as simply a business venture which should be run on business principles. Many contemporary newspapers felt this way and frequently carried editorials promoting municipal reforms. Typical of this view is this comparison of a municipality and a joint stock company:

> If we could only manage our business as private corporations manage theirs we certainly would not have such a queer lot of directors — aldermen we call them — or make presidents — mayors as we call them — out of men who have never proven themselves as good businessmen....[25]

Businessmen were also concerned about the power and narrow focus of ward-based politicians who failed to understand the importance of municipal reforms and hindered their implementation. In many cities these ward politicians were elected from areas where foreigners constituted most of the electorate and as Winnipeg's Mayor Sharpe stated: "The city's many foreigners could not comprehend civic issues and hence

[24]Weaver, "Tomorrow's Metropolis Revisited," p. 42.

[25]*Saturday Night*, 1899, as quoted in Weaver, *Shaping the Canadian City*, p. 41.

the role of the wards which gave them a degree of influence should be reduced in any new system."[26]

Much of the reform fervor was also due to a certain amount of enlightened self-interest as many businessmen stood to gain financially through municipal actions. Winnipeg's Mayor Sharpe was a wealthy contractor who specialized in sidewalks. In Regina the reform candidate was known as "the Merchant Prince;" he claimed that he paid $3 out of every $100 of local taxes. In Montreal the leaders of the business community, including the president of the Street Railway Company, privately financed a plebiscite on structural reforms.[27]

The reforms advocated by the business community really only served to give businessmen a greater hand in municipal affairs. Businessmen had ambitions to have certain public works undertaken, but they found that in city politics they were only one of many competing interests, including newly enfranchised lower classes. Since they were "unwilling to fully accept the realities of political pluralism they worked to scupper the rules of the game."[28] What follows is a discussion of how, specifically, the rules were changed.

The Reforms

The American schemes of municipal reform which were to influence Canadian reformers had two main thrusts: first, to give more power to the mayor and, second, generally to separate legislative and executive powers. Reforms actually implemented in Canada seemed to have been tempered by British traditions and the main concession made toward obtaining a strong mayor was the move to "at large" elections for the head of council. But there was a greater acceptance of the need to remove certain responsibilities from the control of council and in effect create separate executive and administrative bodies.

Changes to the Election Process

One of the structures most under attack was the council-committee system which seemed to allow ward aldermen a great deal of power in

---

[26]*Ibid.*, p. 62.

[27]*Ibid.*, pp. 62-63.

[28]*Ibid.*, p. 64.

specific areas and thus "opened the door to corruption." In a move to reduce this power reformers called for the complete abolition of the ward system in favour of "at large" elections for all of council. One of the more convincing arguments for abolishing wards was that they fostered a parochial view of municipal issues instead of a broader view of city-wide concerns. This situation frequently resulted in "back scratching" and "log rolling," or "I'll give you what you want in your ward if you'll give me what I want in mine." An editorial in the *Financial Post* in 1912 stated that the ward system was one of the dominant evils of municipal life and that "all aldermen should hold their seats by the vote of all the electors and should represent all the city at all times."[29] Of course, at large elections, plus a concurrent move to raise the property qualification for voters, would reduce the influence of foreign born and slum residents. As early as 1857 Montreal changed from aldermen choosing their mayor to the mayor being elected at large and in 1873 Toronto followed suit. In 1891 Toronto reduced the number of wards and in 1894 Saint John and Fredericton abolished wards completely. In Toronto and Montreal an unsuccessful attempt was made to extend the franchise to companies.

Board of Control

Another reform, which was directed at strengthening the executive at the expense of council, was the introduction of the board of control. The board of control made its initial appearance in Toronto in 1896 in response to a water and sewer crisis. It was influenced by local business models and by the commission system popular in the United States. Only one Canadian city, Saint John, New Brunswick, specifically adopted the commission system. In 1912 its council was abolished and provision made for the election at large of a five member commission. Democratic control features included public recall, initiative, and referendum. One of the concepts behind this scheme of government was that each commissioner would become responsible for overseeing a particular field or department and would therefore become an expert in that area.

The Canadian board of control differed significantly from the American commission system in that it retained a council. Initially the members of the board of control were chosen by the councillors from among themselves but subsequently they were elected at large. The purpose of the board of control was to take important executive functions out of the

---

[29]*Financial Post*, February 10, 1912, as quoted in Weaver, *Shaping the Canadian City*, p. 67.

control of council by allowing the board to prepare the budget, appoint and dismiss department heads, and award all contracts. Board decisions could only be overturned by a two-thirds vote of council which was difficult to accomplish since council included the board of control members. This form of executive committee proved to be popular in Ontario where it became mandatory for municipalities of a certain size. It also spread to other provinces and in 1906 was adopted by Winnipeg, in 1908 by Calgary where it was called a commission, and in 1910 by Montreal. The Montreal board of control, which was actually part of a more comprehensive reform which also cut the size of council in half, was seen as a managing commission whose powers were subject to the majority approval of council.

Proponents of the board of control often drew an analogy between the board and the provincial or federal cabinets. Yet the most important element of a cabinet was missing because there was no party loyalty and the controllers were not responsible to the rest of council, but instead to their own electorate. Unfortunately the board of control did not live up to reformers' expectations because the same people were still in the executive and administrative positions and the standing committee structure was usually retained. Friction often arose between the board of control and the committees because of overlapping jurisdiction. It was also far too easy to pass the buck and postpone decisions when contentious issues arose. As one contemporary observer noted:

> Our councillors have long ago discovered the truth of the maxim that there is safety in numbers. When any ticklish matter comes up, the board of control passes it on to the council; council refers it back to the board.[30]

According to this observer, after all have had their say it is customary to ask some senior staff member for a full report and "when that long-suffering individual, after much waste of valuable time, has prepared his report no one any longer has interest enough to read it."

In Western Canada most politicians were reluctant to adopt the extreme measures of the American commission system or even the somewhat more democratic board of control. Western cities adopted a system of appointed commissioners. Instead of electing commissioners who would specialize in specific fields, these cities retained their councils and appointed experts to be administrators without any formal role in policy

---

[30]Frank H. Underhill, "Commission Government in Cities (1911)," in Paul Rutherford (ed.), *Saving the Canadian City*, Toronto, University of Toronto Press, p. 327.

making. Edmonton was the first city to implement this system in 1904; Regina, Saskatoon, and Prince Albert followed in 1911-1912.

Chief Administrative Officer

Another American reform adopted by many Canadian municipalities was the city manager system. This was especially popular in Quebec after 1920. The system entailed the appointment of a chief administrator who was to coordinate and supervise all of the departments and affairs of the municipality. The system was based on the assumption that policy making, which was to be the exclusive concern of a small elected council, could be completely separated from policy implementation. It was an extremely popular reform in the United States where it was expected to solve the problem of coordinating the various people who had been given bits and pieces of power, by centralizing authority in one person. Despite the somewhat different conditions in Canada, the city manager system was appealing to reformers because it appeared to be one step closer to the corporate model. In 1919 Guelph, Ontario, adopted the system and the city clerk described the organization as similar to a joint stock company with the aldermen as directors and the mayor as president. According to him:

> The city manager through his different departments, plans the work, submits same to council for their approval. When approved, it is up to the city manager to carry it out in a businesslike manner, without interference from the aldermen.[31]

In some cities it was even suggested that the elected council should be abolished and local affairs should be managed by an appointed executive. In London, Ontario, it was proposed that this appointed executive should be composed of representatives of special interest groups such as Rotary clubs, ratepayers associations and the Board of Trade. In Montreal it was intended to retain the council with the mayor, two members elected by council, one by the Board of Trade, and one by the Chambre de Commerce as the executive committee. While most of these proposals were not adopted for councils, in the 1940s Montreal did have a council consisting of a mayor and 99 councillors of whom 66 were elected and 33 were appointed by public associations.[32] However, the idea of special

---

[31]*Ibid.*, p. 68.

[32]Paul Hickey, *Decision Making Processes in Ontario's Local Governments*, Toronto, Ministry of Municipal Affairs, 1973, p. 203.

interest group representation became a popular plan when establishing special purpose bodies.

Boards and Commissions

In a further effort to reduce council's control, reformers advocated the creation of various boards and commissions which would oversee activity in a specific area and thus remove it from the political arena. Although these special purpose bodies were not a new phenomenon, Ontario having had police commissions and boards of health as early as the 1850s, they flourished between 1890 and 1920. To some extent this is understandable. The pressures of urban growth and new technological developments made municipal government more complex. Municipalities were now faced with decisions in areas relating to sewers, pumping stations, streetcars, power systems, street and sidewalk paving, building codes, assessments, department budgets, tenders, debentures, and sinking funds.

Goldwin Smith, a member of a Toronto municipal reform group, summed up the general attitude in 1890 when he said that in the past city government was a proper setting for debates on principles, but now "a city is simply a densely peopled district in need of a specially skilled administration."[33] The age of the experts or the professionals had arrived and their coming was seen as the panacea for urban problems. The creation of a committee of experts was that much better.

Another argument in favour of creating special purpose bodies was that a commission could attract "the services of bright, able men who have not the time to serve in the council."[34] What this also meant was that businessmen were more likely to serve in an appointed position than they were to engage in an election contest and, if successful, to endure the tedious task of attending to constituents' requests. In any event, the lobbying for appointed commissions increased; in Toronto for a parks commission, fire commission, hydroelectric commission, and transportation commission; in Montreal for a parks commission; and in Vancouver for a water works commission. As previously discussed, the impetus for town planning also included the creation of a separate planning board or commission. As well, when municipalities took over the operations of street railway systems in the name of efficiency, they usually established a separate body to oversee the administration of this very important function.

---

[33]Weaver, *Shaping the Canadian City, op. cit.*, p. 72.

[34]Mayor Bethune, Vancouver (1907), as quoted in *ibid.*, p. 70.

By 1917 the proliferation of special purpose bodies was causing concern over the amount of decentralization and fragmentation which had resulted. The October issue of *Municipal World* that year carried an article with the following statement:

> Decentralization has been carried too far. Town Planning Commissions, Suburban Road Commissions, Railway Commissions, Police Commissions, Boards of Education, Hospital Trusts, Utilities Commissions have usurped Council powers. The Council today is little more than a tax-levying body with little or no control.[35]

As will be seen in Chapter 5, these criticisms of excessive boards and resulting fragmentation were still being heard when local government reform initiatives were launched in many of the provinces in the 1950s and 1960s. In response, most of the reforms called for the abolition of boards and municipal consolidations to create a more coordinated structure for efficient delivery of services. However, as will also be seen, boards have been making something of a comeback in recent years. They have been established in, or proposed for, a number of urban areas, in part because of the near-impossibility of gaining agreement on municipal boundary changes.[36]

Summary: The Legacy of the Reform Era

Each of the reform movements had its own vision of what tomorrow's city should be like: a city beautiful, filled with parks, trees, boulevards, and stately buildings; a nation full of Garden Cities in which development was controlled to ensure all the basic amenities of life; the Canadian city converted into a Christian community where poverty, crime and vice were eliminated; or an orderly community with a municipal government run on principles of economy and efficiency.[37]

While many of the reformers undoubtedly were sincere in their efforts, others had less noble motives behind their reform proposals. C. S. Clarke,

---

[35]S. M. Baker, "Municipal Government Reform," *Municipal World*, Vol. 27, October 1917, p. 154, as quoted in Weaver, "Tomorrow's Metropolis Revisited," p. 411.

[36]A number of examples are found in Dale Richmond and David Siegel (eds.), *Agencies, Boards and Commissions in Canadian Local Government*, Toronto, Institute of Public Administration, 1994.

[37]Rutherford, *Saving the Canadian City, op. cit.*, p. xvii.

an opinionated Torontonian, denounced those crusaders who wanted to purify city life as "a small group of pious fanatics who bothered the respectable and terrorized the weak."[38] In only slightly more generous terms, Kaplan states that "the reform doctrine was self-congratulatory, contemptuous of outsiders, and thus highly vulnerable to charges of hypocrisy,"[39] especially since, as indicated above, its main advocates were prominent businessmen seeking to expand their influence. Keating describes the concern of the business community and much of the professional middle class about the demands of an increasingly assertive working class, armed with the franchise.[40] These demands had produced "machine politics" in the United States and a socialist movement centred mainly in Western Canada. Both of these troubling developments (in the minds of the business community) could be curtailed by limiting the role of the poor and working class in local politics through institutional reform and by reasserting the ideology of non-partisanship and good government. As Keating points out, "attacks on politics or partisanship often mask objections to the use of political power to counteract inequalities in the social or economic spheres. Non-partisanship thus tends to be a conservative rallying cry."[41] This bias will become evident with the examination of developments in local political parties in Chapter 8.

The reforms pertaining to municipal government were partly meant to eliminate corruption and to improve efficiency. The primary method of achieving this was to remove powers from council control by decreasing the number and importance of ward politicians, by increasing the power of a small executive through the board of control, by increasing the powers of the administration through the commissioner and city manager systems, and finally by creating separate special purpose bodies to take over completely certain important functions which could not be entrusted to politicians. Municipal government was regarded less as a level of government and more as a business. The right to vote was viewed as less important than ensuring a well run municipal organization which

---

[38]Rutherford, "Tomorrow's Metropolis," p. 371.

[39]Harold Kaplan, *Reform, Planning and City Politics: Montreal, Winnipeg, Toronto*, Toronto, University of Toronto Press, 1982, p. 173.

[40]Michael Keating, *Comparative Urban Politics*, Aldershot, Edward Elgar, 1991, pp. 43-46.

[41]*Ibid.*, p. 43.

would provide services efficiently. In discussing the municipal franchise, Goldwin Smith asked:

> What is the power which we now exercise, and which is largely illusory so far as the mass of us are concerned, compared with our health, our convenience, and the rescue of our property from the tax-gatherer?[42]

The net result of the reforms was a more complex, less accountable municipal government, more responsible to economy and efficiency than to the voters. Yet even in these former respects the success of the new municipal organizations was questionable. As early as 1899 there was some recognition in Toronto that structural reforms had not eliminated waste and corruption. A *Toronto Star* editorial claimed that council and the board of control were playing "a game of shuttlecock and battledore."[43] In 1909 the Fort William-Port Arthur Utilities Commission had to admit that service was poor. In 1913 Calgary's commissioners bought a $5 000 car with special paint and a special siren horn for their use,[44] perhaps not the most efficient use of public funds. The problem, of course, was that even businessmen and experts were as prone to self-interest and corruption as those municipal officials they had previously chastised. In 1895 the Telegram had written that "the fault is not with the system but with the people."[45]

It is ironic that while many of these turn of the century reforms were prompted by the excesses of party politics and the "spoils" system in American local government, they were adopted by Canadian municipalities which, for the most part, were not organized on party lines. A number of indigenous factors have been suggested to explain this different pattern of development in Canada.[46] Because urbanization came later to Canada, Canadian cities were smaller and more homogeneous and lacked the patronage potential found in American cities with a heavily immigrant population. In addition, since provincial governments controlled their local governments more than state governments did, "the

---

[42]Weaver, *Shaping the Canadian City, op. cit.,* pp. 45-46.

[43]*Ibid.,* p. 72.

[44]*Ibid.,* pp. 72-73.

[45]*Ibid.,* p. 48.

[46]See J.D. Anderson, "Nonpartisan Urban Politics in Canadian Cities" in Jack K. Masson and J. D. Anderson (ed.), *Emerging Party Politics in Urban Canada*, Toronto, McClelland and Stewart, 1972.

sandbox politics of City Hall offered little incentive for organized partisan activity or division."[47]

These indigenous factors changed with the passage of time, of course, and reference has previously been made, for example, to the extensive immigrant population in Winnipeg by the first decade of the twentieth century and the "Divided City" which resulted. But as Anderson noted:

> By the time Canadian cities reached the size and complexity sufficient to make them attractive to political parties, the reform ideology and the accompanying structural innovations imported from the U.S. had become firmly established, and provided an effective barrier to the entry of parties.[48]

Instead, as already mentioned, what we got in a number of Western Canadian cities was business groups backing slates of candidates for municipal office, ostensibly to keep out political parties, but really to keep the socialist party (first the CCF, then the NDP) from gaining control of city hall.

The legacy of the reform era is evident in the continued existence of many of the structural reforms from the early 1900s and in the continued denial of the relevance of politics at the local level. Yet, as discussed in the next chapter, these nonpolitical traditions became increasingly inappropriate as the twentieth century advanced, as did the historical boundaries of municipalities, their revenue sources and allocation of responsibilities.

---

[47]James Lightbody, "The Rise of Party Politics in Canadian Local Elections," in Masson and Anderson, p. 196.

[48]Anderson, *op. cit.*, p. 12.

CHAPTER 4

Cracks in the Foundation:
The Pressures of Growth and Change

OBJECTIVES:

1. To examine the changing nature of the industrialization and urbanization experienced by Canada in the 20th century.

2. To explore the nature of urbanization and the problems inherent in the urbanization process.

3. To describe the perceived inadequacies of the traditional local government system which gave rise to local government reform initiatives.

Introduction

As described in Chapter 2, the basic municipal system was established 100 to 150 years ago, to serve the limited needs of a primarily agricultural and rural society. Profound changes in the nature of our economy and society have occurred in the intervening years, with Canada going through a period of industrialization and into a new era which is usually called the post-industrial or information economy.

This chapter begins with a very brief outline of the changing nature of the Canadian economy and the changes in population and in urbanization. This is followed by an examination of the nature of urbanization itself and the problems inherent in this process. This latter analysis draws attention to the link between municipal government, urban growth and the overall economic system.

Notwithstanding this link, most assessments of the adequacy of municipal government in the second half of the 20th century focused more narrowly on weaknesses in municipal boundaries, functions and finances — in other words, shortcomings within the municipal *structure* viewed in isolation from the larger economic context. These limited assessments are also summarized in this chapter. They must be understood because — limited in insight or not — they were the stimulus for the local government reforms introduced in most provinces in the post-war period and described in the next chapter.

The Pendulum Swings:
Shifting Patterns of Industrialization and Urbanization

Sir John A. Macdonald has been credited with (or accused of) many things, but it may seem surprising to cite him as a key player in determining the pattern of urban development in Canada. Yet, his "national policy" of 1879, and especially its emphasis on high tariffs to protect the new domestic manufacturing industries of central Canada, was to lead to the early (and continuing) concentration of manufacturing in a central corridor extending from Quebec City to Windsor. This development, in turn, contributed to the growth of a number of cities throughout this area, and to the dominance of the Montreal and Toronto urban areas.

The transformation was described by the Economic Council of Canada in its fourth Annual Review, a document which helped to focus attention on the problems of urbanization.

> ...economic change in Canada has thus been marked by a relative shift in the focus of employment and output from the on-site exploitation of the natural resource base to the processing of materials, to manufacturing and advanced fabrication, and to the provision of a rapidly widening range of modern private and public services. Inevitably this change has implied a shift in the location of economic activity away from the rural area and its small service centres towards the larger urban centre.[1]

Figures on both overall population growth and the growth in urban populations mirror the developments in the Canadian economy. As already discussed in Chapter 2, the early years of the 20th century saw rapid population growth. Almost half of this growth was caused by the extensive immigration of this period. The rate of increase in population then slowed during each successive decade reaching a low of only 10.9% during the intercensal decade of 1931 to 1941. During this period of the "Great Depression" there was not only a decline in immigration but also a marked reduction in the movement of rural populations to urban centres. With jobs hard to find in the cities, many able-bodied adults who had migrated to urban areas moved "back to the land," where they might hope for regular meals.[2] After 1941 population growth again accelerated to a near-record expansion rate of 30.2% between 1951 and 1961. In sub-

---

[1]Economic Council of Canada, *Fourth Annual Review*, September 1967, p. 181.

[2]John U. Marshall, "Population Growth in Canadian Metropolises, 1901-1986," in Frances Frisken (ed.), *The Changing Canadian Metropolis: A Public Policy Perspective*, Toronto, Canadian Urban Institute, 1994, Vol. 1, p. 49.

sequent periods the rate of increase has steadily declined, largely because of the reduction in birth rates.

Of particular interest is the classification of the population as between urban and rural. The Census of Canada defines as urban all persons living in an area having a population concentration of 1 000 or more and a population density of at least 386 per square kilometre. On this basis, Canada's population was classified as 75.5% urban in the 1976 Census. Indeed, at this point Canada's urban growth since the end of World War Two had exceeded that of any Western industrial nation and three-quarters of the nation's population was concentrated on less than one per cent of its land area.[3]

More significant than this general shift from rural to urban has been the concentration of that urban population. In 1871 only nine municipalities had populations of over 10 000, but by 1971 there were 246 such municipalities. Although representing only 5.7% of all municipalities, they contained 62% of the Canadian population.[4]

Even greater concentration is evident from the fact that in 1971 more than 50% of the population was centred in 19 census metropolitan areas (census areas comprised of at least two adjacent municipal entities, each at least partly urban, with an urbanized core of 100 000 or more). By 1991 there were 25 of these areas, containing just over 61% of the Canadian population.[5] In that census year, Ontario had over 70% of its population concentrated in census metropolitan areas, and Alberta, Quebec and British Columbia had over 55% of their populations in these areas.[6]

Compounding this growth and its attendant pressures was what Gertler and Crowley called the "mushrooming growth in a few metropolitan agglomerations" Chief among these were what they identified as the "Lower Mainland" in British Columbia; the Calgary-Edmonton "Transportation Corridor" in Alberta; the "Golden Horseshoe" in Southwestern

---

[3]Len Gertler and Don Crowley, *Changing Canadian Cities: The Next 25 Years*, Toronto, McClelland and Stewart, 1977, p. 41.

[4]Institute of Local Government, *Urban Population Growth and Municipal Organization*, Kingston, Queen's University, 1973, p. i.

[5]From *Statistics Canada, Census, 1991*, as quoted in Richard M. Bird and Enid Slack, *Urban Public Finance in Canada*, Toronto, John Wiley & Sons, 1993, p. 1.

[6]Christopher R. Bryant and Daniel Lemire, *Population Distribution and the Management of Urban Growth in Six Selected Urban Regions in Canada*, Toronto, ICURR, December 1993, p. 10.

Ontario; the "Golden Triangle" in Southern Quebec and the "Central Corridor" in the Maritimes.[7]

Even greater concentration of population is evident in the Toronto, Montreal and Vancouver areas which alone accounted for 32% of the Canadian population in 1991.[8]

In recent years, however, the nature of economic development has been changing, with profound implications for the Central Canadian urban centres. The Canadian economy is going through a pronounced economic restructuring — not only in response to the free trade agreements signed with the United States and Mexico but, more fundamentally, in response to the development of an increasingly integrated world economy. The result has been a shift of industrial capital to countries offering lower labour costs and less restrictive regulatory environments and the downsizing of firms that have stayed behind and are trying to remain competitive in the world market.[9] The proportion of manufacturing jobs in the economy has declined. While the primary sector (agricultural) now accounts for only 10% of employment and the secondary sector (manufacturing) only 20%, the tertiary sector (service industries and government) now accounts for 70%.[10]

One of the results is that cities in the Windsor-to-Quebec industrial heartland are now "at a structural disadvantage when compared with cities in the peripheral regions such as Atlantic Canada and the Western Provinces."[11] For example, Montreal's economy has been severely affected, with the Montreal census metropolitan area losing 10.9% of its manufacturing employment between 1975 and 1985.[12]

Further evidence of the shift in growth momentum is found in the fact that the census metropolitan areas of Western Canada, as a group, have grown more rapidly during the 20th century than those of any other region — including southern Ontario.[13] In part, this growth reflects the fact

---

[7]Gertler and Crowley, *op. cit.*, p. 5.

[8]Bird and Slack, *op. cit.*, p. 1.

[9]Frances Frisken, "Introduction," in Frisken *op. cit.*, Vol. 1, p. 5.

[10]Marshall, in Frisken, *op. cit.*, p. 45.

[11]*Ibid.*

[12]Frisken, *op. cit.*, p. 6.

[13]Marshall, in Frisken, *op. cit.*, p. 58.

that western centres such as the Vancouver and Calgary regions are in the forefront of the rapidly expanding information technology. One estimate states that "half of the labour force of Canada works in occupations involving the collection, processing and dissemination of information."[14] According to Durlak:

> In British Columbia, the software business is already larger than the forest-products business, and computer-related businesses may overtake tourism, mining, and fishing to become that province's largest industry by 1996. Calgary has more than 181 specialty software companies among more than 500 advanced technology businesses.[15]

To take another example, the city of Moncton, New Brunswick has revitalized its urban area by providing telemarketing and other communications services for large parts of Eastern Canada and beyond, and was the only city named both in 1992 and 1993 by the *Globe and Mail Report on Business Magazine* as one of Canada's top five cities in which to do business.[16]

By the very nature of the technology, information-based industries do not need to locate close to raw materials or large populations of consumers, factors which restricted the locations of traditional manufacturing industries. This new economic reality is contributing to the shift of economic activity and population from urban centres to outlying suburbs or even beyond census metropolitan areas. One study found that during the 1980s, "almost 60 per cent of the net growth in Canada's CMAs and almost 50% of Canada's net growth was located in the CMA's fringe areas beyond the urbanized core, and CMA fringe areas account for an increasingly large share of CMA population."[17]

The preceding statements and statistics are sufficient to demonstrate "the fact" of urbanization in Canada, and the shift in its pattern and in the underlying economic forces influencing this pattern. What also has to be understood, however, is the nature of this urbanization and its impact

---

[14]According to Jerome Durlak, "The Effects of Information Technologies on Large Urban Regions," in Frisken, *op. cit.*, p. 75.

[15]*Ibid.*, p. 83.

[16]Cited in Andrew Sancton, *Governing Canada's City Regions: Adapting Form to Function*, Montreal, Institute for Research on Public Policy, 1994, pp. 47 and 54.

[17]Christopher Bryant and Daniel Lemire, *Population Distribution and the Management of Urban Growth in Six Selected Urban Regions in Canada*, Toronto, Intergovernmental Committee on Urban and Regional Research, 1993, p. 14.

on our society. As will be seen, one's understanding of these matters largely dictates the nature of the urban problems which are identified and the solutions which are advocated.

The Nature and Impact of Urbanization

Urbanization involves much more than the concentration of population. It arises from, and gives rise to, fundamental changes in the nature of our economy and society. As noted above, it was industrialization, and especially the development of mass production, which encouraged the concentration of population in cities. With this shift in population, other changes occurred. The movement from farm to factory created growing numbers of workers who were dependent upon industrial employment and its attendant uncertainties instead of being relatively self-sufficient by living off the land. They increasingly turned to government to provide them with some protection and security, and gradually the "positive state" evolved with its elaborate range of services and programs designed to ensure all citizens a minimum standard of living conditions. All levels of government were affected by this development, and the resultant increase in services demanded of local government represented a heavy burden for most municipalities.

The shortage, expense and inadequacy of urban housing led to greater government involvement by all levels. The concentration of low income families in inner city neighbourhoods strained the social service system. The loss of spacious country living, for those who had moved to the city, led to growing demands for parks and recreational facilities. The higher living standards and leisure time of a technological society accentuated this demand. Transportation and traffic movement required increasing government attention, as did the provision of an adequate supply of water and the disposal of domestic and industrial waste. Governments had to deal with air pollution concerns, in large part because of the exhaust from the concentration of motor vehicles. New problems of subdivision control and urban renewal and redevelopment also claimed the attention of the urban municipality. Population sprawl caused the conversion of land from agricultural production to urban uses and government action was needed to protect against developments which had an undesirable impact on the natural environment.

It should be noted that rural municipalities also experienced new servicing pressures, largely because of the influx of the nonfarm rural population. Improved road maintenance and fire protection were demanded and such urban amenities as sidewalks and streetlights were expected in many hamlets. New recreational facilities were requested. Extensive cottage development on scenic lakes and rivers and excessive residential development on unsuitable soil often caused pollution problems requiring government action. Where these problems arose in a concentrated area, the municipality often faced the very heavy financial burden of a water supply and sewage treatment system. Residential development and farming activities proved an uneasy mix and the resulting friction provided one more example of the need for land use planning policies and controls in rural areas.

A number of analysts stress that urban problems are not just found in urban areas but are *inherent in the process of urbanization* itself. For Lithwick, the distinctive feature to be noted is that the growth of cities produces "competing demands for the one common feature of all cities, scarce urban space, driving core prices upward and households outward." He suggests that transportation, pollution and poverty problems flow from this. Moreover, he argues that because of these interdependencies efforts to deal with each problem in isolation have inevitably failed.

> Housing policy has added to the stock of urban accommodations, but has led to urban sprawl and fiscal squeeze for the municipalities. Transport policies have moved people faster initially, but have led to further sprawl, downtown congestion, pollution, and rapid core deterioration.[18]

Fowler is also very critical of the process of urbanization pursued in North America, the urban sprawl and suburban development, and the extensive transportation network criss-crossing the landscape. He describes how we ended up with cities "where we sleep en masse in huge residential complexes and work en masse in huge retail or industrial developments — and spend our lives travelling between them, from living room to kitchen, so to speak."[19] He is even more critical of the built environment of our cities and its lack of physical diversity. He cites the proliferation of large scale projects, the deconcentration and decentralization of development (not just with respect to low-density residential development, but also affecting office and factory space), and the homogeneity of architecture and of land use. Fowler contends that we are squandering billions of dollars in North America because of the built en-

---

[18]N. H. Lithwick, *Urban Canada: Problems and Prospects*, Ottawa, Central Mortgage and Housing Corporation, 1970, p. 15.

[19]Edmund P. Fowler, *Building Cities That Work*, Kingston, McGill-Queen's University Press, 1992, p. 31.

vironment in our urban areas which involves us in "an extravagant transportation system, life-threatening levels of pollution, a needlessly large
infrastructure of utilities such as water mains and trunk sewers, and significantly more expensive housing and consumer goods."[20]

Extensive urban sprawl and suburban development, and attendant
financial problems for central cities, have long been characteristic of
urban areas in the United States.[21] As business, industry and middle class
homeowners moved to the suburbs, the tax base of the cities shrank. Yet
they faced increased expenditures for fire, police, welfare, education and
other services for the primarily lower class population which remained.
The flight to the suburbs intensified as the cities experienced an influx of
Blacks, racial tensions increased, and yet the revenue base of the cities
continued to erode — setting up a downward spiral from which it was
difficult to escape.

Writing in 1986, Goldberg and Mercer contended that Canada's urban experience had been both different and more positive.[22] In comparison to the United States, they found that Canada's cities were more
compact, had not been losing population or jobs to the same extent, were
still attractive as places of residence for middle-class homeowners, had a
much lower incidence of violent crime, and did not have an "urban under-
class" made up of members of one or more racial minorities. As a result,
city and suburb differences in income and population characteristics were
less marked in Canada.[23]

Less than a decade later, Frisken finds that Canadian metropolitan
areas may just be slower to develop many of the features found in their
American counterparts, notably:

> ... a decline in the economic strength of central cities within their
> metropolitan areas, as jobs and middle-class residents relocate to the
> suburbs; the differentiation of peripheral from central city populations
> by income and race, with central cities coming to house a disproportion-
> ately large share of their regions' most disadvantaged residents; and the

[20]*Ibid.*, p. 69.

[21]The description which follows is based on Edward C. Banfield and James Q.
Wilson, *City Politics*, New York, Random House, 1963, p. 14.

[22]Michael Goldberg and John Mercer, *The Myth of the North American City:
Continentalism Challenged*, Vancouver, University of British Columbia Press, 1986,
quoted in Frisken, *op. cit.* p. 2.

[23]*Ibid.*

outward dispersal of population and jobs at densities likely to result in a high level of automobile dependency.[24]

Another similarity between the American and Canadian experiences is the fact that, to varying degrees, the urban problems which developed were caused or aggravated by senior government policies. Describing the American situation, Banfield writes that from the New Deal onward, the flight to the suburbs was encouraged, albeit inadvertently, by the federal government through its transportation and housing policies and programs. Indeed, he contends that these two programs account for 90% of the federal government expenditure for the improvement of the cities, that neither is directed toward the really serious problems of the cities, and that both make the problems worse![25] The improvement of transportation serves to encourage further movement of industry, commerce and relatively well-off residents (mostly white) from the inner city. Federal housing programs have subsidized home building on a vast scale by ensuring mortgages on easy terms, mostly for the purchase of new homes which were being built in the suburbs. Urban renewal initiatives have also been harmful, forcing hundreds of thousands of low income people out of low cost housing to make room for luxury apartments, office buildings, hotels, civic centres, industrial parks and the like.[26] Far from being productive, Banfield demonstrates that these federal programs actually work at cross-purposes. The expressway program and the housing mortgages in effect pay the middle class whites to leave the central city for the suburbs; at the same time, the urban renewal and mass transit programs pay them to stay in the central city or to move back to it.

A rather similar pattern is evident in Canada, particularly with respect to federal housing and urban renewal initiatives. Since the 1935 Dominion Housing Act, and especially the establishment of the Central (now Canada) Mortgage and Housing Corporation (CMHC) in 1946, federal financial assistance for single family dwellings has reinforced low density sprawl.[27] The actions of CMHC also contributed to neighbourhood dislocations and attendant problems because of what has been described as a

---

[24]*Ibid.*, p. 4.

[25]Edward C. Banfield, *The Unheavenly City*, Boston, Little, Brown and Company, 1968, p. 14.

[26]*Ibid.*, p. 16.

[27]For a description of the role of the CMHC, see Donald J. H. Higgins, *Urban Canada: Its Government and Politics*, Toronto, Macmillan, 1977, pp. 76-81.

bulldozer approach to urban renewal. It is evident that in Canada, as well as in the United States, urban growth became a prime instrument of public policy to stimulate and maintain high levels of economic activity.[28] After studying federal housing policy, Fallis concludes that it is mainly influenced by federal macroeconomic policy and he observes that "the federal government has always used housing programs as instruments of fiscal policy."[29]

Lorimer also attributes the developments in our cities to the policies of the federal government. He contends that "most of the development of Canadian cities in the three boom decades from the Forties to the Seventies was a direct consequence of the economic development strategy chosen by Ottawa for Canada."[30] In his view, this strategy had two principal components — exploitation of natural resources for use mainly by the major metropolitan economies, and expansion of a branch-plant secondary manufacturing industry in Southern Ontario. The primary role of local government was to provide the physical services needed to support growth and development. Lorimer charges that local governments became the servants of the development industry that they were supposed to regulate.[31]

Magnusson describes the federal government's efforts to support the housing market to ensure an expansion of the economy.[32] But, he also notes that the provinces were just as concerned as the federal level about removing any possible checks on growth, which was one of their reasons for increasing conditional grants for improving public facilities in the

---

[28]Michael Goldrick, "The Anatomy of Urban Reform in Toronto," in Dimitrios Roussopoulos, *The City and Radical Social Change*, Montreal, Black Rose Books, 1982, p. 264.

[29]George Fallis, "The Federal Government and the Metropolitan Housing Problem," in Frisken, *op. cit.*, p. 376.

[30]James Lorimer, "The post-developer era for Canada's cities begins," in *City Magazine Annual 1981*, Toronto, James Lorimer and Company, 1981, p. 7.

[31]See, for example, *The Real World of City Politics*, Toronto, James Lewis and Samuel, 1970; *A Citizen's Guide to City Politics*, Toronto, James Lewis and Samuel, 1972; *The Developers*, Toronto, James Lorimer, 1978; and *After the Developers* (with Carolyn McGregor), Toronto, James Lorimer, 1981.

[32]Warren Magnusson, "Introduction," in Warren Magnusson and Andrew Sancton (eds.), *City Politics in Canada*, Toronto, University of Toronto Press, 1983, p. 27.

cities. He also suggests that provincial legislation on planning and zoning was based on the assumption that urban development would be undertaken through private initiative, with municipalities playing a regulatory role, but one which facilitated private enterprise.[33]

Yet another viewpoint on the problems in our cities is that they are caused by the excesses of private decision making and the lack of sufficient government intervention into the private domain.[34] Those who hold to this viewpoint have numerous examples to support their contention. Perhaps the most blatant example is the land speculation in and around our cities. The extension of services, at public expense, often brings windfall profits to the private speculator who purchased and held land against such an eventuality. Escalating land costs then push the cost of housing beyond the reach of more and more Canadians.

Another example has been the widespread disruption (some would say destruction) of the city to meet the needs of the private use of automobiles without anything like this degree of support for public transit. Indeed, public transit services have been struggling to maintain ridership, hesitating to increase fares which would likely lose more riders, yet faced with growing deficits and, traditionally, very little financial support from the senior levels of government. According to the Science Council of Canada's Report *Cities for Tomorrow*, "it appears that barely one-half of the cost incurred by the automobile is returned to different levels of government in gasoline taxes and license fees."[35] Not only do public transit services face unfair competition because of this subsidy, but too little consideration is given to the broad social benefits which they bring — and the social costs of our devotion to the automobile.[36] As Richardson notes, economists can be quite explicit about such factors as time saved for truckers or the cost of congestion for businesses, but they seem unable

---

[33]*Ibid.*

[34]See, for example, Boyce Richardson, *The Future of Canadian Cities*, Toronto, New Press, 1972, on which this section is based.

[35]Quoted in *ibid.*, p. 130.

[36]Although provincial governments have played a key role in the development of urban mass transit systems in the Toronto, Montreal and Vancouver areas in the 1970s and 1980s, and without their involvement there would have been a serious decline in service — according to Frances Frisken, "Provincial Transit Policy-making in the Toronto, Montreal and Vancouver Regions," in Frisken, Vol. 2, *op. cit.*, p. 528.

to estimate "the cost of isolation for 200 000 old people; or of congestion, pollution, noise and a general shattering of the urban environment for the entire population."[37]

Private enterprise has also been deficient in providing adequate and appropriate housing for the varied needs of the Canadian population. Here again, the forces of urbanization have played a part by making land very scarce and therefore very valuable. As land prices increase it becomes necessary to have buildings which will generate a large income for the landowner.

> ...poor houses inhabited by poor people must be swept away, their occupants with them; new places go up, let at high rents; young men and women, married couples, or the rich, move in where poor people lived before; the poor people just "disappear" — most of the time we don't even take the trouble to find out where they go to live.[38]

While Richardson's analysis of the shortcomings of private decision making may seem quite critical, to some it is far too tame. A more radical viewpoint is that such "problems" as too many cars in the streets, insufficient affordable housing, lack of green space and environmental pollution are but symptoms of more fundamental causes.[39] According to this view, "it is impossible to understand both the urban sprawl which passes for development and the urban conflict it has produced unless one recognizes the determining power of the capitalist mode of production which governs these processes."[40] Rather than being haphazard and random, city growth is seen as intimately linked with the changing needs of the economic system. "The city is developed, redeveloped and moulded over time according to long term cycles in how profits are made and investment decisions taken."[41] As Western nations emerged from the depression of the 1930s, they faced the need to stimulate consumption to sustain the capitalist system. The response was to introduce a series of policies to facilitate urban growth. By shifting the focus of capital from production

---

[37]Richardson, *op. cit.*, p. 139.

[38]*Ibid.*, pp. 155-156.

[39]Dimitrios Roussopoulos, "Understanding the City and Radical Social Change," in Roussopoulos, *op. cit.*, p. 61.

[40]M. Castells, as quoted in Stephen Schecter, "Urban Politics in Capitalist Society," in Roussopoulos, *op. cit.*, p. 111.

[41]Goldrick, *op. cit.*, p. 263.

to consumption and by emphasizing urban development as a key vehicle to achieve it, these actions effectively changed the function of cities from that of workshops to "artifacts of consumption."[42] The impact of the urban development which resulted has already been described. The chief beneficiaries have been the property development industry, including developers, financiers, real estate companies, construction companies, property managers, and others.

Weaknesses of the Traditional Municipal System

By the early postwar years, there were growing concerns about the ability of the traditional municipal government system (established between 50 and 100 years earlier) to meet the challenges posed by the combined forces of industrialization and urbanization. In particular, questions were raised about outdated municipal boundaries, overlapping responsibilities and inadequate finances. As described in Chapter 5, the response to these questions was municipal reform initiatives in most provinces — focused, not surprisingly, on changes to boundaries, distribution of responsibilities and efforts to achieve greater operating efficiency and economies of scale. Given the limited assessment of "the problem" on which these reform initiatives were based, it will not be surprising to learn (in Chapter 5) that the reforms themselves have been quite limited in their scope and effectiveness.

Structural Limitations

One fundamental weakness was that most municipal institutions had originated in the previous century and had been designed only "to carry out the public functions and to operate within the restricted area boundaries considered appropriate for that time." Yet the pace of change since had brought about "a complex transformation in functions of municipal government and the complete obliteration of many previously significant territorial boundaries."[43] Consider, for example, the 18 metropolitan areas or large city complexes of 100 000 people and over identified in the 1961 Census. Within these 18 areas "there were some 260 separate municipal government jurisdictions, together with an additional unknown number of semi-independent single purpose special authorities such as school

---

[42]*Ibid.*, p. 264-265.

[43]Economic Council of Canada, *op. cit.*, pp. 209-210.

boards, water boards, transit and utility commissions, and sewerage districts."[44] To most observers, such a fragmented structure made concerted action to deal with urban problems both difficult and unlikely. (To keep matters in perspective, however, it should be noted that even *after* municipal restructuring the Montreal census metropolitan area still had 104 lower tier municipalities and 13 upper tier municipalities in 1991.[45])

Functional Fragmentation

In addition to this structural fragmentation, functional fragmentation also inhibited and complicated the ability of municipal government to respond to urban problems. A number of traditionally local responsibilities "outgrew" the local level in terms of their significance, importance and impact. The result, in fields such as health, education and welfare, has been a gradual shift of responsibility to the senior levels of government and an increasing sharing of responsibilities between two or more levels of government.

At the same time, a parallel but reverse trend was under way in which senior governments launched new initiatives but delegated responsibility to the local level for at least some aspects of program delivery. This pattern was evident in such areas as housing, urban renewal and environmental protection. The combined result was that the operations of local government became increasingly intertwined with those of the senior governments.

> In many traditional areas of local competence, provincial supervision, regulation or outright control have been deemed the acceptable solutions....Their overall effect has incorporated municipal affairs more completely in the broader contexts of provincial and federal public administration. Indeed, local autonomy in all but a few ... areas is extinct.[46]

Thus, not only were municipal governments facing the pressures of an urbanizing trend largely shaped by the policies of the senior levels of government but they were also constrained in responding to these pressures by the extent to which their responsibilities were entangled with those senior governments. A number of provinces had established depart-

---

[44]*Ibid.*, p. 210.

[45]Frisken, "Transit Policymaking," p. 511.

[46]H. J. Whalen, *The Development of Local Government in New Brunswick*, Fredericton, 1963, p. 90.

ments of municipal affairs around the turn of the century, but these departments — and often municipal boards as well — really came to the fore during the depression of the 1930s. In the years that followed, their supervision and control of local governments increased steadily. These intergovernmental developments and the experience with federal-local and tri-level relations are examined in Chapter 7.

Financial Constraints

In addition to its structural and functional shortcomings, the traditional municipal government system also faced increasing financial problems. When municipalities were first established, it was expected that they would meet their revenue needs through the real property tax. This tax could be administered effectively on a local basis and it appeared adequate to finance the limited servicing requirements of the day, mainly related to education, local roads and the care of the poor. The property tax seemed appropriate since property was the main form of wealth in the early days, and it wasn't considered particularly burdensome since the local taxpayer was not subject to the income tax and other forms of direct and indirect taxation which subsequently made their appearance.[47]

However, as the twentieth century advanced, a number of the traditional responsibilities of local government became much more significant and costly, including the above-mentioned examples of education, roads and welfare. A growing number of new service demands also arose, largely because of urbanization, as has been amply illustrated in the preceding discussions. Yet the real property tax remained the primary source of municipal revenues.

The inadequacy of this financial base became all too evident during the 1930s, when the entire burden for unemployment relief assistance was initially considered to be within the scope of municipal responsibility for poor relief. Even when the federal and provincial levels had assumed 80% of the costs, municipalities still had difficulty financing their share for the substantial unemployed population of the urban industrial centres. They cut back on services and postponed expenditures for maintenance and new construction. Further postponements occurred with the diversion of resources and the massive centralization of government which occurred during the Second World War.

---

[47]T. J. Plunkett, *The Financial Structure and the Decision Making Process of Canadian Municipal Government*, Ottawa, Canada Mortgage and Housing Corporation, 1972, p. 21.

Thus, an enormous backlog of expenditures had already built up even before the municipalities faced the greatly increased demands of the post-war urbanization. The challenge which this posed is well described by Goldenberg:

> They (the municipalities) faced the problem of financing not only the expenditures which had been deferred during fifteen years of depression and war, but also vast new expenditures on works and services required to meet an unprecedented growth in population and economic activity.[48]

The resultant upsurge in municipal spending in the immediate postwar years is vividly illustrated by the fact that total urban municipal expenditures increased by 131% over the eight year period from 1945 to 1953 compared to an increase of only 13% during the fifteen year period 1930 to 1945.[49]

Not surprisingly, the real property tax couldn't generate sufficient revenues to meet this explosion of municipal expenditures. While this tax was still providing over 80% of municipal revenues in 1930, the proportion had fallen to 53% by 1953 and to 47% by 1963.[50] By 1974-75, the proportion had declined to below 40% according to the Report of the Tri-Level Task Force on Public Finance in 1976. Since the mid-1980s, the proportion has been just over 31%.[51]

The growing shortfall in municipal revenue needs in the postwar period has, until the past decade, been remedied almost entirely by grants from the senior levels of government.[52] By the beginning of the 1970s, this assistance accounted for over 40% of gross general revenues of Canadian municipal governments. While these transfer payments allowed municipalities to meet their expenditure obligations, they were a mixed blessing. The municipal submission to the first national tri-level conference in 1972 noted that approximately 90% of this financial assistance was in the form of conditional grants which reflected the priorities of the senior

---

[48]H. Carl Goldenberg, "Municipal Finance and Taxation: Problems and Prospects," in *Forecast of Urban Growth Problems and Requirements 1956-1980*, Montreal, Canadian Federation of Mayors and Municipalities, 1955.

[49]Plunkett, *op. cit.*, p. 33.

[50]Economic Council of Canada, *op. cit.*, p. 219.

[51]Bird and Slack, *op. cit.*, p. 64.

[52]More recent developments, including arrangements for provincial-municipal revenue-sharing, are discussed in Chapter 7.

levels of government. It warned about the resulting loss of local autonomy — one which threatened to turn local governments into "hollow receptacles into which the values of the federal and provincial governments are poured."[53]

In fairness, one can find considerable justification for a number of the provincial conditional grant programs. Many traditional local government responsibilities are now recognized as having much wider than local significance and it has become necessary to find some means of ensuring that these responsibilities are exercised to at least a minimum standard across the province. Given a multiplicity of municipal jurisdictions with widely varying financial capacities, the most effective means of ensuring these standards has been through the grant structure. Whatever the rationale, it seems clear that this process has been carried too far. A basic difficulty is that "there is a rapidly diminishing relationship between the taxes paid to any one level of government and the services rendered by it."[54] The most fundamental problem with such arrangements, which apply to the federal-provincial relationship as much as to the provincial-local, is well expressed in a pamphlet by the Ontario Economic Council:

> Through the development of a complex transfer system, each level of government can influence the nature and scope of the services provided, take a share in the political rewards, maintain the fiction of autonomy, and have a convenient excuse for avoiding any criticism for inadequate services. The only drawback is that the public never knows who is responsible for what or how much the services provided really cost.[55]

As the 1980s unfolded, however, both senior levels of government became increasingly preoccupied with their annual deficits and accumulated debts. As a result, the Federal Government has tightened up on the amount of money turned over to the provinces in transfer payments, and, the Provincial Governments, in turn, have decreased their transfers to the municipal level. Transfers as a proportion of municipal revenues have declined from 46.4% in 1971 to 37.2% in 1991.[56] But, these transfers re-

---

[53]Municipal Submission to the first National Tri-Level Conference, *Policies, Programs and Finance*, Ottawa, 1972, p. 20.

[54]Ontario Economic Council, *Government Reform in Ontario*, Toronto, 1969, p. viii.

[55]*Ibid.*, p. 19.

[56]Bird and Slack, *op. cit.*, p. 64.

main overwhelmingly conditional in nature. That is, they provide funds, but only if they are spent on the purpose specified and, usually, only if the municipality provides some matching share. Except for New Brunswick, conditional grants make up the vast majority of the transfers to the municipal level by each province.

Unfulfilled Political Role

This lack of a clear focus of accountability and responsibility relates to one of the most important inadequacies of local government to be highlighted by the pressures of post-war urbanization. The traditional system was quite ineffective in fulfilling its political role — that is, in representing the views of the local inhabitants, choosing between alternative courses of action, setting priorities for the allocation of scarce resources, and then answering for these decisions to the local electorate.

As we have seen, the turn of the century reformers vigorously denied the relevance of a political role for local government. They viewed this role much too narrowly, equating politics with excessive divisiveness and abuse of power through patronage and the pork barrel. In addition, many of the reformers who purported to want politics removed from local government actually wanted to impose their own notion of what the local priorities should be. As Leftwich has pointed out, "there is nothing *more political* than the constant attempts to exclude certain types of issues from politics."[57] (emphasis in the original)

Whatever their motivations, however, the reformers bequeathed us a deeply ingrained notion of municipal government as administrative and not political in nature, with the council performing a caretaker or custodial role and preoccupied with considerations of efficiency. According to this viewpoint, councillors were not politicians, but "local worthies who kept an eye on one or two amenities."[58] Also from this reform period came the belief that servicing questions were best resolved by the application of technical expertise, with "politics" being kept entirely out of the picture if possible.

Given the growth pressures and challenges of the post-war period, this concept of municipal government became increasingly unworkable. The issues which now demanded the attention of local governments involved

---

[57]A. Leftwich (ed.), *What is Politics?*, London, Blackwell, 1984, p. 144.

[58]B. Walden, "Apply the brakes to our local politicians," *Sunday Times*, July 26, 1987, quoted in John Gyford, Steve Leach and Chris Game, *The Changing Politics of Local Government*, London, Unwin Hyman Ltd, 1989, p. 1.

widespread controversy about the best course of action. Concern about the quality of life and the preservation of established neighbourhoods increased as rapid development threatened the fabric of the city. The traditional reliance on technical expertise was found unacceptable and the public demanded that decision makers show a greater awareness of social and environmental considerations. For example, whether to meet transportation needs through expressways or public transit has been an ongoing dispute, with the battle over the Spadina expressway in Toronto providing a good illustration, along with similar disputes in Vancouver and Edmonton.[59] The fondness for single family dwellings on sizeable lots, supported by the lending policies of the Central (now Canada) Mortgage and Housing Corporation, has had to be reconciled with the cost and space demands of such housing compared with the economics of higher density construction. Urban renewal projects have aroused strong opposition from neighbourhoods where residents wanted rehabilitation rather than the traditional response of tearing down and building anew.[60]

Nor were the tensions confined to urban areas. Rural residents also debated the desirability of growth and the validity of new service demands. There has been a growing concern about the loss of farmland and, paradoxically, about controls intended to protect the farmland but which were felt to be too restrictive. Conflicting views about both the style and substance of municipal government were presented by the non-farm rural dweller and the farmer, the new resident and the long time settler, the seasonal population and the permanent inhabitants.

Given these developments, the caretaker or custodial role of local government became less and less appropriate, as did the notion of periodic voting as the primary method of citizen involvement. Instead, citizens and citizen groups increasingly questioned the actions of their municipal councils and demanded a more open, consultative decision making process which considered their views at least as much as the technical advice provided by staff. An even more direct response was evident in some cities where reform candidates and local parties ran for municipal office. These developments, which are examined in Chapter 8, were not new. Indeed, Kaplan provides numerous examples of both

[59]See Christopher Leo, *The Politics of Urban Development: Canadian Urban Expressway Disputes*, Monographs on Canadian Urban Development, No. 3, Toronto, Institute of Public Administration, 1977.

[60]For an excellent account of one such battle, see Graham Fraser, *Fighting Back*, Toronto, Hakkert, 1972.

citizen group and party activity in the early years of local government in our major cities and notes that "a culture that ascribed a high mission to local government and forbade all forms of "politics" co-existed alongside an intensive, undignified scramble for specific facilities."[61]

However, the upsurge in this activity in the post-war period reflected a growing public conviction that local governments must demonstrate responsiveness and accountability in the discharge of their responsibilities. But here again the traditional system was inadequate in several respects. The fragmentation of the structure made it very difficult to assign responsibility for action (or inaction). Not only was power divided among the council and varying numbers of local special purpose bodies, but in addition responsibilities were shared between the local and senior levels of government, and an extensive network of conditional grant payments further blurred the focus of responsibility.

Nor was accountability any clearer within the council of most municipalities. All councillors were collectively responsible for everything, and yet none were specifically responsible for anything! Except in the few instances where organized political parties operated, councils were made up of a group of individuals with potentially different interests and concerns and no sense of cohesion or collective purpose. There wasn't any particular governing group responsible for taking the initiative in dealing with the problems facing the municipality. Nor was there any group responsible for scrutinizing and criticizing the initiatives taken to ensure that they were in the best interests of the public. It was almost impossible for citizens to know where to direct criticism or praise. Any particular councillor could claim that he was for (or against) the matter at issue but was outvoted by the other councillors. The chances for buck-passing in this system were endless.

Even if councils wanted to be accountable and responsive, previously mentioned legal and financial limitations acted as severe constraints. Often councils couldn't do what their local citizens wanted them to because they lacked the authority or had failed to receive provincial approval, or felt unable to finance the expenditures involved. These limitations are well summarized by Plunkett and Graham:

> When many of the apparent characteristics of contemporary urban local government in Canada are taken into account (the tendency to adhere to a purely service role, increased dependence on conditional provincial grants, fragmentation of responsibilities, intergovernmental linkages

---

[61]Harold Kaplan, *Reform, Planning and City Politics: Montreal, Winnipeg, and Toronto*, Toronto, University of Toronto Press, 1982, p. 146.

based on professional and functional ties rather than on broad policy issues, lack of policy direction and the failure to furnish an identifiable government), we have to conclude that local governments are adhering to their role as agents of provincial interest to the detriment of their role as interpretors of the local scene.[62]

The explanations for the unfulfilled political role offered above are consistent with the conventional view that the problems lie in inadequacies in the traditional municipal structure. Before leaving this section, however, other factors must be noted.

It would be misleading to leave the impression that a different municipal structure would provide the openness and responsiveness desired by all citizens' groups. First of all, these groups shared no common view about the role which municipal governments should play in creating the ideal urban environment.[63] While some were genuinely committed to various forms of neighbourhood self-government, most were only concerned with the particular issue at hand and were interested in their municipal government only to the extent that it had any decision-making power with respect to that issue. Nobody in the new urban reform movement argued for truly multi-functional municipal governments subject to reduced provincial supervision and control. "In fact, many new urban reformers seemed profoundly suspicious of any political institutions, including municipal governments and local political parties, that would have the potential to overrule the expressed preferences of local neighbourhoods and their leaders."[64]

Sewell goes so far as to suggest that neighbourhood groups, which were the building block for the reform efforts in the 1960s and 1970s, will be the stumbling block for any new reform movement.[65] He describes the earlier reform period as one in which neighbourhood groups fought to preserve the city built before World War Two — a city whose neighbourhoods contained a range of incomes and family sizes, a mix of uses and

---

[62]T. J. Plunkett and Katherine A. Graham, "Whither Municipal Government," in *Canadian Public Administration*, Winter 1982, p. 614.

[63]See Andrew Sancton, "The Municipal Role in the Governance of Cities," in Trudi Bunting and Pierre Filion (eds.), *Canadian Cities in Transition*, Toronto, Oxford University Press, 1991, p. 473.

[64]*Ibid.*

[65]John Sewell, *Prospects for Reform*, Research Paper 180, Toronto, Centre for Urban and Community Studies, University of Toronto, January 1991.

building forms. Residents wanted to preserve that diversity against the destructive impact of urban renewal, expressways and private redevelopment. Then came Don Mills, Canada's first corporate suburb, and a new definition of neighbourhood based on exclusivity. This was the message presented in the carefully designed homes, the enforced colour coordination, the looping, curvy street design and the modern house form.[66] According to Sewell, the land mass of most Canadian cities is now predominantly filled with the progeny of Don Mills. "Exclusivity has become the dominant characteristic of the urban area and the Not in My Backyard (NIMBY) lullaby is frequently sung to consistent applause."[67] Sewell contends that NIMBY has hijacked the neighbourhood concept embraced by the reformers and has used the idea that local decision making is best to create an exclusive closed community and a limiting approach to city possibilities.

As discussed earlier in this chapter, Fowler is also very critical of the lack of diversity in our modern cities. He finds that the physical characteristics of the postwar urban environment do have an adverse impact on our social behaviour, including our political activities. He quotes Theodore Lowi, who contends that suburbs represent a failure of citizenship.

We have removed ourselves not only from the responsibilities of civic participation but also from the challenges of social relations by zoning poor families out of our neighbourhoods. The social and political skills of adults have declined; we have lost the ability, at a personal level, to say how we feel, to negotiate, to solve problems creatively — in short, to be publicly responsible individuals.[68]

According to Jane Jacobs, the physical diversity which has been disappearing from our cities made neighbour contact more likely and encouraged people to care about what went on in the neighbourhood.[69] The mixture of workplaces and residences ensured the presence of users throughout the day. Short blocks maximized the number of corners and

---

[66]*Ibid.*, p. 13. Sewell has since elaborated his views about urban design in *The Shape of the City,*, Toronto, University of Toronto Press, 1993.

[67]*Ibid.*

[68]Theodore Lowi, *The End of Liberalism*, 2nd Edition, New York, W. W. Norton, 1979, p. 267, quoted in Fowler, *op. cit.*, p. 73.

[69]Jane Jacobs, *The Death and Life of Great American Cities*, New York, Random House, 1961.

therefore meeting places. The result was streets filled with activity and under constant observation.

The web of mutual recognition among habitual users of the street, who need be only a minority, is the natural outgrowth of an urge to be responsible for the territory surrounding one's place of work, one's front door, and even the parks and shopping areas one frequents. This is *civic government at its most local*, but perhaps most crucial, level.[70] (emphasis added)

What Fowler terms "authentic politics" is, he contends, only possible in small scale, diverse spaces where a variety of casual face-to-face interactions occur naturally, a development pattern disappearing as our cities have been rebuilt in the post-war period. Moreover, he argues that the lack of physical diversity in our cities "encourages the perception that politics does not take place at the local level, but only at the regional and national levels. Alternatively, local politics is considered petty, and provision of local services is considered an administrative job, not a political issue."[71]

To the extent that there is local politics in our cities, Fowler observes, it is mainly concerned with the planning, approval, and servicing of large new developments. This, of course, is a very widely held view. Indeed, Sancton contends that "Canadian municipal politicians have little choice but to build their political careers on policies designed to make their city more prosperous, more appealing, and more pleasant than other competing cities."[72] For the most part, politically salient cleavages based on class, ethnicity, or even neighbourhood, are absent, so municipal politicians are rarely in a position to profit politically by mobilizing one sector of the community against another. A candidate's election prospects depend on convincing voters that his or her policies and abilities are best suited to promoting the general well-being of the whole city. "This means that Canadian city politics is, above all, about boosterism."[73] It also follows, according to Sancton, that most conflict in Canadian urban politics can be located on a pro-development/anti-development spectrum. Caulfield, however, suggests that division and dispute often relate more to the kind of development that is being promoted by different groups. He cites as an

---

[70]Fowler, *op. cit.*, p. 87.

[71]*Ibid.*, p. 132.

[72]Sancton, "Conclusion," in Magnusson and Sancton, p. 293.

[73]*Ibid.*

example the "reform group" elected in Toronto in 1972, supposedly unified in opposition to development. By 1974, as discussed in Chapter 8, the
group had split apart after it became apparent to its more radical members that no progress was being made on the real issues of redistributing
wealth and power.[74]

Peterson goes even farther by arguing that cities are obliged to pursue
economic development strategies, that they are limited to an urban
growth agenda.[75] According to Peterson, local politics is limited to matters of production while redistribution is, and must be, a matter for the
central governments. Redistributive policies, he contends, will prejudice
a city's chances of attracting growth by driving away high income residents
and business and by attracting welfare claimants. It is clear that Peterson
sees cities as engaged in a zero-sum competition for growth, because of
the porous nature of their economies and the mobility of capital and individuals.[76] It is assumed that cities are engaged in a competition for a fixed
amount of capital, the gain of one being the loss of another. It is further
assumed that all citizens of the city have an interest in economic growth
and development policies, resulting in local politics which is low-key.[77]
While his writings have had quite an impact, and are discussed further in
Chapter 9, Peterson has also been strongly criticized for exaggerating his
case and for ignoring the considerable case study evidence that conflict,
not consensus, is characteristic of redevelopment and expressway issues.[78]

Summary

By the middle of the twentieth century, approximately 100 years after
the establishment of local government in Canada — if the Baldwin Act

---

[74]Jon Caulfield, "Reform as a Chaotic Concept: The Case of Toronto," in *Urban History Review,* October 1988, pp. 107-110.

[75]Paul Peterson, *City Limits,* Chicago, University of Chicago Press, 1981.

[76]Michael Keating, *Comparative Urban Politics,* Aldershot, Edward Elgar, 1991, p. 155.

[77]Clarence Stone and Heywood Sanders (eds.), "Reexamining a Classic Case of Development Politics: New Haven, Connecticut," in *The Politics of Urban Development,* Lawrence, University Press of Kansas, 1987, p. 163.

[78]*Ibid.,* p. 167.

of Ontario is used as a major starting point — the local government system had become increasingly inadequate, largely because of the pressures of industrialization and urbanization. To many observers, the problems went much deeper than the local government system itself. They were inherent in the process of urbanization and in the nature of the built environment of our cities with its lack of physical diversity. They were the result of misguided policies of the senior governments, notably using housing and urban development as tools of economic growth. They were the inevitable result of the capitalist mode of production and of the demands of investment capital.

The more conventional assessment, however, and the one which was reflected in the reforms subsequently introduced, was that the main problems were within the existing local government system, were "cracks in the foundation" that had been established in the previous century. These included:

1. Inappropriate municipal boundaries arising from an excessive number of small municipalities and from the fragmented municipal structure found in most urban centres.
2. An erosion of the powers of the municipality to separate boards and commissions and to the senior levels of government.
3. Insufficient municipal revenue sources and an increasing dependence upon provincial grants, heavily conditional in nature.
4. An incompatibility between the nonpolitical tradition inherited from the turn of the century reform era and the increasingly controversial issues and value judgments facing municipal governments, especially in urban Canada.
5. Municipal governing bodies that were ineffective in providing leadership, coordination, and a clear focus of accountability and responsibility.

As these problems intensified, various adaptations and modifications occurred, culminating in local government reform initiatives in a number of the provinces. These reforms were moderate in nature, directed towards making improvements within the existing system. Even judged on that basis, they do not measure up well. Rather than building new foundations for a modern system of local government based equally on considerations of effective representation and efficient service delivery, most of these reforms did little more than patch up the cracks in the traditional foundation, leaving the structure over-balanced in favour of the service delivery function.

CHAPTER 5

Local Government Reform

OBJECTIVES:

1. To describe and compare the main local government reforms introduced in the various provinces in the post World War Two period.

2. To examine the strengths and weaknesses of these reform initiatives.

3. To assess the overall impact of these reforms on the shortcomings in the traditional system of local government described in the preceding chapters.

Introduction

The present local government system in Canada is the product of extensive reform efforts in a number of the provinces, especially in the first couple of decades following World War Two. A major purpose of this chapter is to examine these reforms and the resulting local government system in relation to the inadequacies identified in the previous chapters.

In addition to the breadth of this topic, a further difficulty is determining the beginning of the reform period since, as has already been demonstrated, the system of local government has undergone considerable adaptation since its establishment. Examples include the shift of functions upward to more senior levels of government, the establishment of intermunicipal special purpose bodies, intermunicipal servicing agreements, boundary extensions through annexations and amalgamations, and increased financial assistance from the senior levels of government.

For our purposes, the modern period of local government reform began in 1953 with the establishment of Metropolitan Toronto. Over the next decade, we witnessed a period of what might be termed *ad hoc metropolitan reform*, extending to Montreal and Winnipeg by the beginning of the 1960s. These reforms were *ad hoc* in the sense that they represented unique responses to serious servicing problems in the three urban areas involved, rather than arising from any comprehensive study of local government in that particular province.

In contrast, the decade of the 1960s can be distinguished by not only a great increase in reform activities but also much more comprehensive approaches in several of the provinces. For example, fundamental examinations of the provincial-local relationship were carried out in New Brunswick in 1963 and in Manitoba in 1964, but only the New Brunswick recommendations were acted upon. Reform initiatives were introduced in British Columbia and Quebec in 1965 with particular emphasis on the creation of upper tier governments for the urban areas and, in the case of Quebec, voluntary amalgamations of small municipalities. The establishment of regional governments was the central feature of Ontario's local government reform efforts during this period.

Reform initiatives were much more limited during the 1970s and 1980s, with the only major structural changes being the creation of Winnipeg Unicity in 1972 and the introduction of regional county municipalities (RCMs) in Quebec in 1979. Major local government studies in both Nova Scotia and Newfoundland were completed in 1974, but were not acted upon except for some gradual changes in recent years.

Since the end of the 1980s, however, there has been renewed activity in local government reform, with initiatives currently underway in all four Atlantic Provinces and some very dramatic school board restructuring taking place in Alberta.

Since a strict chronological presentation would necessitate returning to certain provinces on two or more separate occasions, the complete reform experience of each province will be examined in what follows. The order in which the provinces are examined reflects the timing of the initial reform activities. Where the provincial descriptions are quite lengthy, summary sections are provided in several instances.

Ontario

Since the pressures of change rendering the traditional local government system increasingly inadequate have been previously described as arising because of urbanization, it is not surprising that the first major structural reform in Ontario was introduced in the Toronto area. A brief examination of the background to, and nature of, this reform is useful in assessing subsequent reforms.

Metropolitan Toronto

With the postwar "population explosion," the rapid growth of a number of the municipalities surrounding the city of Toronto produced serious servicing difficulties. Most pressing were the problems of water supply and sewage treatment facilities arising from the fact that only six of the thirteen municipalities involved had direct physical access to Lake Ontario. Arterial road development could not keep pace with the rapidly increasing volume of traffic. Public transportation and the existing highway network were poorly integrated. There was a desperate need for new schools. Many of the outlying municipalities were particularly ill-equipped to finance these service demands since, as dormitory suburbs, they lacked industrial assessment to help relieve the tax burden of the residential taxpayer.

The city of Toronto also faced serious economic and social problems, with a large backlog of public works because of the disruption of the depression and war years, and a greatly increased demand for welfare services. There was growing traffic congestion because of the extent of commuter population, and urban renewal and redevelopment needs were increasingly obvious. With each municipality seeking capital funds on its own credit, borrowing by the burgeoning suburbs became more and more difficult as interest rates rose.

By the beginning of the 1950s it was evident that a radical solution was required to meet existing servicing crises and to ensure orderly future growth. The need for intermunicipal cooperation had already prompted innumerable joint agreements between two or more municipalities and a number of proposals for annexations and amalgamations. Indeed, it was the presentation of three such separate applications to the Ontario Municipal Board in 1950 that brought the matter to a head and led to the recommendations which created Metropolitan Toronto.

This reform, which was radical and yet simple, established a federated form of government embracing the city of Toronto and the twelve surrounding municipalities. As the lower tier in a two tier structure, these thirteen municipalities retained their existing boundaries and continued to exercise a wide range of responsibilities. In addition, an upper tier unit, the municipality of Metropolitan Toronto, was established with the responsibility for such major functions as assessment, debenture borrowing, water supply and trunk mains, sewage treatment works and trunk sewers, and designated metropolitan roads. A number of responsibilities were also to be shared between the two levels of government. The fact that the metropolitan council was indirectly elected, that is composed of individuals elected in the first instance to designated positions on the lower tier councils, made the new structure similar to the century old county system. The major differences were the inclusion of the city in the metropolitan system and the much stronger powers given to the upper tier council.

In its early years, Metropolitan Toronto was substantially successful in combating the servicing problems facing the member municipalities, particularly as regards sewers, water supply, education, and general financial stability. To a considerable extent, these early successes have been attributed to the forceful, skilled leadership of the first chairman of the metropolitan council, Frederick Gardiner, who held this position from 1953 to 1961. Gardiner's personal philosophy was clearly consistent with the founding objectives of the new metropolitan system, to develop the servicing infrastructure needed to accommodate the growth pressures. As Timothy Colton observes, Metropolitan Toronto was invented to promote what was presumed to be a common and profound interest in rapid urban growth.[1]

While Gardiner was quite successful in meeting these initial objectives, Colton notes that doubts were growing even before his retirement.[2] Yes, there was a massive expansion of housing, but primarily in the form of high rise apartment construction which was accompanied by an increasing concentration of power in the development industry. Public transit was upgraded and expanded, but the construction of expressways prompted a growing anti-expressway sentiment, culminating in the "Stop-Spadina" movement. Toronto enjoyed a boom in downtown development but fears mounted about an excessive growth mentality and the disruption of established neighbourhoods — as reflected in the activism of citizens and citizen groups in the 1960s.

Quite apart from these changing public attitudes, Kaplan offers some interesting explanations for the decline in Metropolitan Toronto's momentum after the first few years.[3] He emphasizes the significance of the indirect election of metropolitan councillors, noting that they stood, succeeded, or failed largely on the basis of their records in their local (lower tier) council, only referring to Metro when it was politically expedient to blame it for not delivering enough for the local municipality in question. Ironically, according to Kaplan it was this very parochialism of councillors which helped to explain Metropolitan Toronto's initiatives and successes in the early years. Gardiner astutely avoided issues which would threaten local municipalities, and councillors were largely indifferent to everything

---

[1]Timothy J. Colton, *Big Daddy*, Toronto, University of Toronto Press, 1980, p. 175.

[2]*Ibid.*, pp. 177-178.

[3]Harold Kaplan, *Reform, Planning, and City Politics: Montreal, Winnipeg, Toronto*, Toronto, University of Toronto Press, 1982, pp. 685-690.

else and prepared to accept Gardiner's persuasive leadership. However, when Metro turned to the more complex issues of the 1960s, especially under the less forceful chairmen who succeeded Gardiner, the limitations of this passive support became increasingly apparent. Noting that Metropolitan Toronto's main achievements were between 1953 and 1957, Kaplan contends that "in retrospect, the early burst of activity was the aberration and the subsequent prolonged retreat a more accurate expression of the system's character."[4]

Some problems and limitations were documented by the Royal Commission on Metropolitan Toronto established in 1963 to examine the first decade of operation. However, the Commission's 1965 Report endorsed continuation of the two tier system.[5] The main change, introduced effective January 1st, 1967, was a consolidation of the original 13 municipalities at the lower tier into six. In addition, the metropolitan council was increased to 32 members, with the city retaining its 12 representatives but the five suburban municipalities now sending 20 in recognition of their much greater population growth since the establishment of Metro. A few responsibilities, notably waste disposal and social assistance, were transferred from the lower tier municipalities to Metropolitan Toronto, continuing a trend which had become evident throughout the 1950s.

As Kaplan observes, there was little in these reforms to revive Metro.[6] While the suburban municipalities now enjoyed a majority position, they had no regional aspirations on which to use their power. They had received the necessary expansion of their basic services during the first decade. Now it was the City of Toronto which needed Metro more — to help finance the renewal of aging facilities. But Kaplan concludes that with a complacent suburban majority, Metropolitan Toronto was even less inclined to blaze new trails.

In 1974 another Royal Commission was appointed to review the Metropolitan Toronto system.[7] It recommended retention of the existing structure, including the six lower tier municipalities, with some boundary modifications. Partly in recognition of some of the problems previously

---

[4]*Ibid.*, p. 694.

[5]*Report of the Royal Commission on Metropolitan Toronto* (H. Carl Goldenberg, Commissioner), Toronto, Queen's Printer, 1965.

[6]Kaplan, *op. cit.*, p. 697.

[7]*Report of the Royal Commission on Metropolitan Toronto* (Honourable John P. Robarts, Chairman), Toronto, Queen's Printer, 1977.

discussed, it did recommend changes relating to such matters as the election of the metropolitan council and the division of governmental responsibilities.

No action was taken at that time, but major changes in the election of the Metropolitan Toronto council were finally introduced at the time of the 1988 municipal elections. The size of Metro's council was reduced to 34 members, consisting of the mayors of the six lower tier municipalities as before, and 28 directly elected members — who do not hold any seats on the lower tier councils. Provision was also made for the Chairman of Metro to be chosen by the metropolitan council from among the 28 directly elected members. These changes appear to reflect a belated concern by the Ontario government for the representative role of local government and its accountability and responsiveness — a point returned to at the conclusion of this chapter. As to why the province finally responded after ignoring a number of earlier studies and recommendations, Mellon[8] points to such factors as the use of a Task Force composed largely of municipal appointees and the municipal experience and commitment to change of the then Minister of Municipal Affairs. However, any further discussion of this change will await the next chapter, which deals with internal governing structures.

The area of urban development that Metropolitan Toronto was established to embrace and to stimulate has long since expanded beyond its boundaries. Just as the population growth of the city of Toronto has failed to keep pace with that of the suburban lower tier municipalities within Metro, so too has Metro itself fallen behind the rapid pace of growth of areas adjacent to it. It is "hemmed in" on all sides by four regional governments (and Lake Ontario). Until 1971 Metropolitan Toronto absorbed the bulk of the new population growth in this area — now known as the Greater Toronto Area (GTA) — but since then its growth has dropped off sharply. In fact, Metro's share of the population of the GTA fell from 77% in 1961 to 54% in 1991.[9]

The importance of the Metropolitan Toronto experience lies not only in what was done there, but on the extensive influence which this model wielded on the reforms elsewhere in the province, as described below.

---

[8]Hugh Mellon, "Reforming the Electoral System of Metropolitan Toronto," in *Canadian Public Administration*, Toronto, Spring 1993, pp. 38-56.

[9]Frances Frisken, "Planning and Servicing the Greater Toronto Area," in Donald N. Rothblatt and Andrew Sancton (eds.), *Metropolitan Governance: American/Canadian Intergovernmental Perspectives*, Berkeley, Institute of Governmental Studies Press, 1993, p. 157.

Regional Government: What's in a Name?

A more comprehensive approach to local government reform in Ontario was introduced toward the end of the 1960s although, as will be seen, the actual reforms introduced were considerably more limited than the reform policy. Indeed, well before any governmental policy statement the process began with the appointment of local government studies in several, mostly heavily urbanized, areas — beginning with Ottawa-Carleton in 1964. At this time, significantly, the Metropolitan Toronto system was still in its initial, conspicuously successful phase, and the model was to influence greatly all subsequent reforms.

The actual local government reform policy set out in Design for Development, Phase Two at the end of 1968 was potentially quite broad and imaginative, largely because of guidelines and a philosophical base taken from the Report of the Ontario Committee on Taxation the previous year. The policy recognized the need to provide not only efficient delivery of services but also adequate access and effective representation of local views and concerns. It called for regional governments based on such criteria as community of interest, an adequate financial base and sufficient size to generate economies of scale.[10] The policy also proposed varied structural approaches including both two tier and one tier governments and the direct election of upper tier councillors in the former instance.

In practice, the reforms introduced were all regional governments closely resembling Metropolitan Toronto. As such, they can best be described as a modification of the traditional county system in Ontario. The reformed structures have all contained two tiers with the upper tier closely paralleling the boundaries of one or more counties in most cases. All or major municipal responsibility for such functions as welfare, parks, roads, water supply, sewage disposal, planning, and capital borrowing have been vested in this upper tier. The lower tier units in the structure have been formed by a consolidation of constituent municipalities and have included any cities and separated towns, previously separate under the county system. With minor exceptions and recent changes, election to the upper tier closely resembles the indirect election of county councillors, and the costs of regional services are apportioned to lower tier municipalities in accordance with their assessment in essentially the same manner as under the county system.

---

[10]See the Honourable John Robarts and Darcy McKeough, *Design for Development: Phase Two*, Statements to the Legislature of Ontario, November 28th and December 2nd, 1968, and *The Ontario Committee on Taxation, Volume Two*, Toronto, Queen's Printer, 1967, Chapter 23.

In the decade from the commissioning of the first local government reform study (of Ottawa-Carleton) in May 1964 to the coming into operation of the Regional Municipality of Haldimand-Norfolk in April 1974, eleven regional governments were established,[11] covering over one-third of the population of Ontario. However, well before this time, the regional government program was losing momentum. Indeed, most local government reform studies were undertaken before the government announced its policy on the subject in the aforementioned Design for Development statement. As the unpopularity and political cost of the reforms became apparent, the government increasingly disavowed any intention of introducing new regional government initiatives.

County Restructuring: Regional Government By Another Name?

Instead a County Restructuring Program was announced in February 1974. Under this Program, the Ontario government indicated its willingness to participate jointly with counties in local government studies and to share equally the costs of such studies under certain specified conditions. On the surface this new policy appeared to involve a significant shift toward local initiative in reform. However, the policy went on to identify certain conditions which would have to be met for a county to qualify as a restructured county and thereby be eligible for the additional powers and grants being given to the regional governments. These specified conditions were essentially the basic features of the regional governments already established, and the only restructured county to date (Oxford) has adopted a two tier system basically the same as the regional governments. Therefore, one can reasonably wonder whether the County Restructuring Program was intended as anything more than a change in name and shift in emphasis from provincial to local initiative with the same reform objectives in mind.

The question may be academic since very little action was taken on the studies carried out under this program and the prolonged period of minority government in Ontario in the latter part of the 1970s forestalled any new initiatives. Indeed, the provincial government even appeared unwilling to modify existing reformed structures if there were local objec-

---

[11]These were Ottawa-Carleton, Niagara, York, Waterloo, Sudbury, Peel, Halton, Hamilton-Wentworth, Durham, Haldimand-Norfolk, and Muskoka, with the latter being known as a District Municipality. If we add the prototype, Metropolitan Toronto, and the subsequently established Restructured County of Oxford (described below), there are thirteen regional governments in Ontario, containing two-thirds of its population.

tions. The previously-cited Robarts Royal Commission on Metropolitan Toronto was but one of several reviews appointed in the mid-1970s to examine established regional governments. In spite of a wide variety of recommendations, however, only minor changes were introduced to the existing structures.

County government reform — or what might be termed the "third coming of regional government," as it has been practised in Ontario — resurfaced in the late 1980s.[12] As with the earlier regional government program, a primary impetus for these new county reform proposals was the need to meet certain servicing challenges, including planning and waste management. Once again, much of the emphasis was on strengthening the upper tier by bringing in any cities or separated towns, and strengthening the lower tier through municipal consolidations — although the original population minimum of 4 000 for new lower tier unit was subsequently qualified and essentially abandoned. But, as with the previous county restructuring program of the early 1970s, virtually no action has been taken on the county studies carried out, and the whole county reform initiative has apparently been allowed to lapse.

Instead, Ontario appears to have returned to a traditional method of adapting local government to growth pressures — annexation and amalgamation. The Municipal Boundary Negotiations Act enacted at the end of 1981 provided a new approach to boundary adjustments with procedures somewhat similar to the negotiation process found within collective bargaining. In its first decade, this Act was used to resolve 140 annexation disputes in Ontario, although mostly relating to towns, villages and townships, not major urban areas.[13]

Ironically, it was the failure of this boundary negotiations process that led to one of the most significant annexation decisions in Ontario. Provincial intervention resulted in the city of Sarnia absorbing the neighbouring town of Clearwater in 1991,[14] and also becoming part of a restruc-

---

[12]See Report of the Advisory Committee on County Government, *Patterns for the Future*, Ontario Government Bookstore, 1987, Report of the Advisory Committee to the Minister of Municipal Affairs, *County Government in Ontario*, January 1989, and Ministry of Municipal Affairs, *Toward an Ideal County*, January 1990.

[13]Andrew Sancton, *Local Government Reorganization in Canada Since 1975*, Toronto, ICURR Press, April 1991, p. 13.

[14]This reform is well documented in Byron Montgomery, *Annexation and Restructuring in Sarnia-Lambton*, Local Government Case Studies #4, London, University of Western Ontario, 1991.

tured county of Lambton. These changes were consistent with the thrust of the county government reform program (discussed above) which the Province was by then proposing. In fact, only Lambton county has gone through restructuring since the county reform program was announced.

A second significant annexation decision involved the city of London, which was given a larger area of adjacent territory than it had sought, as a result of the report of a Greater London Area Arbitrator based on planning and economic development considerations. Sancton questions the assumptions (or lack thereof) concerning why the London annexation was needed to ensure future economic growth. The key feature of the annexation was to give London increased industrial land adjacent to Highway 401. But, as Sancton points out, no consideration was given as to whether future economic growth must be centred on manufacturing or whether access to major highways will be critical in the future.[15] With the shift to an "information economy" as briefly described in the previous chapter, both of these traditional assumptions should have been questioned more closely.

Another significant boundary adjustment occurred in south Simcoe county, an area experiencing strong growth pressures extending northward from the Greater Toronto Area. A proliferation of joint servicing arrangements covering such subjects as fire, police, water, sewer, landfill, libraries and building inspection were cited as evidence of the need for restructuring.[16] A full county restructuring which would have brought the cities of Barrie and Orillia into the county system was not pursued, but eight municipalities in south Simcoe were reduced to three through consolidations.

Ontario Highlights

Even if no further major changes are made in Ontario, it is striking to note that, as a result of the reform initiatives which have been introduced, two-thirds of the population of Ontario is under regional governments (including Metropolitan Toronto), so it is important to consider the nature of these reforms. Clearly, they were preoccupied with structural changes designed to improve administrative efficiency and the provision of services. (This emphasis was also evident in the parallel reform in edu-

---

[15]Andrew Sancton, *Governing Canada's City-Regions: Adapting Form to Function*, Montreal, Institute for Research on Public Policy, 1994, p. 32.

[16]Allan O'Brien, *Municipal Consolidation in Canada and its Alternatives*, Toronto, ICURR Press, May 1993, pp. 79-80.

cational administration culminating in the still very controversial county and district boards of education established in 1969.) Service standards have doubtless improved, although some would dispute this, and the division of responsibilities between the upper and lower tiers has caused friction and inhibited coordination.

Moreover, the reforms have been quite narrow in focus. Until recently, the political role of local government has been largely ignored and little attention has been given to ways of making municipal governments more representative and more accountable to their inhabitants. The consolidation of lower tier municipalities reduced the number of elected councils and, with the enlarged areas, many citizens felt that their municipal government was less accessible and less sensitive to their particular needs. The feeling of alienation was even stronger with respect to the regional councils, which not only appeared remote but also had taken over a number of responsibilities previously exercised at the lower tier. The increase in regional staff made the system seem increasingly bureaucratic and the essentially indirect election of regional councillors did little to generate public involvement in, and support for, the regional system.

One analysis of the reformed structures in Ontario discerns a change in the balance of power at the local level and describes "a major increase in the influence of public servants, especially regional ones, at the expense of local elected officials and residents."[17] Because of the municipal consolidations there are fewer elected representatives and their role has changed. Rather than being closely involved in the operations of the municipality (perhaps too closely at times), councillors appear relegated to a role of responding to policy proposals put forward by the bureaucracy, especially at the regional level. This analysis further notes that with fewer councils and councillors and more formal, streamlined procedures for handling business, the nature of citizen participation in local government has also changed. "The emphasis now was on scheduling an appointment before a council and presenting a brief outlining one's arguments...instead of a spontaneous appearance and an informal discussion...." The result was a shift of power among citizens since "the new technical rules of citizen participation not surprisingly favour those with formal argumentative skills or those who can afford to hire people with these skills."[18]

---

[17]Henry J. Jacek, "Regional Government and Development: Administrative Efficiency versus Local Democracy," in Donald C. MacDonald (ed.), *The Government and Politics of Ontario,* Toronto, Nelson, 1985, p. 111.

[18]*Ibid.,* p. 112.

Reforms in the composition of the council of Metropolitan Toronto in 1988 have been cited as a belated response to the political and representative role of municipal government and, as discussed in the next chapter, other changes in election and composition have been introduced for the Hamilton-Wentworth and Ottawa-Carleton regional councils. On the other hand, the Province seems prepared to expand the responsibilities of county government, notably in the planning field, even though county reform has not been successful and even though the make-up of most county councils makes a mockery of the concept of "representation by population."

In spite of the fact that the main reforms in Ontario have been preoccupied with creating regional government structures more effective in delivering services, it is increasingly apparent that the boundaries of many of these governments are no longer appropriate. This deficiency has become particularly evident in the Toronto area. The growth pressures in this area and the lack of coordination in managing this growth led in 1988 to the creation of the Office of the Greater Toronto Area (OGTA), reporting directly to a Provincial cabinet minister. The OGTA does not have any legislative mandate, but defines its role as one of fostering communication among government bodies, seeking solutions to immediate problems that no single government can solve on its own and helping governments in the area develop a consensus on what the GTA should look like 20 years from now.[19] The OGTA acts as a secretariat for the Greater Toronto Coordinating Committee, which includes senior staff representatives from the five upper tier municipalities in the GTA (Metro Toronto, Halton, Peel, York and Durham) and the 30 lower tier municipalities in this area.[20]

Sancton refers to "the tragedy for the municipal system in the GTA," in that this area has had more municipal reorganization and upheaval than any other part of Canada and yet the municipal boundaries bear little relationship to urban reality.[21] His sobering conclusion bears repeating as a fitting epitaph to the Ontario municipal reform experience and should also be borne in mind in the ensuing discussions of reforms in other provinces.

---

[19]Frisken, *op. cit.*, p. 161.

[20]Sancton, *Canada's City Regions*, p. 78.

[21]Andrew Sancton, "Canada as a Highly Urbanized Nation," in *Canadian Public Administration*, Fall 1992, p. 290.

The simple truth is that urban areas in Canada, and elsewhere, have become too big to be governed by metropolitan or regional authorities of the type introduced in Canada from the 1950s to the 1970s. *Their time is past.*[22] (emphasis added)

Manitoba

Local government reform activities in Manitoba have been concentrated on Winnipeg, which, as the provincial capital and the centre for over half of the population of the province, understandably dominates the local government scene.[23] However, the opportunity for a more comprehensive reform affecting the overall system of local government was presented by a major Royal Commission study in the early 1960s.

Missed Opportunities in Manitoba?

In 1963 the Manitoba government appointed a commission:

to inquire into all aspects of the powers, responsibilities and organization of local government in Manitoba, its financial structure and resources, and in particular to examine the division of responsibilities between the municipalities and the Provincial Government.[24]

The Commission's 1964 Report attempted a new delineation of provincial and municipal responsibilities, fairly similar to the services to people versus services to property distinction used by the Byrne Commission in New Brunswick as described later in this chapter. The Report called for the division of Manitoba into eleven administrative regions.

Each region was to have a regional council composed of elected representatives from municipalities within the region. However, these

---

[22]*Ibid.*, p. 292.

[23]Indeed, by 1971 (the year the present Winnipeg Unicity structure was introduced), the city accounted for over 65% of the province's labour force, 70% of its personal income, 80% of its industrial production, 62% of its retail sales, fully 95% of its wholesale sales, and nearly 70% of total provincial tax revenue. See Mathew J. Kiernan and David C. Walker, "Winnipeg" in Warren Magnusson and Andrew Sancton (eds.), *City Politics in Canada*, Toronto, University of Toronto Press, 1983, p. 225.

[24]*Report of the Manitoba Royal Commission on Local Government Organization and Finance* — popularly known as the Michener Report, after its chairman, Roland Michener — Winnipeg, Queen's Printer, 1964.

regional councils were not to constitute another level of government, as do the county councils in Ontario for example, but were to serve as a forum for developing and carrying out joint works of the municipalities. Executive authority and the responsibility for formulating policy and imposing taxes would remain with the individual municipal councils. The municipalities themselves would be considerably changed, however, with the Report recommending that the existing 106 municipalities in Manitoba be amalgamated to form 40 or 50 units.

Whatever its merits, this major study was largely ignored. With strong opposition to the creation of larger municipal units, the Province moved instead to formalize a system of single purpose districts for joint municipal services.[25] The system involves a combination of intermunicipal and provincial-municipal services for rural residents on a more affordable basis than a single municipality could deliver. Examples include planning districts, conservation districts, regional development corporations, community round tables, weed control districts, veterinary services districts and a recreational opportunities program.

Metropolitan Winnipeg

As indicated above, municipal reform efforts in Manitoba have been concentrated on its dominant urban centre, the city of Winnipeg. The factors leading to this reform were quite similar to those leading to the establishment of Metropolitan Toronto. The population growth after World War Two brought the by now familiar urban problems. Expenditures soared, notably in education, while the revenues were distributed unevenly and there were wide variations in property assessment. There was inadequate sewage disposal for the area and water rationing became common. A considerable number of intermunicipal special purpose bodies operated in the Greater Winnipeg area and, while they enjoyed some success, their very existence pointed to the need for some form of area-wide government. In fact, it has been suggested that the Metro Planning Commission established in 1943 helped to shape thinking about wider planning issues and thus to create the more unified outlook which was needed for subsequent reforms.[26]

A Greater Winnipeg Investigating Commission was established in 1955 and reported in 1959 with recommendations for the establishment of a two tier system of metropolitan government in the area. Apparently

---

[25]The description which follows is based on O'Brien, *op. cit.*, p. 31.

[26]Kaplan, *op. cit.*, pp. 501-504.

the Commission was strongly influenced by the newly created system of Metropolitan Toronto and frequent consultations were held with its chairman, Fred Gardiner.[27]

The reform introduced by the Manitoba government in 1960 was more modest than the Commission's recommendations and it also differed from Metropolitan Toronto in certain significant respects. A two tier system of municipal government was established with ten municipalities completely within Metro's jurisdiction and nine more partly in the Metro area and partly in the outlying "additional zone" where Metro had planning authority. The metropolitan government was given full authority over all planning, zoning, and issuing of permits as well as such operating functions as assessment, civil defence, flood protection, sewage disposal (but not collection), and water (excluding local distribution). Many responsibilities which had previously been exercised by separate special purpose bodies were vested directly in the metro council and no new boards were established — in marked contrast to the Metropolitan Toronto system in which the numerous separate boards were retained.

In a notable departure from the Toronto approach, the ten members of the metropolitan council were directly elected from special pie-shaped districts including both central and suburban areas. Moreover, metro councillors could not also hold local office. It was hoped that this type of district and method of representation would encourage area-wide thinking. This it did do, but almost too successfully! The metropolitan council contained a strong core of metro supporters and with more specific, parochial demands being directed at lower tier councils, they were able to take the broader view. However, in their enthusiasm they were rather aggressive in their initiatives and insufficiently sensitive to the concerns of the local councils. Municipalities which questioned whether they were receiving a share of metro expenditures commensurate with their financial contribution were informed that decisions were made objectively, in the public interest, not on the basis of the pork barrel.

This approach certainly contrasts with Gardiner's skilful balancing of city and suburban benefits in the Metropolitan Toronto system. As Kaplan points out, if Metropolitan Toronto had insufficiently strong boundaries between it and its lower tier and could not avoid being exploited and manipulated by the municipal governments (especially after Gardiner), "Metro Winnipeg's problem was that it forged impermeable boun-

---

[27]T. Axworthy, "Winnipeg Unicity," in Advisory Committee on Intergovernmental Relations, *A Look to the North: Canadian Regional Experience*, Washington, D.C., 1974, p. 90.

daries between it and the municipalities and thus remained singularly obtuse about the wishes of those municipalities."[28] Adding to the problems was the extent of the opposition to the new metropolitan system. Some negative reaction had been expected since the suburbs had wanted the status quo and the City of Winnipeg had wanted complete amalgamation.

> What occurred instead was a virtual municipal insurrection, an assault on metro far exceeding anyone's expectations. During its ten year history, but especially in 1961-65, metro lived under a state of siege.[29]

In the face of these attacks, "metro became even more insular and self-righteous."[30]

The attack on the metropolitan system was led by Stephen Juba, the long time mayor of the city of Winnipeg, "conducted without restraint or let-up in the mayor's characteristically strident, affectively charged, assaultive style."[31] The criticisms were kept up partly because of the provincial government's lukewarm support for its creation. Premier Roblin had stated that there wouldn't be any review of the new system until 1965, but in the face of mounting criticism of the system he appointed a review commission in 1962. The Commission's Report in 1964 reaffirmed the basic system, although some changes were made in the status of municipalities partly in and partly without metro's jurisdiction.

Attacks on the system subsided somewhat after 1965, with Premier Roblin's assertion of stronger support. Instead, attention increasingly shifted to the possibility of amalgamation of the municipalities within the system. The 1969 election of an N.D.P. government suddenly made such a change quite probable because of the N.D.P.'s long time support for an amalgamated approach. Indeed, even though a Local Boundaries Commission appointed by the previous government was still continuing its studies, the new provincial government began preparation of a White Paper "Proposals for Urban Reorganization," released December 22, 1970. From this initiative came an exciting and imaginative new structure for urban government with the establishment of Winnipeg Unicity, effective January 1st, 1972.

---

[28]Kaplan, *op. cit.*, p. 684.

[29]*Ibid.*, p. 554.

[30]*Ibid.*, p. 556.

[31]*Ibid.*, p. 562.

Winnipeg Unicity

As its name implies, Unicity replaced the two tier metropolitan system with one enlarged city government. Much more than amalgamation of municipalities was involved, however, and the administrative centralization for efficiency in service delivery was to be offset by a number of provisions for political decentralization. To understand the new structure, it is important to bear in mind the philosophy and objectives of local government on which the reform was based.

Of particular note was the emphasis on the representative role of local government and the importance of citizen access and participation. In part, this was reflected in the provision for an unusually large council of fifty members, each elected from a separate ward. In addition, the Unicity legislation established thirteen community committees, each covering a number of wards and consisting of the councillors from these wards. The committees were originally seen as providing a forum for public involvement and for the political decentralization of certain functions. They were to maintain close two-way communication between Unicity and its residents concerning present and potential policies, programs, and budgets. Each committee was also to be responsible for preparing its own budget for services with a local orientation which were assigned to it, a provision which suggested the possibility of some variation in local services. To advise and assist each committee, the legislation also provided for the election of a resident advisory group (RAG).

A second significant feature of the new system was the attempt to build in the elements of the parliamentary   model of government, particularly in terms of a separate executive responsible for providing leadership and answering to the elected council. A key provision of this model, which was proposed in the White Paper but deleted from the legislation, was the stipulation that the mayor be chosen by and from elected members of council. Through this process, mayors could provide leadership on council because of majority support. At the same time, they would only remain in this position so long as they retained the confidence of the councillors. It was envisaged that the members of the executive committee would be chosen in the same way and, with the mayor as chair, this body would be akin to the cabinet in the parliamentary system. An important element, of course, was the existence of organized political parties. Some form of political party activity had been evident in Winnipeg since 1919, but it was hoped that a more formalized party system would evolve to complement the new government structure.

A third distinctive feature of Unicity was the amount of emphasis given to the internal organization of the municipality. It is clear that an attempt was made to concentrate council's role on representation and policy making while delegating much of the executive power of council to committees and staff, and attempting to ensure coordination of the administrative activities of the municipality. To this end, a fairly elaborate internal structure was established, details of which are found in the next chapter.

Unfortunately, the actual performance of Unicity has been increasingly disappointing. To some extent, this was inevitable, given the innovative, ambitious objectives which had been initially set for the system. Other difficulties and shortcomings were inherent in the Unicity structure or were created by changes introduced over the intervening years.

A Committee of Review appointed in 1975 found that the principle of unification under a one tier government had apparently been well accepted.[32] The Committee also noted that greater equity in distributing the burden of taxation had resulted from the establishment of a single tax rate throughout the urban area, and that disparities in the level of services provided in the former separate municipal jurisdictions had been considerably reduced. On the other hand, Axworthy claims that capital works expenditures between suburbs and inner city ran as high as 7-1 in favour of the suburban areas.[33]

The Committee of Review also found, that a number of the primary objectives of the new structure had not been realized. It laid much of the blame for Unicity's shortcomings on the fact that the mayor was directly elected rather than chosen from council, thereby removing the focus of leadership and accountability central to the parliamentary model. This lack of strong political leadership was especially significant given the large size of the council and the potentially fragmented outlook inherent in election by ward. Indeed, there is considerable evidence to suggest that traditional attitudes, outlooks and practices continued to prevail within the council in spite of the changes in approach envisaged in the legislation.[34] Parochialism remained, and considerable attention was directed

---

[32]*Report and Recommendations, Committee of Review, City of Winnipeg Act*, Winnipeg, Queen's Printer, October 1976.

[33]Lloyd Axworthy "The Best Laid Plans Oft Go Astray: The Case of Winnipeg," in M.O. Dickerson, S. Drabek, and J.T. Woods (eds.), *Problems of Change in Urban Government*, Waterloo, Wilfrid Laurier Press, 1980, p. 114.

[34]According to P.H. Wichern, Jr., *Winnipeg's Unicity After Two Years; Evaluation of an Experiment in Urban Government*, a paper prepared for the 46th annual meeting of the Canadian Political Science Association, Toronto, June 3-6, 1975.

to the securing of public services for particular wards — often taking the form of a city/suburbs division, rather than the establishment of overall policies for the Unicity area. After reviewing the new system, Plunkett and Brownstone concluded that "city policy making has not been altered drastically, and that it has only been improved slightly from what it seems likely to have been if the former structure had remained unchanged."[35]

Gerecke and Reid[36] are much more critical, labelling Unicity "a disaster." In their view, because only 16 of Unicity's original 50 seats on council were allocated to the inner city, suburban interests have dominated ever since. While the amount of economic development in the Metropolitan Toronto area allowed both the city of Toronto and the suburbs to enjoy considerable growth (especially with the skillful balancing act of Fred Gardiner, the first Metro chair), much slower growth in Winnipeg resulted in suburban development taking place at the expense of the city.[37] As discussed below, the Unicity council has been twice reduced in size, down to only 15 in 1992, with inner city representation shrunken to only three seats, leaving the old city of Winnipeg as "nothing more than three wards on the rump of a suburban council."[38]

So much has the power of the inner city declined, argue Gerecke and Reid, that the fringes of Unicity are being allowed to crumble away. This comment stems from legislation in 1992 which allowed a part of Winnipeg known as Headingley to secede from Unicity and to become the 106th rural municipality in Manitoba. When presenting the legislation, the Minister characterized Headingley as a semi-rural community with no municipal water or sewer service and more in common with neighbouring rural municipalities than with Winnipeg.[39] He stressed that the secession of Headingley was not setting a precedent, and that the government remained fully committed to the concept of Unicity. However, Gerecke and Reid note that this development has caused other fringe communities

---

[35]Meyer Brownstone and T. J. Plunkett, *Metropolitan Winnipeg: Politics and Reform of Local Government*, Berkeley, University of California Press, 1983, p. 173.

[36]Kent Gerecke and Barton Reid, "The Failure of Urban Government: The Case of Winnipeg," in Henry Lustiger-Thaler (ed.), *Political Arrangements: Power and the City*, Montreal, Black Rose Books, 1992, pp. 123-142.

[37]*Ibid.*, p. 132.

[38]*Ibid.*, p. 127.

[39]O'Brien, *op. cit.*, p. 32.

on the edge of the city, such as St. Norbert and St. Germain, to consider leaving as well. They express concern that Winnipeg may be "unravelling as a coherent unit of government."[40]

Another major issue of concern with respect to Unicity's performance has been the effectiveness of the new structure in facilitating citizen involvement, especially through the community committees and the resident advisory groups. The roles of these bodies were insufficiently clear from the outset, although the Unicity legislation certainly gave them less power than had been envisaged by the White Paper. The community committees were not lawmaking bodies and they had no taxing powers. While there were suggestions that they would in some respects fulfil the role of the former lower tier municipalities, Higgins provides a more accurate description in calling them "sub-committees of the city council."[41]

Even less specific was the mandate of the resident advisory groups — to advise and assist the community councils! As Higgins outlines, the initial response from local citizens was strong, with almost 500 advisors elected at the first meetings of the resident advisory groups.[42] Disillusionment set in, however, with the realization that these groups had little influence and that even if their particular community committee was responsive to their views, the committee only comprised from three to six of the fifty-one members (including the mayor) of council.

Other analysts haven't even been as positive as Higgins. Axworthy, for example, feels that the consultative mechanisms made very little impact and notes that in a 1973 survey "less than 5% of citizens recalled ever having contact with the RAGs or community committees."[43] He also describes an increasingly centralized system characterized by bureaucratic "stonewalling." According to Axworthy, "Civic administrators became notorious for not divulging information, for controlling the activity of the junior members of departments in their public dealings, and for refusing public access to information."[44] Another study notes that in 1976 the

---

[40]Gerecke and Reid, *op. cit.*, p. 127.

[41]Donald J. H. Higgins, *Urban Canada: Its Government and Politics*, Toronto, Macmillan, 1977, p. 150.

[42]*Ibid.*, p. 203.

[43]Axworthy, "The Best Laid Plans," *op. cit.*, p. 117.

[44]*Ibid.*, p. 116.

Unicity Council prohibited the community committees from continuing with the allocation of modest sums to various community cultural and recreational groups. This action also blocked the limited financial support which had existed for the RAGs, and in 1981 — 10 years after the creation of these much-heralded instruments of citizen participation — council was allocating RAGs on average $400 each![45]

In June 1977 the Manitoba government adopted a number of amendments to the Unicity structure but, ironically, these changes did little to resolve the weaknesses identified and, in some cases, have intensified them. In several respects, the amendments undermined the recommendations of the Committee of Review just as the original Unicity legislation had weakened the approach of the White Paper. The Committee of Review had recommended that the mayor be elected from within the council and that the mayor appoint the chairs of the standing committees. These chairs and certain other specified members would constitute the executive and would be given the powers necessary to function as a cabinet. The Committee had further recommended that the mayor and executive committee should be confirmed or replaced in their positions annually by a vote of council and that a chief critic should also be elected annually by those councillors not voting for the mayor. While it could not legislate a party system, the Committee expressed the hope and conviction that such a system would evolve "under the influence of the parliamentary characteristics of our model."

Instead, however, the revised legislation removed the mayor from the board of commissioners, and he was also replaced on the executive policy committee by a council-elected chair. These changes, together with the continuation of direct election of the mayor, seemed intended to reduce the position to the largely ceremonial role found in most Canadian municipalities. A further change saw the reduction in the size of council from fifty to twenty-nine. The number of community committees (twelve since 1974) was reduced to six and their vague and limited powers were further reduced. They now exercised discretion only with respect to libraries, parks and recreation and some planning functions,[46] a reflection of the growing trend toward centralization in program design and service delivery. Moreover, with greatly increased areas and populations of approx-

---

[45]Kiernan and Walker, *op. cit.*, pp. 236-7.

[46]Lionel G. Feldman Consulting Ltd. and Institute of Local Government, Queen's University, *Evaluation of Alternative Structures and A Proposal for Local Governance in the Edmonton Region*, January 1980, p. 67.

imately 100 000, the community councils and RAGs lost the close contact and familiarity with local issues which had been their main (and just about only) strength.

In June 1984, the Manitoba government appointed a Committee to review the Unicity legislation and governing system. The committee's 1986 Report found a lack of identifiable and consistent leadership within the Unicity Council, as well as confused roles and relationships among the various elements of the city governing machinery.[47] The Committee recommended that significant powers of the city be delegated to an executive committee composed of six councillors and chaired by the mayor.

The Review Committee also recommended that the community committees be given greater powers concerning the initiation, preparation and approval of local plans and zoning. It further recommended that these bodies be allocated financial resources for expenditures on local services, programs, and facilities according to their individual priorities and needs.

The government's response, in a 1987 White Paper,[48] was mixed. It rejected any change which would eliminate the standing committee system. While it agreed with the mayor chairing the executive committee, the Government proposed that this committee consist of 12 members not six, with the additional members being councillors from each of the community committees as elected by those committees. Once again, therefore, the Government's approach seemed designed to prevent the mayor from exercising the kind of strong leadership intended. There is no reason why these additional six members of the Executive Committee would necessarily follow the mayor's direction. The Government agreed with increasing the planning powers of the community committees, but without any increase in financial resources to these committees — here again limiting the potential of the change.

With the defeat of the NDP Government and the election of a minority Conservative Government at the end of the 1980s, a Winnipeg Wards Review Committee was appointed (in February 1991) and charged with recommending a new Unicity council of between 12 and 15 members. The resulting legislation (Bill 68) reduced the Unicity council from 29 to

---

[47]Ministry of Urban Affairs,*Discussion Paper*, "Strengthening Local Government in Winnipeg: Proposals for Changes to The City of Winnipeg Act," Winnipeg, February 27, 1987, p. 10. The summary of recommendations which follows is based on this Discussion Paper.

[48]*Ibid.*

15 members. This change was supposed to reduce parochialism and encourage the council to take a broader, city-wide approach to planning. It was also expected to streamline and speed up the decision-making process. The result was to be a smaller and more cohesive group to manage city hall.[49]

Other changes in Bill 68 saw the community committees further reduced in number from six to five, and the RAGs abolished outright. The bold experiment in citizen participation launched in 1972 was all but gone twenty years later!

Manitoba Highlights

For a quarter of a century Winnipeg's Unicity has been cited by those seeking an example of municipal restructuring which paid attention to the political role of municipal government, to the importance of public access and accountability. Ironically, as has been outlined, many of the key features which were designed to ensure this political role have been undermined or abandoned. Reviewing the most recent changes introduced by Bill 68, Leo[50] concludes that their main theme is narrowed participation in public decision making. In adopting such reforms, and especially in increasing the size of wards, he suggests that the Provincial Conservative Government "is following the time-honoured tradition of conservative governments seeking to enhance the business community's control over civic affairs."[51]

Even viewed from the narrower perspective of service delivery, the Unicity structure has not stood the test of time all that well. It is true that Unicity still contains most of the population of Winnipeg's census metropolitan area (94.5% in 1991), but much urban-related development has been taking place beyond the Unicity boundaries in recent years.[52] The 1986 report of the Review Committee (described above) recognized this trend by recommending the establishment of a new advisory and coordinating organization which would link all municipalities within the Winnipeg commuting area. While stressing that it was not recommending a new

---

[49]O'Brien, *op. cit.*, pp. 31-32.

[50]Chris Leo, "The Erosion of Unicity and the 1992 Civic Election," in *Institute of Urban Studies Newsletter*, Winnipeg, University of Winnipeg, Autumn 1992.

[51]*Ibid.*, p. 3.

[52]Sancton, *Canada's City Regions*, p. 27.

layer of regional government, the Committee acknowledged that the boundaries of Unicity were too limited for such municipal purposes as regional planning, environmental assessments and refuse disposal.[53]

In 1989 the Manitoba Government established what has become known as the Capital Region Committee, comprising three provincial ministers and the heads of council for Winnipeg and 14 surrounding municipalities. To date the committee's limited meetings have focused mainly on developing a strategy for sustainable development.[54] There is no indication that this committee will restrict the operations of Unicity, but its very existence demonstrates that even Unicity's major restructuring has not avoided municipal servicing problems which overlap municipal boundaries.

New Brunswick

The first province to undertake comprehensive local government reform initiatives in the 1960s was New Brunswick, and it did so by appointing a Royal Commission on Finance and Municipal Taxation. The emphasis on fiscal matters implicit in the title reflected the difficulties facing local government in New Brunswick at the time. The level of municipal services compared unfavourably with other provinces and there were wide variations in the standard of service within New Brunswick, notably in education. A multitude of assessment and tax acts resulted in a variety of taxes, again differing from one municipality to the next. There were marked inequities in municipal taxation and high tax arrears. Moreover, municipalities faced increasing difficulties financing their servicing demands and by the 1960s three of the single tier rural counties were virtually bankrupt.

To its credit, the Byrne Commission, as it came to be known, did contend that the problems facing local government in New Brunswick were not just a matter of allocation of tax fields but also involved government organization and structure. In its 1963 Report it made an attempt to distinguish between services appropriate for the provincial level and for the local level. On this basis it recommended the transfer of a number of functions to the provincial level and called for the New Brunswick government to provide services directly for rural areas, hitherto governed

---

[53]*Ibid.*

[54]*Ibid.*, pp. 27-28.

by the counties. Recommendations such as these caused some observers to conclude that the Commission's preoccupation with finances had led it to overemphasize efficiency and administrative rather than representative considerations.[55]

Equal Opportunity Program

Following extensive public discussions the government of New Brunswick launched a Program for Equal Opportunity in 1967 under which the main recommendations of the Byrne Commission were implemented. The provincial government took over responsibility for the administration of justice, welfare and public health, and also financial responsibility for the provision of education, with the number of school districts reduced from 422 to 33. All types of municipal taxation except the real property tax were abolished, and assessment — now to be at market value — and tax collection became provincial responsibilities. The fifteen single tier rural counties were abolished and, in partial compensation, some ninety new villages were created. Nonincorporated local service districts were also created, as administrative units for the province to provide services which had been provided by the now-abolished county councils. Provision was made for the establishment of advisory local service district committees, if a sufficient number of local inhabitants actively participated in forming them.[56] To meet their expanded responsibility, the province established a number of field offices in rural areas.

The reforms were beneficial in bringing about a substantial improvement in the quality of such services as education, justice, health and welfare — although this gain was essentially at the expense of the municipal level, which lost all or partial responsibility for these functions to the province. As the years passed, however, two areas of concern came increasingly to the fore. One was the lack of municipal government in rural New Brunswick after the abolition of the counties; the other was the failure to deal with boundary changes needed in urban areas. The subsequent response to each of these issues is examined next.

---

[55]Indeed, T.J. Plunkett in his "Criticism of Byrne Report," in Donald C. Rowat, *The Canadian Municipal System*, Toronto, McClelland and Stewart Limited, 1969, p. 180, charged that the Commission's proposed solutions "make the continuance of municipal government in New Brunswick of doubtful value."

[56]Edwin G. Allen, *Municipal Organization in New Brunswick*, Ministry of Municipal Affairs, Fredericton, 1968, p. 12.

Governing Rural New Brunswick

One major problem not resolved — indeed, some might argue, worsened — by the Program for Equal Opportunity, concerned the approximately 250 000 people (one-third of the population of New Brunswick) left without any form of municipal government.[57] These people looked to nearby villages and towns for some local services. They demanded some form of municipal government and, at the same time, the incorporated municipalities complained that these residents of non-incorporated areas were not paying fully for some local services they received.

In response to this situation, a Task Force on Nonincorporated Areas was established in June 1975. The resultant Report[58] found not only the predictable concern about the lack of elected councils to represent the people but also inequities in the financing of services. It noted that many services underwritten by property taxation in the incorporated municipalities were, in the case of the unincorporated areas, provided by the New Brunswick government without the imposition of any property taxation. Moreover, the Report stated that some of the services provided by the provincial government, notably community planning, could not be implemented effectively by that level of government and that more opportunity for local citizen input was necessary. As a result of these and other considerations, the Report recommended that all existing legislation pertaining to local service districts be repealed and that eleven new municipalities with the status of "Rural Municipalities" be incorporated. No action was taken on this recommendation, and one analysis concluded that the Report was a piece-meal response to the problems facing the New Brunswick municipal system, handicapped by narrow — and narrowly interpreted — terms of reference.[59]

In the years since, a number of intermunicipal single purpose boards have been established for regional planning and the provision of such regional services as economic development, sewage, transit, hospitals, ambulance service, emergency planning, pest control, libraries and solid waste management. Many of these boards have representation from both municipalities and local service districts. For example, Moncton, River-

---

[57]See Harley d'Entremont and Patrick Robardet, "More Reform in New Brunswick: Rural Municipalities," *Canadian Public Administration*, Fall 1977.

[58]*Report of the Task Force on Nonincorporated Areas in New Brunswick*, Fredericton, Queen's Printer, 1976.

[59]D'Entremont and Robardet, *op. cit.*, p. 480.

view and Dieppe are involved in some ten separate regional single purpose agencies which also serve the unincorporated areas in the adjacent
geographic counties of Albert and Westmorland.[60]

A more comprehensive response to the problems of the rural areas
may be in the offing as a result of the recommendations of the Commission on Land Use and the Rural Environment, established in January
1992. In its April 1993 Summary Report, it expressed great concern about
the general lack of support and priority for planning, and the amount of
sprawl and ribbon development which had been occurring in the unincorporated areas — resulting in an increase in the population of these
areas from 36% of the provincial total in 1976 to 40% in 1991.[61] It also
noted that a great deal of antagonism and dissension existed between incorporated and unincorporated areas of the province.

In response, the Commission recommended a number of structural
changes, at the provincial, regional and local levels. At the local level, it
called for the rationalization of existing local service districts into "Rural
Communities." These communities would have elected councils which
would appoint members to sit on District Planning or Management Commissions along with members representing municipalities within the districts. This change would, according to the Commission, provide better
representation for rural residents, more accountable decision making and
more integrated planning for urban and rural areas.[62]

The Commission indicated that these new Rural Communities would
be made up of combinations of the existing local service districts, with one
councillor elected from each district to the new community council. The
Commission emphasized that these Rural Communities would *not* be
municipalities in the same sense that cities, towns and villages are. The
responsibilities of their councils would initially be limited to dealing with
local planning matters.

Strengthening Urban Centres

While the Byrne Commission and Equal Opportunity Program failed to
address the issue of restructuring in New Brunswick's urban areas, some
boundary changes were introduced in the Fredericton and Saint John

---

[60]O'Brien, *op. cit.*, p. 14.

[61]Government of New Brunswick, *The Commission on Land Use and the Rural
Environment: Summary Report*, Fredericton, April 1993, p. 3.

[62]*Ibid.*, p. 7.

areas, and in the Moncton area with the consolidations which created Dieppe and Riverview, respectively, out of the Acadian and English-speaking suburbs.

A December 1992 government Report[63] acknowledged that the Equal Opportunity reforms had not addressed the problems of urban areas. Seven of these have populations of 20 000 or more, and the Report noted that they have been developing a variety of ad hoc regional bodies to deal with the provision of local services to their region — a trend cited above. The proliferation of these boards, according to the Report, weakened the accountability and added to the fragmentation within urban centres.

Options for restructuring were considered and some, like two tier or regional governments, were found to be inappropriate for New Brunswick. The preferred options cited in the Report were amalgamations to produce larger single tier municipal units or a formalized regional structure which would preserve existing municipalities but with an intermunicipal body to coordinate and administer regional services.[64]

To recognize the unique features of each of the seven urban areas, and to minimize disruption, the Report called for a phased approach, with a limited number of areas considered at any one time. The first two areas selected for study were the Moncton and Miramichi areas, with Reports appearing in April 1994.[65] The latter Report proposes the amalgamation of all 11 communities in the study area (only five of which are incorporated municipalities) into one municipality — a restructuring which would make Miramichi the fourth largest municipal unit in New Brunswick. The Moncton Report acknowledges the distinctive French and English communities of Dieppe and Riverview in ruling out amalgamation as the response. Instead, it calls for a joint services board comprised of elected and appointed officials from the three municipalities.[66] The Board would exist at the pleasure of the municipal governments to perform a municipal-like function. The Report emphasized that it should

---

[63]Ministry of Municipalities, Culture and Housing, *Strengthening Municipal Government in New Brunswick's Urban Centres*, December 1992.

[64]*Ibid.*, p. v.

[65]See Local Government Review Panel, *Miramichi City: Our Future — Strength Through Unity* and *Greater Moncton Urban Community: Strength Through Cooperation*, Government of New Brunswick, April 1994.

[66]For details on this interesting concept, see Moncton Report, *op. cit.*, pp. 37-38, on which the following description is based.

not be allowed to become a new level of government, but rather a mechanism to permit the three municipalities to work in greater harmony. Funding for the board would be through the three councils, with their shares based on their proportions of the total tax base of the three communities. Whether any of the existing single purpose agencies would be replaced by the new joint services board would be the decision of the three councils. In the interim, the new board was expected to provide coordination, liaison and financial control over those special purpose bodies providing municipal services to two or more municipalities in the Greater Moncton area.

New Brunswick Highlights

The reforms introduced in New Brunswick under the Equal Opportunity Program are a striking example of what happens when service delivery considerations are over-emphasized to the neglect of the political role of municipal government. The result was the loss of a number of responsibilities from the local to the provincial level and also the loss of municipal government in rural areas. It remains to be seen whether or not the New Brunswick Government will proceed with the municipal government reforms which have been proposed for both their rural and urban areas. Action on these proposals would help to "close the gap" left by the Byrne Commission and the Equal Opportunity Program.

Commendable in the approach being taken with the reform of urban areas is the willingness to recommend a variety of changes. This approach contrasts sharply, for example, with what has happened in Ontario, where the local government reform policy (as expressed in *Design for Development — Phase II*) suggested that experimentation would occur, but where the changes actually introduced were essentially transplants of the Metropolitan Toronto model.[67] On the basis of the two areas studied to date, New Brunswick appears much more prepared to contemplate varied approaches.

While the details are still unclear, the concept of a joint services board for the Greater Moncton area is at least refreshing in its conception. Ontario's approach in recent years has been to use intermunicipal servicing agreements as evidence that restructuring (and municipal consolidation)

---

[67]In fairness, it should be noted that many of the local government studies in Ontario did call for varied approaches to reform; it was the Provincial Government that ended up introducing a fairly standard package over and over. It remains to be seen whether the Government of New Brunswick will have the courage to try new approaches.

are needed. In contrast, New Brunswick accepts and builds on the presence of these arrangements. Its study praises the Greater Moncton urban community for being comprised of "three proud and distinct municipalities working together on joint ventures to bring about regionalized services for the benefits of all its citizens."[68] Rather than taking such cooperation as proof of the need for municipal consolidation, New Brunswick decided to build on that approach. In the words of the Moncton Report, it chose to "Go with the winner," rather than restructure and risk disruption.

British Columbia

In contrast to the comprehensive studies carried out in Manitoba and New Brunswick, British Columbia's approach to local government reform has been very pragmatic and directed to specific problems as perceived by the provincial government. To a large extent these problems were related to the absence of a municipal structure over much of the province. In 1966 only 2 870 square miles out of the 266 000 square miles in British Columbia were within organized municipalities.[69] The remainder of the province, containing one-sixth of B.C.'s population, received services directly from the provincial government although much of the affected populace resented paying taxes without some form of municipal government. The provincial administration was felt to be too small to deal with the vast territory involved, particularly when people moved into this unorganized area to avoid municipal taxes and then expected municipal services.

The organized municipalities also faced problems, with small, financially weak areas finding it difficult to provide necessary services. Some municipalities suffered from sprawl and poor land use, and the need for a joint approach to the provision of services in the Greater Vancouver area had already prompted the establishment of a number of regional special purpose agencies — the Greater Vancouver Sewerage and Drainage District (1914), the Greater Vancouver Water District (1926), four area health boards (set up between 1936 and 1948), the Lower Mainland Regional Planning Board (1948), the Greater Vancouver Parks District

---

[68]Moncton Report, *op. cit.*, p. 76.

[69]The figures are from D.W. Barnes, "The System of Regional Districts in British Columbia," in Advisory Commission on Intergovernmental Relations, *op. cit.*, p. 110.

(1966) and the Greater Vancouver Hospital District (1967). A form of metropolitan government for the Greater Vancouver area had been recommended in 1960, but the government did not act on this proposal.

Strategy of Gentle Imposition

Instead, the British Columbia government provided for the creation of regional districts to administer certain functions over wide areas. The specific objectives of this reform were not made clear by the government. However, this may well have been deliberate since one analysis[70] contends that the provincial government was especially interested in the potential of these regional districts in the two major urban centres of Vancouver and Victoria. It argues that the government used a strategy of "gentle imposition" to implement potentially significant regional governments, particularly for Greater Vancouver.

Whatever the government's motives, since the enabling legislation was passed in 1965, twenty-nine regional districts have been established, covering all of British Columbia except the northwest corner. Each district is governed by a regional board of directors comprising representatives from incorporated municipalities within the regional district and from the population of the unorganized territory. The regional districts vary greatly in size.[71] The Greater Vancouver Regional District is a major metropolitan area encompassing seven cities, eight districts (urban municipalities, not to be confused with regional districts), three villages and three unincorporated areas, known as electoral areas. In contrast, the Central Coast Regional District, with a population of just over 3 000, does not have any municipalities within it, but encompasses five electoral areas.

Because of the previously referred to strategy of gentle imposition, the regional districts originally did not have any assigned responsibilities. Instead it was left to the board of directors of each district to decide on the responsibilities they wished to assume. Individual municipalities or unorganized electoral areas were free to opt in or opt out of any of the servicing arrangements at their own discretion. Gradually, however, this discretion was reduced with certain responsibilities becoming mandatory and the opting out provision being removed. Thus, all regional districts became responsible for the adoption of an official plan, for the development

---

[70]Paul Tennant and David Zirnhelt, "Metropolitan Government in Vancouver: the strategy of gentle imposition," in *Canadian Public Administration*, Spring 1973, pp. 124-138.

[71]The two examples which follow are from O'Brien, *op. cit.*, p. 53.

of community planning services in their constituent electoral areas, for building inspection, and for certain "local works and services." In addition, individual districts voluntarily adopted a variety of other responsibilities including ambulance service, pest control, recreation facilities, refuse disposal, sewers, and water.[72] The end result is that regional districts are hybrids, delivering a mixture of upper and lower tier services.[73]

The regional districts do not levy taxes. They send a separate requisition for each service, which includes the appropriate share of the administrative costs, to each municipality — and the municipality must pay.[74] In the case of services provided to unincorporated areas, the requisition goes to the Province which, in turn, collects property taxes from inhabitants of these areas.

The overall impact of the British Columbia reforms is difficult to assess. There was some feeling that the regional districts would be a transitional stage toward a strong regional government system in which the existing municipalities would be amalgamated. There is no indication, however, that this was the provincial government's intention and, except for the Greater Vancouver and Victoria (Capital) areas, the regional districts have not developed into an important level of government. But if, as previously mentioned, the government's main purpose was to strengthen local government in these two metropolitan areas, it may feel that this objective has been largely met.

The regional districts have proven to be a flexible structure for dealing with a variety of considerations. They have assumed direct responsibility for the provision of municipal services to the population in unorganized areas. They have also acted as the administrative agency for certain functions or projects which some of their member municipalities wished to pursue jointly. In addition, they have assumed responsibility for various functions delegated to them by their constituent municipalities and they can acquire functions through the affirmative vote of two-thirds of the Directors of the regional district having among them at least two-thirds of the votes of the Board.

One analysis of the regional district scheme cites several positive features. Existing municipal units are allowed to continue under this structure thereby contributing to the preservation of an existing sense of

---

[72]Barnes, *op. cit.*, p. 116.

[73]Brian Walisser, *Understanding Regional District Planning: A Primer*, Ministry of Municipal Affairs, June 1987, unpaginated.

[74]O'Brien, *op. cit.*, p. 53.

community, allowing for diversity within the regional area, and helping to ensure accessibility and responsiveness in the municipal system. At the same time, the services provided by the regional districts have promoted the common interests of area municipalities and the fact that these regional services have been assigned by the area municipalities means that they are determining their common interests themselves rather than having this definition imposed from above.[75]

However, this analysis also identified certain problems or issues of concern. Because of the structure of the regional districts, notably the indirect election of members to the regional board, there appears to be little public discussion of board activities and decision making appears very insulated. The one exception to this pattern has been in the field of planning and development. Both the Capital and Greater Vancouver Regional Districts have undertaken regional planning exercises accompanied, in the latter case, by an elaborate public participation program. However, the results have been controversial in that future development has been restricted beyond the core municipalities and suburban areas have complained about undue limits on their rights of self-determination.

Some difficulties have also been noted with respect to coordination and information exchanges between the staffs of the regional district and its member municipalities. There have been complaints by incorporated municipal members that the regional boards spend too much time on the administration of the unorganized areas and that some of the overhead costs of this administration are borne by the incorporated municipalities. Finally, where a regional district is responsible for provision of a particular service over only part of its area, as in the Capital Regional District, there have been complaints that the committees of the regional district board which deal with these partial functions are not limited to representation by board members from only those affected areas.

A Regional District Review Committee was set up by the government in 1977. Its Report, the following year, identified several problems.[76] The relationship between the public and the regional district was found to be negative, with the public feeling that the district was inaccessible, dictatorial and a secretive organization. The Committee felt that the regional districts needed to do more to explain their responsibilities and to encourage public involvement. The Review Committee Report also described

---

[75]Feldman Consulting Limited, *op. cit.*, especially pp. 37-42.

[76]Regional District Review Committee, *Report of the Committee*, Victoria, Ministry of Municipal Affairs and Housing, 1978.

problems in the provincial-local relationship, stemming from the heavy-handed way in which the provincial level, and particularly the Ministry of Municipal Affairs and Housing, dealt with the regional districts.

Feldman and Graham concluded that the regional districts were "basically a low-profile nonthreatening system of area-wide responsibility for the delivery of certain local government services."[77] They correctly observed, however, that because of the limited scope of the regional district reforms and the reluctance of the provincial government to introduce more major changes, the issues arising from urban growth pressures, especially in the Vancouver and Victoria areas, had not been resolved.

The provincial government showed more inclination to act in the 1980s, although not in ways which the regional districts would have preferred. Patrick Smith describes the changed situation as being "regional structures under attack."[78] He examines two provincial initiatives which have limited the regional districts — the 1983 legislation declaring null and void all regional plans and removing the right of regional districts to plan for their regions as a whole, and the 1985 legislation centralizing the transit function at the provincial level. In spite of these developments, Smith argues that the need for regional institutions is evident. He notes that the number of functions which have been assumed by the regional districts indicates that they fill an important gap. He also points out that bilateral arrangements in planning are still permitted, and the fact that, for example, 14 of the 15 municipalities in the Greater Vancouver area participate voluntarily in such arrangements shows the necessity for the broader perspective brought by the regional districts.[79]

Oberlander and Smith explain the loss of the regional district planning function as the result of a continuing conflict between the Greater Vancouver Regional District (GVRD) and the provincial government.[80] Agricultural land reserves had been created under the provisions of the 1973 Land Commission Act, passed by the NDP Government of that time. But

---

[77]Lionel D. Feldman and Katherine A. Graham, "Local Government Reform in Canada," in Arthur B. Gunlicks (ed.), *Local Government Reform and Reorganization: An International Perspective*, London, Kennikat Press, 1981, p. 156.

[78]Patrick J. Smith, "Regional Governance in British Columbia," in *Planning and Administration*, 13, 1986, pp. 7-20.

[79]*Ibid.*, p. 14.

[80]See H. Peter Oberlander and Patrick J. Smith, "Governing Metropolitan Vancouver," in Rothblatt and Sancton, *op. cit.*, pp. 361-363.

appeals to the cabinet to release such lands for other (development) purposes became increasingly frequent with the return to power of Social Credit. Matters came to a head over a land reserve in the metropolitan Vancouver suburb of Delta. The GVRD opposed provincial plans to release this land from the agricultural designation. The Government responded, in October 1983, by stripping regional districts of their planning and zoning authority.

Some changes were introduced at the end of the 1980s as a result of another Review Committee which was appointed in 1983 and reported in November 1986.[81] This Committee reiterated the concern about lack of public understanding about the roles of regional districts. It observed that the provincial level had reduced its support for the regional districts over the years and was sending out very mixed signals about the future of these organizations (as described above). The Committee called for, among other matters, closer liaison between the regional districts and the Ministry of Municipal Affairs and clear and consistent statements of public policy with respect to the regional districts.

In 1989 the legislation governing the regional districts was revised. There were no drastic changes, but for the first time the local services that potentially fall within regional district jurisdiction are listed in the statute. It is still left to each regional district to determine the functions it will provide. However, they can now make service decisions by by-law, rather than by getting the Province to revise letters patent as was formerly required.[82] To provide a degree of self-government in isolated rural areas, the 1989 amendments encourage regional districts to create community commissions to cover part of an unincorporated area.[83] These commissions would consist of four specially elected commissioners and the director who would be elected to the board from the surrounding unincorporated area. The by-law setting up the commission sets out the administrative powers being delegated to it.

British Columbia Highlights

Municipal government reform in British Columbia has resulted in one of the most imaginative and flexible governing arrangements found any-

---

[81]Regional District Survey Committee, *Summary Report of the Regional District Survey Committee*, Victoria, Queen's Printer, 1986.

[82]O'Brien, *op. cit.*, p. 52.

[83]The description of these bodies is based on *ibid.*, p. 53.

where in Canada. The regional district structure allows existing municipalities to continue, with whatever communities of interest they represent, provides for the delivery of a variety of services by a regional authority, and avoids the bureaucratic buildup and duplication often associated with full-blown two tier regional governments. Its flexibility in being able to provide services to both incorporated municipalities and unincorporated areas is especially important, given British Columbia's population pattern. At the same time, the regional district structure does not measure up well in terms of representing and being accountable to the local public. It is more of an administrative contrivance of considerable ingenuity than it is an effective political entity.

One other difficulty with the British Columbia structure has been previously noted with respect to Ontario. That is, the fact that municipal government boundaries, even of new upper tier structures, are rarely large enough to encompass complete urban areas over which planning needs to be done. The "Lower Mainland" of British Columbia is one such major urban area, and it is interesting to trace briefly the planning efforts within it.

Originally, provision was made for land use planning over this area through the establishment in 1948 of the Lower Mainland Regional Planning Board (LMRPB). Working through a regional board composed of representatives of the 28 municipalities within its boundaries, the LMRPB achieved the not inconsiderable feat of gaining approval of a regional official plan, in 1966. Its very success, however, led to friction, jealousy in local bureaucracies and conflict with the Provincial Government.[84] The LMRPB also became critical of the Ministry of Municipal Affairs program of establishing regional districts, beginning in 1965. The Government's response, without much warning or public debate, was to dissolve the LMRPB in 1968 and to divide its territorial responsibilities among the four regional districts which had been established within the Lower Mainland area.[85]

Not only does no one municipal government have jurisdiction for planning the whole Lower Mainland area, but the appropriate area for planning may even be larger still, extending to the Fraser Valley and including those watersheds which flow into the Fraser River. This definition reflects an ecosystem approach to regional planning and boundaries. This approach is also expounded by David Crombie in his report on the Toronto

---

[84]Oberlander and Smith, *op. cit.*, pp. 358-359.

[85]*Ibid.*, p. 359.

waterfront[86] Yet attempting to create regional governments or planning structures large enough to encompass such sizeable areas would make it almost impossible to retain a sense of local community.

Quebec

By the 1960s, the local government system in Quebec had evolved, after more than a century of existence, into a very fragmented system, characterized by an excessive number of very small municipalities. Over 90% of the more than 1 600 municipalities had less than 5 000 population and nearly 50% had less than 1 000 population. At the same time, problems of urban concentration and sprawl were evident, with the cities of Montreal, Quebec, and Hull (Outaouais) containing 30% of the population.[87]

After the election of the Liberal government in 1960, a "Quiet Revolution" brought a variety of reforms at the local level. As Sancton outlines, this led to:

> the replacement of classical colleges by public colleges for general and professional education (CEGEPS), the consolidation of school boards into regional units, and the establishment of a completely new network of health and social service institutions to replace hospitals and agencies which had previously been controlled by the church or private charities.[88]

Municipal Consolidations

Dealing more specifically with municipal government, the major Liberal response was the Voluntary Amalgamation Act of 1965, which allowed two or more municipalities to amalgamate following a council's resolution to that effect. Not surprisingly, however, this voluntary approach was ineffective, with fewer than 100 municipalities abolished between 1965 and 1971, hardly enough to reduce the badly fragmented municipal structure in Quebec. While new legislation in 1971 gave the Minister of Municipal Affairs more power to force amalgamations where he felt that it was

---

[86]*Royal Commission on the Future of the Toronto Waterfront*, 1992.

[87]These figures are from Jean Godin, "Local Government Reform in the Province of Quebec," in Advisory Commission on Intergovernmental Relations, *op. cit.*, p. 50.

[88]Andrew Sancton, "The Impact of Language Differences on Metropolitan Reform in Montreal," in Lionel D. Feldman (ed.), *Politics and Government of Urban Canada*, Toronto, Methuen, 1981, p. 369.

desirable, this power was little used because of opposition and because (as will be seen) the government was by then preoccupied with metropolitan reforms. According to O'Brien,[89] the peak period for municipal consolidations was between 1971 and 1975, when the number of municipal units was reduced by 84. A limited number of voluntary consolidations (and a few forced ones) have continued in the years since — although provincial government financial policies which give larger subsidies to smaller municipalities than to larger ones have certainly not encouraged the consolidations. Two recent consolidations are Lévis and Lauzon (located across the river from Quebec City), which after amalgamation were joined by adjacent St. David, and — in 1992 — the city of Sorel and the parish of St. Pierre de Sorel.[90]

Metropolitan Government for Montreal

Annexations were also used early and often in response to problems of urban sprawl in the Montreal area. Indeed, beginning as early as 1883, Montreal proceeded to annex thirty-three municipalities in roughly as many years. By 1920 this policy had halted, but the provincial government wanted the city to annex four island municipalities recently declared bankrupt. Instead, a regional agency was established — the *Montreal Metropolitan Commission* — which was to have the authority to approve or veto all local decisions on borrowing and capital expenditures of Montreal and fourteen island municipalities. Under pressure from Montreal, however, the province amended the legislation to remove the Commission's authority over the city's financial decisions. The Commission was governed by a sixteen member Board, eight named by Montreal, seven by the suburbs and one by the provincial government.

With its limited jurisdiction, the Montreal Metropolitan Commission was never a very significant body and by the 1950s two studies had confirmed that it was not settling basic intermunicipal problems and that its existence was no more than a make-shift solution to a financial dilemma.

In 1959 the Commission was replaced by the *Montreal Metropolitan Corporation*. At the outset the new body appeared to represent much more than a change in name. It was authorized to exercise a number of important functions including sewers, water distribution, arterial roads, planning, mass transit, major parks and all other services considered as

---

[89]O'Brien, *op. cit.*, p. 39.

[90]Details on these consolidations are provided in *ibid.*, pp. 41 and 46.

intermunicipal by agreement among the municipalities or by decision of the Corporation. Moreover, its jurisdiction extended to the City of Montreal as well as to the fourteen island municipalities which had come under its predecessor.

The governing body comprised fourteen representatives from the city, fourteen from the suburbs and a chairman appointed by the province. This balancing of city and suburbs ensured the vigorous opposition of Montreal's Mayor Drapeau who was like most central city mayors in resisting any form of metropolitan government which he could not control.[91] As Sancton points out, another and unique reason for Montreal's opposition was the concern that any metropolitan government, by extending to the suburbs and their higher proportions of English-speaking citizens, would decrease the influence of the French.[92] In any event, Montreal's refusal to cooperate effectively sabotaged the new Metropolitan Corporation, which was never a major innovation in spite of its greatly expanded terms of reference.

As an alternative approach, Drapeau and his chief lieutenant, Lucien Saulnier, pursued annexation with a view to establishing one city covering the entire island. The provincial government, not surprisingly, had no desire to see Montreal grow so large as to rival the importance of the province itself, and the city only managed the annexation of three virtually bankrupt suburbs in 1963, 1964 and 1968 respectively.

In the meantime, the Liberal government had been defeated (in 1966) without acting upon the recommendations of a study committee on the future government of the Montreal metropolitan area. The new Union Nationale government apparently had little interest in urban reform. But civil servants in the Municipal Affairs Department were impressed with structural reforms introduced in France in the form of "communautés urbaines," upper tier, indirectly elected governments. In June of 1969 the Minister of Municipal Affairs tabled plans for the creation of communautés urbaines in Montreal and Quebec City and a communauté regionale around Hull. Strong negative reactions, especially from Montreal, caused the Minister to announce postponement of the plan for one year.

Ironically, just three months later, January 1, 1970, the *Montreal Urban Community* (MUC) came into existence (as did two others around Hull

---

[91]Sancton, *The Impact of Language Differences*, p. 372. Note the similar response by Winnipeg's Mayor Juba, discussed earlier in the chapter.

[92]*Ibid.*

and Quebec City, discussed below). The governing council of the MUC consisted of the mayor and councillors of the city of Montreal and one delegate from each of the other twenty-nine municipalities under its jurisdiction, with the city having seven of the twelve members on the powerful executive committee and providing the first chairman in the person of Lucien Saulnier.

The new structure owed little to the prior recommendations of the Quebec civil service; instead it was a hastily implemented response to the devastating effect of a police strike which hit Montreal on October 7th, 1969. A prompt end to the strike was engineered by none other than Lucien Saulnier, whose strategy was "in essence, to promise to pay the police what they wanted and then to force the suburbs and the provincial government to finance the increases."[93] The vehicle for this redistribution of funding was the new MUC, "organized such that in many ways it was a mere extension of the City of Montreal."[94] Contrast the background to the establishment of Metropolitan Toronto, with Frederick Gardiner having several months to acquire staff and organize his approach even before the new structure came into effect. As Sancton observes, the way in which the MUC came into existence without planning or any administrative structure "is a vivid illustration of the fact that its original purpose was to act as a conduit of funds rather than as an important force in the management of Montreal's urban development."[95]

By January 1, 1972 all of the police forces on the island had been unified into the MUC Police Department but controversy over this decision and related policing issues dragged on for a number of years. It is important to realize, however, that while public security still accounts for almost half of the annual budget of the MUC, the new upper tier government has also become involved in several other areas of activity. In financial terms, the major initiatives have been with respect to subways and sewers, although these projects have come under considerable provincial influence because of the extent of provincial funding. The provincial government has also been extending its influence with respect to regional planning issues. In part, this may reflect the more interventionist philosophy of the Parti Québécois, which came to power in 1976. To a large extent, however, it results from the failure of the MUC to take initiative

---

[93]*Ibid.*, p. 376.

[94]*Ibid.*

[95]*Ibid.*

in this area, largely because of a city-suburb split and the effectiveness of the suburban veto. While the City of Montreal has a majority of the votes on the MUC, reflecting its population dominance, a motion cannot pass unless supported by at least half of the suburban delegates present.

An analysis by Sancton concludes that the original hopes that the MUC would evolve into a genuine metropolitan government have never been realized.[96] He notes that suspicion between the City of Montreal and the suburbs has paralyzed the structure from the beginning. While the original legislation contemplated that internal boundary adjustments would be made, any such changes would have involved some merging of French-speaking and English-speaking populations — a task no politician wanted to tackle. Without significant boundary changes, Sancton observes, it was only possible "to tinker with the Community's clumsy institutions."[97] The principle that a double majority (city and suburb) was needed before action could be taken meant that often no decision was made. As a result, the provincial government, which held most of the financial power anyway, seized most of the initiative. Instead of being a counterweight to provincial influence, the MUC "passively accepts provincial funds and implements provincial decisions."[98]

The population of the suburbs has been increasing at a faster rate than that of the city of Montreal. As a result, the suburbs have been gaining more voting strength on the MUC governing council, where votes are weighted according to population. Amendments to the MUC Act in 1982 also provided parity between the suburbs and Montreal on the executive committee. At the same time, changes were made in the selection of the chair of the MUC, the ostensible political leader of the metropolitan government. Under the new arrangements, the chair must still be a member of council to be chosen, but must resign his or her local municipal position on taking office for a four year term.

Sancton uses experiences under these new arrangements to demonstrate how little importance is attached to the metropolitan government.[99] He refers to what happened after the election of Michel Hamelin as chair of the MUC executive committee in December 1985. Hamelin

---

[96]Andrew Sancton, "Montreal's Metropolitan Government," Hanover, *Quebec Studies*, No. 6, 1988, p. 23.

[97]*Ibid.*

[98]*Ibid.*, p. 24.

[99]Sancton, *Local Government Reorganization*, p. 27.

was one of Jean Drapeau's Civic Party councillors and a member of the city of Montreal executive committee. Less than one year later, almost all of the incumbent Civic Party councillors were defeated in the municipal election which swept Jean Doré into power. Hamelin served out his four year term, apparently working smoothly with the new city administration controlled by the Montreal Citizens' Movement. Moreover, he was then reelected chair of the executive committee. Sancton concludes that this experience indicates that few in Montreal consider the MUC to be an important political institution. "Its leadership can be entrusted to someone with no political base and with no particular political agenda."[100]

Another problem facing the MUC is the declining relevance of its boundaries. In 1971 it contained 71% of the population of the Montreal census metropolitan area, but by 1991 the proportion was down to 57%. The MUC does not have any jurisdiction where most development is now taking place — in the outer suburbs.[101] Expansion of the MUC boundaries seems unlikely, since the adjacent areas have now been established as regional county municipalities (discussed below) — rather like the situation in which Metropolitan Toronto finds itself, hemmed in by adjacent regional governments.

In April 1992, the Minister of Municipal Affairs established a Task Force on Greater Montreal, an area encompassed by the MUC and the 12 regional county municipalities surrounding it. The mandate of the Task Force was essentially concerned with issues of "governance," that is, how responsibility for planning and management within the metropolitan area should be shared among the various municipalities and levels of government.[102] The main recommendation of its December 1993 Report was that a Montreal Metropolitan Region be established, "the territory of which would correspond exactly to that of the CMA and which would automatically be adjusted to match future CMA boundary changes."[103] The governing body of the new region would be comprised of 21 mayors and city councillors from the different municipalities in the region.

Even though there are more than 100 municipalities within this area (as contrasted with the 30 lower tier municipalities in the Greater Toron-

---

[100]*Ibid.*

[101]Sancton, *Canada's City Regions*, p. 84.

[102]Canadian Urban Institute, *The Future of Greater Montreal: Lessons for the Greater Toronto Area?*, Toronto, 1994, p. 13.

[103]Sancton, *Canada's City Regions*, p. 88.

to Area), the Task Force did not recommend any amalgamations. It called instead, it called for the abolition of the 12 regional county municipalities and the creation of four Intermunicipal Service Agencies or ISAs.[104] The ISAs would be legal entities with authority to borrow money, but they would only take on responsibilities if enabling motions were approved by a two-thirds vote (weighted by population) of their member municipalities.[105] Concerns have been expressed that these proposals would, in effect, establish three levels of municipal government in the Montreal area. At this point, it is not known what action will be taken on the proposals.

Other Urban Communities

The December 1969 legislation which created the Montreal Urban Community also provided for an urban community for Quebec City and for a similarly constituted regional government for Hull and environs known as the Regional Community of Outaouais.

The latter municipality has been hampered by municipal opposition based on a feeling that the reform was introduced without sufficient prior consultation. A primary motivation for its establishment was apparently the perceived need to provide a counterweight to the adjoining Regional Municipality of Ottawa-Carleton in Ontario, and to represent the area's interests to the National Capital Commission. A somewhat more positive attitude was evident in the Quebec Urban Community where more advance consultation with local leaders occurred.

In neither instance, however, has the regional level attracted much feeling of loyalty. Instead, there has been some movement for municipalities to consider amalgamation to better defend their interests against the new regional units. Indeed, the number of lower tier municipalities within Quebec and Outaouais has been reduced from 26 to 13 and from 32 to 8 respectively — a consolidation which is even more striking when compared with the total absence of any such change in the Montreal Urban Community.

The extent of the change within the Outaouais Urban Community may partly reflect the fact that, unlike Montreal and Quebec City, it contained major portions of rural as well as urban territory. This resulted in an uneasy partnership which placed strains on the organization. In 1989, for example, only 23% of the budget went for services used in common, with

---

[104]Canadian Urban Institute, *op. cit.*, p. 26.

[105]Sancton, *Canada's City Regions*, p. 89.

the rest going to services which were largely urban.[106] Following a Ministerial statement and a study (the Giles Report) in 1990, two new structures were put into place effective January 1, 1991 — a new regional county municipality covering the rural areas, and a modified Outaouais Urban Community confined to the urban areas of Gatineau, Hull, Aylmer, Buckingham and Masson. A proposal to amalgamate the first three of these municipalities was put to a referendum and failed to win majority support in all three municipalities as required.

Regional County Municipalities

As a result of legislation passed in 1979 (the Land Use Planning and Development Act), the three upper tier urban communities were joined by a network of 95 new upper tier units called regional county municipalities or RCMs. These new units replaced all the 72 former county municipalities, which had consisted entirely of rural units and had exercised very limited responsibilities.

Municipalities were grouped together to form these RCMs on the basis of "affinity" — a criterion which was very similar to the community of interest concept specified (but almost never applied) in Ontario's regional government program. The specific boundaries for the RCMs and the exact composition of their governing councils were worked out locally, often with great difficulty and under threat of withdrawal of provincial funds, through tripartite committees comprising representatives of the old counties, the lower tier municipalities and the Minister of Municipal Affairs.[107] Under the terms of the legislation, cities (which had been politically separate from their surrounding counties) had to become part of the new RCM system. In addition, each RCM had to adopt a regional land use plan, and was also to take over the functions of the old counties, at least for the mainly rural areas in which counties had been operating.[108]

Each RCM is governed by a council composed only of the head of council (or representative) of each member municipality. According to Sancton, the message was clear: "a new source of elected political authority was *not* being established." The RCMs were, in his view, to represent

---

[106]O'Brien, *op. cit.*, p. 48.

[107]Sancton, *Local Government Reorganization*, p. 15.

[108]Louise Quesnel, "Political Control over Planning in Quebec," *International Journal of Urban and Regional Research* 14, 1990, pp. 25-48, quoted in Sancton, *Local Government Reorganization*, p. 16.

existing municipalities acting together — nothing more.[109] In about half of the RCMs, voting rules give each representative a number of votes proportional to the population of his or her municipality, and 38% of them have some form of veto as part of the delicate balancing of city and rural interests.[110] A further complication is that when the RCMs are performing the functions of the old county councils, representatives from the cities are excluded altogether and the remaining mayors have one vote each, as had been the case under the former county system.[111]

Concerns about the adequacy of the representation arrangements have increased as the expenditures of the RCMs have grown. Costs are shared by municipalities in proportion to their share of the area's taxable assessment. Cities with a healthy assessment base are, not surprisingly, critical of the fact that their voting strength on council is not nearly as large as the expenditure burden they are required to assume.

In response, the Quebec government passed legislative amendments in 1987 which set out three options relating to the voting arrangements within the RCMs, including an opportunity for member municipalities to determine their own rules if agreement could be reached by municipalities representing at least 90% of the population of the area. The amendments also set forth conditions under which RCMs could acquire new responsibilities, where supported by a majority vote of two-thirds of the members of an RCM council.[112]

The future of the 12 RCMs in the Greater Montreal area is now in doubt, however, as a result of the Task Force recommendations previously discussed and the possible creation of a new Montreal Metropolitan Region.

Intermunicipal Agreements

Since 1979, the Cities and Towns Act has authorized three types of intermunicipal agreement: for a municipality to purchase a service from another, for one municipality to delegate its authority to another in order to pursue a defined objective, and for the establishment of intermunicipal corporations to deliver particular services agreed to by the participating

---

[109]*Ibid.*, p. 16.

[110]These figures are from Quesnel, *op. cit.*, p. 33.

[111]Sancton, *Local Government Reorganization*, p. 17.

[112]O'Brien, *op. cit.*, pp. 36-38.

municipalities.[113] These arrangements have been used mainly for leisure programs and fire protection. They have been particularly useful in situations in which residents of a rural municipality (parish) use services of a nearby village.[114]

Quebec Highlights

Like Ontario, Quebec has had too many municipalities, many of them with very small populations. Efforts to deal with this situation through municipal consolidations have had very limited success. Three upper tier structures, somewhat like Ontario's regional governments, were set up in the Montreal, Quebec City and Hull areas of Quebec — although, for reasons discussed above, these urban communities have not developed into strong upper tier governments. Nor were the Regional County Municipalities established for the rest of Quebec in 1979 given much of a role beyond their mandated regional planning function.

However, these RCMs differ from Ontario's county governments in several key respects. First, negotiations leading up to the establishment of the RCMs led to boundaries quite different from the old counties — something Ontario has been unable to achieve even with its restructured counties and regional governments. Second, cities are included within the RCMs, but cities remain separate from the 25 unreformed county systems still found in Ontario. Third, for better or worse, RCMs are designed as flexible mechanisms through which the province and the existing municipalities can better perform their assigned responsibilities, not as genuine political institutions. In that regard, they are probably closer to the regional districts of British Columbia than to Ontario's county and regional governments.[115]

The pattern of urban development has made the boundaries of the Montreal Urban Community increasingly irrelevant, paralleling the problem which has arisen with Metropolitan Toronto's boundaries. As a result, consideration is being given to a new and broader governing body, the Montreal Metropolitan Region. Unlike the Greater Toronto Area (GTA) structure, which has representation from municipal staff, the proposed Montreal governing structure would be composed of mayors and councillors from member municipalities. Another difference is that

[113]Sancton, *Local Government Reorganization*, p. 39.

[114]O'Brien, *op. cit.*, p. 38.

[115]Sancton, *Local Government Reorganization*, p. 23.

the regional county municipalities established in 1979 would be abolished, whereas Ontario seems reluctant to consider changes in the boundaries of its regional governments created almost a decade earlier.

Nova Scotia

Major local government reform initiatives in Nova Scotia have come in two main waves, almost 20 years apart. As discussed below, a comprehensive report and recommendations appeared in the early 1970s, with some changes gradually introduced over the ensuing decade. The early 1990s have seen a return of very significant studies and recommendations.

Graham Commission: Too Much at Once?

June 1974 saw the release of the massive Report of the Royal Commission on Education, Public Services, and Provincial-Municipal Relations in the Province of Nova Scotia. Established in March 1971 under the chairmanship of Professor John F. Graham, this study dealt with not only local government organization but also with the reorganization of provincial departments and agencies, although the latter proposals are of less relevance for our purposes.[116]

As with the previously discussed Byrne Commission in New Brunswick a decade earlier, the Graham Report examined the most appropriate distribution of provincial and local responsibilities and concluded that municipal government should be relieved of such "general services" as education, health, social services, housing, and administration of justice. It also called for the Nova Scotia government to provide such "support services" to municipal governments as capital borrowing, assessment, tax billing and collection, water and sewer user billing and collection, and the administration of municipal staff pension funds.

In relation to the municipal structure, the Graham Report recommended that eleven one tier counties be established throughout Nova Scotia replacing the existing rural municipalities, towns and cities. To facilitate citizen participation in this new structure, the Report called for the establishment of community associations supported by county council staff in areas of common interests. Considerable attention was devoted to the

---

[116]For a useful summary of the main recommendations of the Graham Commission, see the Appendix prepared by W. Hooson in C. Richard Tindal, *Structural Changes in Local Government*, Toronto, Institute of Public Administration of Canada, 1977, on which this section is partially based.

internal organization of the new county system, with specific recommendations offered concerning the make-up of councils, and the use of executive committees and chief administrative officers.

The lack of action on the Graham Report has been attributed, in at least one analysis, to "the degree of detail, the vast and comprehensive nature of the recommendations, the lack of detailed argumentation of alternatives....."[117] Instead, informal discussions involving representatives from the Union of Nova Scotia Municipalities and the Department of Municipal Affairs evolved into what became known as the Task Force on Municipal Reform.[118] Their deliberations culminated in a departmental White Paper in February 1978 titled "New Directions in Municipal Government in Nova Scotia."

The main emphasis of the White Paper was on the reform of some aspects of provincial-municipal financial relations, although not in relation to the most expensive local services such as education, health and social services, housing and justice. Proposals included an unconditional general grant, provincial grants in lieu of taxes, road user charges, and a revenue guarantee. Strong emphasis was given to the expansion of user-related charges, such as in relation to water and sanitary sewerage. While the proposals were relatively modest, their positive reception is a tribute to the consultative process which was followed.

In the ensuing years, most of the major proposals of the 1978 White Paper have been implemented.[119] These include the development of an unconditional municipal operating and capital grant program and a restructuring of educational administration which saw the municipal school districts consolidated into 21 district school boards comprised of one-third municipally appointed, one-third provincially appointed and one-third elected representatives.

While the major boundary changes inherent in the restructuring recommendations of the Graham Commission were not pursued, a number of boundary changes have been occurring over the three decades as a result of annexations. The cities of Halifax and Dartmouth both secured large annexations in the 1960s. In 1961 Dartmouth annexed portions of

---

[117]Feldman and Graham, *op. cit.*, p. 164.

[118]See Donald J. H. Higgins, "Nova Scotia's New Directions in Municipal Government" in *Urban Focus*, Institute of Local Government, Queen's University, March-April 1979.

[119]Correspondence from Shingai Nyajeka, Nova Scotia Department of Municipal Affairs, April 17, 1989, on which this section is based.

adjacent Halifax County, increasing its population by 90% and increasing its area by nine times. A 1969 annexation by the City of Halifax nearly quadrupled its area and increased its population by a third.[120] In 1980 Bedford was carved out of Halifax County to provide a focal point for urban development at the head of the Bedford Basin, which separates Halifax from Dartmouth.[121]

The increasingly intertwined relationships between the municipalities in this greater Halifax area was reflected in the establishment of the Metropolitan Authority of Halifax. It was originally established to operate a regional jail and after experiencing many incremental changes over the years, it now operates a regional transit system and a sanitary land fill operation.[122] Bedford became the fourth member of this metropolitan authority in 1986, joining Halifax, Dartmouth and the County of Halifax. The authority is governed by a twelve member Board of Directors comprised of elected representatives appointed from the councils of each of the four member municipalities.

Task Force on Local Government

Major new reform initiatives returned in Nova Scotia beginning with the establishment by the Minister of Municipal Affairs in late 1991 of a *Task Force on Local Government*. Its April 1992 Report recommended a significant realignment of functions between the province and municipalities, including: that rural municipalities would have to start providing their own policing and their own roads (as the urban municipalities had been doing) and that the province would take over the administration and financing of the non-federal share of the costs of general welfare assistance. As discussed further in Chapter 7, these proposals are very similar to the "disentanglement" process launched by Ontario during this period.

In addition, the Task Force recommended a major restructuring of municipal governments in the five most urbanized counties in the province (containing 67% of the total population of Nova Scotia). After considering a number of options, the Task Force stated that one tier municipal governments would be the preferred model for the restructuring in these areas, with existing county boundaries representing the likely

---

[120]These figures are from David M. Cameron and Peter Aucoin, "Halifax," in Magnusson and Sancton, *op. cit.*, p. 183.

[121]*Ibid.*, p. 184.

[122]Sancton, *Local Government Reorganization*, p. 35.

maximum sizes for any such new units.[123] As for possible changes outside of these five urbanized counties, the prospect of the amalgamation of many of the smaller rural municipalities in the province was raised.

June 1993 saw the release of the *Report of the Interdepartmental Committee on Municipal Reform.* This Committee had been established to report on the implementation of the transfer of services between the provincial and municipal levels of government, as had been proposed by the earlier Task Force on Local Government. The original timetable suggested that the realignment of responsibilities would take place effective April 1, 1995. However, recent indications are that the provincial government may be backing off somewhat, partly because some of the shifts in responsibility — notably social services to the provincial level — are now seen as too expensive to absorb.

Initial municipal restructuring efforts, however, seem to still be on track. July 1993 saw the release of Interim Reports from the Municipal Reform Commissioners of both Cape Breton County and Halifax County. Here again, these studies were follow-ups to the recommendations from the Task Force. Both Reports recommended the amalgamation of all municipal units within their study areas into a single municipality. Legislation to implement the Cape Breton amalgamations passed in mid-1994. The limited resistance to this significant change may reflect a recognition of the serious financial difficulties which have been facing a number of the municipalities in this area, and also some public willingness to consider fewer governments and less bureaucracy in the hope that savings can result. The Cape Breton Report[124] had estimated that the establishment of a unitary government should result in annual savings of $6.5 million or more — although municipal personnel can be forgiven if they react to such a projected windfall with some suspicion or disbelief.

Prince Edward Island

The need for municipal reform in Canada's smallest province was raised in a 1990 *Royal Commission on the Land* Report.[125] It commented on the

---

[123]Task Force on Local Government, *Report to the Government of Nova Scotia*, April 1992, p. 33.

[124]*Interim Report of the Municipal Reform Commissioner, Cape Breton County*, Department of Municipal Affairs, July 8, 1993, p. i.

[125]The summary of its findings which follows is based on O'Brien, *op. cit.*, p. 27.

failure in the past to adjust municipal boundaries to reflect population overspill, and took the position that "where the outlying ribbon development begins, so should the municipal borders."[126] The Report gave particular attention to the Charlottetown area, where nine suburbs and the city have struggled with what the Commission termed the "herculean" task of achieving a coordinated approach on a volunteer basis. The Commission contended that the municipal consolidation needed for the area would only come about through strong provincial leadership.

June 1993 saw a *White Paper on Municipal Reform*, whose objectives included strengthening the urban centres of the province, improving the decision-making process, achieving greater equity, effecting economies of scale, and improving land use planning. In particular, the White Paper singled out restructuring for the Charlottetown and Summerside areas, which it found to be over-governed. It considered several reform options and expressed a preference for amalgamation, while not ruling out annexation or regionalization. A Commissioner was appointed to examine further the implications of municipal reform in these two areas.

The *Report of the Commission on Municipal Reform (Charlottetown and Summerside Areas)* was completed in December 1993. It recommended three sets of amalgamations in the Charlottetown area, one creating an enlarged city of Charlottetown, and the complete merger of the municipalities in the Summerside area. Bills implementing these changes were given 1st reading on May 5th, 1994, but there is fierce municipal resistance to the impending consolidations.

Newfoundland

Major changes in the municipal structure in Newfoundland were recommended by a Royal Commission study completed in 1974 (the Whalen Commission). It called for the gradual creation of as many as twenty regional governments envisaged as two tier structures with the upper tier units similar to, but much stronger than, British Columbia's previously described regional districts.[127] It also recommended a tightening up of incorporation procedures and some modifications in municipal classifications, as well as the introduction of the real property tax because of the poor financial conditions in most municipalities. The latter recommen-

---

[126]*Ibid.*

[127]Higgins, *op. cit.*, pp. 127-128.

dations were gradually incorporated into revisions to the Municipalities Act, but no action was taken with respect to a system of regional governments.

Studying St. John's

Considerable attention was directed, however, to the government structure in the St. John's area. This area had been excluded from the Royal Commission study, but it has been the subject of at least four other studies of its own. The St. John's metropolitan area is comprised of the central city of St. John's and about 20 smaller surrounding municipalities which are largely dependent on the central city for employment and retail services.[128] The initial study of this metropolitan area in 1957 led to one change — the creation in 1963 of the St. John's Metropolitan Area Board (discussed below). A second study in 1971 offered three alternative reforms for the area, and this prompted the government to appoint a commission to conduct hearings and make specific recommendations concerning an appropriate governmental structure for the metropolitan area.

The Henley Commission, as it came to be known, recommended in January 1977 that a two tiered structure of regional government be established along with an expanded city of St. John's. The Commission's recommendations generated considerable controversy. Draft legislation was introduced twice, with the Henley recommendations substantially incorporated except for the lack of a provision for the enlargement of St. John's. Following the defeat of the second bill, the regional government concept appeared to be dropped. The Municipalities Act of 1979-1980 included enabling legislation for the establishment of regional governments anywhere in the province without further legislative approval, but no action has been taken in this regard.

In the meantime, the St. John's Metropolitan Area Board continued to grow and evolve.[129] It spent its first six years developing a municipal plan. It then began to supply urban services in a number of subdivisions outside the towns and city. In 1978, the Board took over responsibility for administration of the regional water supply system on behalf of the province. During the 1980s, the Board had nine members appointed by the province, two of whom represented the city of St. John's and one the

---

[128]See Peter G. Boswell, "Regional Government for St. John's?" in *Urban Focus*, Institute of Local Government, Queen's University, January-February 1979, on which this section is based.

[129]The summary which follows is based on O'Brien, *op. cit.*, p. 24.

town of Mount Pearl, a major suburb of the city. It employed a staff of 37 and generated revenues by levying property taxes and user fees.[130]

Municipal Consolidations

Shortly after the election of the Liberal government headed by Clyde Wells in 1989, Newfoundland launched an ambitious program of municipal consolidations. When the program commenced, the province had 310 municipalities and 165 local service districts, ranging in size from 15 to 95 000 (in the city of St. John's).[131] Not surprisingly, many of these municipalities operated on very high Provincial subsidies to provide even a basic level of services.

The community consolidation program (as it was called) identified communities on the basis of physical proximity and a combined population of 1 250. Some 110 municipalities were identified using these criteria, and the declared objective was to reduce these to 43.[132] Municipal objections to this reform process centred particularly on what was perceived to be insufficient consultation — both in advance of the reform initiative and during each of the consolidation studies — and on the perceived bias of Commissioners carrying out the consolidation studies, since they were also senior staff of the Ministry of Municipal Affairs.

By the time the consolidation program was put on hold in 1992, to allow for a review of the process and its accomplishments, 31 former communities had been reduced to 13. The main changes have occurred in the Northeast Avalon area, which included the cities of St. John's and Mount Pearl, 17 towns and the St. John's Metropolitan Area Board. Originally, the Department of Municipal Affairs discussed converting these 20 municipal organizations into two cities and four towns. However, after studies and public hearings, it was recommended that two cities and nine towns be created, with some territory left unorganized.[133] Somewhat different changes were incorporated into the legislation dealing with these consolidations. The final result was still the creation of two cities and nine

---

[130]*Ibid.*

[131]Donald Peckham, "Amalgamation Program Undertaken in the Province of Newfoundland and Labrador," in *The Boardroom Files*, Halifax, Maritime Municipal Training and Development Board, Spring/Summer 1993, p. 15.

[132]*Ibid.*, p. 16.

[133]O'Brien, *op. cit.*, p. 25.

towns, but provision was also made for the abolition of the Metropolitan Area Board. The new arrangements call for St. John's to provide the regional services which other municipalities require, with regional service committees being set up for each function involved. Initially only fire and water committees were established.[134]

According to an Assistant Deputy Minister in the Department of Municipal Affairs, the government is continuing with the consolidation process, but at a much slower pace and with much more consultation with the municipal units involved before final decisions are made.[135]

Alberta

In one respect Alberta might have come first among the various provinces we have been discussing instead of last. It initiated the earliest local government reform of the post-war period, when it embarked on a program of consolidating rural units of both municipal and educational administration which culminated in the County Act of 1950. Under this Act, the educational and municipal units were combined, initially on a voluntary basis, to form one tier county governments which now cover the majority of the populated rural area of the province.

No such comprehensive restructuring was introduced in urban areas, although the population increase which accompanied the development of the petroleum industry strained the existing municipal organization, especially in the Calgary and Edmonton areas. The result was the frequent annexation of adjacent territory — some 19 separate annexations involving Edmonton between 1947 and 1980 — usually at the initiative of landowners and developers wishing an extension of services. However, this piece-meal approach frustrated both Calgary and Edmonton and further concern arose when the Alberta government, between 1974 and 1976, unilaterally imposed restricted development areas around both cities. While intended as utilities and transportation corridors, these RDAs were also seen as potential barriers to future expansion.

Edmonton's response was a March 1979 application to the Local Authorities Board for a massive annexation, including the City of St. Albert and the entire county of Strathcona (an application which would add over 467 000 acres to the city's existing 80 000). The subsequent

---

[134]*Ibid.*

[135]Peckham, *op. cit.*, p. 17.

Board hearings extended from September 1979 to the end of June 1980, comprising 106 days of testimony, the hearing of about 200 witnesses, the examination of 299 official exhibits and the generation of 12 235 pages of transcript — at a cost of over $6 million! After all of that, the outcome was a compromise solution. While the Local Authorities Board approved a very large expansion of Edmonton's boundaries in December 1980, the Cabinet issued a revised order in June 1981, in which it awarded the city some 86 000 acres of land but not its dormitory suburbs. As Feldman observes, there weren't really any winners or losers and none of the protagonists was severely harmed.

> Edmonton got land on which to expand, possibly not the lands and assessment it really wanted. St. Albert ... lost no territory. Strathcona saw 54,000 acres ... go to Edmonton.[136]

Quite apart from the great cost involved, this approach to developing reformed structures for Alberta's major urban areas has other drawbacks. It is at best a piece-meal, fragmented approach which does not consider the overall needs of the entire urban area, but instead focuses on particular territories affected by proposed annexation, and does so in an inevitably confrontational atmosphere. Nonetheless, this annexation process has kept 73% of Edmonton's census metropolitan area within its boundaries and 94% in the case of Calgary. This has meant that the governing arrangements in these major urban areas have been spared the extensive fragmentation of boundaries which is so common in metropolitan areas and the duplication and division of responsibilities inherent in two tier municipal systems.

Intermunicipal Agencies

The local government arrangements in Alberta include provision for a number of regional bodies providing specialized services. Regional Planning Commissions were authorized in 1929 legislation, although the first (in the Edmonton area) wasn't established until 1950. There are now 10 of these covering about 70% of the area of the province.[137] Their most important function is to prepare a regional plan with which the plans of all member municipalities must conform. The members of the regional

---

[136]Lionel Feldman, "Tribunals, Politics and the Public Interest: The Edmonton Annexation Case — A Response," in *Canadian Public Policy*, Summer 1982, p. 371.

[137]O'Brien, *op. cit.*, p. 60.

planning commissions are elected representatives from the councils of the member municipalities. According to Masson,[138] even though the larger municipalities have been given multiple votes, they are still underrepresented on these commissions — which has been an ongoing source of friction.

Alberta also has another intermunicipal agency known as the regional services commission. According to the 1981 enabling legislation, the objective of these commissions is to provide water, sanitary and storm sewerage and waste management services, or any of them, with respect to more than one municipality. Of the 14 in existence, six are established for water, three for sewer, one for sewer and water, three for solid waste management, and one for sewage collection and waste management.[139] Members of the commission are representatives from the councils of member municipalities — the same indirect election arrangement found with the regional planning commissions described above. Masson claims that "it is not coincidental that the functions and political structures of regional service commissions closely resemble those of the regional service districts in existence in British Columbia for a number of years."[140]

Yet another example of the intermunicipal activity in Alberta is found in the more than 500 intermunicipal agreements through which municipalities purchase and sell municipal services to each other. The services most commonly subject to these arrangements are fire protection, ambulance service, recreation facilities, garbage disposal, libraries, family and community support services, airports, roads, and disaster services.[141]

Education Reform

Since Alberta had the earliest post-war local government reform initiative with its combination of rural and educational administration into one tier county governments, it is noteworthy that almost half a century later it is again undertaking educational restructuring. As part of the restraint measures introduced by the Conservative Government of Ralph Klein, Alberta announced in January 1994 that the number of school boards in

---

[138]Jack Masson, *Albert's Local Governments and Their Politics*, Edmonton, University of Alberta Press, p. 269.

[139]O'Brien, *op. cit.*, p. 60.

[140]Masson, *op. cit.*, p. 126.

[141]O'Brien, *op. cit.*, p. 60.

Alberta will be reduced through amalgamation and regionalization from 141 to about 60 by 1995. School boards have been given until August 31st, 1994 to develop plans for voluntary regionalization. This fairly tight deadline is designed to ensure that changes — whether voluntary or imposed — can be implemented in time for the school board election of October 1995.

In addition, the province will assume full responsibility for the funding of public and secondary education, currently financed in part through local property taxes. Effective for the 1994 tax year, the provincial government will collect and redistribute all property taxes to fund education and will phase in uniform mill rates by 1997.[142]

Summary

In the more than four decades since Metropolitan Toronto launched the modern era of local government reform in Canada, there have been extensive changes introduced or proposed in most provinces. Indeed, the only province not discussed in this chapter is Saskatchewan — whose residents may feel angered at their exclusion or relieved that they have thus far been spared the unsettling experience of any major municipal restructuring. Not that the Saskatchewan municipal structure has been without change, however. A large number of annexations have been approved over the past couple of decades, twelve of them involving annexations to Regina and Saskatoon.[143] Inter-municipal agreements are also widely used, especially for fire protection and road maintenance.

What kinds of reforms have been introduced, and to what extent do they resolve the problems which prompted their introduction? The types of reforms can be briefly summarized as follows:

1. The creation or strengthening of upper tier municipal governments, as with Ontario's regional governments, British Columbia's regional districts and the urban communities and regional county municipalities in Quebec.
2. The use or revival of annexation to bring about boundary adjustments, especially in Alberta, Saskatchewan and Ontario.
3. The increased use of intermunicipal boards and servicing agreements, as in Fredericton, Saint John and Moncton, New Brunswick,

---

[142]Government of Alberta, *News Release*, January 18, 1994.

[143]O'Brien, *op. cit.*, p. 58.

St. John's, Newfoundland, and the 14 regional service boards in Alberta.

4. New approaches to representation and decision making, particularly with the initial Unicity arrangements, and with the increasing introduction of direct election in Ontario's regional governments.

5. A new delineation of provincial and local responsibilities, widely studied and recommended, but only introduced to any significant degree in New Brunswick.

Most of the reforms discussed above, however, have been concerned with improving the delivery of services. For example, in somewhat oversimplified terms it can be said that Metro Toronto was created as a vehicle for tapping the city's revenue base to extend services to the growing suburbs, while the Montreal Metropolitan Community was set up to access suburban funds to pay for regional policing. But an approach to municipal government reform which establishes structures to optimize service delivery is doubly flawed. The search for appropriate boundaries fails to solve the servicing challenges even as it succeeds in diverting attention away from the political role of municipal government.

Taking the first flaw, it has been amply illustrated above that whatever new boundaries are created are inevitably outstripped by the pace and pattern of urban development. The result is that the reformed municipal structures are still unable to meet the servicing needs of the urban area. Sancton illustrates this point well by explaining how public transit, water supply and garbage disposal issues in the Metropolitan Toronto area have increasingly become the concern of the Provincial Government. He wonders what role metropolitan and regional governments are supposed to play if they cannot handle functions such as these.[144]

The second flaw, of course, is that even though regional and other reformed structures find themselves too small to tackle effectively the servicing challenges of their areas, they are also too big for fulfilling their representative role. This is especially true where the regional councils are indirectly elected and have a weak link to the local citizens.

One possible way out of this impasse is to create structures appropriate for *governing* rather than structures designed for administering services. This can be done if we free municipalities from the need to be comprehensive service providers and allow them to become service arrangers instead. This relates back to the concept, introduced in Chapter 1, of defining the municipality in terms of the community it serves rather than the services it provides. If municipalities are viewed mainly as service

---

[144]Sancton, *Canada as a Highly Urbanized Nation*, pp. 292-296.

arrangers rather than as service providers, it follows that finding the boundaries that are best for providing a particular mix of assigned functions becomes much less of an issue. "Municipal boundaries can then be used to delineate real communities, and optimal boundaries for service production can be worked out by other agencies and even by the private sector."[145]

[145]Sancton, *Canada's City Regions*, p. 43.

CHAPTER 6

The Governing Machinery

OBJECTIVES:

1. To examine the weaknesses in the traditional internal machinery of municipal government.

2. To describe and assess the various forms of chief administrative officer system established to provide administrative leadership.

3. To describe and assess the various forms of executive committee system established to provide political leadership.

4. To identify the potential strengths and limitations of the reforms introduced.

Introduction and Overview

The preceding chapter examined the main local government reform initiatives across Canada in the postwar years. Most of these reforms focused on changes in municipal boundaries and on reallocation of responsibilities — whether between lower and upper tier municipalities or municipalities and the provincial level. Very few reforms concentrated on the internal governing arrangements within municipalities. Yet the traditional internal structures — consisting mainly of councils, staff and probably a standing committee system — were also becoming increasingly inadequate as the pressures and societal changes resulting from industrialization and urbanization increased.

This chapter begins by examining the traditional internal governing structure and its shortcomings. This is followed by an assessment of the the effectiveness of the internal structural reforms which have been introduced. The two main reforms are the establishment of some type of chief administrative officer (CAO) position at the staff level and/or some type of executive committee at the council level. As with the analysis in the preceding chapter, what will become apparent is that reform efforts have been preoccupied with the service delivery role of municipal government to the relative neglect of its representative and political role.

The Traditional Machinery

For our purposes, the traditional machinery of municipal government will be defined to comprise the municipal council, the municipal staff (usually organized into a number of functionally specialized departments, depending on the size of the municipality), and a number of standing committees providing a link between councillors and staff. It is appreciated that other structures, notably the chief administrative officer or CAO system, are also fairly common — but these are examined in a subsequent section as part of the reforms or modifications to the municipal machinery.

The Municipal Council

All municipalities in Canada are corporate bodies and as such exercise, and are limited to, the powers granted by their creators, the provincial governments. These powers are exercised on behalf of the inhabitants by an elected council. The provincial legislation usually includes provisions for the form of council and such details as the number of councillors and whether election is by general vote or by ward (a distinction discussed below).

Municipal councils in Canada consist of a head (known as warden or chair in counties and other upper tier governments, as mayor in cities and towns, and as reeve, chairman, or overseer in villages and townships) and a widely varying number of other councillors. While the total membership varies greatly, there has been a tendency to have small councils of from five to fifteen members, largely on the grounds that a small group is less unwieldy and more efficient in making decisions. Notable exceptions include the city of Montreal with its 51 members and, initially, Winnipeg Unicity — which also started out with 51 members but has since been reduced twice to a current membership of 15.

Perhaps the most distinctive feature of the council as a governing body is that it combines both executive and legislative responsibilities. As an executive body it initiates proposals for municipal action, makes a myriad of specific decisions — such as hiring a particular employee — and supervises the administration of the policies and programs of the municipality. As a legislative body, it makes by-laws which are the laws governing its citizens. At the senior levels of government, these functions are the responsibility of two separate branches: the Cabinet and the Legislative Assembly (House of Commons). The fact that these functions are combined in the council means, among other things, that the line between making policy and administering policy is often quite blurred at the local level. The combination of diverse responsibilities may also help to explain why there has often appeared to be a preoccupation with specific servicing considerations to the neglect of the other roles of municipal government.

Methods of Election

One of the distinguishing features of municipal governments is the election of members of the municipal councils, a process which supposedly ensures representativeness and accountability. In practice, however, there are three key variables in connection with the municipal election process:

1. Whether election is by general vote, or on the basis of wards.
2. Whether election is for a short term or a long term of office.
3. Whether members are elected directly or indirectly.

All three of these variables have changed over the years, and all are the subject of lively debate and divided opinions. As will become evident from the examination of these three variables, the differing arguments reflect an underlying preoccupation with either the service delivery or the political role of municipal government.

Ward Versus General Vote

While directly elected heads of council are chosen by a general vote of the entire municipality, members of council may be elected on the basis of a ward system. If so, the municipality is divided into several geographic areas with a number of members (usually an equal number) to be elected from each of these areas. Candidates don't campaign over the whole municipality but only in "their" ward, and the voters are limited to choosing from among the candidates in their particular ward. Whether election is by general vote or ward may be dictated by statute; it may be at the discretion of the local council; or it may be decided by council subject to the approval of the municipal electors.

Both methods of election have their proponents and their alleged advantages and disadvantages. Supporters of the ward system argue that under this approach the voters are much more likely to be familiar with the limited range of candidates from whom they must choose and the candidates will be more aware of the particular needs and interests of their constituents. It is also contended that ward elections ensure that all areas of the municipality will be represented on council, that they mean less expensive campaign costs and that they bring a higher voting turnout, an assertion which appears to have some validity.

On the other hand, those supporting election by general vote claim that ward elections tend to perpetuate and even accentuate differences and divisions within the municipality. It is argued that a ward council is very parochial in outlook with councillors worrying about their individual bailiwicks wherein they must seek reelection rather than being concerned about the good of the whole municipality. It is also contended that some representatives get elected on a ward basis who would not have been chosen if they were running over the entire municipality. Election by general vote is therefore felt to result in stronger, better qualified candidates since they must have support throughout the municipality. It also avoids the apparently unfair situation in which one candidate receives, as an example, 2 000 votes in a ward but finishes out of the running while another candidate receives 1 800 votes and tops the polls in a different ward. While such situations will inevitably arise since the populations of all wards do not stay equal even with periodic attempts at redistribution, they add to the feeling that the "best" person may not be elected under a ward system. Finally, proponents of a general vote assert that it results in a council more capable of taking a broad view of the overall needs of the municipality.

Whatever the respective merits of the two methods of election, it might be assumed that beyond a certain size of population (which is difficult to specify precisely) election by ward becomes almost inevitable to ensure that the citizen will have some prospect of knowing the candidates and that the candidates will not be faced with the financial and time demands of canvassing an excessively large population. While this relationship between the population of a municipality and the method of election holds generally true, there are exceptions, the most notable being election at large in the City of Vancouver. The ward system in this city was abolished before the 1936 municipal election and has not been reinstated in spite of several local initiatives over the years.

Moreover, even where a municipality utilizes a ward system, there are wide variations in how effectively it achieves its alleged advantages. Particularly since the turn of the century reform era, those opposed to the notion of "politics" in local government have sought to eliminate wards or to reduce their influence in representing the diverse interests of the municipality. For example, in 1891 the size of Toronto's city council was reduced from forty to twenty-five and the existing wards were replaced with six elongated strips running north from the lake — supposedly to enlarge the political vision of the aldermen.[1] Almost seventy years later strip wards were still being used in Toronto, but a proposal to extend this

[1]Warren Magnusson, "Toronto," in Warren Magnusson and Andrew Sancton (eds.), *City Politics in Canada*, Toronto, University of Toronto Press, 1983, p. 100.

pattern in 1969 at the time of an expansion from nine to eleven wards provoked a strong opposition from local citizen groups. Of particular concern was the fact that the heterogeneous areas embraced by these elongated strips militated against the representation of the varied local concerns and, instead, ensured that the upper middle class neighbourhoods prevailed at the expense of the lower class areas.[2] The Ontario Municipal Board, which had the responsibility for approving changes in ward boundaries, rejected the city's strip plan in favour of a block plan.

Efforts to design wards in which it is difficult to represent specific neighbourhoods or communities of interest have been fairly widespread. One is reminded, for example, of the special pie-shaped districts created for the election of members to the Metropolitan Winnipeg government created in 1960, districts whose combination of central and suburban areas was supposed to engender area-wide thinking.

Edmonton's experience is also instructive.[3] Following a positive plebiscite on this issue, the city moved to develop a ward system for the 1971 elections. As with Lorimer's description of the Toronto experience, Edmonton's new wards were designed by a municipal employee who "certainly had a strong sense of political reality and knew that he was not being asked to prepare a map which would make the task of re-election for the sitting aldermen any more difficult than necessary."[4] He proposed the establishment of four strip wards running the length of the city and completely ignoring community, economic and ethnic differences. As one observer described the change: "By establishing four wards completely heterogeneous in terms of socioeconomic composition, the council in effect provided four at-large elections at every municipal election"[5] — but at a quarter of the cost. Unlike the Toronto experience, local opposition did not materialize to block the new ward boundaries for Edmonton. If the new ward boundaries were supposed to protect the incumbents, they were successful; only one incumbent who sought re-election was defeated. However, revisions at the 1980 election did provide for six new wards

---

[2]See James Lorimer, *The Real World of City Politics*, Toronto, James Lewis and Samuel, 1970, Chapter Two.

[3]See James Lightbody, "Edmonton," in Magnusson and Sancton, *op. cit.*, pp. 272-273.

[4]Lorimer, *op. cit.*, p. 38.

[5]Jack K. Masson, "Decision-Making Patterns and Floating Coalitions in an Urban City Council," *Canadian Journal of Political Science*, March 1975, p. 128.

having more of a block nature, and Lightbody speculates that "a local community attachment will play an increasing role in successful candidatures."[6]

As these examples illustrate, it is necessary to look at the specific system in place, not just whether it is election by general vote or ward, in order to judge its likely impact on the municipal operations.

The recent experience of the city of Kingston, Ontario offers an interesting variation on the issue of election by ward. Over the years, council had often considered reducing the size of its 15 member council and perhaps abolishing the ward basis of election as well. The rationale for such proposed changes was always couched in terms of the need for a smaller body to provide more expeditious decision making and reduced "politicking." Following a recommendation from a report prepared by Frank Collom of Queen's University, the city introduced, effective the November 1994 municipal election, a change which managed to reduce the size of council while at the same time enhancing its representative dimension. This combination was achieved by reducing the number of representatives from each ward from two to one, while increasing the number of wards from seven to ten. The net result was to reduce the overall size of council (including the mayor) from 15 to 11. The change was not without its critics, with some expressing concern about the lack of population balance among the new wards created. The city's position was that the population imbalances were unavoidable if the wards were to embrace rather than divide neighbourhoods and areas with an established sense of community.

Short or Long Term of Office

Another variation in municipal elections concerns the term of office, which has ranged from one to four years. Those favouring the short term argue that it is more democratic because the electorate can retain closer control over the elected representatives. Since an ineffective council can be turned out of office quite promptly it is felt that councillors elected for a short term are more sensitive to public views and concerns. On the other hand, it is argued that too much of the time of a short term is used learning the job and gearing up for re-election. The lack of long term planning exhibited by most councils may be caused, at least in part, by frequent elections. According to Munro,[7] the historical Canadian one year

---

[6]Lightbody, *op. cit.*, p. 273.

[7]W. B. Munro, *American Influences on Canadian Government*, Toronto, Macmillan, 1929.

term was influenced by the American practice prevalent in the nineteenth century but subsequently abandoned as unworkable. Brittain makes the same observation and goes on to argue that:

> This one year term is probably the most effective method ever devised for preventing the adoption of bad measures, but it is equally effective in preventing or delaying good measures.[8]

In his view the one year term grew out of a lack of faith in representatives and electors and should be abandoned.

In recent decades, the term of office has gradually been extended in most provinces. Three year terms are now in effect for all or some classifications of municipalities in eight of the provinces and in the Northwest Territories and the Yukon. Four year terms are found in the remaining two provinces, Newfoundland and Quebec. Most local government reform studies have reflected this trend to a longer term, usually because of their preoccupation with improving the service delivery role of municipal government.

Yet there is little solid evidence to demonstrate that a longer term leads to improved planning and priority setting on the part of councillors. Whether or not that desirable activity takes place seems to be much more a function of how progressive councillors (and senior staff) are, not such structural features as the term of office. Illingworth reviews the Ontario experience with the standard three year term since 1980 and remains unconvinced of its benefits over the two year term which was previously in place.[9]

Even if the longer term could be shown to benefit the service delivery role of municipal government, it is not seen as reflecting its representative role. Citizens are increasingly cynical and disillusioned about government at all levels. They want more involvement in decision making, more opportunities to have their say. This is reflected in the public interest expressed in the use of plebiscites and referenda, and even in the concept of public recall of elected representatives during their term — for unacceptable performance. In this connection, Rossland, British Columbia has introduced a municipal constitution authorizing citizen-initiated referenda. The Rossland experiment is examined in Chapter 10.

---

[8]H. L. Brittain, in the annual report of the Bureau of Municipal Research, 1945, quoted in K.G. Crawford, *Canadian Municipal Government*, Toronto, University of Toronto Press, 1954, p. 82.

[9]Dick Illingworth, "Is the Longer Term Better?" in *Municipal World*, St. Thomas, September 1994, pp. 22-23.

Direct or Indirect Election

A third variation in the method of election, and one which has been the subject of increasing debate in recent years, is whether it is considered to be direct or indirect. In most cases, election is direct in that the voters choose a candidate for a particular position and none other. Examples of indirect election are found with respect to the upper tier county councils in Ontario and Quebec (although the latter were replaced by regional county municipalities in 1979). The councils are considered to be indirectly elected because they are composed of members who were directly elected to the constituent lower tier municipalities and as a result automatically became county councillors.

In Ontario, for example, all townships, villages, and towns are lower tier units in the two tier county system of government. Each of their councils includes a reeve and also, if they are entitled by the number of electors, a deputy reeve. Informed voters know when they are voting for their reeve and deputy reeve that the successful candidates will not only take office locally but will become that municipality's representatives on county council. In that sense they are indirectly elected to county council.

This form of indirect election has often been criticized, particularly on the grounds that it results in a parochial council with each representative feeling loyalty to his own municipality and no one taking a broader view of matters — essentially the same criticism as that which is made against election by ward. However, the traditional defence of the arrangement is that it provides valuable liaison between the two levels of government since the reeve and deputy reeve "wear two hats" and can represent the concerns of each level of municipal government to the other.

This concept of indirect election has been used, in whole or in part, for most of the strengthened upper tier governments created as a result of the local government reforms efforts in the various provinces. This is true of Quebec's urban communities, the regional districts in B.C. and Ontario's regional governments. Where members are being elected in a lower tier municipality to serve on a regional council, however, the ballot specifies both offices — unlike the situation with respect to county council — so the term "double direct" or "joint seat" is sometimes used instead of indirect to describe the method of electing these regional councillors in Ontario. In any event, as noted in Chapter 5, this method of election appears to have contributed to a feeling of alienation towards these upper tier governments and reinforced their image as bureaucratic, unresponsive regimes. In addition, councillors elected on this basis have little incentive to identify and deal with regional concerns since their re-election depends on satisfying much more specific, localized concerns.

Similar observations are made by Sancton, who notes that most Canadian two tier systems have been structured so that all members of the upper tier council have also been members of the lower tier councils.[10] The advantages of this arrangement are that the upper tier has had to be extremely responsive to the expressed desires of the politicians who run the lower tier units and the potential for jurisdictional squabbles between the two tiers is reduced. The big disadvantage is that politicians and voters have focused most of their attention on the lower tier, leaving regional staff and, in some cases, the indirectly elected chair, in charge.[11]

Perhaps partly in response to these criticisms, a number of recent local government reviews in Ontario have given particular attention to questions of representation and accountability and their implications for the method of electing upper tier councillors.[12] As a result, there has been increased emphasis on the potential benefits of direct election of upper tier councillors. As mentioned in Chapter 5, a major change was introduced for the Metropolitan Toronto council at the time of the 1988 municipal election. It is now composed of 34 members, 28 directly elected by wards, and the mayors of the six lower tier units comprising Metro. At the same time, provision was made for the direct election of the regional chair in both the Hamilton-Wentworth and Ottawa-Carleton regional governments. Effective the November 1994 municipal election, a further change in Ottawa-Carleton provides for the direct election of all regional councillors from new wards which, in many instances, cut across the boundaries of lower tier municipalities. The regional chair will continue to be directly elected as well. Unlike Metro Toronto, the mayors of the lower tier municipalities are *not* ex-officio members of the upper tier, making the entire regional council directly elected.

As noted, some of the recent changes have affected the selection of head of council, a particularly controversial issue. While most heads of

---

[10]Andrew Sancton, *Local Government Reorganization in Canada Since 1975*, Toronto, ICURR Press, April 1991, p. 8.

[11]*Ibid.*

[12]See, for example, Brian Koscak and David Siegel, *Accountability and Representation*, Background Study, Niagara Falls, Niagara Region Review Commission, September 1988; Task Force on Representation and Accountability in Metropolitan Toronto, *Analysis and Options for the Government of Metropolitan Toronto*, Toronto, Ontario Government Bookstore, November 1986; and Ottawa-Carleton Regional Review, *Accountability and Representation, Phase I Report*, Toronto, Ministry of Municipal Affairs, December 1987.

council are directly elected, at large, there are some instances of indirect election. For example, the warden of the county in Nova Scotia and Ontario and the regional county municipality (RCM) in Quebec are chosen by and from the council membership. This selection process was also adopted for the various regional governments in Ontario except in the first instance when the chair, as the head is called, was appointed by the Ontario cabinet. A similar approach was adopted for the selection of the head of the Montreal Urban Community.

This practice has been strongly criticized as undemocratic in that it does not give the electorate an opportunity to choose directly the occupant of the most important municipal office. On the other hand, the practice has been persuasively defended in a number of local government studies[13] as being a central feature of a more effective organization of the municipality modelled upon the parliamentary system. It is argued that heads of council chosen by their fellow councillors have, in effect, been given an indication of majority support for their leadership whereas this situation may not apply at all when the heads are directly elected. Moreover, having given their support, council can also take it away again in a vote of nonconfidence by not reappointing the particular head of council, thereby adding an important element of accountability. Dennis Flynn's unsuccessful attempt to obtain reappointment as Chair of Metro Toronto after the 1988 election can be seen as an illustration of this point.

Especially controversial has been the usual provision in Ontario's regional governments that the chairs need not have — and cannot retain — a seat on a lower tier council. As a result, the electorate may not even have chosen the regional chairman indirectly. This has been the case with several long-serving chairmen of Metropolitan Toronto, such as Paul Godfrey, who were appointed to several terms by the metropolitan council without holding any elected office within the system or having any form of accountability to the electorate.

This situation will no longer arise, however. Changes introduced in 1988 stipulate that only the directly elected members of council are now eligible to be chosen as chair. It is no longer possible for someone who is not on council to be chosen as chair of the metro council. Nor can the metropolitan councillors who are there by virtue of being heads of local municipalities be chosen. The reason for their exclusion was a concern

---

[13]Notably the *Report and Recommendations, Committee of Review, City of Winnipeg Act,* Winnipeg, Queen's Printer, 1976, and the *Report of the Royal Commission on Education, Public Services, and Provincial-Municipal Relations in Nova Scotia,* Halifax, Queen's Printer, 1974.

that serving as the head of two councils could create situations in which there would appear to be a conflict of interest.[14]

The Underlying Question

As stated at the outset, the differing viewpoints about the three aspects of election just discussed reflect the underlying conflict between the two fundamental roles of local government — the representative, political role and the administrative or service delivery role. Those who emphasize the representative role and who recognize the political nature of local government tend to favour election by ward, while supporters of at large elections show their concern for service delivery when they emphasize the prospect of a stronger calibre of candidate capable of taking a broad overview of the municipality's needs. Similarly, those who argue for a short term of office are emphasizing the representative role, but proponents of a longer term are concerned about the increasingly complex demands requiring attention. Finally, direct election of councillors is seen as more democratic, and is therefore favoured by those who emphasize the representative role. However, those concerned with the need for strong leadership and improved priority setting in the face of growing local responsibilities are drawn to the concept of a head of council chosen by, supported by, and responsible to, the council.

The Administration

In addition to the council, the government of the municipality includes the appointed staff who are responsible for administering the programs and policies of council and for assisting council in making decisions by providing expert advice. Because they may be in frequent contact with the public, the staff are also potential public relations ambassadors for the municipality. Some staff have the responsibility for supervising a number of subordinates and demonstrating managerial skill and, as described later in this chapter, some have a special role as a coordinating officer.

There is, of course, a tremendous variation in the number and organization of staff depending on the population of the municipality and the range of functions. At one extreme, and still found in some Canadian municipalities, is the staff of one, perhaps part-time at that. This individual may act as clerk, treasurer, tax collector, by-law enforcement officer, dog catcher, and building inspector while performing a variety of other duties and all without any formal job description whatsoever.

---

[14]Koscak and Siegel, *op. cit.,* p. 9.

At the other extreme is the staff of thousands, grouped into twenty-odd functionally specialized departments, with detailed job descriptions and operating manuals and an elaborate hierarchy. In this latter instance, the municipality obviously has much greater staff resources and expertise available. Bigger is not always better, however, and as with all larger organizations, the municipality may have difficulty drawing these resources together into a coordinated operation.

Probably the most common approach traditionally used to oversee administrative operations has been the establishment of standing committees although, as discussed below, these have often been abandoned or modified in recent years because they were perceived as contributing to the problems of fragmentation and lack of coordination.

Standing Committees: The Council-Administration Link?

Standing committees normally exercise both executive and legislative responsibilities. They provide a general oversight of the operations of one or more municipal departments and they also make reports and recommendations as requested by council. In large municipalities the committees may be policy-advisory only, without any responsibility for supervising the departments. Standing committees are composed of councillors, sometimes with citizen members as well, and the extent of their use depends upon the size of the council, the volume of business and local customs and administrative arrangements.

The use of a standing committee system is held to be advantageous because it speeds up work in council since the committee sifts through the details of an issue and presents a positive recommendation to council. It also allows councillors to specialize in the fields of administration under the jurisdiction of their standing committees rather than to attempt to be knowledgeable in all fields. It is also alleged that the informal atmosphere of a committee meeting encourages more "give and take" in debate, facilitates participation by municipal officials and also provides a good opportunity for interested groups or individuals to be heard. In this latter connection, it is argued that the delay built in when matters are referred to committee gives public opinion a chance to develop and be heard and guards against overly precipitous action.

However, there are also a significant number of alleged disadvantages of the standing committee system. While some delay in decision making may be regarded as beneficial, referrals from council to committee to another committee and back to council can create a very slow process and some opportunity for buck-passing. If committee discussions are duplicated in the council chamber, much time is wasted and the value of the committee's specialized scrutiny is lost. There are often too many committees and one result is that a councillor's already limited time is seriously overburdened. An associated problem in many smaller municipalities is the tendency to establish standing committees when they are not necessary given the volume of work. Often such committees have no terms of reference, no regular schedule of meetings, and no systematic procedure of reporting to council. As a result, they are not an effective addition to the management of the municipality.

Another criticism, and one of particular relevance for the ensuing discussion, is that standing committees tend to reinforce the departmentalism inherent in the municipal organization and contribute to a fragmented outlook. This is because members of a committee may put the interests of their particular department or departments first, an attitude which is hardly conducive to a coordinated approach or to a broad view of the municipality's needs. Often difficulties arise in this respect because the committee system has simply expanded with the increase in municipal departments. Yet the departments themselves may have grown without sufficient forethought, and if this structure is poorly organized for coordination then what can one expect from a committee system similarly designed? Finally, it is argued that committee members tend to become overly preoccupied with matters of administrative detail and internal management of the departments under their jurisdiction. This is a criticism of councils generally but it is felt to be accentuated by the greater contact and familiarity with administration that the specialized scrutiny of the committee system permits.

Shortcomings in the Traditional Machinery

Just as the pressures of growth and change undermined the traditional boundaries, responsibilities, and revenues of municipal government as discussed in earlier chapters, so these pressures increasingly called into question the traditional internal governing structure and operation of the municipality. In particular, there were growing problems related to leadership, planning and priority setting, accountability and coordination.

Problems of Political Leadership

These weaknesses were focused at the top, in the limited powers given to the head of council. To illustrate, let us consider the Ontario legislation concerning the head of council and then note any significant variations. Perhaps the most striking feature of the Ontario Municipal Act's section on heads of council is that it is identical to the statement in the Act of 1877.[15] As a result, it is hopelessly out-of-date, deals mostly with matters of administration, and does not recognize that the important duties of heads of council are "to lead, to initiate, and to coordinate the efforts of the councillors, the officers, and the many groups in the local communities that work for the betterment and the enrichment of the local citizens."[16] Briefly, the Ontario legislation requires the head of council to preside at council meetings, cause the municipal laws to be executed and obeyed, oversee the conduct of the officers, cause negligence, carelessness, and violation of duty by officers to be prosecuted and punished, and make recommendations to the council to improve the finances, health, security, cleanliness, comfort, and ornament of the municipality.

While many provinces have comparable provisions, some of the legislation gives the head of council other duties which strengthen his role as leader of the council. For example, the legislation in Manitoba, British Columbia and Quebec provides a limited form of veto by authorizing the head of council to return any matter to the council for its reconsideration. The latter two provinces and Saskatchewan grant the head of council the power to suspend any officer or employee, subject to subsequent confirmation by council. In no instances, however, do the heads of council possess significant executive powers. While they are not limited to the largely ceremonial role of their British counterparts, neither are they comparable to the American "strong mayor" who has extensive authority in connection with the preparation of current and capital budgets, planning, hiring and firing. Heads of council in Canada must rely heavily on their personality and persuasive skills and attempt to enlist council's cooperation. According to Levine, the power exercised by mayors in Canada has historically depended on their personal and popular appeal. The record indicates that Canadian mayors, even facing opposition from council members, can accomplish a good deal "if they are competent, shrewd and, most important, popular with the electorate."[17]

Part of the difficulty for any head of council is that the council itself has serious limitations as a governing body. Except in those few instances

---

[15]According to Paul Hickey, *Decision-Making Processes in Ontario's Local Governments*, Toronto, Ministry of Treasury, Economics and Intergovernmental Affairs, 1973 — and there has been no significant change since his report.

[16]*Ibid.*, p. 62.

[17]Allan Levine (ed.), *Your Worship: The Lives of Eight of Canada's Most Unforgettable Mayors*, Toronto, James Lorimer and Company, 1989, p. 2.

where organized political parties operate, the council is made up of a group of individuals with potentially different interests and concerns and no sense of cohesion or collective will. This situation is accentuated when councillors are elected on a ward basis and parochial views are allowed to predominate over any concept of the good of the municipality. As a result, support for a particular measure is often arranged on the basis of trade-offs. This "log-rolling and back scratching" makes voting patterns even more unpredictable and further complicates the efforts of the head of council to develop a consensus for action. On the other hand, election by general vote, as espoused by the turn of the century reformers, has been increasingly criticized as providing insufficient representation of the diverse interests and needs of many municipalities today. According to Masson, when partisanship is eliminated and council members are elected at large, council policy choices are narrowed and political accountability becomes blurred. He argues that:

> Even in a small, relatively homogeneous community there are social and economic cleavages. Non-partisan and at large elections blur neighbourhood and minority interests in the "public interest," which is seldom, if ever, defined.[18]

Efforts to get councils to undertake long term planning or even to take the long view on a particular issue have been hampered by the relatively short term of office, although, as described above, this term has been extended in a number of provinces in recent years. Planning and priority setting have also been hampered by the limited control actually exercised by council over its activities and finances. Because of the dependence on conditional grants from the senior levels of government, municipal decisions often reflect the priorities of these governments rather than local priorities. The municipal council's control over its expenditures has also been eroded by the financial demands of various special purpose bodies, particularly the school boards as they operate in most provinces. Technical resources to undertake research, analysis and long term planning have not been widely available to municipalities.

Because of the lack of cohesion on council, coordination of the activities of the municipality is difficult. This is particularly the case as the range of responsibilities increases and a large number of functionally specialized departments are established. At the provincial and federal levels, each government department is headed by a minister, an elected representative, and all ministers belong to the cabinet where the twin

---

[18]Jack Masson, *Alberta's Local Governments and Their Politics*, Edmonton, University of Alberta Press, 1985, p. 22.

forces of party loyalty and cabinet solidarity serve to facilitate coordination. At the local level, however, there is no comparable arrangement. Perhaps the closest approximation is the establishment of standing committees of councillors to supervise each of the municipal departments, as described above. But it is generally agreed that these committees tend to perpetuate a fragmented outlook on municipal operations by being overly preoccupied with their particular department(s).

There is also a serious lack of accountability within most municipal councils. Granted, all members are normally elected and must regularly seek re-election. But who is responsible for taking the initiative in dealing with the problems facing the municipality? Who is responsible for scrutinizing and criticizing the initiatives taken to ensure that they are in the best interest of the public? Unlike the senior levels, there is no "government" or "official opposition" at the municipal level. Because these matters are the responsibility of everybody on council and yet of nobody, it is almost impossible for citizens to know where to direct criticism or praise. Councillors can claim that they attempted to represent a citizen concern but were outvoted by other councillors, and the possibilities for evading responsibility are all too evident.

Problems (and Possibilities?) of Boards

Problems of accountability are also caused by the existence of special purpose boards and commissions at the local level. As with so many features of local government, we are indebted to the turn of the century reformers who urged the creation of boards as a way of insulating responsiblities from the control of councils and hence from politics and as a means of obtaining expert assistance. Some boards came even earlier, of course — notably the school board which dates from the early 1800s and preceded the creation of municipalites — and some came later, particularly in the form of intermunicipal bodies designed to help overcome the fragmented municipal structure in Canada's urban areas. The existence of these separate boards is most prevalent in Ontario, less so in the Atlantic and Western provinces, and least so in Quebec. According to a recent study,[19] virtually every province has separate boards dealing with recreation, planning, trade and commerce and housing; many provinces have boards dealing with policing, transit, health care and conservation; and only a few provinces have boards dealing with children's services,

---

[19]Dale Richmond and David Siegel (eds.), *Agencies, Boards and Commissions in Canadian Local Government*, Toronto, Institute of Public Administration, 1994.

licensing, solid waste disposal, fire, water, electricity, sewage treatment, transportation and parking.

Almost all of these bodies are appointed rather than elected, many operate quite independently of council, and collectively they provide a wide range of services that ought to be, but often are not, closely integrated with the services provided by the municipality. It is hoped that the classic example of the street being paved by the council and then being torn up by the utility commission for sewer work is seldom in evidence. But there are many other, more subtle examples of lack of coordination or insufficient liaison between boards and council. School board decisions concerning the location of new schools or the closing of existing ones have an important bearing on the pattern of growth within a municipality. Municipal planning efforts may also be affected by decisions made by such bodies as utility commissions, park boards, conservation authorities, industrial commissions, and planning boards. A coordinated approach to social services administration by the municipality may be complicated by the fact that relevant programs are under the jurisdiction of such separate bodies as children's aid societies, health units, housing authorities, and library boards.

Quite apart from the problems of fragmentation, these boards increase the problem of accountability since most are not responsible to council or to the electorate in any very direct or effective mannner. As has been noted, the rationale behind the establishment of some of these boards, such as planning boards and police commissions, was the presumed desirability of keeping the issue in question "out of politics," and as a result these bodies are not meant to be particularly responsive to public opinion. Not only are the boards themselves not accountable, but their separate existence presents a very confusing picture to the citizen and the divided jurisdictions which result give both the council and the boards an opportunity to indulge in buck-passing.

As Masson summarizes the problem:

> Boards, commissions and committees do not take particular functions out of politics; rather they remove these functions from the control and scrutiny of the citizenry to those of special interests in the community.[20]

Have We Gone "Overboard" About Boards?

The preceding criticisms reflect what might be termed the "conventional wisdom" concerning boards and commissions. Much of this criticism is a reaction against the turn of the century reformers and what is now seen

---

[20]Masson, *Alberta's Local Governments*, p. 47.

as their misuse of boards for the purpose of taking issues out of politics. The criticism also reflects the view that fragmented local government is inevitably inefficient, lacking in accountability and coordination, and unresponsive.

In fairness, there is another point of view concerning local boards and their value. It is also evident that a new generation of boards is emerging, in many instances to provide some mechanism for intermunicipal servicing arrangements in the absence of suitable municipal boundaries — as indicated in some of the reform initiatives discussed in Chapter 5. It is important, therefore, to consider the contrary viewpoint — that boards may have positive benefits to offer.[21]

Recent public choice theory embraces that opposite viewpoint in arguing that fragmentation in local government also means multiple suppliers of services, hence competition, and therefore the probability of greater efficiency. This competition, it is argued, also may lead to greater responsiveness to local clients on the part of the multiple service providers.[22]

In addition, there are increasing examples of municipalities making innovative use of boards, often in partnership arrangements with other bodies. To illustrate:[23]

1. The Forks Renewal Corporation was established with tri-level funding to develop the Winnipeg Core Area.
2. The Peterborough Public Buyers Cooperative Association has since 1968 achieved considerable savings through bulk purchasing for area municipalities, hospitals and educational institutions.
3. The Meewasin Valley Authority in Saskatoon, established in 1979, brings together the city, the province and the University of Saskatchewan to preserve the natural features of the South Saskatchewan River Valley.
4. Saskatchewan Rural Development Corporations are an example of public-private partnerships to promote economic and social development within rural areas of the province.

---

[21]The discussion which follows is based on Richmond and Siegel, *op. cit.*

[22]See Mark Sproule-Jones, "The Pragmatics of Special Purpose Bodies: A Public Choice Analysis of Special Purpose Bodies in Canadian Urban Public Economies," in Richmond and Siegel, *op. cit.*, pp. 71-82, and also the discussion of public choice theory in Chapter 9.

[23]These examples are taken from Brian Smith, "Innovative Uses of Agencies, Boards and Commissions," in *ibid.*, pp. 38-44.

5. Public-private partnership is also evident in the Halifax Human Resources Development Association, a non-profit corporation established in 1978 to provide long term employment for people who would otherwise be on social assistance.

Siegel reviews the main rationales for the use of boards and offers some guidelines as to when their use would be appropriate.[24] He acknowledges the value of boards when the optimum service delivery area for a function does not coincide with municipal boundaries and *is unlikely ever to coincide*, as in the case of the watershed requirements of conservation authorities. But when a number of services are being provided across municipal boundaries by one or more intermunicipal boards, Siegel sees this development as suggestive of outmoded municipal boundaries which should be reviewed. He sees value in multi-jurisdictional boards, such as the previously-cited Forks Renewal Corporation, where a function or project crosses over more than one level of government. He also concedes the usefulness of boards in providing more flexible operations, and cites the ability of the Halifax Human Resources Development Agency to administer short term contracts in a way that would not be possible under the city's regular collective agreements. But he cautions against overuse — or abuse — of the flexibility argument as an excuse to avoid legitimate controls and accountability. Finally, Siegel also offers only a qualified support for the argument that boards are needed to keep certain matters at arm's length from the political process. This justification has been used far too often in an attempt to remove matters from politics and therefore from democratic control. Even where there may be some grounds for a separate board, this doesn't mean that every aspect of its operations should be removed from council control. Siegel cites the example of policing, noting that a separate commission helps to ensure that there is no direct political involvement in day-to-day enforcement decisions. But he disagrees with the fact that such commissions are used to keep all aspects of policing policy, including expenditures and hiring decisions, removed from council control — especially when municipal governments, in Ontario at least, are obliged to pay 100% of the costs of local police forces.

If separate boards are going to remain a fixture of local government — and probably even increase in usage — municipalities will have to get beyond their all-too-common posture of either ignoring the boards or regarding them as "the enemy" — the typical stance vis-à-vis school boards.

---

[24]David Siegel, "The Appropriate Use of Agencies, Boards and Commissions" in *ibid.*, pp. 83-110.

Here again, Siegel offers a number of very useful suggestions.[25] While boards commonly have representation from a number of different municipalities (and often the province, as well), they should have to be accountable to one government — usually the one which provides the majority of the board's funding. That *lead* government should also make the majority of the appointments to the board, reflecting the "pay for say" principle. That *lead* government, and all others making appointments to the board, should exercise great care in the selections they make. Siegel provides a very colourful example of the difficulties which can arise when this appointment power is exercised carelessly, citing a municipality which belatedly discovered that one of its appointments to the local hydro-electric commission was "an outspoken, iconoclastic morning disk jockey who specialized in raunchy bathroom humour and sexist antics."[26]

Making appointments carefully should extend to some type of orientation for new appointees, providing at least some general guidance about council's expectations. These expectations could include that the board would consult with the council about certain actions before it undertakes them, and that the board would provide some sort of annual report as part of its accountability. While the specifics of any such expectations and reporting arrangements would obviously vary with the board and its degree of operating independence from council, efforts to define the relationship more clearly could certainly help to reduce misunderstandings and conflict.

It is hard to imagine a better (or worse) example of a council-board conflict than the one currently affecting the city of Kingston and the area Separate School Board — a conflict which has gained national prominence thanks to the efforts of Bloc Québécois to distort it into an issue of language and of anti-French sentiment. The basic facts are that the Separate School Board determined that under existing zoning it could build a new separate school within a city industrial park. Such a development is not possible under the policies of the city's new official plan, but the zoning by-law has not yet been amended to bring it into conformity with that official plan, and it is the zoning by-law which dictates land use in Ontario. Whatever the legal provisions and possibilities, an industrial park is certainly an unusual and, it is contended, questionable location for a school. Moreover, if this land is developed as a school the city will lose the municipal taxes which it could reasonably have anticipated.

---

[25]*Ibid.*, pp. 94-105.

[26]*Ibid.*, p. 100.

The impasse between the city and the school board has delayed any resolution of this matter for six months. There has been a hardening of positions, with neither side apparently willing to compromise. Having taken the by now highly publicized decision to locate the school in the industrial park, the Separate School Board would presumably find it very difficult to back down. One can't help thinking that, had there been more open communications between school board trustees and city councillors *before* any decisions were taken and lines hardened, this damaging deadlock, now before the courts, might have been avoided. While school board-council relations in Ontario have never been characterized by open and frequent communications and joint meetings, seldom have they resulted in such an unfortunate incident.

Fragmented Administration

Even without the divided jurisdictions which arise with separate boards and commissions, there have traditionally been serious problems of fragmentation and lack of coordination with the administrative structure of municipalities. As municipalities have grown, more and more departments have been established. Organized on a functional basis, these departments are usually headed by a specialist in that particular discipline, and they tend to be preoccupied with their own area of expertise or specialty. This narrow focus is reinforced by the existence of provincial departments similarly specialized, each of them maintaining close contact with their municipal counterparts. These provincial departments deploy a variety of conditional grant programs to ensure that the municipal departments give high priority to their specialized area. While all of this is understandable, it results in little attention being paid to the overall needs of the municipality.

Where municipalities use a standing committee system, it has already been noted that these committees often tend to reinforce a narrow focus on the activities of "their" departments, to the neglect of a broader consideration of overall municipal needs.

Modifications to the Machinery

In response to the kinds of weaknesses described above, many municipalities have modified their internal governing machinery, especially over the past few decades. At first glance the resulting organizational forms seem quite diverse. However, there have only been two main types of change:

1. The establishment of some form of chief administrative officer to provide leadership and coordination at the staff level.
2. The introduction of some form of executive committee of council to provide stronger political leadership.

Chief Administrative Officer Systems

Chief administrative officers (CAOs) are found in Canadian municipalities under a variety of names and with a variety of powers and responsibilities. Titles used include city administrator, commissioner, city manager, director general, and chief commissioner. Plunkett, in a recent publication,[27] uses the term CAO to encompass all types of structure (including manager systems) which have a single appointed officer as the head of the administration. On this basis, he finds that by 1989 some 170 urban municipalities in Canada had adopted this structure.[28] Among the larger cities in this category are Vancouver, Edmonton, Calgary, Winnipeg, Saskatoon, Regina, Windsor, Hamilton, Metro Toronto, Quebec City, Ottawa, and the regional municipalities of Ottawa-Carleton, Hamilton-Wentworth, Durham, Halton, Niagara, Peel, Sudbury, Waterloo, Quebec City, Saint John, Halifax, and St. John's.[29]

The earliest and most powerful form of CAO is that of the city manager or council manager system which spread into this country from the United States in the early 1900s. The first Canadian city manager was appointed in Westmount in 1913 and the system is still found particularly in Quebec, where legislation has authorized municipal councils to appoint a manager since 1922. In contrast, until a 1970 amendment, Ontario's Municipal Act did not give municipalities the authority to appoint any type of CAO. While the number of CAO positions has increased markedly since, most are not full-fledged managers but rather weaker forms of coordinating officer or expanded clerk-treasurer, as described below.

In the Western provinces, the principal form of CAO has been the commissioner, usually found in a group of three or four operating as a board of commissioners. As described in Chapter 3, the commissioner system, like the council manager system, arose out of the turn of the century reform era and was first established in Edmonton in 1904. Within a

---

[27]T. J. Plunkett, *City Management in Canada: The Role of the Chief Administrative Officer*, Toronto, Institute of Public Administration of Canada, 1992.

[28]*Ibid.*, p. 21.

[29]*Ibid.*, p. 25.

decade Regina, Prince Albert, and Saskatoon followed suit. In a number of respects, the commissioner system is comparable to a multiheaded council manager system, as can be seen from the examination of the two which follows.

The Council Manager System

As it developed in the United States, this system is predicated on a complete separation of the policy and administrative activities of the municipality. It involves the appointment of a professional administrator — the manager — to whom is delegated complete responsibility for administering the programs of the municipality including the supervision and coordination of staff. The council is elected at large and on a nonpartisan basis and directs its attention to its representative role and the formulation of overall policies for the municipality. In the "pure" council manager systems found in the United States, there are not usually any standing committees and therefore not any regular council contact with the administration except through the manager.

The duties of the manager may be summarized as follows:[30]

1. To see that all laws and ordinances are enforced.
2. To exercise control over all departments and in accordance with civil service regulations appoint, supervise, and remove department heads and subordinate employees of the city.
3. To make such recommendations to the council concerning the affairs of the city as may seem to him desirable.
4. To keep the council advised of the financial conditions and future needs of the city.
5. To prepare and submit the annual budget to the council.
6. To prepare and submit to the council such reports as may be required by that body.
7. To keep the public informed, through reports to the council, regarding the operations of the city government.

Proponents of the council manager system contend that it provides for greatly improved coordination of administrative activities, frees the council from unnecessary detail, and allows councillors to concentrate on their primary role of policy making. While there is considerable potential for improved coordination in the organization of the manager system, its greatest weakness is the premise on which it is based, that it is possible to separate policy and administration in municipal government. To the contrary, it is very difficult to identify in advance whether a particular issue

---

[30]From the *City Manager Directory*, quoted in T. J. Plunkett, *Urban Canada and its Government*, Toronto, Macmillan, 1968, p. 38.

is a routine administrative matter or has political implications. Even if this distinction could be made, it is not desirable to rigidly separate the two activities. In practice, much policy arises out of ongoing administration and the council's complete separation from the administrative activities of the municipality leaves it "making policy in a vacuum."

Moreover, while the system provides for a more effective administrative structure, it does not provide for strong political leadership. Indeed, because of the focus on the manager, he or she is often a more conspicuous public figure than the members of council including the mayor. In addition to producing friction and jealousies which frequently result in the dismissal of managers, this situation also leads to managers becoming publicly identified with particular viewpoints and policies. If, as a result, they become embroiled in political controversies, their role as administrative leaders is impaired and they will likely be replaced. One author dryly observes that a manager's departure from work is often the result of illness or fatigue: "The council was sick and tired of him."[31] Thus the successful operation of the council manager system not only requires a manager who does not dominate his council and usurp its policy making role but also one who does not seem to do so.

The Commissioner System

The commissioner system has traditionally been found only in Western Canada and except for Winnipeg has been confined to the provinces of Alberta and Saskatchewan. Cities such as Saskatoon, Regina, Moose Jaw and Red Deer have appointed city commissioners — although Regina subsequently changed the designation to city manager.[32] In Edmonton (until 1984), Calgary and Winnipeg, this system has involved the appointment of a limited number of commissioners[33] who are delegated administrative responsibilities by council. As individuals, these commissioners are charged with supervising and coordinating the activities of the departments under their jurisdiction. In addition, the commissioners may meet together as a board of commissioners with responsibility for overall man-

---

[31] Wayne Anderson, Chester A. Newland and Richard J. Stillman, *The Effective Local Government Manager*, Washington, International City Management Association, 1983, p. 68.

[32] Plunkett, *City Management*, p. 24.

[33] In fact, some cities such as Red Deer, Alberta and Prince Albert and Estevan, Saskatchewan have established a single council-appointed commissioner as described by Plunkett, *City Management*, p. 53.

agement and coordination of the municipality's activities. The head of council is also usually a member of this board.

To illustrate this structure, consider the example of Calgary as described by Masson in 1985.[34] There was then a chief commissioner, a commissioner of planning and transportation, a commissioner of finance and administration, and a commissioner of operations — each directly responsible for the supervision of a number of municipal departments. These four commissioners together with the mayor constituted the commission board which was responsible for determining how council's general policy directions were to be carried out through the administrative structure. The commissioners were also resource persons for the standing committees of council, and actively participated in their discussions, but did not have the voting rights accorded to full members.

The commissioner system is similar to a council manager system except in two important respects. The fact that there is more than one commissioner permits a degree of specialization not possible under the manager system where one person must supervise the entire administrative structure no matter how large and complex. Typically, one commissioner is concerned with hard services (such as water and sewerage facilities and roads), another with soft services (such as health and welfare programs and libraries) and a third — if available — with finance and planning. Moreover, the commissioners provide a two level approach to administrative coordination, both as individual commissioners in charge of a group of related departments and as a board of commissioners in charge of the entire administrative structure.

The second difference from the manager system is the somewhat less marked separation of policy and administration found in the commissioner system. This is particularly reflected in the mayor's membership on the board of commissioners, although this combination has not been without problems. On the one hand, Plunkett, while acknowledging the delicate relationships involved, endorses this combination on the grounds that the mayor participates:

> in the vital stage when problems are being analyzed, as well as when recommendations are formulated for presentation to the council. Under this arrangement direction and leadership in civic affairs is provided by the city's recognized political leader, supported by the managerial coordination of the appointed city commissioners.[35]

---

[34]Masson, *Alberta's Local Governments*, pp. 36-37.

[35]Plunkett, *Urban Canada*, p. 54.

Masson also favours combining these two elements. He describes as retrogressive Calgary's 1968 change which transferred the chairmanship of the commission board from the mayor (who remains an ex-officio member) to the chief commissioner. The more limited role played by the mayor is unfortunate in his view, "since the mayor is the linchpin in the whole system, the bridge between the formulation of policy on council and its administration through the commission board."[36]

A consultant's report to Edmonton city council in 1982 was much more critical.

> It is our view that when the mayor chairs the Commission Board there is ambiguity regarding the nature of recommendations emanating from the board as to whether they are politically or administratively generated and endorsed.... The political and administrative responsibilities and authority are blurred and the authority of the Chief Commissioner to manage and exercise administrative authority is undermined.[37]

This report also concluded that the mayor's chairmanship of the Commission Board had been a factor in the high level of conflict between council and administration. As previously noted, at the beginning of 1984 Edmonton replaced its Commission Board with a City Manager and established an Executive Committee of Council.

The city manager who came to Edmonton in 1985, Cy Armstrong, sees several problems with the commission board system which preceded his arrival.[38] He notes that a key difference from the CAO system is that an administrative board is responsible for the administration of the city, with no one person clearly in charge. He also expresses concern about having the mayor as a member of such a board. Noting that councils want reports and recommendations from staff to be professional, Armstrong wonders whether the board's activities might be unduly influenced politically by the mayor. He also suggests that a mayor could be placed in a difficult position of being overruled by his staff. He is also critical of the commission board for meeting in private to discuss the "politics" of issues, when debates on public policy should be held in public and by council. Not surprisingly, in light of the foregoing, Armstrong concludes that the

---

[36]Masson, *Alberta's Local Governments*, p. 36.

[37]Norm Duce and Associates Ltd., *Final Report: Review of Organization —
Council and Commission Board in the City of Edmonton*, Edmonton, July 8, 1982,
p. 2.

[38]Cy Armstrong, *Thoughts on Canadian Municipal Management*, Local
Government Case Studies #5, London, University of Western Ontario, 1992.

commission board is no longer appropriate and predicts that it will gradually fade away as the CAO system continues to grow in popularity.[39]

Lightbody also found several problems with Edmonton's commissioner system.[40] He points out that some conflicts are inevitable given the attempt to group departments under three broad functional areas headed by the three commissioners and cites, as an example, the fact that land use planning is under public affairs while transportation planning is under utilities and engineering. More serious is his allegation that internal struggles over policy alternatives are almost never allowed to reach the public and that "upwardly mobile civic managers do not upset applecarts in Edmonton."[41] Lightbody goes on to observe that commissioners "have usually been recruited from the world of hard services and, by virtue of their training, have not been overly sympathetic to the direct intrusions of citizen amateurs into civic policy-making."[42] Masson also expresses concern about this lack of citizen involvement.[43]

What can be seen as a variation of the commissioner system has been appearing in a number of Ontario cities in recent years. This has involved grouping together related departments and appointing commissioners to oversee the department heads within the groupings. This structure often includes a CAO — who then operates as the equivalent of the chief commissioner. However, in at least some instances, one of the main purposes of the change has apparently been to reduce what was considered an excessively heavy span of control for the CAO. It is held that this Ontario variation is not really the same as the traditional commissioner system; moreover, the addition of an extra layer of senior management is hardly consistent with the general thrust in organizations toward "de-layering" and "down-sizing" and it will be interesting to see how widely this innovation is used.

The Manager System in Canada

As adapted to Canada, the council manager system has undergone certain modifications which minimize some of the problems noted above

[39]*Ibid.*, p. 27.

[40]Lightbody in Magnusson and Sancton, *op. cit.*, pp. 274-275.

[41]*Ibid.*, p. 275.

[42]*Ibid.*

[43]Masson, *Alberta's Local Governments*, p. 38.

and, at the same time, minimize somewhat its strength and coordinating potential. Not surprisingly, these modifications reflect both the different governing principles of the two countries and the differing conditions which prevailed at the time of the system's introduction.

In most Canadian cities in the early years of the 20th century the need for such an administrative reform seemed less pressing or necessary than in American cities. Corruption and the worst excesses of local party politics were much less evident in Canadian cities, and appointments based on merit were much more prevalent. Moreover, administrative coordination was being achieved informally by utilizing the potential of certain key municipal positions, notably that of clerk and treasurer. Especially where the positions were combined in people with leadership skills, their overall knowledge of the municipality's operations and the influence inherent in their responsibilities for preparing agendas, background reports, minutes, by-laws, budgets and financial reports, often made them unofficial chief administrative officers. Some municipalities confirmed the coordinating potential of these positions by formally designating the clerk or treasurer as something more — resulting in such positions as Clerk-Comptroller, Clerk-Treasurer-Administrator, and Clerk Coordinator.

Even where the council manager system was adopted, the Canadian version usually incorporated certain features designed to maintain the significance and prestige of the elected council.[44] First, the Canadian council manager system does not attempt to enforce a complete separation between administration and policy. The council usually has a direct relationship with at least its main department heads as well as the manager — normally accomplished "by the attendance of the department heads at a meeting of a limited number of standing committees of council when matters affecting their particular areas of jurisdiction are under review."[45] Second, the responsibility for the appointment of staff is exercised by council, not the manager, although often council only exercises this responsibility after receiving recommendations from the manager.

With such modifications, Young feels that the Canadian version has managed to avoid the fundamental problem of council's complete separation from administration. As he explains, the council in a Canadian coun-

---

[44]See Dennis A. Young, "Canadian Local Government Development: Some Aspects of the Commissioner and City Manager Forms of Administration," in Lionel D. Feldman and Michael D. Goldrick (eds.), *Politics and Government of Urban Canada*, Toronto, Methuen, 1976, pp. 276-278.

[45]*Ibid.*, p. 277.

cil manager system continues to concern itself with administration but "does so from a much broader viewpoint." The advice and recommendations of staff are coordinated by the manager and "it is this opportunity and ability to place such recommendations within the broader perspective of the city's needs as a whole which represents his greatest value to the council in his capacity as policy advisor."[46]

Canadian CAOs Today

Plunkett sees the growth of the CAO system in Canada as the result of the growth in municipal departments with the urbanization following World War Two and the recognition that the issues confronting municipal governments today require more analysis and synthesis than could be provided through such a fragmented departmental structure.[47] He explains that most municipalities can now appoint a CAO under the general municipal legislation of their province. In some cases, the legislation provides for the position only in general terms, but in provinces such as British Columbia and Quebec, duties are specified in the statute. For example, the British Columbia legislation stipulates that the incumbent shall, under the control of the council:[48]

a) supervise and direct municipal affairs and employees;
b) put into effect and carry out council policies;
c) advise the council on matters within its control; inspect and report on municipal works as council requires;
d) be responsible for preparing for council the estimate of revenue and expenditures annually or as council requires;
e) prepare and award all contracts as council prescribes;
f) carry out other duties as prescribed by by-law or resolution.

Another difference is that while most provincial statutes simply authorize council to establish the position, both British Columbia and Saskatchewan require that the appointing by-law be passed by two-thirds of all council members, and the former even requires that this by-law be approved by the electors.[49]

The success of any particular CAO will depend, in large part, on how well the individual is able to work with the diverse mix of department

---

[46]*Ibid.*, p. 278.

[47]Plunkett, *City Management*, pp. 25-26.

[48]From *ibid.*, pp. 28-29.

[49]*Ibid.*, p. 28.

heads in the municipality. Some of these managers may have been strongly opposed to the introduction of a "senior coordinating officer," while others may have unsuccessfully sought the position themselves. In either case, they are unlikely to welcome a new CAO or to support the position. Where standing committees have been retained, department heads may attempt to use these as a buffer or a means of blocking CAO initiatives.

Plunkett suggests that relationships between CAOs and department heads tend to fall into three categories.[50]

1. *Passive:* CAOs who simply forward, without comment, reports received from department heads.
2. *Active:* CAOs who include with departmental reports an accompanying memo setting out their comments.
3. *Dominant:* CAOs who attempt to hold back reports from departments until these conform to their general policy viewpoint.

The second category is probably the most common and certainly the most desirable. It ensures that both the technical knowledge of the specialist department head and the broader perspective of the CAO are sent forward, and it gives council the benefit of the most complete range of information on which to make a decision.

Another problematic relationship which can arise is between the CAO and the head of council, given the way the latter position is defined in provincial legislation. Consider the Ontario legislation which states that it is the duty of the head of council:

a) to be vigilant and active in causing the laws for the government of the municipality to be duly executed and obeyed;
b) to oversee the conduct of all subordinate officers in the government of it and as far as practicable, cause all negligence, carelessness and violation of duty to be prosecuted and punished; and
c) to communicate to the council from time to time such information and recommend to it such measures as may tend to the improvement of the finances, health, security, cleanliness, comfort and ornament of the municipality.[51]

Plunkett indicates that virtually the same language is used in the other provincial statutes with respect to the responsibilities of the head of council. The potential for a clash is evident if a mayor has a strong personality and a determination to provide "hands-on" leadership consistent with the

---

[50]The descriptions which follow, but not the categorical terms used, are based on *ibid.*, p. 42.

[51]*Municipal Act*, R.S.O. 1990, c.M.45, s.70.

statutory authority to oversee subordinate officers. While a CAO faced with such a conflict could appeal to the council, which is ultimately responsible for the management of the municipality, such a course of action is by no means certain of success — especially since councillors are all too inclined to view CAOs with suspicion and to fear that they will become too dominant. Prudent CAOs usually make every effort to avoid an overt power struggle.

No matter how effectively a CAO system may work, it provides administrative, not political, leadership. As we will see, the search for new forms of municipal machinery which can provide the latter has proven to be even more elusive.

Executive Committees

Over the years the most persistent method of attempting to deal with the various problems of political leadership has been the establishment of executive committees of council. As had been the case with the establishment of CAO systems, a major impetus was the turn of the century reform movement, which emphasized a strong executive along with such measures as smaller councils and at large elections in its concern to make municipal government more efficient and less political. This prompted the introduction of boards of control, a form of executive committee which became quite prominent in Ontario during the first half of the 20th century. Other forms of executive committee have also been established in a number of large cities or metropolitan municipalities in an effort to duplicate a cabinet organization and a semblance of the parliamentary system.

Board of Control

The board of control first appeared in Canada in the City of Toronto in 1896, and within a decade it had spread to Winnipeg (1907) and then Montreal (1910). It didn't last long in either of those latter cities, however, and became an exclusively Ontario structure. In fact, it became mandatory for cities over 100 000 population in Ontario, although it could be dispensed with by a two-thirds vote of council if affirmed by the Ontario Municipal Board. In addition, cities and towns over 45 000 and other local municipalities over 100 000 could establish a board of control if approved by a two-thirds vote of council and affirmed by the Municipal Board. Given these statutory provisions, the board of control became a prominent feature of the government system of many of Ontario's largest municipalities — although this is no longer the case, as will be noted.

As historically constituted, the board of control was made up of the head of council and two or four (usually) members elected at large. All were full members of the municipal council, the other members of which were elected by ward. The responsibilities of the board of control included:

1. The preparation of annual estimates.
2. The calling of tenders and awarding of contracts.
3. The supervision of works in progress.
4. The nomination of all heads and subheads of departments and other permanent employees and the suspension or dismissal of department heads.
5. The submission of proposed by-laws to council.
6. Any other duties as assigned by council.

It can be seen that a number of important executive responsibilities were assigned to the board of control. Significantly, these powers were not delegated by council at its discretion but were assigned by statute, and the board was not responsible to council but to its electorate. Indeed, major decisions taken by the board can only be altered or overturned by a two-thirds vote of council. This concentration of power within a special group of councillors may seem a curious arrangement until one recalls the conditions and attitudes at the time the board of control was originally established. Controllers were deliberately given the more important responsibilities because they were elected at large and therefore were expected to be a better calibre of representative than the ward politicians who comprised the rest of the council. It was anticipated that the board of control would provide effective leadership and contribute to a more efficient management of the affairs of the municipality.

In practice, however, the board of control system experienced a number of difficulties and fell into increasing disfavour. The limited number of members involved became increasingly overburdened in attempting to oversee the administrative activities of the municipality. Nor was the board very effective in attempting to coordinate the ever more complex, fragmented administrative structures which evolved. The board's supposed similarity to a cabinet was shown to be very superficial at best. Instead of a body unified by the glue of party loyalty and discipline, the board of control was made up of individuals without necessarily any collective purpose. Indeed, it was not uncommon for one or more of the controllers to be eyeing the mayor's job, with resultant infighting.

An added problem was that many municipalities with boards of control also retained standing committees of council. This arrangement not only reinforced a fragmented departmental outlook inimical to coordination, but also caused conflict between the board of control and the standing committees in terms of the responsibility for supervising administration. The overall complexity of the municipal organization was also a problem with, typically, a board of control, a council, standing committees, and a variety of special purpose bodies. As a result of this complexity, the decision making process was often slow, discussion was duplicated, buck-passing was common, and the lack of clear lines of authority and responsibility also confused the public and undermined the accountability of the system.

Probably the most serious difficulty was the pronounced and persistent friction between the board of control and the rest of council. In effect, there were two classes of councillor and those considered second class were acutely aware of it. They resented the controllers' argument that election at large had given them (the controllers) a stronger mandate and they resented the special powers given to the controllers. But most of all, the rest of the councillors resented the provision that a two-thirds vote was required to overturn board of control decisions. Since the members of the board had a vote as councillors, there had to be near unanimity among the rest for the necessary votes to be marshalled. Consider, for example, the City of Hamilton as it was structured some years ago. With a council which was composed of a mayor, four controllers and sixteen councillors, it was necessary for fifteen of the sixteen councillors to join together to defeat a recommendation supported by all members of the board of control. Not surprisingly, it was felt that the board of control enjoyed excessive power and that the result was too often a case of "the tail wagging the dog."

Given all of these difficulties, it is not surprising that the board of control system fell into increasing disfavour. A Report at the beginning of the 1970s noted that "16 of the 25 councils that are required or authorised to establish the system ... have sought and obtained approval to reject the system."[52] By the time the Royal Commission on Metropolitan Toronto had reported in 1977, the number of board of control systems had been further reduced to seven. Four of these were in the boroughs of Metropolitan Toronto and the Commission recommended their abolition — a step which was finally taken at the time of the 1988 municipal elections.[53] Of the remaining three, those in Hamilton and Ottawa have

---

[52]Hickey, *op. cit.*, p. 158.

[53]Following a further study, the Task Force on Representation and Accountability in Metropolitan Toronto, *op. cit.*

been abolished — leaving London as the only municipality featuring this once so prominent form of executive committee. Moreover, legislation has removed the two-thirds vote provision for the London board.

Given its virtual extinction, one might wonder why so much attention has been given to the board of control. Part of the reason is that an appreciation of the difficulties faced by this type of executive committee is helpful when considering some of the alternative forms which have been attempted or contemplated. Moreover, some of the other forms, as we will see, are essentially variations of the board of control.

Other Forms of Executive Committee

Apart from the board of control, a variety of other forms of executive committee are found in Canadian municipalities. Some of these are similar to the board of control in having a statutory foundation, including those established in a number of the reformed local government structures.

There are also nonstatutory executive committees. By their nature they are much harder to categorize, and often are not even called "executive" committees. However, their purpose is reflected in their composition, which usually comprises the chairs of the major standing committees in the municipality plus the head of council, and in their mandate, which includes responsibility for the budget and for providing leadership and coordination in most cases.

The few examples that follow are designed to illustrate the nature of statutory executive committees and their operation.

Montreal is likely the Canadian city with the longest experience with an executive committee, since there are references to such a body as early as the 1850s. Montreal did, as previously mentioned, establish a board of control in 1910, the result of a new charter prompted by councillors endorsing the views of the reform movement of that time. However, charter revisions in 1921 abolished the board of control and provided for an executive committee to be named by council. The mayor was made a voting member of this executive committee but could not be its chairman, a deliberate arrangement to attempt to curb the power of the mayor.

Montreal's executive committee, which has continued to the present, was authorized to initiate legislation and to supervise the municipal departments, with each member normally assigned a number of specific departments to oversee. Its powers were similar to those of an Ontario board of control, even to the extent of the two-thirds vote provision for council to overturn most major decisions of the committee.

By the 1960s, the executive committee had evolved into quite a different, and more powerful, position because of the emergence of dominant political parties within Montreal's council. The Civic Party, under the leadership of Jean Drapeau, controlled a majority of the council seats from 1960 until Drapeau's retirement in 1986. The result was that Drapeau's personal choices for membership on the executive committee were ratified by council and the committee could initiate actions with every expectation that they would be supported by council.

Party domination has continued since Drapeau with the election of a large majority of members of the Montreal Citizens' Movement (MCM), including Jean Doré as mayor, in both 1986 and 1990. If anything, the domination by the executive committee is even more pronounced now — and even more disappointing since the MCM had presented itself as offering a much more open, consultative government. "No matter what happens in City Hall, or the various new bodies created by the MCM, the final decision is always made by the executive committee."[54]

An executive committee is also found in the *Montreal Urban Community* set up in 1969. Initially this executive committee consisted of the city of Montreal's seven member executive plus five suburban representatives, an arrangement which reflected Montreal's dominant position within the new upper tier government. As discussed in Chapter 5, however, amendments to the legislation in 1982 provided parity between the suburbs and Montreal on the executive committee. Apart from the chair, who is elected by the entire council and must resign his or her municipal position before accepting the position, the other 12 members of the executive committee are the chairs and vice-chairs of the MUC council and each of its five standing committees.[55]

The cities of *Quebec*, *Hull* and *Laval* established executive committees in the mid-1960s after studies which found that the existing government machinery exhibited weaknesses of excessive council involvement in administrative detail, lack of executive direction, and uncoordinated administration. These executive committees are composed of the mayor (as chair) and four councillors selected by the mayor. According to Hickey, the system was based on the premise that a candidate for mayor runs as the head of a team of like-minded councillor candidates.[56] The existence of what is, in effect, a local political party provides the strong political leadership previously noted with respect to the City of Montreal.

---

[54]Karen Herland, *People, Potholes and City Politics*, Montreal, Black Rose Books, 1992, p. 15.

[55]*Ibid.*, p. 82.

[56]Hickey, *op. cit.*, p. 199.

One of the earliest executive committees in Ontario was established by the new *Municipality of Metropolitan Toronto* in 1954 under the council's general authority to establish "standing and other committees." This committee was given powers almost identical to Ontario's board of control, but unlike the board it was not directly elected. Instead it was composed of the chair of the metropolitan council, the mayors of the six lower tier municipalities in the system, and seven other specified representatives from the lower tier councils. Therefore, each member of the executive committee was there because of a prior position in the government structure.

The 1977 Robarts Commission recommended that the metropolitan council be given a general power of delegation which would authorize it to elect from its own membership an executive committee and any number of standing committees and to vest them with such responsibilities as council sees fit.[57] No action was taken on this recommendation — as with virtually all of the recommendations of the Commission — and yet the lack of strong political leadership in the Metropolitan Toronto system must be attributed, at least in part, to the way in which the executive committee has been chosen and the absence of organized political parties on council. Under these past arrangements, the executive committee members have not been responsible to the full metropolitan council for their selection nor could they depend on continuing majority support for their proposals. Indeed, there was not even any certainty that the executive committee members themselves would agree on what needed to be done in particular circumstances. They were individuals with different constituencies, different viewpoints, and different — perhaps competing — ambitions.

Following a Task Force on Representation and Accountability in Metropolitan Toronto[58] changes were finally made in the executive committee at the time of the 1988 municipal elections. As previously recommended by the Robarts Commission, the legislative requirement for an executive committee has now been abolished. It is left to the discretion of the Metropolitan Toronto Council whether or not it establishes such a committee, how it is composed, and what it does.

Winnipeg Unicity in its philosophical base and its actual experiences provides the most striking example of the link between organized political

---

[57]*Report of the Royal Commission on Metropolitan Toronto* (John Robarts, Commissioner), Toronto, Queen's Printer, 1977, p. 113.

[58]Task Force Report, *op. cit.*, Chapter Six.

parties and the operation of an executive committee. It will be recalled from Chapter 5 that a major objective of those designing the government machinery of Unicity was the development of a parliamentary model at the local level. A central feature was the provision for an executive policy committee chaired by the head of council and including the chairs of the three major standing committees established as part of the new structure. From the outset, however, the potential of this arrangement was weakened by the fact that the mayor was directly elected, rather than being chosen from among the councillors as had been proposed in the White Paper which led to the new structure.

A Committee of Review of Unicity reporting in 1976 offered forceful arguments in favour of the development of the parliamentary model at the local level, but acknowledged that the political parties which are an essential component of such a model are not warmly welcomed by the local electorates. The committee felt that it could not legislate the development of a party system but would have to hope for "a full fledged party system to evolve over the course of time, under the influence of the parliamentary characteristics of our model."[59] These hopes have not been well realized, as will be evident when local political party activity in Canada is examined in Chapter 8.

Edmonton established an executive committee in 1984, replacing the commissioner system which had prevailed for three-quarters of a century. According to Edmonton's mayor at the time, a major reason for this change was that the commissioners had become too powerful, more powerful than the elected representatives. He also felt that pushing decisions back down to the departmental level had led to more imaginative and creative decisions.[60] Described as "the nerve centre of city government," Edmonton's executive committee is directed to prepare the annual budget and monitor the administration's financial performance, call for tenders and award contracts, develop long-range policies, act as policy coordinator between the city manager and the council's standing committees, draft by-laws for council's consideration, enter into collective bargaining agreements with city staff, set the council's agenda and direct and coordinate the flow of information and business between council, its committees and the administration.[61]

---

[59]Committee of Review, *op. cit.*, p. 57.

[60]"A Better Deal for Cities," (Interview with Mayor Laurence Decore), *City Magazine*, Vol. 8, No. 3 & 4, Fall 1986, pp. 31-34.

[61]Masson, *Alberta's Local Governments*, p. 40.

Summary: *Assessing the Modifications*

As noted earlier in the chapter, the pressures of growth and change highlighted a number of weaknesses in the internal governing machinery of
Canadian municipalities. In particular, concerns were expressed about
the need for stronger political leadership and executive direction from
within council, a clearer focus of accountability and responsibility within
the municipal decision-making process, and greater coordination and
integration of municipal programs and activities. To what extent have
these problems been overcome by the modifications in municipal machinery described above?

Administrative Leadership Improved

It would appear that the establishment of a chief administrative officer
system has the potential to effect improved coordination and integration
of municipal programs and activities. This system may help to develop an
expanded research and analytical capability and the provision of more
comprehensive advice and recommendations to council, although much
depends on whether complementary changes are introduced in the management and decision-making process of the municipality. Designating
a chief administrative officer also provides a specific focus of accountability and responsibility for the administrative performance of the municipality.

By itself, however, the establishment of a chief administrative officer
system does nothing to strengthen *political* leadership and accountability;
to the contrary, as discussed above such a system may even detract from
the latter objectives by creating a very bureaucratic system and by under-
mining the power and public status of the council. In fairness, CAOs may
also find themselves drawn into the council's realm of activities to fill the
void created by the absence of any form of political executive — and this
added role may detract from the fulfillment of their primary responsibilities as coordinator.

Political Leadership More Difficult

The establishment of an executive committee system has proven to be a
less effective structural reform in most instances. Most of these committees have lacked political cohesion and have not had any means, except
persuasion, to ensure that their initiatives receive the necessary support
of council. The effectiveness of these committees has been dependent
upon their method of selection and whether or not they were reinforced

in their position and activities by the existence of organized political parties on council. As discussed in Chapter 8, however, even where political parties have captured a majority of the seats on council, they have usually been groups alleging a nonpartisan approach who evaded responsibility for council's performance. Instead of strong political leadership, the result was usually the protection of the interests of this group, and accountability was certainly not enhanced. The main exception to this pattern has been in a number of the Quebec municipalities, notably the City of Montreal, where council's domination by a political party has provided the basis for strong leadership. While accountability has also been present in that one group was clearly in charge, the overwhelming dominance of one party — first the Civic Party under Drapeau and then the MCM — has afforded the public little in the way of alternatives.

The establishment of a stronger executive without an accompanying reform in the administrative structure has also hampered the intended benefits. For example, Hickey notes that while Montreal, at the time of his study in the early 1970s, had an executive secretary to link the executive and the department heads, "he has been granted neither the authority nor the staff to exercise essential leadership, coordination and direction among the directors."[62] After taking power, however, the MCM created the post of Secretary-General, staffed it with a leading Quebec civil servant, and streamlined the organization of services.[63]

Another problem arises when executive committees are not authorized to delegate any administrative powers to the directors of the departments and thus are overly immersed in administrative detail to the neglect of their responsibility for policy development. In contrast, such cities as Quebec, Hull and Laval have attempted to overcome this situation by appointing chief administrative officers (managers) to complement and support the work of executive committees responsible to and supported by the council.

CAO systems seem to be gaining increasing recognition as the preferred model for providing administrative leadership. In contrast, the search is still on for a comparable model at the political level. Ontario's board of control was rejected because it was regarded as too powerful; many of the nonstatutory executive committees in existence today are seen as too weak — since their members may not work together well and since their recommendations may not be supported by the full council.

---

[62]Hickey, *op. cit.*, p. 197.

[63]*City Magazine*, Vol. 10, No. 2, Winnipeg, 1988, p. 6.

The attempt to create a strong executive committee based on political party support has foundered on the widespread public antipathy to party politics at the local level. The one other obvious change which might have been attempted — the strengthening of the position of mayor in the direction of the "strong mayor" system found in the United States — has not really been pursued in Canada. As a result, our municipalities face the approach of the 21st century without, in most instances, any internal structures which provide political leadership and executive direction. While such leadership is found in a number of municipalities, it is because of the forcefulness and personality of certain individuals and, as a result, is very vulnerable to changes in the make-up of the council.

Over-emphasis on Service Delivery

Another deficiency with the modifications to municipal machinery described in this chapter is the fact that they have been preoccupied with improving the administrative efficiency of municipal government. Not only have they neglected the representative and political role of municipalities, some of the modifications have weakened or undermined that role.

This consequence should not be surprising when it is remembered that both the city manager and board of control systems originated as part of the turn of the century reform era. The manager system was consistent with efforts to take politics out of local government, in this case by turning over the running of the municipality to a professional administrator. The board of control was devised as a way of shifting power to a handful of people elected at large, thereby reducing the influence of ward politicians. More recent modifications to internal machinery have, for the most part, also served to undermine the political role of municipal government — by creating powerful and secretive executive committees (as in Montreal) or by establishing boards of commissioners heading influential and equally secretive bureaucratic regimes (as in Edmonton).

CHAPTER 7

Intergovernmental Relations

OBJECTIVES:

1. To examine the subordinate legal position of municipal governments as provided in Canada's constitution and reinforced by judicial interpretation.

2. To trace the evolution of the relationship between municipalities and the senior levels of government, and the consequences for municipal operations today.

3. To offer suggestions for improving municipal relations with the senior levels of government.

Introduction

The examination of the local government system which has been the focus of much of this text to this point would not be complete without some reference to the senior levels of government with which local governments have become increasingly intertwined. Intergovernmental relations can be examined from a number of perspectives. In this chapter we will concentrate on the following seven areas:

1. The subordinate constitutional position of municipalities.
2. The way this legal subordination to the provincial governments has become even more limited by judicial interpretations over the years.
3. The patterns in the evolution of the municipal-provincial relationship during this century.
4. Disentanglement exercises undertaken by various provinces, and the possibilities and pitfalls of these exercises.
5. The changing nature of the provincial-local financial relationship, including the concept of revenue-sharing.
6. The nature of, and future prospects for, federal-municipal relations, and why they exist in spite of the constitutional arrangements.
7. Mechanisms for municipal consultations with the senior levels.

The Constitutional Relationship

Any discussion of intergovernmental relations usually begins by emphasizing the subordinate constitutional position of municipal governments. The basic point is that municipalities, unlike the provincial and federal levels of government, do not have any guaranteed right to exist under the constitution. From a strict legal viewpoint, therefore, they only exist and take such form as their respective provincial governments see fit to provide.

Amazingly, the last serious attempt to guarantee municipal institutions was also the first; it occurred in 1839, and reflected the recommendations of the Durham Report. The Act of Union proposed that year established municipal institutions in a united Canada. It was broadly criticized and withdrawn, but a similar act was then proposed by the new Governor of Canada, Lord Sydenham, whose view was that:

> The establishment of municipal government, by Act of Parliament, is as much a part of the future scheme of government for Canada as the Union of the two Legislatures, and the more important of the two.[1]

However, the provisions relating to municipal institutions were quite controversial and were omitted when the act was passed. The significance of this omission was emphasized in Chapter 2. Had the Union Act included clauses providing for a system of municipal government, then such clauses might well have been reproduced in the British North America Act which brought Canada into existence. Instead, municipalities are mentioned in the B.N.A. Act (now part of the 1982 Constitution Act) only as one of the areas of jurisdiction given to the provinces. L'Heureux states that "there has never been another attempt to guarantee municipal institutions in the Canadian constitution."[2] While municipal associations have proposed such a guarantee on numerous occasions, notably during the period of formal tri-level relations in the 1970s (discussed later in this chapter), he is correct that such a change has never received serious consideration from the senior levels of government.

Any discussion of constitutional relationships, then, is really about federal-provincial relations. It is only the two senior levels of government

---

[1]Quoted in Jacques L'Heureux, "Municipalities and the Division of Powers," in Richard Simeon (ed.), *Intergovernmental Relations*, Royal Commission on the Economic Union and Development Prospects for Canada, Vol. 63, Toronto, University of Toronto Press, 1985, p. 200.

[2]*Ibid.*

which are given a guaranteed right to exist and a list of assigned powers. Municipal governments enjoy neither of these benefits. Their subordinate constitutional position is fundamental to understanding their relationship with other levels of government and the constraints under which they operate. Yet, important as it is, it is by no means a complete explanation of the position of municipal government in Canada.

There are other considerations, both practical and political, that also affect the relationship. It is noteworthy that the basic structure of municipal government was already in place in some provinces before the provincial governments came into existence. To that extent, provincial governments did not really have a choice of whether or not to establish municipal institutions. Rather, the question was how the provinces would deal with the municipal system that they had inherited, especially as demands on government increased with fundamental changes in the nature of the Canadian economy and society.

In other provinces where there wasn't already a municipal system in existence, the provincial governments were often the main protagonists in the establishment of such a system — to relieve their administrative burden and/or to shift some of the expenditure burden to the local level. As noted in Chapter 2, this was the case, for example, in several of the Western Provinces and in Newfoundland. Indeed, as the demand for services grew, all provincial governments came to regard a network of municipal governments as not just administratively convenient but almost essential. Without such municipal governments, the provincial authorities would face an overwhelming administrative burden. They would also be deluged by a myriad of local grievances and concerns that would compete with broader provincial issues for their attention.

In addition to these practical considerations, of course, there was also a recognition of the political reality that local governments could not be dealt with in too heavy-handed or arbitrary a manner without adverse public reaction. Even in provinces where the populace was at first reluctant to have municipal institutions, once they were in place they developed a legitimacy of their own in the eyes of the local inhabitants, and a resulting security of status which belied their subordinate constitutional position. Dramatic evidence of just how deep rooted this public feeling became over the years is provided by the strong opposition to local government reform efforts in the postwar period which sought to consolidate municipalities or even alter existing boundaries. David Cameron[3] suggests

---

[3]David M. Cameron, "Provincial Responsibilities for Municipal Government," in *Canadian Public Administration*, Summer 1980, p. 234.

that "the political process has bequeathed a de facto security to municipalities" and that they "may be said to occupy a quasi-constitutional position vis-a-vis the provinces."

The Role of the Courts

The lack of constitutional status for municipal governments did not have to result in the very narrow, limited role for municipalities that is found in most provinces today. That sorry state of affairs reflects the way provinces chose to exercise their powers: by passing acts which imposed detailed controls over specific municipal actions, rather than authorizing municipalities to exercise their discretion within a broadly defined area of responsibility.

Perhaps even more so, the limited scope of municipal action reflects the way courts have chosen to interpret statutes which grant powers to municipalities. There are innumerable texts documenting how the Judicial Committee of the British Privy Council (as the Supreme Court for Canada at the time) made a series of decisions which interpreted the British North America Act in such as way as to increase the powers of the provinces much more than Sir John A. Macdonald would ever have intended. It appears much less widely recognized how influential the courts also were in shaping the fate of municipal governments — although in the opposite direction.

The courts have traditionally interpreted very narrowly statutes which grant powers to municipalities. Their position has been that a municipality may exercise only those powers expressly conferred by statute, those powers necessarily or fairly implied by the express power in the statute, and those indispensable powers essential and not merely convenient to the effectuation of the purposes of the corporation.[4] This approach is often described as "Dillon's Rule," in reference to Judge John F. Dillon, a circuit judge and Chief Justice of the Supreme Court of Iowa, and author of *A Treatise on the Law of Municipal Corporations*, first published in 1872. His attitude toward municipal government was one shared by many during the second half of the 19th century. In the fifth edition of his treatise he writes that municipal government "... has been impaired by evils that are either inherent in them or that have generally accompanied their workings." He goes on to justify this view by pointing out that the best

---

[4]Stanley Makuch, *Canadian Municipal and Planning Law*, Toronto, Carswell, 1983, p. 115.

candidates are not always elected (a phenomenon hardly unique to the local level), that those chosen act differently in their public role than they do in private life (implying that public office corrupts), and consequently that the local administration is unwise and extravagant.[5]

Perhaps because many early municipalities were established by charter in a manner similar to the incorporation of private companies (at least in the United States and Britain, the two countries on which his treatise was focused), Dillon and his contemporaries on the bench treated both types of corporation in much the same way. In their view, corporations can only exercise their powers for the accomplishment of limited and defined objects. They saw a clear need "to protect citizens from the excesses of the municipal corporations to which they belong."[6] Their jaundiced view of municipal government reflected the conditions of their time, the municipal inefficiencies and corruption that were to give rise to the turn of the century reform movement, described in Chapter 3.

Why should we care about the views on municipal government of an Iowa judge from a century ago? Because Dillon's views were to influence the Canadian judiciary as well, and "Dillon's Rule" has been frequently cited in support of narrow, literal interpretations of provincial statutes. The result of this approach is that a general grant of power to municipalities, as found in many statutes, has been interpreted in such a way as to render it meaningless. For example, the Ontario Municipal Act contains a general grant of power to municipalities that states that:

> Every council may pass such by-laws and make such regulations for the health, safety, morality and welfare of the inhabitants of the municipality in matters not specifically provided for by this Act as may be deemed expedient and not contrary to the law.

The intention here seems clear enough. The granting of a blanket power is certainly not as wide open as the provisions commonly found in federal and provincial statutes that the Minister, in furtherance of the powers granted by the statute, may make such rules and regulations as are considered "necessary and expedient." Yet, in the leading case on this section, *Morrison v. City of Kingston*, the court stated that very few subjects falling within the ambit of local government are left to the general provisions of the section in question. In addition, the court stated that matters

---

[5]John F. Dillon, *Municipal Corporations*, Boston, Little, Brown & Company, 1911, p. 30, quoted in Susan Nobes Tindal, *Dillon's Rule Over-Ruled*, unpublished paper, April 1990.

[6]*Ibid.*, p. 5.

of "health" are generally dealt with by provincial legislation affecting health and that "morality" is generally dealt with in the federal Criminal Code, so that these areas are beyond the sphere of municipal legislation. The court also held that the power to legislate for the "welfare" of the inhabitants is too vague and general to be defined. It cannot include powers that are otherwise specifically given, nor can it be taken to confer unlimited or unrestrained power.[7] Similarly, the courts have rendered ineffective the provision of the Vancouver Charter that "council may provide for the good rule and government of the city."

It is argued that judicial interpretation, not only of general grants of power such as the two cited above, but also of specific powers given to municipalities, has been overly narrow and confining. Makuch is very critical of the fact that by-laws are not examined in the context of the reason for the legislative provisions purporting to grant the authority to pass them. The problem to be overcome by the legislation granting the power is not considered. He concludes that in a desire to limit the authority of municipalities and thereby protect individuals from abuses of municipal power, the courts have adopted an arbitrary, if not irrational, approach to interpreting municipal powers.[8] We concur, and would add that this narrow approach by the judiciary is particularly inappropriate to the extent that it continues to reflect "Dillon's Rule." Rather than regarding municipalities as analogous to private corporations, as corporate bodies which must be tightly controlled to protect citizens from their excesses, it is suggested that the courts should be more appreciative of municipalities as a level of government with a mandate from the electorate and with a legitimate political role to fulfill.

A striking contrast is provided by the situation in many European countries where municipalities are given a power of "general competence."[9] This is the power to take action on behalf of the community beyond the powers given or the duties laid down in specific statutes. The important thing about this power is that it is *not* added on to a long list of specific duties; rather, it is the starting point in defining the municipality. It reflects the concept of municipal government as the community governing itself. In that respect, the importance of the power of general competence lies less in the activities that it makes possible and more in

---

[7]This summary is based on Makuch, *op. cit.*, p. 116.

[8]*Ibid.*, pp. 118-119.

[9]Michael Clarke and John Stewart, *The Choices for Local Government*, London, Longman, 1991, pp. 16-17.

what it symbolizes about the nature of municipal government. Municipalities need not search for specific powers, because the powers derive from the concept of the municipality as the community governing itself. As a result, the municipality is, or can be, concerned with "any needs or problems faced in the community, and not merely the services it provides directly."[10]

More will be said about this concept of municipal government in the final chapter; for now, it is sufficient to note how dramatically it contrasts with the very narrow, constraining view enforced by judicial interpretations in Canada.

The intergovernmental relations affecting municipalities are the product of much more than constitutional provisions and judicial decisions, however. To a large extent, they result from the varied ways in which all levels of government have responded over the past century to the impact of such forces as economic growth and depression and extensive urbanization.

The Evolution of Provincial-Local Relations

The evolution of provincial-municipal relations in Canada has involved, for the most part, a pattern of increasing provincial supervision, influence and control. In the early years of their existence, municipalities often had considerable operating freedom, especially where their provincial governments were still in their infancy. As Crawford describes the considerable local autonomy enjoyed by Ontario municipalities following the 1849 Baldwin Act:

> Within the scope allowed, and the scope was extensive, the municipalities had gained the right to local self-government with a minimum of parliamentary or executive control, the elected representatives being answerable in matters of policy to their electors and in matters of law to the courts.[11]

Before long, however, provincial governments began to exercise a growing supervisory role. Departments of municipal affairs were established by the turn of the century in a number of the provinces, "to give

---

[10]John Stewart, "A Future for Local Authorities as Community Government," in John Stewart and Gerry Stoker (eds.), *The Future of Local Government*, London, Macmillan, p. 239.

[11]K. G. Crawford, *Canadian Municipal Government*, Toronto, University of Toronto Press, 1954, p. 32.

leadership and guidance in municipal development and to provide for the continuous study of the problems of the municipalities."[12] This need was first evident in the Western provinces, where a rapid development of local government institutions was made necessary by a sudden expansion of population. Manitoba established a Department of Municipal Commissioner as early as 1886, with Saskatchewan following suit in 1908 and Alberta in 1911. British Columbia appointed an Inspector of Municipalities in 1914, but a full department was not created until 1934. Ontario's experience was somewhat similar, with an office of Provincial-Municipal Auditor as early as 1897 and a Bureau of Municipal Affairs from 1917, but no department until 1935. That same year Nova Scotia created a Department of Municipal Affairs and in 1936 New Brunswick established a Department of Education, Federal, and Municipal Relations.

The common factor here, of course, was the Depression of the 1930s and attendant municipal defaulting on financial obligations. In response, provincial governments established or expanded not only municipal departments but also boards with a variety of administrative and quasi-judicial responsibilities relating to local government. A number of these bodies had originally been formed to regulate public utilities and their relations with municipal authorities. As a result of the financial difficulties of the 1930s, many of these bodies were assigned responsibility for controlling municipal financing as well as jurisdiction in other areas such as zoning and assessment. As an example, the Ontario Railway and Municipal Board, created in 1906 primarily to deal with railway matters, was reconstituted as the Ontario Municipal Board in 1932. That same year, the Municipal and Public Utility Board of Manitoba, which had been established in 1926, was given the responsibility for approving debenture issues and the Quebec Municipal Corporation was established.

By the mid-1930s, all but one of the then provinces[13] provided extensive supervision and control over municipalities through a department and, in most cases, a board. In several instances this control was quite sweeping. Nova Scotia provided that every municipal by-law was subject to the Minister of Municipal Affairs, and the Lieutenant-Governor-in-Council in Quebec was empowered to disallow any municipal by-law. All of the provinces except Prince Edward Island required approval of by-laws to incur debt. Other types of by-laws, such as those relating to public

---

[12]*Ibid.*, p. 345. Chapter 17 of Crawford, on which this section is based, provides a good description of the historical evolution of provincial-local relations.

[13]The exception was P.E.I., no doubt because it had few municipalities.

health, traffic, and zoning, were also made subject to approval by the appropriate provincial departments and boards. In many cases, municipalities were authorized to exercise specific powers only subject to review or control by some provincial authority. Provincial control was also gradually extended over personnel and the conditions of employment of municipal staff. This included provincial standards of qualification for appointees and the limitation of the right of councils to dismiss employees without provincial approval. In addition, provision was made for the inspection or investigation of the affairs of a municipality both on a regular basis and as a special inquiry at the request of council or citizens or on the initiative of the province.

The postwar period brought a further increase in provincial supervision and control, largely because of the growing service demands on local government arising from the extensive urbanization of the time. As the revenues from the real property tax became less and less adequate to finance the growing expenditures of municipal government, the provinces increased their financial assistance. Most of this increased assistance, however, was in the form of conditional grants, as described below. By attaching conditions, provinces were attempting to ensure that certain services were provided to at least a minimum standard regardless of the varying financial capacities of their individual municipalities. But as municipalities participated in more and more of these conditional grant and shared cost programs, their local expenditures increasingly reflected provincial priorities.

In some instances, provincial intervention was even more direct, with the provincial government taking over all or partial responsibility for functions traditionally exercised by the local level on the grounds, often quite valid, that the function had outgrown local government — or at least its limited boundaries — and now had much wider implications. This pattern of responsibilities shifting upward to more senior levels occurred with respect to such matters as roads, assessment, the administration of justice, education, public health and social services. A related development in some of the provinces saw the establishment or enlargement of a number of intermunicipal special purpose bodies which were ostensibly part of the local government structure and yet came under increasing provincial influence and control. Here again there was a valid concern on the part of the province about minimum standards in such areas as health and education, but the end result was a further weakening of municipal government in relation to the provincial level. As one analyst saw it:

> The succession of efforts to enlarge local administrative structures in education, public health, welfare, and toward regional municipalities has

simply reduced the number of units confronting the provincial administrator at any one time .... The taxpayer's dollar has been the fulcrum of power for the bureaucrat to use in organizing things, ostensibly for the citizen's benefit but inevitably for the bureaucrat's benefit as well.[14]

By the 1960s then, local governments had been subjected to three decades of developments which undermined their operating independence and brought them increasingly into the orbit of the senior levels of government.

1. As a result of the Depression of the 1930s, municipalities experienced increased provincial surveillance over their financial activities and they lost their historical place in the social services field to the senior governments, increasingly the federal government.

2. During the 1940s, massive centralization occurred because of the war effort. As part of the tax-rental and then tax-sharing agreements brought on by the wartime emergency, municipal governments were squeezed out of such fields as income tax and sales tax, and confined to their historical dependence upon the real property tax as their main source of revenues.

3. By the 1950s, the greatly increased demands of the postwar period resulted in further provincial and federal encroachment on the operations of local government.

Kitchen notes that the areas of health, education and welfare have evolved from predominantly local to predominantly provincial responsibilities, promoted in part by federal government programs.[15] While municipal governments funded the majority of the combined municipal-provincial expenditures on schooling in the first quarter of this century, by 1980 they accounted for only 10% of that total.[16] Indeed, provinces such as New Brunswick and Quebec have assumed total responsibility for education costs — although financed partly by provincial collection of property taxes.

Even where municipalities retained some jurisdiction over traditional functions, they found themselves increasingly entangled with the senior levels of government. Typical of the pattern which had evolved by the

---

[14]Vernon Lang, *The Service State Emerges in Ontario*, Toronto, Ontario Economic Council, 1974, p. 61.

[15]Harry Kitchen, "Local Government and Canadian Federalism," in Simeon, *op. cit.*, p. 224.

[16]*Ibid.*

early postwar years is the situation below, describing developments in New Brunswick:

> In many traditional areas of local competence, provincial supervision, regulation or outright control have been deemed the acceptable solutions.... Their overall effect has incorporated municipal affairs more completely in the broader contexts of provincial and federal public administration. Indeed, local autonomy in all but a few ... areas is extinct.[17]

To a considerable extent, this intertwining of activities is inevitable, and reflects the interdependence of the programs and policies of all three levels of government. As O'Brien points out, the various functions of government are interrelated in ways which would require intergovernmental activity even if they were all parcelled out in separate pieces to one level only — which they aren't and can't be.

> The line between health and welfare is not always easy to find. Welfare and social housing are part of one policy. Housing density depends on transit or the automobile. The latter affects the environment and depends on energy policy. Add the need for planning and financing and there is no escaping the fact that governance in our society requires a lot of communication among governments at various levels.[18]

To combat this extensive overlapping of responsibilities, a number of provinces have recently undertaken studies to reallocate and simplify the distribution of responsibilities between the provincial and municipal levels. As outlined below, however, the concept of "disentanglement" is neither new nor as advantageous for municipalities as its proponents would have us believe.

The Potential and Pitfalls of Disentanglement

When municipal institutions were established, their limited role consisted mainly of providing services to property, financed — quite logically — by a tax on property. The property tax came under increasing criticism as the 20th century advanced not only because it was no longer adequate to

---

[17]H. J. Whalen, *The Development of Local Government in New Brunswick*, Fredericton, 1963, p. 90.

[18]Allan O'Brien, "A Look at the Provincial-Municipal Relationship," in Donald C. MacDonald (ed.), *Government and Politics of Ontario*, Toronto, Van Nostrand Reinhold, 1980, p. 167.

generate all of the revenues required but also because it was seen as no longer appropriate to finance the services to people which were becoming part of municipal operations. Those looking for a rationale for a new distribution of provincial and municipal responsibilities — a disentanglement of the existing pattern of overlapping responsibilities — often seized upon this services to property versus services to people distinction for their purposes. They argued that services to people should be handled by the provincial level. They pointed out that services such as education provided benefits well beyond the boundaries of any one municipality and should be financed appropriately. They also noted that social services involve an income redistributive function tied to broad provincial (even national) standards and objectives, should not be open to local variation and hence was not appropriate for local administration.

As noted in Chapter 5, a number of the local government reform studies of the postwar period attempted to draw such distinctions and to recommend reallocation of responsibilities. Such was the approach, for example, of the Byrne Commission in New Brunswick (1963), the Michener Commission in Manitoba (1964), and the Graham Commission in Nova Scotia (1974). To illustrate, the Graham Commission contended that municipal responsibilities should be divided into two groups: "...local services, which are of primarily local benefit or which might best be provided by municipal government, and general services, which are of more general benefit to the province or which the province might best provide."[19]

As Cameron pointed out, however, there are two shortcomings with this type of analysis.[20] First, it suggests that municipal responsibilities don't extend beyond the provision of services, however defined, and it therefore ignores the representative and political role of municipal government. Second, the specific distinction used is vague and inevitably requires an arbitrary allocation of responsibilities. For example, Cameron finds no evidence to support the Graham Commission's assertion that sidewalks provide a local benefit while education is a general benefit.[21] He suspects that the key distinction is found in the Commission's observation that education is one of the most important and costly services provided, and questions whether municipal government can have any serious role to

[19]Nova Scotia, *Royal Commission on Education, Public Services and Provincial-Municipal Relations, Report*, Halifax, Queen's Printer, 1974, Vol. II, p. 3:22.

[20]Cameron, *op. cit.*, pp. 222-235.

[21]*Ibid.*, p. 226.

play in our governmental system if it is to be responsible only "for that which is unimportant or inexpensive."

Nonetheless, efforts to reallocate and disentangle municipal and provincial responsibilities have been recently undertaken or are currently underway in several provinces, as briefly outlined below.

Quebec undertook a significant realignment of responsibilities and financing in 1980. School board revenues from property taxes were substantially reduced and their revenues from provincial transfers were increased. To offset its increased costs for education, the province also significantly reduced its transfer payments to municipalities, thereby increasing municipal reliance on the property tax.[22] As a result, the share of school board expenditures financed by provincial transfers increased from 60 to 93% between 1969 and 1989. Even more dramatic, with these changes Quebec municipalities were meeting 96% of the cost of local services through their own fees, charges and local taxes[23] — a degree of fiscal autonomy not approached in any other province.

Two further changes were introduced at the beginning of the 1990s, prompted by the provincial government's concern about its growing expenditure burden and its perception that the revenue-raising potential of the property tax had not yet been fully tapped.[24] In 1990 the province transferred to Quebec school boards the expense of maintaining school facilities while authorizing the boards to levy a property tax (which is to be collected by municipalities) covering up to 10% of their expenditures.[25] The result has been to reduce the share of provincial financing of school board operations to about 88%.[26] The following year the Quebec government introduced changes which will shift to municipalities greater responsibility and financing obligations for public transit, roads and policing. Thus both of these changes can be seen, at least in part, as an attempt by

---

[22]F. Vaillancourt, "Financing Local Governments in Quebec: New Arrangements for the 1990s," in *Canadian Tax Journal*, 1992, Vol. 40, No. 5, pp. 1123-1139.

[23]Canadian Urban Institute, *Disentangling Local Government Responsibilities — International Comparisons*, Toronto, January 1993, p. 27.

[24]This view is frankly expressed by Claude Ryan, Minister of Municipal Affairs, in a December 14, 1990 statement, *The Sharing of Responsibilities Between The Government and Municipalities: Some Needed Adjustments*.

[25]*Ibid.*

[26]Vaillancourt, *op. cit.*, p. 1137.

the province to shift back to the property tax the burden for financing some of the expenditures which had been assumed by the 1980 reforms. Nonetheless, municipalities in Quebec are in an enviable position compared to those in other provinces in the extent to which they are able to finance their expenditures out of their own revenue sources.

While education provided the initial stimulus for changes in Quebec, in *Ontario* it was social services which launched what became a wide-ranging disentanglement process.[27] The *Report of the Provincial-Municipal Social Services Review* (PMSSR) recommended in 1990 that Ontario follow the lead of most other provinces and take complete responsibility for the cost of social assistance. The province agreed in principle but was not prepared to absorb the approximately $800 million in extra costs that this would entail.

The way out of this dilemma was to put more items on the table, and the *Report of the Advisory Committee to the Minister of Municipal Affairs on the Provincial-Municipal Financial Relationship* (with a title that long, it soon became known as the Hopcroft Report after its chairman) provided this broader approach.[28] Established in April 1989 and reporting in January 1991, the Hopcroft Report recommended that the entire division of powers between the provincial and municipal governments and the accompanying financial arrangements be reconsidered. It further recommended that:

1. Functions should be assigned clearly and unambiguously to one level to the extent possible.
2. The financial relationship should be simplified so that the province would continue to provide conditional grants to municipalities only in areas where there is a legitimate provincial interest.

Once again the province accepted the recommendations in principle, while worrying about the financial implications of some of the shifts in responsibility being advocated — especially since the Hopcroft Report calculated[29] that the changes it was recommending would decrease municipal operating expenditures by about $709 million and capital expen-

---

[27]The summary which follows is based on David Siegel, "Disentangling Provincial-Municipal Relations in Ontario," in *Management,* Toronto, Institute of Public Administration, Fall 1992.

[28]*Ibid.,* p. 29.

[29]*Report of the Advisory Committee to the Minister of Municipal Affairs, on the Provincial-Municipal Relationship,* Toronto, January 1991, p. 42.

ditures by about $18 million. The response of the newly elected NDP government was to invite the Association of Municipalities of Ontario to appoint municipal representatives to a working group including an equal number of provincial cabinet ministers to look at the possibility of reallocating provincial and municipal responsibilities. The stated objectives were to create better, simpler government; improve the efficiency and effectiveness of service to the public; clarify which level of government is responsible for what services; and improve financial accountability and fiscal management.[30] A key guiding principle was that the exercise had to be "fiscally neutral," leaving neither level of government better or worse off financially as a result of any reallocation of responsibilities. Thus began Ontario's disentanglement process.

From the outset, the province expressed a willingness to take over the municipal share of the cost of general welfare assistance. To maintain the concept of fiscal neutrality, this meant that municipalities would have to assume additional costs in other areas. A draft agreement reached in January 1993 called for the municipal level to assume responsibility for certain provincial highways serving primarily local traffic and for municipalities to pay for the property assessment services provided by the province. There would also be a reduction in provincial unconditional grants, with the effect of all three of these adjustments supposedly offsetting the cost burden associated with the shift of welfare to the provincial level.

In the months that followed a number of concerns were expressed about the draft agreement. Many on the municipal side felt that the province was assuming welfare costs which were inflated because of the prolonged recession and which would gradually decline, whereas the offsetting road costs being shifted to municipalities would remain high or would increase. Underlying the concern was an apparent lack of trust in the motives of the province — understandable given the "downloading" of responsibilities and costs which had been taking place in recent years.[31] Small and rural municipalities were especially troubled by the proposed changes since roads are their primary function. Overshadowing all of these specific concerns, however, was a growing controversy about the

---

[30]Ian Connerty, "Disentanglement: Changing the Provincial-Municipal Balance," in *Municipal Monitor*, Association of Municipal Clerks and Treasurers of Ontario, Richmond Hill, Kenilworth Publishing, October 1992, p. 182.

[31]See *Municipal World*, St. Thomas, July 1990 for a list of examples cited by the Association of Municipalities of Ontario at a 1990 conference; see also Nasreine Canaran, "Facts about Provincial Funding," in *Municipal World*, October 1989.

province's quaintly-termed "social contract" initiative. A central thrust of this initiative was to help reduce the provincial deficit by imposing very significant cuts in transfer payments to the local level. The arbitrary nature of these cuts, announced as they were after municipalities had already set their budgets and were more than one-third of the way through their fiscal year, prompted a very negative reaction from the municipal sector and led the Association of Municipalities of Ontario to reject the draft disentanglement agreement. For the moment, disentanglement is dead in Ontario, as is any kind of trusting relationship between the municipal and provincial levels — without which the revival of discussions is very unlikely.

The disentanglement process in *Nova Scotia* arose out of a provincial government initiative which was originally focused on reducing, in the name of efficiency, the number of municipalities in the province. The *Task Force on Local Government* reported in April 1992 and called for a major restructuring of municipal government in the five most urbanized areas of the province, as discussed in Chapter 5. In addition, The Task Force called for a revenue-neutral reallocation of responsibilities — reflecting the prior position of the Union of Nova Scotia Municipalities, which was represented on the Task Force. More specifically, the Task Force proposed that rural municipalities would have to start providing their own policing and roads (as urban municipalities had been doing) and that the province would take over the municipal share of the administration and financing of general welfare assistance.[32] In one of several interesting parallels with the Ontario experience, these disentanglement proposals caused greater concern among rural municipalities than urban. The urban municipalities have larger social assistance obligations (which the province would assume) and were already paying their own way with regards to policing and roads.

In December 1993 the Nova Scotia government released *Provincial-Municipal Service Exchange: A Discussion Paper,* with proposals which were said to be based on consultations with municipal governments and especially the Union of Nova Scotia Municipalities. The principle underlying the proposed reallocation of service responsibilities[33] was that municipal units should be providing local services, that is services of primary

---

[32]Allan O'Brien, *Municipal Consolidation in Canada and its Alternatives,* Toronto, ICURR Press, May 1993, p. 18.

[33]Department of Municipal Affairs, *Provincial-Municipal Service Exchange: A Discussion Paper,* p. 5.

concern to a community rather than to the entire province, and the provincial government should be responsible for the provision of services in which the entire province is concerned. The Discussion Paper proposed that the province assume complete responsibility from municipalities with respect to social assistance, that it assume all costs of the administration of justice, and that the responsibilities of municipal boards of health be transferred to the province. In return, municipalities would be given responsibility for defined local roads and local police services (but not highway patrol). Most shared-cost programs are to be ended, although not with respect to capital expenditures. The cost of the property assessment function carried out by the province is to be shared equally by the municipal level.

The Discussion Paper had set out a fairly ambitious schedule which called for implementation of the proposed changes by April 1995. However, there has been some recent indication that the government may be backing off, partly because the shifts to the province — notably of social assistance — are seen as too expensive to absorb.

From this admittedly brief overview of a complex process, several observations can be made. First, disentanglement has been studied far more than it has been actually carried out. While a reallocation of functions has been recommended over the past three decades in Manitoba, New Brunswick, Nova Scotia, Quebec and Ontario, only Quebec and New Brunswick introduced changes.

Second, the changes which are introduced can vary considerably — both in their scope and in their impact on municipal operations. This is evident from a comparison of the New Brunswick and Quebec experiences. Following the recommendations of the Byrne Commission, the New Brunswick government launched a Program for Equal Opportunity in 1967 which saw the province take over responsibility for the administration of justice, welfare and public health, and also financial responsibility for the provision of education. Property assessment and municipal tax collection also became provincial responsibilities. As discussed in Chapter 5, the extent of the provincial takeover, coupled with the abolition of municipal government in rural areas, caused some observers to worry about the continuance of municipal government in New Brunswick. On the other hand, the shift in Quebec was much more limited, being mainly related to education, but it did result in a dramatic improvement in the fiscal autonomy of municipalities. Most of the disentanglement exercises have attempted to distinguish between local services and those of a more general nature, and have usually called for provincial assumption of the municipal responsibility for social assistance in exchange for greater municipal responsibility for roads, property assessment and policing. Adjustments in provincial grants have also usually been part of the package, ostensibly to provide adjustments needed to maintain the goal of fiscal neutrality. While there is insufficient information on which to make a firm judgment, there is a widespread municipal perception that underlying the recent rounds of disentanglement has been a provincial objective of downloading responsibilities and costs.

This last observation leads into the third, and most important, observation about the concept of disentanglement, that is, its overall impact on the continued functioning of a healthy municipal government system. While a recent survey of disentanglement experiences concluded that the exercise was valid, even essential, in the Ontario context, it also found that disentanglement is not a concept widely used in other jurisdictions where the degree of centralization or decentralization of authority and the scope of municipal responsibility were viewed as more important concepts.[34] Yet, as Sancton has pointed out, disentanglement inevitably means a narrower range of municipal functions.[35] He is critical of disentanglement's underlying rationale that municipal governments should concentrate on those responsibilities which are inherently local, echoing Cameron's concerns, already noted above. Sancton describes the faulty assumption made by municipal advocates of disentanglement as follows:

> To base municipal government's existence on a mission to concern itself with inherently local issues is to insure its quick death. Does anyone really believe that there *any* issues which are still inherently local?[36]

He points out that there are provincial rules and regulations in place for almost any municipal function one can cite, and notes as examples sewers and garbage disposal — which were once thought of as local matters. Indeed, Sancton has demonstrated elsewhere[37] that even metropolitan and regional governments have not been able to handle functions such as public transit, water supply and garbage disposal, which have increasingly come under provincial jurisdiction. To illustrate, consider these two developments relating to garbage disposal in the Toronto area: (1) the pro-

---

[34]Canadian Urban Institute, *op. cit.*, pp. 81 and 85.

[35]Andrew Sancton, "Provincial-Municipal Disentanglement in Ontario: A Dissent," in *Municipal World*, July 1992, p. 23.

[36]*Ibid.*

[37]Andrew Sancton, "Canada as a Highly Urbanized Nation," in *Canadian Public Administration*, Fall 1992, pp. 281-316.

vincial establishment of an Interim Waste Authority whose mandate is to seek out and operate new landfill sites within the Greater Toronto Area; and (2) the provincial rejection of an agreement between Metro Toronto and the city of Kirkland Lake which provided for Metro shipping garbage to an abandoned gold mine.[38]

It is contended that a major weakness of the disentanglement concept is that, once again, there is an overpreoccupation with the service delivery role of municipal government and a relative neglect of its representative and political role. Granted, the disentanglement proponents argue that the exercise will result in a greatly simplified structure and one more easily held accountable. Yet almost all of the discussions and the changes proposed or introduced relate to which services are to be provided by which level of government. As Sancton has observed, the process has given too much emphasis to "political and administrative tidiness."[39]

We concur with Sancton that municipal government is not just about using local resources to provide local services. As indicated at the beginning of this text, the other primary purpose of municipal government, and the one that should be paramount, is to act as a political mechanism through which a local community can express its collective objectives. If that is the case, then it is essential that municipalities be involved in as many activities as possible that are of interest and concern to the local community. This means expanding, not reducing, their sphere of influence. It means becoming (or staying) involved in functional areas in which the municipalities cannot expect to be autonomous. As Sancton wryly observes: "If municipal politicians are not interested in *all* government policies that affect their community, they can hardly complain if many in the community are not interested in municipal government."[40]

There is yet another problem with the service delivery focus of disentanglement. It accepts and even reinforces the notion that municipalities exist to provide services. This, in turn, directs attention to the adequacy of existing municipal boundaries for providing those services which are to remain at the local level. This can lead to suggestions for enlarged municipal jurisdictions which are farther removed from local participation and yet given fewer responsibilities to exercise — a scenario that might be considered "the worst of both worlds." In this connection, the pre-

[38]*Ibid.*, pp. 295-296.

[39]Sancton, *Disentanglement Dissent*, p. 24.

[40]*Ibid.*

viously cited analysis which endorsed disentanglement for Ontario also concluded that for the changes to be effective municipalities would have to cover the territory of urban regions — so that local or regional issues that may now spill over municipal boundaries can be internalized.[41]

A way out of this difficulty is provided if we stop accepting the view that municipal governments must *provide* whatever services are left to the local level. What has been termed "this assumption of self-sufficiency"[42] is deep-rooted in British local government and has been taken to mean that when local authority has been given for a responsibility the municipal government must have sufficient staff and resources to look after this responsibility on its own. The result of this line of thinking has been the creation of progressively larger units of municipal government in Britain. Municipalities have been defined in relation to administrative require- ments, not political requirements. But what if one accepts the concept, introduced in Chapter 1, of municipalities being defined by the communi- ties they serve, not the services they provide?[43] Such municipalities are likely to be much smaller and will not have the capacity to provide, to- tally, many of the services required by their inhabitants. Instead, they obtain such services through a wide range of agreements — with other municipalities, with various local boards, even with public-private partner- ship arrangements. Such municipalities recognize that their role is to give expression to the collective concerns and desires of the community. This role includes identifying those services which the community wants to have, but it doesn't necessarily mean providing those services. Obviously, this concept of municipal government, about which more will be said in the final chapter, is at odds with the tidy, self-contained structure implicit in the concept of distentanglement.

Disentangling Finances: The Buck Stops Here

One area in which more disentanglement is likely to occur is provincial- municipal finances. As discussed below, this change will be driven by the increasingly severe financial and deficit problems affecting the senior

---

[41]Canadian Urban Institute, *op. cit.*, p. 82.

[42]Clarke and Stewart, *op. cit.* p. 17.

[43]In addition to the Clarke and Stewart reference already cited, see John Stewart and Gerry Stoker, *The Future of Local Government*, London, Macmillan Education Ltd., 1989, especially Chapter 12.

levels of government. The federal level has no choice but to continue reducing its transfer payments to provinces; they, in turn, will reduce the transfer payments to the local level. Municipalities have nowhere to "pass the buck" and are also required to balance their current budgets every year. The net result will be that the municipal level will find itself funding an increasing proportion of its expenditures out of its own revenue sources. While the adjustment will be painful, it will mean municipalities with greater financial independence. Before examining this trend, however, some background on the provincial-municipal financial relationship is in order, partly based on the discussion in Chapter 4.

The fundamental problem facing local government finances has been that the revenue sources under the control of the municipalities have been increasingly inadequate in meeting their greatly expanded expenditures, largely caused by the extensive urbanization of the postwar period. The provincial and federal governments have also faced greatly increased expenditures but they have been able to impose a variety of new taxes to finance their needs. While the federal government has unlimited taxing powers under the constitution and the provincial governments can levy any form of direct tax, municipalities are restricted to those tax sources which their provincial governments have seen fit to delegate to them. A number of different taxes have been available to municipalities over the years, but most of these have since disappeared or been reclaimed by the senior levels of government as part of the centralization of finances referred to above. The mainstay of municipal revenues has always been the tax on real property, supplemented in some provinces by an additional tax on business at a rate on a stipulated percentage of the assessed value of the property.[44]

While the property tax was still providing over 80% of municipal revenues in 1930, that proportion had fallen below 50% by the beginning of the 1960s.[45] In its place, grants from the senior levels of government became increasingly prominent, accounting for over 40% of the gross general revenues of Canadian local governments by the beginning of the 1970s. As discussed in Chapter 4,[46] the overwhelmingly conditional nature

---

[44]For a detailed outline of municipal revenues see *Provincial and Municipal Finances*, a biennial publication of the Canadian Tax Foundation, Toronto.

[45]Economic Council of Canada, *Fourth Annual Review*, Ottawa, September 1967, p. 219.

[46]Municipal Submission to the first National Tri-Level Conference, *Policies, Programs and Finance*, Ottawa, 1972, p. 20.

of these grants threatened to reduce municipal governments to "hollow receptacles into which the values of the federal and provincial government are poured." A major Ontario study in the mid-1970s identified the following problems with grants:

1. Too many grants.
2. Confusion and uncertainty among recipients.
3. Excessive administrative requirements.
4. Too much entanglement of jurisdiction.
5. Too many special purpose bodies.
6. Obsolete grants.
7. An inconsistent variety of equalization programs.[47]

One change which appeared to offer the possibility of overcoming at least some of the above-noted difficulties was provincial-municipal revenue-sharing, introduced in a number of the provinces in the 1970s. However, some of the early promise of this concept has not been realized, especially with cutbacks in federal and provincial transfers as both of the senior levels of government grapple with their growing deficits and debt load.

Revenue-Sharing Arrangements

Ontario was the first province to introduce revenue-sharing, but also the first to abandon it. Known as the "Edmonton Commitment" because it was first announced at the national tri-level conference in Edmonton in October 1973, the revenue-sharing policy was officially introduced in the 1974 Ontario Budget. The Ontario government pledged that it would increase its transfers to local governments and agencies at the rate of growth of total provincial revenues. This appeared to guarantee the municipalities at least a minimum level of provincial financial support while introducing a greater degree of certainty and stability.

Unfortunately, the implementation of this revenue-sharing scheme was plagued by problems of interpretation and growing controversy. The final straw from the municipal viewpoint was a provincial redefinition of the Edmonton Commitment to include certain existing assistance programs of direct financial benefit to local government such as the Teachers' Superannuation Fund, payments in lieu of taxes and farm tax rebates. Whether or not this redefinition was valid, municipalities resented the

---

[47]From the *Report of the Provincial-Municipal Grant Reform Committee*, Toronto, Queen's Printer, 1977, as summarized in Canadian Urban Institute, *op. cit.*, p. 14.

fact that it was imposed without consultation and they saw it as an attempt to reduce the province's financial support for local government. The Municipal World editorialized that the Edmonton Commitment had been brutalized, depleted and changed almost beyond recognition before being laid to rest.[48]

In the ensuing years a variety of new financial arrangements were suggested, but none were agreed upon. Provincial transfers reverted to an ad hoc basis. Municipal governments were back in the familiar position of having to wait each year for provincial announcements before they knew what their financial position would be. In early 1989 the Ontario government introduced a freeze on both the Municipal Unconditional Grants Program and the Municipal Roads Subsidy Program. The result was an emergency session of the Association of Municipalities of Ontario at which concern was expressed about not only the reduction in financial support but also the province's activities in shifting a number of responsibilities and expenditure burdens to the local level.

All of this was but a warmup, however, for what was to follow. In April 1993 the government announced its Expenditure Control Plan and Social Contract initiatives to reduce the growing provincial deficit. These reductions initially included an approximately $450 million cut in transfers to municipalities. As indicated earlier, such provincial action in the middle of a disentanglement process that was supposed to be "fiscally neutral" caused angry municipal representatives to abandon that process. Far from the certainty and stability of a revenue-sharing agreement, Ontario municipalities now face a completely unpredictable situation in which a deficit-obsessed provincial government is quite prepared to take any steps — including the violation of existing municipal collective agreements — to achieve its own financial objectives.

Manitoba enacted a Provincial-Municipal Tax Sharing Act in 1976 which provides municipalities with specified portions of the yield from personal income taxes and corporation taxes. At present the Act assigns 2 percentage points of personal income tax and 1 percentage point of corporation tax to local governments in the form of per capita payments which vary with the size and type of municipality. The Manitoba government also introduced a new unconditional grant, the Local Government General Support Grant.

British Columbia has had a Revenue Sharing Act since 1977, providing both conditional and (mostly) unconditional grants based on 1 percentage point of personal income tax, 1 percentage point of corporation tax and

---

[48]*Municipal World*, St. Thomas, October 1977, p. 255.

6 percentage points of revenue from other revenue sources.[49] The amount of assistance for each municipality is based on population, total expenditure and relative assessment deficiency. In addition, in the Greater Vancouver Regional District and elsewhere, provincially defined levies on commercial properties are used to support public transit.[50]

Provincial restraint measures have also had an impact in British Columbia, with municipalities expressing concern about the resulting decline in the level of financial support for the local level. According to one study, while revenue-sharing grants made up 19% of local government budgets in 1981, this figure had declined to 12% in 1982 and 10% in 1986.[51]

Saskatchewan began a revenue sharing program in 1978. In the first year a base amount was determined which was equivalent to the amount of certain conditional grants which were being eliminated. All revenue-sharing transfers to urban municipalities are now unconditional. They are composed of foundation, basic and equalization grants. As in most provinces, revenue sharing has been reduced in recent years. In 1992 transfers represented 8% of urban revenues, down from almost 11% in 1988.[52] Revenue-sharing to rural municipalities is approximately one-third unconditional (equalization payments) and two-thirds conditional. The latter payments are mainly targeted to road and bridge construction and maintenance. These transfers accounted for 22.1% of rural revenues in 1992, down from 27.4% in 1988.[53]

The financial arrangements in *Quebec* have been outlined previously, in the section on disentanglement. Changes introduced in the Municipal Finance Act of 1979, which came into effect January 1, 1980, greatly simplified the financial relationship. The number of conditional grants was reduced from 45 to seven and the previous revenue-sharing arrangement was abolished.[54] The province took over 94% of the financial responsibil-

---

[49]Canadian Urban Institute, *op. cit.*, p. 20.

[50]*Ibid.*

[51]Ministry of Municipal Affairs, Recreation and Culture and the Union of B.C. Municipalities, *Financing Local Government*, September 1988, p. 28.

[52]Figures provided by Patrick Hall, Information Officer, Saskatchewan Municipal Government in correspondence dated August 5, 1993.

[53]*Ibid.*

[54]Canadian Urban Institute, *op. cit.*, p. 26.

ity for elementary and secondary schools (since reduced to 88% with the transfer of some costs back to the property tax). With this major change, municipalities found that they could finance 96% of the cost of local services through their own revenue sources.[55]

Nova Scotia introduced a new unconditional grant program in 1980, as a result of the deliberations of a Joint Union of Nova Scotia Municipalities-Department of Municipal Affairs Task Force. It was calculated by taking as a base the payments which were made under certain previous grant formulas and increasing this figure by the percentage increase in gross provincial revenues.[56] The basic operating grant is escalated annually to reflect growth in provincial revenues. It includes an allocation formula that takes into account municipal expenditure needs by size and type of municipality, as well as each unit's ability to pay.[57]

As part of local government reform initiatives underway in Nova Scotia, the government has called for the end of a number of conditional grants in areas such as public transit, building inspection, and recreation and culture. It suggests that elimination of these shared cost programs will remove a source of near-perpetual friction between the province and the municipal units and will minimize the time and effort now being put into "grantsmanship."[58] A new revenue-sharing scheme is proposed as well, but rather different in nature than the kind we have been discussing in this section. The government proposes that all municipalities contribute a uniform levy on their commercial assessment to a revenue-sharing fund that would then be distributed among the municipal units according to their needs.

New Brunswick made a number of changes to strengthen the financial position of its municipalities, particularly as a result of the Equal Opportunity Program introduced in 1967 following the Byrne Commission. Municipal expenditure pressures were relieved by the transfer of a number of responsibilities to the provincial level — a mixed blessing as discussed in Chapter 5. In addition, a new unconditional grant program was intro-

---

[55]*Ibid.*, p. 27.

[56]David Siegel, "Provincial-Municipal Relations in Canada: An Overview," in *Canadian Public Administration*, Summer 1980, p. 309.

[57]Canadian Tax Foundation, *Provincial and Municipal Finances 1991*, Toronto, 1992, p. 13:14.

[58]Government of Nova Scotia, *Task Force on Local Government*, April 1992, p. 16.

duced, its grant formula largely derived from a Task Force Report on Municipal Structure and Financing (the Allen Report). The amount of the grant was calculated as a percentage of municipal expenditure (net of non-tax revenue), with grant increases annually in line with the growth of net provincial revenues.[59]

While New Brunswick was the only province during the 1970s in which unconditional grants were a more significant revenue source for municipalities than conditional grants, the proportion of conditional grants began to increase by the end of the decade.[60] In 1983 the province announced that it was freezing the 1984 unconditional grant at the 1983 level as part of a series of restraint measures.[61] Growing municipal concern about the grant prompted a provincial review which reported in 1986. A new unconditional grant formula was introduced the following year, and was supposed to increase at the rate of 4% per year. However, the province announced a freeze for 1989, prompting municipal demands for a royal commission. According to the municipalities, unconditional grants as a percentage of gross budgets in New Brunswick cities have declined from 49.8% in 1974 to 34.9% in 1988.[62] Currently, the Municipal Assistance Act provides for an unconditional grant to municipalities and specifies the formula to be used for its distribution.[63]

Summary: Revenue-Sharing Arrangements

Even this brief outline provides a number of insights into revenue-sharing and the provincial-municipal financial relationship generally. At the outset, one is struck by the potential complexity of the concept of revenue sharing. Among the variables are the way in which transfers are indexed or increased annually, the base to which such an index is applied, the way in which the transfers are distributed to municipalities, and the method of determining which municipalities are most in need of such transfers.

---

[59]Siegel, *op. cit.* p. 310.

[60]*Ibid.*, p. 303.

[61]Department of Municipal Affairs and Environment, *Review of New Brunswick's Unconditional Grant to Municipalities*, February 1986, p. 41.

[62]Brief to the Policy and Priorities Committee of the Government of New Brunswick, *Re The Unconditional Grant to Municipalities and Related Matters*, Provincial-Municipal Council, Inc., October 11, 1988, p. 3-3.

[63]Canadian Tax Foundation, *op. cit.*, p. 13:15.

While the concept of revenue-sharing is welcome, its significance should not be exaggerated. The basic financial problem of municipal governments remains — their expenditures far exceed the revenue sources directly available to them. Accordingly, they must obtain a major portion of their funding in the form of financial assistance from the provincial level. While the basis of this funding and its continuance *can be* made more clear and secure in a number of provinces with revenue-sharing arrangements, the fact remains that the bulk of the transfer payments are still conditional.

Recent transfer payment freezes and reductions have done nothing to alter Richmond's critical assessment of the provincial-municipal financial relationship and the changes which have been made to it. He compares the approach used quite unfavourably with that of the provincial and federal levels in resolving their problems of fiscal imbalance.[64] Generally, Richmond finds that greater centralization and control by the provinces over local governments has been the result and notes that:

> In contrast to the federal-provincial response, the provincial-municipal mechanism for dealing with financial dilemmas was generally characterized by unilaterally determined transfer mechanisms, a proliferation of conditional grants, an irrational equalization system and a large number of special purpose bodies.[65]

He also points to the harmful effects of the financial restraint experienced by provincial governments and observes that some provinces such as Ontario and British Columbia have frozen their contribution to shared cost programs and "left the municipal sector out on a limb when attempting to budget for an ongoing responsibility."[66] Two examples involving Ontario illustrate the difficulty.[67] In 1971 the provincial government increased its support for the capital costs of public transit systems from 25% to 75% and, in addition, agreed to pay 50% of the operating deficit of transit systems — changes which prompted some municipalities to expand their transit facilities. But in 1975 the province imposed a ceiling on the amount it would contribute to operating deficits and the following year it limited its contribution to a 5% increase from the previous year,

---

[64]Dale Richmond, "Provincial-Municipal Transfer Systems," in *Canadian Public Administration*, Summer 1980, pp. 252-255.

[65]*Ibid.*, p. 253.

[66]*Ibid.*, pp. 258-259.

[67]Kitchen, *op. cit.*, pp. 384-385.

at a time when operating costs were increasing much more rapidly. Similarly, municipalities greatly expanded their day care facilities when the province funded 80% of the costs. Here again, 1976 saw the province limit funds for this service to a 5.5% increase, with municipalities locked into more rapidly expanding expenditures over which they had little control.

Siegel explains how this uncertainty surrounding conditional grants can leave municipalities very vulnerable to shifts in provincial policy.[68] Because of initial provincial interest in some program, the municipality is encouraged to develop extensive delivery systems on which local citizens come to rely. Then the provincial government's priorities change, and it shifts its financial support elsewhere. The municipality cannot shift its operations so easily; it has a delivery system in place and a clientele that has come to depend on the service or program in question. The result is that the municipality feels compelled to continue providing the service, but without the provincial funding which first tempted it into this area of activity.

Reference has already been made to declining provincial financial support in recent years in provinces such as British Columbia, Ontario and New Brunswick. Significant improvements in provincial support are unlikely since provinces will continue to have their own difficulties in maintaining what they regard as adequate levels of financial support from the federal level. Given these circumstances, even in those provinces where municipalities are part of a revenue-sharing agreement, there can be very little assurance about ongoing financial assistance. What can be predicted with some certainty is that the level of provincial transfers will continue to decline and an increasingly heavy expenditure load will be left to be financed out of municipal revenue sources. It is also likely that the "pain" of this adjustment will be softened in many instances by shifting the remaining transfers to more of an unconditional basis — thereby giving municipalities greater financial autonomy.

In that respect, recent developments in *Alberta* may represent a vision of the future. If so, that vision is very much a "good news, bad news" story. On the positive side, the Alberta government has just passed a new Municipal Act which apparently provides much greater scope for municipalities to pass by-laws within broad "spheres of jurisdiction," instead of following the traditional approach of itemizing the specific matters on

---

[68]David Siegel, "The Financial Context for Urban Policy," in Richard Loreto and Trevor Price (eds.), *Urban Policy Issues: Canadian Perspectives*, Toronto, McClelland & Stewart Inc., 1990, p. 27

which municipalities can take action. We will have more to say about this new approach in the final chapter. Also positive is the shift to unconditional financing. The Municipal Assistance Grant is being terminated and funds transferred to a new Unconditional Grants Program. Funds from four other conditional grant programs (relating to urban parks, public transit, policing and family and community support services) are also being transferred into the new unconditional program.[69] Now for the bad news! The budget for this new unconditional program will shrink from $169 million in 1994/95 to $126 million the next year and to $88 million in 1996/97.[70] The government anticipates that the dissolution or restructuring of municipalities with a weak financial base will likely occur.[71] Given these announced changes, the Alberta municipal system faces a future with increased legislative and financial autonomy, but also a future which may require some amalgamations of smaller municipal units and will require the municipal level to finance a much larger proportion of municipal expenditures itself.

The Potential of Municipal Revenue Sources

The "new financial reality" facing municipal governments will mean increased funding from the two local sources of revenue: (1) the real property tax, and (2) the catch-all category of miscellaneous local revenues.

The property tax — the tax we all love to hate — has been the subject of increasing criticism over the years, much of it unfair or misplaced. Indeed, complaints that it is a slow growth tax, which does not respond to changes in the general level of economic activity, and that it is inequitable because of varying degrees of underassessment between and within municipalities, are really criticisms of the underlying system of property assessment.

While progress has been slow in some instances, the desire for an improved system of assessment was a factor in the provincial assumption of responsibility for this function in a number of the provinces. Assessment remains a completely local responsibility only in Alberta and Quebec.[72] It is all or primarily a provincial responsibility in the remaining

---

[69]Alberta Municipal Affairs, *News Release*, February 24, 1994.

[70]Alberta Municipal Affairs, *Business Plan 1994-95 to 1996-97*, p. 7.

[71]*Ibid.*, p. 13.

[72]Based on information in *Provincial and Municipal Finances 1991, op. cit.*.

provinces and is a territorial responsibility in the case of the Northern Territories. Although all provinces ostensibly assess property at its "actual," "real," "fair" or "market" value, differences in the frequency of assessment, valuation methods, and definitions of value lead to wide variations in the assessed value of comparable properties.[73] Particularly striking is the unsatisfactory situation in Ontario. Twenty-five years after the province took over responsibility for the assessment function, for the purpose of introducing full market value assessment, and almost twenty years since the province abandoned that commitment and left such a decision to individual municipalities, more than one-third of the population of Ontario lives in the 13% of municipalities that have not been reassessed at all, and still have assessment systems and values dating from the 1940s. A further 10% of the population lives in municipalities in which the assessment base is more than 15 years old. Only 6% of Ontarians live in municipalities in which all properties have been reassessed on the same market value basis.[74] If Ontario municipalities are going to have to rely increasingly on the property tax, then the base for that tax — the assessment value of real property — must be placed on a more equitable and consistent foundation.

Changes are also needed with respect to lands exempt from taxation. Many of these exemptions are mandatory under provincial legislation; others are provided to particular properties by individual municipalities acting under permissive legislation. A major category of tax-exempt property is that owned by federal, provincial or municipal governments.[75] Such lands can represent a significant amount of the property assessment within an individual municipality and yet the payments-in-lieu of taxes provided by the senior levels of government are claimed by the municipal level to yield far less than would have been available had these lands been subject to regular taxation. For example, the city of Kingston — which has the largest proportion of tax-exempt property of any Ontario

---

[73]*Ibid.*, p. 12:3.

[74]Figures from Fair Tax Commission, *News Release*, December 16, 1993. See also Fair Tax Commission, *Report of the Property Tax Working Group*, December 1992.

[75]This statement must be qualified in the case of Prince Edward Island and New Brunswick, where property tax is imposed on provincial and municipal properties. These are also the only two provinces which impose province-wide property taxes at the provincial level. See Provincial and Municipal Finances 1991, *op. cit.*, pp. 12:2-12:3.

municipality — has calculated that it will lose $5.1 million in 1994 on the provincial payments-in-lieu for schools and hospitals.

While provincial payments-in-lieu are not always at the level which municipalities find acceptable, at least the provinces normally make their payments. In contrast, the Municipal Grants Act which governs federal PILs stated that no right to a payment is conferred by the Act but that Public Works Canada may make payments in lieu on federal real property. Moreover, the federal level reserves the right to make its own determination of the value of its properties, regardless of what assessment may have been placed on such properties by provincial assessors.[76]

The uncertainty and arbitrary action that can result is illustrated by Kingston again, which was informed in May of 1994 (after its budget had been set) that the federal government was cutting its PIL by $1.6 million, after deci-ding that its properties in Kingston were not as valuable as provincial assessors had estimated. Led by Treasurer, Rick Fiebig, the city fought back with detailed facts and figures of its own and succeeded in getting the federal cutback reduced by two-thirds.[77] However, this will not be the last battle that municipalities will have to fight with the federal level to retain the level of payments in lieu to which they feel entitled.

If municipalities are to be expected to finance a growing portion of their expenditures from the real property tax, it seems more than reasonable to require that the federal and provincial levels commit to the provision of payments-in-lieu on tax-exempt lands which are both fair and immune to arbitrary reinterpretation.

However the property tax may be reformed, there are obviously limits on how much additional revenue can be generated from this source — given the strong public antipathy to further tax increases, and especially increases in a tax as highly visible as the property tax. It is clear, therefore, that as the responsibility for raising revenues shifts more heavily to the municipal level, it will be necessary to make greater use of "miscellaneous local revenues," including such funding sources as licenses, fees, permits, fines and penalties, user charges and developer charges. Once largely ignored by many municipalities, this category is now recognized as having considerable untapped potential.

Ridler documents a growing use of these miscellaneous revenues, particularly with respect to user fees. Examining the period between 1973

---

[76]Association of Municipal Tax Collectors of Ontario, *Municipal Tax Administration Program*, Unit Two, Lesson 5, p. 9.

[77]*Kingston Whig Standard*, October 1, 1994, p. 8.

and 1982, he notes that transfer payments as a share of gross municipal revenues remained relatively stable, as did the yield from the property tax. In contrast, the share from user fees increased from 5.4% to 9.2% during this period.[78] This expansion occurred particularly in recreational services, but was also evident in areas such as waste removal and police control. Ridler cites a number of potential advantages of the increased application of user fees,[79] and concludes that their expanded use resulted in a slight reduction in fiscal imbalance for municipalities (the difference between expenditures and revenues from own sources) in 1982 as compared to 1973.

This pattern continued through the 1980s, and Nowlan notes that revenues from the property tax and related taxes have fallen from close to 90% of municipal own-source revenue in the 1950s to approximately 70% by the late 1980s, while the revenues from user fees were increasing to near 20%.[80]

While user charges are on the increase because of the growing revenue squeeze facing municipalities, there are also economic arguments in favour of their use.[81] The two main arguments are that they are equitable and that they advance economic efficiency. The equity argument is based on the notion that where specific groups benefit from a service, they should pay for that service (rather than having the cost borne by all taxpayers in the municipality, as happens when a service is financed from the property tax). The economic efficiency argument is that a charge on a service helps to demonstrate how much people are really interested in that service, and also stimulates them to use it sparingly. The widespread shift to metered water billings is an example of a user charge designed to promote conservation. Other examples are increased "tipping" fees at municipal dumps and the introduction of paid "tags" for garbage bags. The Ontario Fair Tax Commission has recently recommended that on

---

[78]Neil B. Ridler, "Fiscal Constraints and the Growth of User Fees among Canadian Municipalities," in *Canadian Public Administration*, Fall 1984, pp. 429-436.

[79]*Ibid.*, pp. 435-436.

[80]David Nowlan, "Local Taxation as an Instrument of Policy," in Frances Frisken (ed.), *The Changing Canadian Metropolis: A Public Policy Perspective*, Vol. 2, Toronto, Canadian Urban Institute, pp. 811-812.

[81]The discussion which follows is based on Siegel, *The Financial Context for Urban Policy*, p. 24, which in turn draws from Richard Bird, *Charging for Public Services: A New Look at an Old Idea*, Toronto, Canadian Tax Foundation, 1976.

both fairness and environmental grounds, sewer, water and solid waste services should be funded from user fees that vary with the amount of service used.[82]

User charges are not without problems, however, and Siegel notes that their application for such services as recreational facilities "can be a political minefield."[83] This is especially true where sports groups are well organized and can exert strong pressure on council. Such groups may also have enjoyed a high degree of voluntarism in the past — manifested in considerable fund-raising and in time spent maintaining recreational facilities. Opponents of user fees argue that they threaten this volunteer spirit and can lead to an attitude of "let the government do it since they are charging for it anyway."

Federal-Local and Tri-Level Relations

In addition to their involvement with provincial governments, municipalities have also long been affected by federal programs and policies. The fact that they are "creatures" or "creations" of provincial governments does not make municipalities immune to the impact of federal government actions. As described in Chapter 4, there is no better example than the federal contribution, through financial assistance under the Dominion Housing Act of 1935 and then the Canada Mortgage and Housing Corporation of 1946, to low density sprawl and all of its associated municipal servicing problems. The actions of CMHC also contributed to neighbourhood dislocations and attendant problems because of what has been described as a bulldozer approach to urban renewal.

To be fair, not all federal urban renewal experiences have been this negative. Gutstein details the experiences of the Strathcona Property Owners' and Tenants' Association, established in 1968 to oppose urban renewal initiatives in Vancouver which were displacing large numbers of families. The following year the federal government announced that it would not provide funds for the urban renewal projects in Strathcona Park unless the residents were involved in the planning process.[84] The result was a working committee comprising government officials and mem-

---

[82]Fair Tax Commission, News Release, *op. cit.*

[83]Siegel, *The Financial Context for Urban Policy*, p. 24.

[84]Donald Gutstein, "Vancouver" in Warren Magnusson and Andrew Sancton (eds.), *City Politics in Canada*, Toronto, University of Toronto Press, 1983, p. 201.

bers of the Association, "one of the first instances in Canada of citizens sharing this kind of decision making with government."

Decisions by the Department of Transport concerning rail services have had a critical impact on the economic vitality of communities as have various industrial incentive and other programs offered by such departments as Regional Economic Expansion. One well documented example shows the federal Minister of Regional Economic Expansion playing a leading role in securing the removal of railway tracks from the centre of Quebec City — an objective that had apparently been voiced for sixty years.[85]

Immigration policy is another federal government responsibility which has affected municipalities, dramatically so in the case of Canada's largest urban centres. But as Frisken points out, "federal immigration policy makes little attempt to ease the strains imposed on cities or city neighbourhoods by large influxes of new immigrants."[86]

These examples should suffice to demonstrate that a kind of federal-local relationship existed long before it was given any formal recognition during the 1970s. Indeed, one study found that by the late 1960s, "more than 117 distinct programs administered by 27 departments in Ottawa influenced metropolitan development plans."[87]

In almost every case, however, the federal programs were introduced without regard for their possible impact on the local level and municipalities had no opportunity for advance consultation and little hope of obtaining adjustments after the fact. Indeed, in many cases, the varied federal initiatives were not even coordinated with each other. For example, during the 1960s the CMHC financed extensive residential construction in the vicinity of the Malton Airport near Toronto.[88] When the Ministry of Transport sought to expand the airport in 1968 it found that an entire

---

[85]See Lionel D. Feldman and Katherine A. Graham, *Bargaining for Cities*, Toronto, Butterworth and Co., 1979, pp. 60-63 and Louise Quesnel-Ouellet and Gilles Bouchard, "Urban Transportation: Politics in Search of a Policy," in Lionel Feldman and Michael Goldrick, *Politics and Government of Urban Canada*, Toronto, Methuen, 1976, pp. 219-245.

[86]Frances Frisken, "Introduction," in Frisken, *op. cit.*, p. 19.

[87]Elliot J. Feldman and Jerome Milch, "Coordination or Control? The Life and Death of the Ministry of Urban Affairs," in Lionel D. Feldman (ed.), *Politics and Government of Urban Canada*, Toronto, Methuen, 1981, p. 250.

[88]*Ibid.*, p. 251.

residential community had been constructed on what had been uninhabited farmland, and it turned its attention to seeking a new site.

By this time, however, developments were underway which appeared to offer the possibility of a much more coordinated approach to the handling of federal activities which affected urban Canada. Two major factors were combining to produce strong pressure for a closer and more formalized federal-local relationship. First, there was a growing municipal interest in the possibility of increased federal funds being made available to deal with major service demands, especially in urban areas. Doubtless this interest was stimulated by the fact that requests to the provincial governments for more financial assistance were constantly rebuffed on the grounds that the provinces were short of funds because of federal dominance of the main revenue fields. [Yes, there was a time in Canada's history when the federal level was seen as the one which might have money to spare!] As the only national municipal body, the Canadian Federation of Mayors and Municipalities (now the Federation of Canadian Municipalities) took the initiative in espousing the municipal cause, especially after discussions on constitutional reform commenced in 1967. A joint Municipal Committee on Intergovernmental Relations was established and prepared an excellent paper on *The Municipality in the Canadian Federation* for presentation to the annual conference of provincial ministers of municipal affairs in Winnipeg in August 1970.

In the meantime, the second factor encouraging a federal-local relationship was developing with the growing federal appreciation that because of the large number of Canadians living in urban areas the ability of municipal governments to meet their needs was of more than local, or even provincial, interest. In this connection, December 1967 saw a Federal-Provincial Conference on Housing and Urban Development and this was followed by a conference of civil servants in April 1968 at which the federal government outlined a number of specific shared-cost proposals. Within a few months a Federal Task Force on Housing and Urban Development was appointed and its January 1969 Report called for a greatly expanded federal role. Headed by the then Minister of Transport, Paul Hellyer, the Task Force did not hesitate to make a number of recommendations involving matters within the jurisdiction of the provincial and municipal governments and appeared to incorporate a number of the proposals which had been made by federal officials at the above-noted April 1968 conference of federal and provincial civil servants.

Thus, for example, the Task Force recommended that the federal government make direct loans to municipalities to assist them in assembling and servicing land for urban growth, acquiring dispersed existing housing for use by low income groups and developing urban transit systems. Noting that urban planning must be undertaken on a regional basis to be effective, the Report called on the provinces to establish a system of regional governments for each major area. In addition, it recommended that the federal government establish a Department of Housing and Urban Affairs. The Task Force envisaged that the CMHC would retain its role as administrator and implementor of federal housing policy, while the new department would concentrate on advising on policy and coordinating research activities, at least at the federal level and possibly with other governments and agencies as well.

Initially, the federal cabinet appeared not ready to accept such an enlarged role and within a few months Hellyer resigned as Minister of Transport, expressing dissatisfaction with the lack of government action on housing and urban questions generally. He later claimed that he was sabatoged by senior civil servants opposed to his recommendations.[89] While there was undoubtedly some truth to this charge, David Cameron notes that by using "outsiders" on his Task Force, Hellyer was bound to create opposition from the bureaucracy, especially when the tight schedule for preparation of the report left insufficient time for the accommodation of views. Moreover, by making himself chairman, Hellyer "forged an identity between the results of the policy recommendations and his own political future."[90]

The Rise and Fall of MSUA

Ironically, within a year of his resignation Hellyer's successor, Robert Andras, was designated Minister of State for Urban Affairs and the establishment of a Ministry of Urban Affairs was announced. This reversal of position was unquestionably influenced by a report by Harvey Lithwick, commissioned by Andras while he was minister without portfolio, which strongly criticized the federal government's failure to integrate and coordinate policy decisions having urban ramifications. As recommended by the Hellyer Task Force, the new ministry was not to be a traditional operating department but was to concentrate on policy development and on coordinating the projects of other departments. Also emphasized was the need to increase consultation and coordination among all three levels of government in dealing with the challenges of urbanization. Here again,

---

[89]See Hellyer's comments in *City Magazine*, Toronto, December 1977.

[90]David M. Cameron, "Urban Policy," in G. Bruce Doern and V. Seymour Wilson (eds.), *Issues in Canadian Public Policy*, Toronto, Macmillan, 1974, p. 231.

the influence of the Lithwick Report was apparent; it had called for "a new kind of vertical integration within the hierarchy of government."[91]

The new ministry began with ambitious objectives considering "the absence of any authority with which to control the legislative or spending proposals of other agencies."[92] One analysis observed that "it was created as a new David without a sling; the new ministry of state could fulfil its mission only with mutual trust and goodwill."[93] These commodities turned out to be in short supply and none of the approaches attempted by the ministry had much success.

Initially, in an attempt to gain credibility, "MSUA offered to represent the interests of municipalities and provincial governments in discussions with other federal agencies."[94] But this approach brought it into direct confrontation with other federal agencies and little was accomplished. By 1972 MSUA had adopted a new strategy — it would promote coordination by arranging meetings among representatives of all three levels of govern-ment and the various federal ministries whose programs affected urban areas. This approach had already been advocated by the Canadian Federation of Mayors and Municipalities and partly through the efforts of the Federation the first ever national tri-level conference was held in Toronto in November of 1972. The fact that the municipal level was represented in its own right was in itself a breakthrough, but the extent to which the conference might be considered a success depends upon the expectations of those participating in it. A Joint Municipal Committee on Intergovernmental Affairs presented several well researched papers but little progress was made because of the uncompromising attitude of the provinces, particularly Ontario.[95]

A second national tri-level conference was held in Edmonton in October 1973. It was decided to undertake a study of public finance with particular reference to the adequacy of municipal revenue sources, a devel-

---

[91]N. H. Lithwick, *Urban Canada, Problems and Prospects*, Ottawa, Canada Mortgage and Housing Corporation, 1970, p. 178.

[92]Cameron in Doern and Wilson, *op. cit.*, p. 245.

[93]Feldman and Milch in Feldman, *op. cit.*, p. 254.

[94]*Ibid.*, p. 255.

[95]For a thoughtful assessment of this first conference see *Urban Focus*, Vol. 1, No. 2, "The Tri-Level Conference — The Morning After," Queen's University, Institutes of Local Government and Intergovernmental Relations, January-February 1973.

opment seen optimistically as "the first important piece of firm evidence of the success of the tri-level process."[96] But difficulties and delays were encountered in launching the Tri-Level Task Force on Public Finance and the third national tri-level conference was accordingly postponed, forever as it turned out.

In the meantime, however, agreement had been reached to hold tri-level meetings at the provincial and city level. A regional tri-level meeting was held, for example, in Peterborough, Ontario in May of 1973, and at the city level a number of tri-level meetings have been held in such places as Halifax, Quebec, Calgary, Fredericton, Montreal, Saint John, Regina, Toronto, Winnipeg and Vancouver. Developments in the latter city illustrate the useful role of such meetings. The Ministry of Transport's plans for the expansion of Vancouver Airport were strongly opposed at the local level. Through the mediation efforts of the MSUA at a tri-level meeting in March of 1973, Transport agreed to establish an Airport Planning Committee, although they refused to let MSUA chair it.[97] These types of tri-level meeting continued for a while even after the demise of MSUA,[98] a reflection of the need for a more coordinated approach to urban issues.

With the national tri-level conferences stalled by provincial intransigence, MSUA adopted another strategy. It attempted to move from persuasion to power — which it sought through the Canada Mortgage and Housing Corporation which controlled major expenditures.[99] Here again, however, successes were limited and by 1975 there was "a state of open warfare between MSUA and CMHC."[100] To resolve this conflict, William Teron was brought in as both Secretary of MSUA and Chairman of the Board of the CMHC. Within 18 months the number of MSUA personnel had been slashed by 40%. It adopted yet another approach at this point. It made no effort to initiate meetings, but let it be known that it would organize them if requested. "MSUA thus evolved from an agency that

---

[96]*Urban Focus*, Vol. 2, No. 1, November-December 1973.

[97]Feldman and Milch in Feldman, *op. cit.*, p. 256.

[98]See J. M. Brodie, "Tri-Level Meeting — The Windsor Experience," in *Urban Focus*, Vol. 10, No. 2, November-December 1981.

[99]Feldman and Milch, *op. cit.*, pp. 257-258.

[100]*Ibid.*, p. 258.

had flirted with the imposition of policy to an urban consultant active only on invitation."[101] This final phase of MSUA activity was received more favourably, but this was largely because of its much more modest mission, not because of any real support. By the spring of 1979 it had fallen victim to the politics of austerity. "Total savings would be less than $4 million (and perhaps closer to $500,000), but the public would be impressed by a government pre-pared to abolish a whole ministry in the name of fiscal responsibility."[102]

While the reasons for the failure of MSUA are fairly obvious for the most part,[103] viewpoints vary on its original appropriateness or the consequences of its demise. While conceding that "responsibility for urban policy — as policy for cities — must rest with the provinces," Cameron concludes that there still could be an important role for a federal body like MSUA "to concentrate on analyzing the impact of federal activities on cities and in turn interpreting provincial and municipal urban policy to federal agencies."[104] What is clear is that because of the failure of MSUA we continue to have federal policies enacted without regard to their urban impact. "Federal initiatives in the cities have been not only incoherent and irrational, often they have been inconsistent and unequal."[105]

In spite of the experience of MSUA, we will continue to have some form of tri-level relations in Canada. Such a relationship is unavoidable given the interdependence of programs and policies at all three levels of government. The need for such a relationship also derives from the very considerable influence which the federal government exerts over Canadian municipalities. To take but one example of the interdependence of the various levels of government, consider the issue of the transportation of hazardous goods. The Canadian Transport Commission held a series of hearings in the mid-1980s on the rail transportation of hazardous materials to the Vancouver port area, only to conclude that broader ques-

---

[101]*Ibid.*

[102]*Ibid.*, p. 260.

[103]In addition to the frequently cited article by Feldman and Milch, see Cameron in Doern and Wilson, *op. cit.*, and Allan O'Brien, "The Ministry of State for Urban Affairs: A Municipal Perspective," in *Canadian Journal of Regional Science*, Halifax, Spring 1982.

[104]Cameron in Doern and Wilson, *op. cit.*, p. 249.

[105]Feldman and Milch in Feldman, *op. cit.*, p. 263.

tions of all forms of movement of dangerous goods were beyond its jurisdiction but needed to be addressed. The result was a tri-level task force to conduct the first such comprehensive study in the Vancouver metropolitan region.[106]

There is ample evidence to demonstrate that the federal government has continued to influence the way Canadian cities develop even with the death of the MSUA. In fact, the federal influence may have been greater during the 1980s — as reflected in major development projects in almost all of Canada's major metropolitan areas.[107] Some of these projects (such as Harbourfront in Toronto and the Rideau Centre in Ottawa) were the result of election promises, while others reflected the regional influence of a cabinet minister — such as the Winnipeg Core Area Initiative promoted by Lloyd Axworthy.[108] Whatever their impetus, they demonstrated the continuing significance of the federal presence in urban Canada.

The end of the 1980s saw repeated calls by municipalities and some provincial governments for a tri-level approach to the funding of infrastructure investment in Canadian cities. Without such support, it was alleged, many basic municipal services which provide the basis for growth and development would begin to crumble. A 1987 study by the Federation of Canadian Municipalities determined that $15 billion in infrastructure investment was needed across Canada.

One is reminded of the situation just two decades earlier, when municipal concerns about the high costs of such items as urban transportation systems helped to precipitate the previously described period of formal tri-level relations. The difference is that in that earlier period the federal government was actively interested in pursuing a more formal tri-level relationship; today, no such interest is apparent, especially with the federal government trying to reduce its financial commitments wherever possible. Nor have the provinces shown any more willingness to contemplate federal incursions into their jurisdiction over municipalities.

The election of a federal Liberal Government in 1993 did lead to one tri-level initiative relating to the infrastructure. As part of a job-creation

---

[106]Peter Oberlander and Patrick Smith, "Governing Metropolitan Vancouver," in Donald Rothblatt and Andrew Sancton (eds.), *Metropolitan Governance: American/Canadian Intergovernmental Perspectives*, Berkeley, Institute of Governmental Studies Press, 1993, p. 341.

[107]Caroline Andrew, "Federal Urban Activity: Intergovernmental Relations in an Age of Restraint," in Frisken, *op. cit.*, p. 430.

[108]*Ibid.*

program promised during the election campaign, the government introduced the *Canada Infrastructure Works* program. Over a two year period ending on March 31, 1996, it pledged to provide $2 billion in federal funding for approved projects, to be matched by the same amount of funding from provinces and municipalities, directed toward upgrading the quality of the physical infrastructure in local communities.[109] Whatever the economic benefits of this initiative — and they have been the subject of some debate — it is a "one shot" joint venture not unlike the public works programs which were long a staple of federal governments seeking to rejuvenate the economy. It does not herald a new, ongoing federal-local or tri-level relationship.

Municipal Consultation with the Senior Levels

While the nature of any formal future relationship is especially dependent on the attitudes and willingness of the senior governments, municipalities must also make every effort to articulate their views in a forceful, consistent fashion. As indicated below, such has often not been the case.

Discussions of intergovernmental relations affecting municipalities tend to portray the municipal level as a passive observer; it is dictated to by the province or adversely affected by thoughtless federal action. Such a focus is much too narrow. It ignores the important role played by local government and the extent to which all levels of government have now become dependent upon each other. It overlooks the extent to which municipal governments can take the initiative in pressing their viewpoint upon the senior levels and attempting to obtain concessions from them. Accordingly, this closing section will briefly consider the consultative mechanisms available to municipalities and the apparent effectiveness of their consultative efforts.

The Federation of Canadian Municipalities

The one national association of municipalities is the *Federation of Canadian Municipalities*. It was founded as the Canadian Federation of Mayors and Municipalities during the Great Depression (1937)[110] and one of its

---

[109]From Canada Infrastructure Works, *News Release*, February 18, 1994.

[110]Gregory Brandsgard, "Regina and Saskatoon's Troubled Membership in the Federation of Canadian Municipalities," in Christopher Dunn (ed.), *Saskatoon Local Government and Politics*, University of Saskatchewan, 1987, p. 78.

main objectives was to pressure the federal government for financing of an unemployment relief program. Efforts to improve the financial position of the municipal level have remained a major concern of the Federation over the ensuing years. The Federation has suffered from some internal squabbling about urban versus rural considerations. In 1973, for example, David Crombie organized a meeting at which Toronto, Montreal, Vancouver and Calgary discussed the possibility of withdrawing from the Federation.[111]   Another problem is that the need to find a middle ground has forced the Federation to espouse generalized positions which reflect the lowest common denominator at times. Its position may also be weakened by the existence of a number of very active provincial associations of municipalities, and there have been recurring suggestions that it become a federation of these bodies.[112]

During the constitutional debate of the late 1970s and early 1980s which led to the patriation of the constitution, FCM established a Task Force on Constitutional Reform which called for the entrenchment of municipalities into the Constitution of Canada.[113] In a 1980 Task Force Report on *Municipal Government in a New Canadian Federal System*, it called for constitutional recognition of autonomy for municipalities in areas relating to law making, finances and governing structures. When the Canadian constitution was repatriated in 1982, however, there was no recognition of the municipal level of government.

The Federation has rebounded from this setback and has experienced considerable growth since. Its membership more than tripled from 1983 to 1990, going from about 200 members to some 600.[114] Its staff and budget have also enjoyed a healthy expansion. It gained national profile with its "big fix" campaign to rebuild Canada's infrastructure, described earlier. The Federation has also developed a new approach to the issue of the constitutional recognition of municipal government, one which seems more realistic.

As part of this new approach, FCM has established, along with the Canadian Association of Municipal Administrators, a task force charged

---

[111]*Ibid.*, p. 84.

[112]Siegel, *Provincial-Municipal Relations in Canada*, p. 314.

[113]The discussion of FCM's efforts to gain constitutional recognition for municipalities is based on Association of Municipalities of Ontario, *Local Governance in the Future: Issues and Trends*, Toronto, 1994, pp. 60-66.

[114]Andrew, *op. cit.*, pp. 440-441.

with creating a mechanism to foster and augment the leadership role of municipal government in Canada. The task force is expected to complete a document which presents a renewed vision of municipal government, one which can be used to promote an improved understanding of municipal government in the media, educational institutions, other orders of government and the public.[115] With strong public resistance to any new round of constitutional talks, and with the likelihood that any such talks would almost certainly be preoccupied with Quebec yet again, it appears that FCM is taking a new approach which seeks to build wider public appreciation of the importance of municipal government — perhaps as a basis from which a new effort at constitutional recognition could be launched in more propitious times.

Municipal Associations at the Provincial Level

Most provinces have a number of municipal associations representing both staff and councillors, although it is the political associations which are critical to the consultations with the senior governments. Some provinces have several of these associations while others have only one. Obviously, one large association representing all municipalities has the potential to speak with a more powerful voice. This potential may not be realized, however, since the attempt to represent a variety of municipal viewpoints may cause internal strife and foster excessive compromising which pleases no one.

Ontario's experience is interesting in this regard, and it also illustrates the workings of a formalized municipal-provincial consultative process.[116] In 1969 a Municipal Liaison Committee (MLC) was established to provide more coordinated activity on the part of the four political associations then in existence. A series of joint meetings were held between a committee of cabinet ministers and the MLC, and by 1972 these sessions had become regular monthly meetings of what became known as the Provincial-Municipal Liaison Committee (PMLC).

During 1973 the PMLC was involved in discussions leading up to the previously described revenue-sharing arrangement known as the Edmonton Commitment. Other important issues included a proposal to move toward a system of unconditional grants. The consultation mechanism

---

[115]*Ibid.*, p. 66.

[116]The analysis that follows is partly based on Sheila Gordon, *Intergovernmental Relations*, a paper presented to the Ontario Conference on Local Government Seminar, September 26, 1978.

appeared to be working and municipalities were encouraged. However, the provincial government appeared less and less responsive with the financial restraint and minority government position of the second half of the 1970s. Some ministers tended to consult with the MLC only when it was in their interests to do so, and one analysis suggests that the MLC was occasionally used as a scapegoat to cover up for Provincial mistakes or to shift the blame for unpopular policies.[117]

The MLC itself was hampered by limited staff and financial resources. It also had difficulty deciding on its proper role. If the MLC was essentially a federation and a policy-presenting body rather than one which made policy, then its members had to reconcile their desire to reach a consensus with their responsibility to represent the potentially diverse views of their respective associations. Making this reconciliation even more difficult was the fact that the associations tended to compete with one another for profile and recognition.[118] In late 1979 the largest political association withdrew from the PMLC and within a short time the regular monthly meetings had ceased.

By June of 1980, however, a new umbrella municipal organization had been recommended, and the founding convention of the new Association of Municipalities of Ontario (AMO) was held in October 1981. The new structure attempted to combine for strength while still preserving the diversity of viewpoints which often arise on municipal issues. Thus, it contained within it five sections: Large Urban, Small Urban, County and Regional, Rural and Northern Ontario. Its principle of operation was that all viewpoints would be forwarded on any issue which comes to it for comment.

The second half of the 1980s was a difficult period for AMO. Without the formal consultative mechanism which had existed in the days of the PMLC, it found it difficult to obtain adequate consultation from provincial administrations preoccupied with reducing their budget deficits and quite prepared to download in fulfillment of that objective. There was also considerable turnover among its limited staff complement. At the beginning of this decade, AMO found itself playing a central role in Ontario's disentanglement exercise, discussed earlier in this chapter. However, the tentative agreement reached on the first phase of this exercise was lost when the province arbitrarily imposed major cuts in transfer

---

[117]T. J. Plunkett and G. M. Betts, *The Management of Canadian Urban Government*, Kingston, Institute of Local Government, Queen's University, 1978, p. 90.

[118]Gordon, *op. cit.*, p. 14.

payments to the municipal level as part of its deficit-reduction efforts. Most recently, AMO seems to have gone "back to the basics" in an approach not unlike that undertaken by FCM and described above. In 1993 it initiated a special project to develop a position on local governance in the future. This has led to a policy paper, *Ontario Charter: A Proposed Bill of Rights for Local Government*, about which more will be said in the final chapter.

One of the oldest municipal associations in Canada is found in *Nova Scotia*, where the Union of Nova Scotia Municipalities was established in 1906. It repeatedly endorsed the need for rationalization of municipal political boundaries and for a reallocation of provincial and municipal responsibilities, and with these objectives in mind participated in the 1992 *Task Force on Local Government*, described in Chapter 5. However, it has since had misgivings about the recommendations in the Report and the government's declared intention to proceed with these recommendations. The Association has expressed concern about the lack of clear evidence to demonstrate the savings which will result from any changes to be introduced and the lack of adequate time and opportunity for public consultation in the process.[119]

Like Ontario, the Nova Scotia association is also pursuing the development of a municipal charter. It has presented to the provincial government a paper in this regard and has received, in principle, the support of the Premier.[120]

The Federation of Prince Edward Island Municipalities was formed in 1967, and currently represents 39 municipalities comprising 80% of the population living in incorporated areas.[121] Its description of what it does for its members is not untypical of such associations:

a) represent the interests of local government and act as a spokesperson for the membership.
b) protect the rights and privileges of municipal governments.
c) carry out research activities for individual members.
d) act as a clearing house for information.
e) further municipal interests through cooperation between municipalities.
f) provide avenues of training, development and education of municipal officials.

---

[119]Union of Nova Scotia Municipalities, *UNSM Concerns with the Current Process of Municipal Reform*, 1993.

[120]AMO, *op. cit.*, p. 59.

[121]*History of the Federation of Prince Edward Island Municipalities*, 1993, p. 2.

As discussed in Chapter 5, the Prince Edward Island government is undertaking a program of municipal reform, including substantial amalgamations in the Summerside and Charlottetown areas. The Federation's response to the government's *White Paper on Municipal Reform* is revealing in demonstrating the difficulty all municipal associations seem to have in reconciling the diverse views of their membership. In its response, the Federation refers to the difficulty of an association of "diverse units" responding definitively and indicates that it is impossible "to manifest a single compatible response." Instead, it has chosen to act as a "facilitator of communication."[122]

To take one more example, *Alberta*'s most prominent municipal association is the Alberta Urban Municipalities Association (AUMA). But Masson has noted that even though this association's membership consisted of 100% of the province's cities and towns and 94% of its villages, it has been limited in its influence because of internal tensions.[123] He describes a picture very reminiscent of the experience of other associations, explaining that in many policy areas small towns and villages have had much different concerns than large cities, and that these differences have made it very difficult for AUMA to take a firm position.

Notwithstanding the activities of the various municipal associations, Feldman and Graham suggest that since these associations are not accountable to the public and are "somewhat immune to public opinion," their use for the conduct of important intergovernmental affairs may have stifled the emergence of much public concern about important municipal (intergovernmental) issues.[124] They question whether or not an association can represent adequately an individual municipality's specific concerns, arguing that associations generally represent "the lowest common denominator" of opinion among their members, thereby blurring the interests of individual municipalities. They raise a concern that municipal associations partially financed by the provincial level may be unduly influenced accordingly. They also point out that provincial governments can sometimes subvert the focus of a municipal association so that it becomes a vehicle for disseminating information about provincial policy, rather than for expressing municipal views and concerns. In this situation,

---

[122]Federation of Prince Edward Island Municipalities, *Response to the White Paper on Municipal Reform*, p. 1.

[123]Jack Masson, *Alberta's Local Governments and Their Politics*, Edmonton, University of Alberta Press, 1985, p. 201.

[124]Feldman and Graham, *op. cit.*, pp. 21-27.

Feldman and Graham conclude, "municipal representatives tend to be thought of at best as glorified office boys and at worst as whipping boys." In their view, intergovernmental concerns should be addressed by individual municipalities, particularly in the case of Canada's larger municipalities. Yet it is the actions of very large municipalities like Metropolitan Toronto and some of the regional governments in Ontario in seeking to look after their own interests that is felt to have weakened the bargaining position of the Association of Municipalities of Ontario. Nor should one rule out the possibility that provincial governments might encourage such "one-on-one" negotiations as a means of keeping the municipal level off balance through a "divide and conquer" strategy.

Highlights and Concluding Observations

This chapter began by tracing the general pattern of provincial-municipal relations in Canada. This pattern has been one of gradually increasing provincial supervision and control over local governments, an increase given particular impetus by the combined impact of the financial pressures of the Great Depression, the centralization of government during World War Two and the upsurge in service demands because of rapid post-war urbanization. The local government reforms which were introduced in various provinces, as discussed in Chapter 5, did little to arrest this trend.

The generally unsatisfactory nature of the provincial-local relationship is also evident in the field of finances. The traditional mainstay of municipal revenues, the real property tax, was providing less than 50% of these revenues by the 1960s and only about one-third by the 1980s. Municipalities were able to generate additional revenues through a substantial increase in the yield from their miscellaneous local revenues, particularly user charges. For the most part, however, the shortfall in the real property tax yield was made up by transfer payments from the senior levels. The overwhelmingly conditional nature of these payments (about 90%) raised concerns about the survival of municipal autonomy.

Improvements brought about by the introduction of revenue-sharing agreements in a number of the provinces have proven to be somewhat illusory. Even with these agreements, municipalities have still found themselves vulnerable to unilateral provincial freezes or reductions of transfers to meet provincial restraint objectives.

In fact, municipalities in some provinces have been experiencing what they see as a double or triple "revenue squeeze." In addition to cutbacks in transfer payments, municipalities claim that there has also been an attempt by their provincial government to solve their own financial problems by shifting certain responsibilities and expenditure burdens to the local level. Third, they charge that the province has extended existing programs or imposed new ones without providing corresponding funding support.

The provincial restraint which has prompted this revenue squeeze on municipalities is itself being caused, at least in part, by actions of the federal government motivated by its desire to put its own financial house in order. This is but one example of the many ways in which federal action (or inaction) can significantly affect the operations of local government. For a few years in the 1970s, it appeared that formal tri-level consultative machinery might develop, largely through the initiative of the federal Ministry of State for Urban Affairs. MSUA was short-lived, but there remains a clear need for some mechanism through which municipalities can have a voice in the many senior level decisions which affect them.

Whatever consultative mechanisms might be established, however, a continuing problem has been the determination of who speaks for Canada's 4 500 municipalities. There are numerous municipal associations within the provinces, some organized into a provincial-municipal consultative structure. There is also one national body, the Federation of Canadian Municipalities, which has attempted to represent municipal concerns to the federal level. It has been shown, however, that many of the larger municipalities prefer to deal with intergovernmental problems by acting on their own, and some reservations have been expressed about the suitability of municipal associations for dealing with intergovernmental issues. Yet only a few of the largest municipalities can be expected to have much success attempting to deal with the provincial or federal levels on their own. For the vast majority of Canadian municipalities, then, an attempt must be made to organize and put forth a united position on the issues which concern them. Ironically, efforts to develop this united position and to bargain from strength are undermined to the extent that large and potentially influential municipalities are inclined to act on their own.

Intergovernmental relations, and the general operations of municipal governments, will continue to be greatly influenced by the "new financial reality" facing all of our governments. The well is dry. Public tolerance for further tax increases has vanished, as is evident by the taxpayer revolt triggered by the GST and by the ever-growing "underground economy." Without major tax increases the only way the federal government can bring its massive deficit and debt problems under control is through expenditure cuts — including continuing cuts in transfer payments to the provinces. The same story applies at the provincial level, with the same result in the form of reduced transfer payments to the local level. While there will probably always be some special funding initiatives such as the current infrastructure program or grants for particular capital expenditures, it is entirely possible that there won't be *any* regular, ongoing provincial transfer payments to municipalities by the year 2000! Prudent municipalities will start working toward the goal of financial self-sufficiency in anticipation of that eventuality.

These fundamental financial changes mean a dramatic change in the provincial-municipal relationship as it existed even a decade or two ago. At that point, municipalities were still looking to their provincial governments for their salvation, to be achieved mainly through the provision of additional financial assistance. For a long time the provincial funds continued to flow, allowing municipal governments to provide a growing number of services without significant increases in the property tax. The only flaw in this apparently attractive scenario was that most of the provincial financial assistance throughout this period was conditional — money with strings attached — and municipalities were drawn ever more into the orbit of provincial priorities.

That "cosy" arrangement has changed for the foreseeable future and probably forever. A painful adjustment period faces municipalities as they learn to operate on the basis of those revenues which they are able to generate for themselves. This adjustment will involve much more than cutting expenditures, as will be discussed in Chapter 10. As a result, however, municipalities could emerge as stronger and more independent units of government. Whether or not they do largely depends on their own ingenuity in dealing with the challenges which face them. Senior governments can also play a key role in this reinventing of municipal government, in at least the following ways:

1. By providing a constitutional recognition that municipalities constitute a separate level of government within Canada, not just an administrative agency for the delivery of senior government programs.
2. By endowing municipal governments with a broader mandate for exercising its powers within spheres of jurisdiction, rather than authorizing only those powers specifically delegated by statute.
3. By giving municipalities a binding commitment (probably in some form of revenue-sharing arrangement) that the limited senior government financial assistance to be provided (including payments-in-lieu of taxes) will not be suddenly or arbitrarily changed.

Given the magnitude of the changes which municipalities will be required to make, many of them to be previewed in the chapters ahead, these are modest commitments to ask of the senior levels of government.

CHAPTER 8

The Local Political Process

OBJECTIVES:

1. To examine the nature of the local political process and differing views as to its primary features.

2. To explore the historic and continuing relationship between local government and property.

3. To assess the prevalence and impact of citizens' groups and of political parties on the operations of municipalities, through profiles of four large Canadian cities.

4. To examine the arguments for and against the introduction of political parties into municipal government.

Introduction

Thus far in this book, much of the emphasis has been structural. The system of local government in Canada has been traced from its historical origins, through various pressures of change and reform programs, to the present governing arrangements. The interaction between these evolving local government institutions and their environment has also been highlighted through the preceding chapters. In the remainder of the text more emphasis is given to process — to the way in which local governments operate, make decisions, determine priorities, and allocate resources. These activities of local governments largely determine the character of their communities and the quality of life of their inhabitants.

Officially, local decisions are made by representatives elected by, and responsible to, the local electorate. These representatives are advised by staff who provide expertise and continuity. The decisions of local governments are often made subject to provincial approval, or under constraints imposed by the province (and to some extent, the federal government as well). In practice, however, there are a number of other potentially important players in local decision making. These players include local interest groups, the media and political parties. It is also evident that local decisions are not made "in a vacuum," but in response to various realities and pressures found in the external environment. Chief among these, in the view of many, is the nature of economic development and of the distribution of economic power.

We begin by examining the nature of the local political process and some of the conflicting views held about this process. This is followed by a description of the principal players in local politics, both official and unofficial. Examples from political activities in a number of Canadian cities are used to illustrate the local political process.

Nature of the Local Political Process

As stated in Chapter 1, politics is an inherent part of local government operations, in that decisions must be made about how scarce local resources will be allocated among the many wants and needs of the local community. On what basis do municipalities decide who gets what? In the admittedly brief overview which follows, a number of quite different, sometimes conflicting, perspectives are offered. Most striking is the contrast between those who extol the democratic nature of local politics and those who denounce the domination of the property industry in the local political process. Further insights into municipal decision making will be found in the next chapter, which explores the policy making process in theory and in practice.

Local Politics and Democracy

Various writers from de Tocqueville and John Stewart Mill to K. Grant Crawford[1] have emphasized the democratic features of local government. To some, such as Mill, local government constituted a training ground for democracy, wherein elected representatives would "learn the ropes" before going on to service at a more senior level, and local citizens would learn about exercising their democratic rights in the context of issues which were relatively simple and understandable. No better expression of this sentiment can be found than the Durham Report. In commenting on the lack of municipal institutions in the colony in the 1830s, Lord Durham expressed concern that "the people receive no training in those habits of

---

[1]See Alexis de Tocqueville's *Democracy in America*, J. S. Mill's *Considerations on Representative Government* and *On Liberty*, and *Canadian Municipal Government* by Crawford.

self-government which are indispensable to enable them rightly to exercise the power of choosing representatives in parliament."[2]

Others, such as de Tocqueville, with his oft-quoted statement that "municipal institutions constitute the strength of free nations," saw municipal government's democratic role in a much more direct, fundamental light. Indeed, Crawford saw municipal government as far from just a training ground, but as the level at which the democratic ideal was most likely to be fulfilled. The citizen is more likely to understand the issues under consideration locally than the increasingly complex, technical matters which predominate at the senior levels of government. Moreover, because the results of local decisions (or indecision) are readily apparent in the local community, citizens should be able to evaluate the effectiveness of their municipal government and the degree to which elected representatives have fulfilled their campaign pledges.

A contrasting viewpoint is provided by Langrod, who viewed municipal government as "but a technical arrangement within the mechanisms of the administrative system, a structural and functional detail...."[3] Langrod not only rejected the assumption that municipal government is vital to democracy, he also contended that local government could be contrary to the democratic process.

> In some countries local government, with its structured anachronisms, the high degree of its internal functionalisation, the preponderance in practice of the permanent official over the elected and temporary councillor, its methods of work and its obstinate opposition to all modernization, can ... act as a brake on the process of democratisation.[4]

It must be recognized, however, that municipal governments were never intended to be instruments of mass democracy — a point made clear in Chapter 2. Indeed, Magnusson argues that "by putting great numbers of people under the same authorities and giving exclusive powers of decision to elected or appointed officials, early municipal reformers made sure that democracy would not be government by the masses and

---

[2]Quoted in Engin Isin, *Cities Without Citizens*, Montreal, Black Rose Books, 1992, p. 132.

[3]Georges Langrod, "Local Government and Democracy," in *Public Administration*, Vol. XXXI, Spring 1953, pp. 25-33. The oft-quoted Langrod and Panter-Brick exchanges on the subject of local government and democracy are reprinted in Lionel D. Feldman (ed.), *Politics and Government of Urban Canada*, Toronto, Methuen, 1981, Section A.

[4]*Ibid.*, pp. 5-6.

so would not be a threat to property." He observes that even such oft-quoted "local democrats" as de Tocqueville and Mill favoured the creation of larger units of local government which made mass participation impracticable.[5]

Preoccupation with Property

The bias in favour of the propertied classes and the lack of participation by the masses is evident from the restricted franchise given to early municipal governments. In the early years only property owners were allowed the right to vote. It is instructive to recall the boards of police established in Upper Canada in the early 1830s and heralded as the breakthrough which transferred power from the appointed courts of quarter sessions to elected councils. As discussed in Chapter 2, membership on the board (council) was limited to freeholders (householders who paid a certain amount of rent per annum for their dwellings). In effect, provision was made for a governing elite. Similarly, Higgins observes that when Halifax was incorporated in 1841, its charter limited the vote to only about 800 people who could meet a property qualification, and restricted candidacy for office to a fraction of that number.[6] To take another example, Baker's study of St. John's, Newfoundland, notes that the incorporation of the city in 1888 was accompanied by strict property qualifications for both voters and candidates. He describes a number of measures which had the effect of ensuring that it was the merchants, lawyers and shopkeepers who dominated — within the colonial legislature as well as within the city council.[7] Similarly, Artibise has shown that the municipal governments of the major cities of western Canada were dominated by a business elite, "partly because of a restricted franchise which effectively limited opposition."[8]

---

[5]Warren Magnusson, "Community Organization and Local Self-Government," in Feldman, *op. cit.,* pp. 61-65.

[6]Donald J. H. Higgins, *Local and Urban Politics in Canada*, Toronto, Gage, 1986, p. 39.

[7]M. Baker, "William Gilbert Gosling and the Establishment of Commission Government in St. John's, Newfoundland, 1914," *Urban History Review*, Vol. IX, No. 3, February 1981, pp. 37-39.

[8]Gilbert Stelter and Alan Artibise (eds.), *Shaping the Canadian Landscape: Aspects of the Canadian City-Building Process*, Ottawa, Carleton University Press, 1982, p. 21. See also the Artibise article on pp. 116-147.

In addition, businessmen were able to convince many others that their interests and those of the general community coincided.

Magnusson stresses the importance of the fact that the notion of municipal governments reflecting the interests of the propertied classes was well established *before* the franchise was extended to people without real property. This caused a strong resistance to political change even when the franchise was gradually extended.[9]

This resistance was evident in the turn of the century reform movement described in Chapter 3. The reformers claimed that their objective was to remove the harmful influence of politics from municipal government. What many of them meant by removing politics, however, was removing the political influence which could now be exercised by growing city populations. In this respect, the reformers were quite undemocratic or anti-democratic. As Plunkett and Betts describe the situation:

> ... their intention was not to try to halt the process of making decisions on public policy at the local level. Their intention, rather, was to exclude various groups from the process.... The reformers were interested in restoring the efficiency and effectiveness of municipal service delivery. At the same time, they were plainly concerned with restricting the influence of the cities' burgeoning population of working people upon the conduct of municipal affairs.[10]

This latter viewpoint reflected the fact that many of the reformers were middle-class merchants and businessmen who had little sympathy for the democratic aspects of local government. In their minds, the solution was to run local government more like a business. This, of course, also meant that citizens should elect more business people to councils — an argument which demonstrated the self-interest within the reform movement.

It will be recalled that the reformers tried to reduce the influence of the ward politician, either by pushing for at large elections or for the establishment of boards of control, elected at large, which took over many of the important decisions from ward politicians. Yet it was these ward politicians who helped to ensure representation from all areas of the municipality, including economically disadvantaged and ethnic neighbour-

---

[9]Warren Magnusson, "Introduction," in Warren Magnusson and Andrew Sancton (eds.), *City Politics in Canada*, Toronto, University of Toronto Press, 1983, p. 12.

[10]T. J. Plunkett and G. M. Betts, *The Management of Canadian Urban Government*, Kingston, Queen's University, 1978, p. 27.

hoods. Election at large was intended to favour the election of people of class and property. As with the boards of police of the 1830s, an attempt was being made to secure the position of a governing elite.

The local political process and the opportunities for lively political debate were also adversely affected by the reform movement and its fondness for separate boards and commissions. The establishment of these boards removed from the jurisdiction of elected councils many of the potentially most important public issues and activities — such as planning, policing, public health, childrens' aid, and public transit. Indeed, this erosion of municipal political vibrancy began much earlier, and Magnusson notes that "some of the heat was taken out of municipal politics in the nineteenth century by the separation of the school boards from the municipal councils and the effective assignment of charitable functions to the churches and other voluntary institutions."[11]

The Narrowing Scope of Municipal Government

This narrowing of municipal jurisdiction — and, therefore, of the potential scope of the local political process — has continued during the 20th century. The possibility of municipal governments becoming involved in the provision of a wide range of services financed by a variety of sources appears to have been largely undermined by the impact of the Depression, World War II and rapid post-war growth. When the Depression began, local governments exercised the main responsibility for the limited social service programs then in existence. Up until World War II, municipalities could finance their expenditures on these and other programs from local sales tax and even income tax as well as from the property tax. With the onset of the Depression, however, municipalities could not afford the financial burden of relief payments. Neither could a number of provincial governments for that matter, and the result was federal government intervention which has since evolved into the modern welfare state. "Canadian municipalities are now almost totally excluded from this crucial area of government policy."[12]

A similar pattern is evident in the health field. One hundred years ago, municipal governments were prominent in the public health movement and its preoccupation with reducing the spread of contagious disease. Much attention was focused on sanitation, sewage and the treatment of drinking water, and in many municipalities the public works de-

---

[11]Magnusson and Sancton, *op. cit.*, p. 10.

[12]Andrew Sancton, "Conclusion," in Magnusson and Sancton, *op. cit.*, p. 313.

partment grew out of the public health movement, as did urban planning, parks, housing and social service functions.[13] Granted, many of these functions were allocated to separate boards rather than being under the direct control of an all-purpose municipal council, but at least *local* government was a primary player in this field. Before the 20th century had progressed very far, however, powerful new diagnostic and therapeutic tools shifted attention from the public health movement to the "medical model" in which better health became equated with doctors and hospitals.[14] The result was increasing federal and provincial involvement in health and a corresponding reduction in the public health movement and the municipal government role therein. Whether the recent revival of the "Healthy Communities Movement" can restore a more prominent role for municipal governments remains to be seen.

The outbreak of World War II brought about a centralization of finances in Canada which ushered in an era of federal-provincial tax-rental and tax-sharing agreements. As the federal and provincial levels competed for the largest possible share of the major tax fields, municipal governments were increasingly squeezed out, reverting to their historical dependence upon the property tax. For example, Ontario introduced its first unconditional grant in 1936 when it preempted municipal governments from the income tax field. Access to the corporate tax field was lost just five years later when the various provincial governments entered into a wartime agreement with the federal government which included the "rental" of this field to the federal level. Instead of tax sources, municipalities were offered an increasing number of conditional grants directed to ensuring the provision of services and servicing standards felt to be important to the senior levels of government.

The rapid urbanization of the post-war period further confirmed the narrowing of municipal government's primary role to that of providing the physical services needed to support the continued growth and expansion of our cities, as discussed in Chapter 4. The primary thrust of federal and provincial policies and financial assistance was clearly in this direction, as evidenced by the lending policies of the Central (now Canada) Mortgage and Housing Corporation, and the grants for road construction

---

[13]For a good summary of these developments, see Trevor Hancock, Bernard Pouliot and Pierre Duplessis, "Public Health," in Richard Loreto and Trevor Price (eds.), *Urban Policy Issues: Canadian Perspectives*, Toronto, McClelland & Stewart, 1990, pp. 189-206.

[14]*Ibid.*, p. 192.

and for the provision of water supply and sewage disposal systems. Consistent with this viewpoint is Timothy Colton's observation that Metropolitan Toronto was invented to promote what was presumed to be a common and profound interest in rapid urban growth.[15]

Limited Participation by Municipal Electorate

Whatever its democratic virtues in theory, municipal government in practice has always shown a preoccupation with property owners and with the provision of services to property. The promise of a much broader scope for municipal activities did not survive the combined centralizing effect of two world wars and a prolonged and severe depression.

Municipalities are also limited as democratic institutions by the relatively low level of public participation in their activities. This is evident from an examination of the most fundamental form of participation — voting in municipal elections. While the local electors *ought to be* key players in the local political process, a disappointingly low proportion of voters take advantage of their democratic opportunities every municipal election year. While the approximately two-thirds voting turnout in federal and provincial elections is not great, it certainly contrasts with the 40% or fewer who vote at the municipal level.[16]

A number of factors are commonly cited as influencing the municipal vote. Studies of voter turnout lend some support to the notion that the turnout is higher in smaller municipalities than in larger ones.[17] The same type of population-to-turnout relationship helps explain why the voting turnout in populous municipalities tends to be higher with a ward system than with elections at large. Socio-economic factors such as the educational level of the electorate and the proportion of home-owners versus tenants also have an influence.[18] Voting turnout is also affected by the

---

[15]Timothy J. Colton, *Big Daddy*, Toronto, University of Toronto Press, 1980, p. 175.

[16]For more detailed statistics, see Higgins, *op. cit.*, pp. 311-313.

[17]See, for example, J. M. Mackenzie, *Ontario Municipal Elections: An Overview (Or Who Cares Anyway?)*, Kingston, Institute of Local Government, Queen's University, undated.

[18]R. Vaison and P. Aucoin, "Class and Voting in Recent Halifax Mayoralty Elections," in L. D. Feldman and M. D. Goldrick (eds.), *Politics and Government of Urban Canada: Selected Readings*, Toronto, Methuen, 1976, pp. 200-219.

extent of competition for the seats available. Acclamations for the head of council position usually result in a reduced turnout, while a close race for that position can have a very positive impact on turnout. A higher voting turnout is also common when there are "questions" on the ballot in the form of plebiscites or referendums.[19] Indeed, there is an old saying which suggests that the most effective way to increase voter interest is to add a liquor licensing question to the ballot.

It is widely held that a major negative influence on voting turnout is the complicated nature of the municipal election process. At the provincial and federal levels, voters are accustomed to selecting one name from three or four, all of them normally identified by a party label. In contrast, the municipal voter must make choices within several different categories (or from multiple ballots) from among many dozens of individual candidates.

> In the 1984 civic elections in Vancouver, for example, each voter had to choose one of five candidates for mayor, ten of twenty-seven candidates for alderman, nine of twenty-seven for school board seats, and seven of twenty-nine candidates for the parks board.[20]

The rather daunting task facing each Vancouver voter, therefore, was to choose a total of twenty-seven from a list of eighty-eight names, while also answering "yes" or "no" to a plebiscite on the question on the testing of the cruise missile in Canada.

A further complication arises in urban areas like Toronto and Ottawa where both lower tier and upper tier councils are now directly elected.

Voting turnout may also be low because the act of voting has little meaning for many citizens. Many municipalities today have retained historic boundaries that bear little relation to the living patterns of today. Citizens are unlikely to take an active interest in the activities of their municipality if their normal circle of movement for work, shopping, and recreation embraces quite different — and usually larger — areas. The relevance of municipal decision making may also be limited in the minds of citizens because so many of the issues which concern them are not handled by municipal councils but by separate boards. This is true in most jurisdictions for such matters as education and public health. Yet, where there are elected school boards, voter turnout is usually even lower than

---

[19]For a discussion of these forms of "direct democracy" which are relatively common at the municipal level, see Patrick Boyer, *Lawmaking by the People: Referendums and Plebiscites in Canada*, Toronto, Butterworths, 1982.

[20]Higgins, *op. cit.*, p. 315.

that experienced for the municipal elections. School boards in Ontario, for example, spend more than half of the property taxes which are levied by municipal councils. There is apparently widespread dissatisfaction with the quality of education being provided. Yet only about 1 voter in 4 casts a ballot in school board elections.

The narrowing and limited scope of municipal activities may contribute to the low voting turnout. If municipalities do little more than provide the physical services to support growth and development, as suggested above, what is there about this administrative role which will generate citizen interest and involvement? Consider the issues and themes raised by candidates during recent election campaigns. Are voters given competing "visions" about the future of their municipality? Are they made part of an effort to define local interests and concerns, to identify the priorities that the community wants to address together? Is there even a hint in most municipal election campaigns that a fundamental democratic exercise is underway? The answer to all these questions is no. By far the most common message offered to voters in municipal elections is "vote for me and I won't increase your taxes." While this is a popular thing to say — except to those voters who have stopped believing such promises — it is simplistic and probably also unrealistic. It says nothing about how and where tax dollars should be spent, or about what difficult choices must be made *if* tax increases are to be curtailed. A municipal election campaign affords an excellent opportunity to educate local citizens about the tough choices and exciting opportunities which face the municipality. If some of that excitement could be communicated to the voters, they might gain an understanding of the importance and significance of casting their ballots. Instead, the election campaign is reduced to a parade of would-be councillors attempting to convince us of how frugal they would be if put in charge of our tax dollars.

It is acknowledged that promising no tax increases may work as a strategy for the election of individual candidates. But, the issue here is a much broader one — the general lack of voter interest and voting turnout in municipal elections. If the only point is to get individuals elected, then let them promise whatever the voters want to hear. But if the point is to develop an appreciation for the political role of municipal government and the vital issues which a municipal council can help its citizens to face and manage, then the campaign needs to be conducted quite differently.

Potential voters may also be disillusioned by the realization that they are not able to enforce any real accountability for actions through the mechanism of periodic elections. How can accountability be allocated, and criticism or praise handed out where warranted? The fact is that there is no clear focus of accountability and responsibility within virtually any of our municipal councils. Without organized political parties, there is no "Government" and no "Official Opposition." Everyone is responsible for everything, which also means that no one is really responsible for anything.

For the minority who do exercise their franchise, voting in municipal elections is, at best, an infrequent and rather passive activity. Many citizens want more continuous, direct involvement. They want the opportunity to participate in the process of making decisions, not just to pass judgment "after-the-fact" by voting for or against certain councillors. For such citizens, the normal recourse has been to form or join local groups.

Local Groups

Such groups are not new, of course, and Chapter 3 described a number of local groups which spearheaded the turn of the century reform movement. Also of long standing are various residents' and ratepayers' associations established to protect the interests of the property owner as principal taxpayer. Groups representing the business community and the middle class have also been prominent in a number of cities for more than half a century, often promoting the election of like-minded councillors and attempting to prevent the election of candidates representing labour or socialist viewpoints. More will be said about these "non-party parties" in a later section of this chapter.

The 1960s and 1970s saw a great increase in local citizens' groups, often representing local citizens and neighbourhoods that had not previously been active or influential in public affairs. In addition, a number of these groups attempted to broaden their concerns beyond one specific issue (although it may have caused their initial formation) and sought to change the municipal decision-making process by building in a consultative element. If there was one common feature of most of these groups over the years, it was their attitude toward growth and development. Just as many of the earlier groups, especially those representing the business community, were pro-growth, so many of the more recent groups, representing neighbourhoods, were concerned with stability and the preservation of existing lifestyles.

According to Magnusson,[21] a new reform politics grew out of this process, one which questioned long held views about "sacrificing the neigh-

---

[21]Magnusson and Sancton, *op. cit.*, pp. 33-34.

bourhood to the larger community, observing the proprieties of bureaucratic procedure, respecting the judgments of professional planners, and
accepting the leadership of elected officials...." Part of this new way of
thinking was the belief that municipal politics should be rooted in the
ward or neighbourhood, at the level where people would and could be
more directly involved in political activity. This view is similar to Fowler's
notion of "authentic politics," discussed in Chapter 4.[22]

Groups representing the business community merit separate mention.
They offer quite a contrast to most citizens' groups, which rely heavily on
volunteers, lack funds, have difficulty getting access to information and
often face an unsympathetic city hall. By comparison, business groups
usually have a solid financial base, full time staff to provide continuity and
ready access to information. In addition, "there tends to be an affinity
between the interests of the corporate sector and the business or professional background and perspectives of a large proportion of local elected
officials."[23] Research by Lorimer and Gutstein in the early 1970s showed
that sometimes up to eighty percent of city councils and land use advisory
bodies in Canadian local governments were members of the development
industry.[24]

Higgins suggests that the elements of the corporate sector with the
greatest interest in municipal operations include real estate agencies,
construction companies (and unions), and their associated contractors in
areas such as electrical and plumbing work, property development companies, and firms of architects and engineering consultants.[25] Among
their associations, he cites the Canadian Real Estate Association, the
Canadian Construction Association, and the Canadian Home Builders
Association (formerly the Housing and Urban Development Institute of
Canada).[26]

---

[22]Edmund P. Fowler, *Building Cities That Work*, Kingston, McGill-Queen's
University Press, 1992, pp. 120-133.

[23]*Ibid.*, p. 291.

[24]James Lorimer, *A Citizen's Guide to City Politics*, Toronto, James Lewis and
Samuel, 1972, Chapters 7 and 8, and Donald Gutstein, *Vancouver, Ltd.*, Toronto,
Lorimer, 1975.

[25]Higgins, *op. cit.*, pp. 291-292.

[26]See *ibid.*, pp. 290-299 for a discussion of the influence of the private corporate
sector, and of property development associations and individual companies.

Profiles of Local Political Activity

In an attempt to provide a clearer picture of the nature of local political activity, this section offers brief profiles of political activity in four major Canadian cities. These examples reveal both the citizen activism since the 1960s and also the efforts of business groups to elect coalitions of like-minded candidates (essentially local political parties) for the avowed purpose of keeping party politics out of local government.

I Winnipeg

Local political activity in Winnipeg received a great stimulus in 1919, when the General Strike of that year polarized the city. A Civic Election Committee was formed by downtown businesses to endorse, and raise funds for, anti-labour candidates. Until the end of the 1980s, this organization, later known as the Metropolitan Election Committee, then the Greater Winnipeg Election Committee, and finally the Independent Citizen Election Committee (ICEC), continued to elect a majority of the members of council against the efforts of the Independent Labour Party, the CCF and, most recently, the NDP.

While essentially a pro-business local political party, the ICEC insisted that it was not a party at all and that support for its candidates would prevent parties — especially socialist parties — from bringing their politics and policies into the municipal council chamber. As a result, the ICEC was able to avoid accepting the responsibility for leadership in spite of its dominant numerical position within Winnipeg council over the decades.

The year 1972 was a watershed for Winnipeg, ushering in the new Unicity structure of government. A major objective of the new system was the fulfillment of the representative role of municipal government and the encouragement of increased public participation through special consultative machinery. The anticipated increase in citizen participation in the decision-making process did not materialize, however, for reasons discussed in Chapter 5.

The ICEC continued its domination through the first decade of new Unicity government in Winnipeg. By the 1980 municipal election, however, ICEC's veneer of nonpartisanship had worn quite thin, and the NDP scored a breakthrough by capturing seven seats on the Unicity council, with another nine going to independent candidates and the remaining twelve to ICEC candidates. Shortly before the 1983 election, the ICEC announced that it was disbanding. One analyst interpreted this step as a clever ploy rather than a sign of collapse. It removed from the scene a name associated with the past council's record, it put off the need for a consensus among the traditional ICEC candidates until after the election, and it avoided the necessity of providing an alternative to the NDP program.[27]

Whatever the motives underlying the dissolution of the ICEC, the election results were quite disappointing for the NDP. They lost one of their seven seats, and nearly lost two others. The local party was undoubtedly hurt by the controversial attempt by the NDP provincial government of Howard Pawley to entrench French as an official language in Manitoba, especially after this became a local referendum issue. In addition, however, the local party was hurt by its own internal divisions between "old guard" members and newer, more progressive members.

The NDP presence on Unicity council was reduced even further, to just two members, in the 1986 municipal elections. The other 27 members elected were all independents, although the majority of them represented the now-disbanded ICEC. Indeed, one assessment identified 20 of these 27 "independents" as actively involved with the Progressive Conservative or Liberal parties,[28] continuing the domination of the ICEC type of candidate. According to one observer,[29] the provincial NDP again contributed to the poor showing of the local NDP, this time much more directly. He claimed that the provincial party created confusion for the local party by overruling its decisions, deciding for the local party that it would not run a candidate for mayor, and redirecting key party workers to the elections in Saskatchewan and British Columbia, thereby weakening the local campaign.

In 1989 a reform coalition composed of New Democrats and Liberals was formed under the hopeful name of WIN (Winnipeg into the Nineties).[30] It succeeded in electing members to one-third of the seats on council, establishing for the first time a cohesive reform block on Winnipeg city council. In the most recent election (1992), WIN candidates

---

[27]Dave Hall, "Twisted Tale of Intentions," in *City Magazine*, Winnipeg, April 1984, p. 14.

[28]This is the assessment of Jeff Lowe, "Winnipeg: User-Unfriendly," in *City Magazine*, Winnipeg, Spring 1988, p. 9.

[29]Kent Gerecke, "Winnipeg Hits Bottom," in *City Magazine*, Winnipeg, Winter 1986-87, p. 35.

[30]Barton Reid, "City Beat," in *City Magazine*, Winnipeg, Winter '92/93, p. 5.

retained their minority position, holding five seats on a council reduced from 21 to 15.

II Vancouver

As with Winnipeg, it was the threat of political gains by the left which prompted the establishment of a pro-business party in Vancouver. The year was 1936, and three CCF candidates were elected in the city's first at large municipal election. In response, business interests founded the Non-Partisan Association (NPA), its very name designed to conceal its real status as a local political party.

The NPA began to run into increasingly strong citizen opposition in the 1960s, concerning both the pace and the location of developments. The city's urban renewal initiatives, for example, were typical of the time in that they involved the displacement of large numbers of families. The Strathcona Property Owners' and Tenants' Association was established in 1968, devoted to halting further such projects in its neighbourhood. The following year the federal government announced that it would not provide funds for the urban renewal project in Strathcona unless the residents were involved in the planning process. The result was a working committee comprising government officials and members of the Association, "one of the first instances in Canada of citizens sharing this kind of decision-making with government."[31] As launched in 1972, the rehabilitation plan became a model for other such programs. Rather than expropriating homes, it emphasized repairs and renovations and provided stability for the Strathcona neighbourhood.

Vancouver's various expressway schemes also prompted strong public opposition which led to their rejection on several occasions. The June 1967 release of the Vancouver Transportation Study triggered a prolonged debate. Leo notes that "citizen protest against the expressway system culminated in November in an acrimonious public meeting attended by five hundred citizens. Some thirty organizations and individuals prepared briefs for submission at the meeting."[32] More significantly, new political parties were formed to challenge the NPA vision of the city.

An important breakthrough appeared to occur in 1972 with the defeat of the NPA and the election of a municipal government controlled by

---

[31]Donald Gutstein, "Vancouver," in Magnusson and Sancton, *op. cit.*, p. 201.

[32]Christopher Leo, *The Politics of Urban Development: Canadian Urban Expressway Disputes*, Monographs on Canadian Urban Government - No. 3, Toronto, Institute of Public Administration, 1977, p. 46.

TEAM (The Electors Action Movement). A coalition of reformers, especially antiexpressway forces, and more conservative business interests, TEAM did make some noteworthy changes.[33] It restructured the bureaucracy, replacing the commissioner system with a single city manager with reduced executive powers, and made some moves to open up city hall to public involvement. Leo concedes that TEAM was a liberal, establishment party, focused on middle class issues, and with only a limited concern for matters like "affordable housing, inner-city education, homelessness, racism, and womens' issues."[34] But he contends that TEAM made a valuable contribution by shifting attention from a conservative, development-oriented approach to city planning to one which addressed issues of "livability."[35] Whatever its accomplishments, within four years TEAM was badly divided and in the 1978 election the NPA re-emerged as the major party on council.[36]

But control of council by right-wing interests faced a new challenge in 1980 when Mike Harcourt, a New Democrat, won the mayoralty and the Committee of Progressive Electors (COPE) elected three councillors. COPE had been formed in 1968 by the Vancouver and District Labour Council with the objective of bringing together labour ratepayer groups, the NDP and other interested groups to establish a base to enter municipal politics. The left was still in a minority on the 1980 council, however, and discussions were often bitter, with members of the NPA, TEAM and COPE increasingly polarized. In addition to this constraint on the mayor's initiatives, the Social Credit provincial government continued to protect business interests and obviously had misgivings about the election of an NDP mayor.

Harcourt was returned as mayor in 1982, along with four COPE councillors and two independent NDP councillors. Gutstein[37] refers to this

[33]Gutstein in Magnusson and Sancton, *op. cit.*, pp. 206-209.

[34]Christopher Leo, "The Urban Economy and the Power of the Local State," in Frisken, *op. cit.*, p. 690.

[35]*Ibid.*, pp. 690-691.

[36]For an analysis of Vancouver's political parties by a founding member of TEAM, see Paul Tennant, "Vancouver City Politics," in Feldman, *op. cit.*, pp. 126-147.

[37]Donald Gutstein, "Vancouver: Progressive Majority Impotent," in *City Magazine*, Winnipeg, Vol. VI, No. 1, p. 12.

election result as the "first successful challenge to business dominance at the local level in the city's 96 year history." However, there were some difficulties in maintaining a progressive voting bloc on council, and continuing problems with interference from the Social Credit provincial government. Indeed, one book during this period[38] expressed concern that local autonomy was being threatened by the neo-conservative forces in power provincially and their view that local authorities should not be allowed to follow policies contrary to the market-oriented revival being promoted provincially.[39]

On the surface, the 1984 election results were quite similar to those of 1982. Harcourt was re-elected mayor, along with five progressive members — four of them from COPE. Opposing them were three members from the NPA and two from TEAM. According to Gutstein,[40] the polarization of the city was completed with this election. As he saw it, Vancouver is really two cities: a working class east side city and a middle class west side city — which elect two entirely different councils.

The 1986 election results were quite dramatic, bringing Vancouver's developers back into power at Vancouver's city hall. The NPA captured nine of the eleven seats on council — including its mayoral candidate, developer Gordon Campbell — and eight of nine seats on the School Board. According to Gutstein,[41] Campbell was successful in attracting the moderate voters in spite of his right wing, pro-development record, especially when the alternative was Harry Rankin of COPE, a long time socialist councillor who was seen by many as quite radical.

Campbell easily won re-election in 1988 and in 1990, but COPE managed to increase its representation on council to three and then to five. The 1993 election was a near-sweep for the NPA, with COPE winning

---

[38]Warren Magnusson, William K. Carroll, Charles Doyle, Monika Langer and R. B. J. Walker (eds.), *The New Reality: The Politics of Restraint in British Columbia*, Vancouver, NewStar Books, 1984.

[39]A very similar pattern, even more pronounced, was also evident in British local government during this period, as Margaret Thatcher attempted to impose her view of the appropriate scope of government activity on resistant labour-controlled municipal councils. See, for example, Gerry Stoker, *The Politics of Local Government*, London, Macmillan Education Ltd., 1988, chapters 7 and 8.

[40]Donald Gutstein, "Civic Election Wars," in *City Magazine*, Summer 1985, p. 12.

[41]Donald Gutstein, "Vancouver Voters Swing Right," *City Magazine*, Winter 1986-87, p. 30. The brief outline which follows is based on the Gutstein article.

only one of the ten seats on council. The NPA also captured the mayoralty, although with one-third less popular support than Campbell had received in the preceding election.[42] In an ironic twist of fate, the right-wing city council must contend with an NDP provincial government led by Mike Harcourt — much as Harcourt, when head of a left-leaning council a decade ago, had to contend with interference from the Social Credit provincial government.

III Montreal

The modern period of local politics in Montreal can be dated from 1914, according to Guy Bourassa.[43] Since that time, we have witnessed a succession of powerful and popular mayors, often gaining re-election. The regimes over which they presided, however, were often corrupt and financially strapped, and the provincial government had to intervene on a number of occasions, notably in 1918 when the province virtually took over the running of the city by appointing a five member administrative commission.[44] Corruption within the city government finally led to a judicial inquiry, prompted by the urgings of the Civic Action League and its offshoot the Committee for Public Morality. One of the investigators for this inquiry was Jean Drapeau, then a young lawyer. When the inquiry ended in 1953, the Civic Action League decided to run candidates in the upcoming 1954 election. Drapeau became the League's successful candidate for mayor, and the rest, as they say, is history!

Drapeau's first term of office was a difficult one, because the Civic Action League had not gained control over the council itself. After losing the 1957 election, Drapeau disassociated himself from the Civic Action League but managed to attract most of their city councillors to his new Civic Party. It was as head of this highly disciplined party that he returned to power as mayor in 1960 — a position he was to hold until his retirement prior to the 1986 election.

By the end of the 1960s, however, there were signs of growing citizen activism in Montreal. Potentially strong opposition to Drapeau first sur-

---

[42]Barton Reid, "Civic Elections 1993," *City Magazine*, Fall/Winter '93/'94, p. 8.

[43]Guy Bourassa, "The Political Elite of Montreal: From Aristocracy to Democracy," in Feldman and Goldrick, *op. cit.*, pp. 146-155.

[44]Andrew Sancton, "Montreal," in Magnusson and Sancton, *op. cit.*, p. 67. The following outline of events leading up to Drapeau's long tenure in office is largely based on Sancton's material.

faced in 1970 in the form of the Front d'action politique (FRAP), which was a grouping of trade unions and left-wing nationalist organizations.[45] Whatever prospects this organization had were dashed by the FLQ kidnapping crisis and Drapeau's success in linking FRAP with the outlawed terrorist group and in capitalizing on the public's desire for stability and security.

Over the next several years opposition to Drapeau grew, not only from radicals who deplored his failure to provide sufficient housing and social and recreational services in the poorer sections of the city but also from middle class groups concerned with stopping high-rise development, saving the city's older buildings and neighbourhoods, and forcing a more democratic, open system of government.[46] These opposition forces came together in 1974 to form the Montreal Citizens' Movement (MCM), which made a dramatic impact on the November municipal elections. Drapeau received only 55.1% of the popular vote for mayor — almost a rebuff in relation to his past results — and his Civic Party won only thirty-six seats on council, with the MCM winning eighteen and a group called Democracy Montreal winning another.

The following year the provincial government took over responsibility for the preparations for the 1976 Olympic Games because of the city administration's poor performance. For the first time there was also clear evidence of corruption within the city administration. One might have expected, therefore, that the opposition forces would consolidate their position and prepare for the overthrow of the Drapeau regime in the 1978 election. Instead, the MCM split apart and was taken over by a group of radical socialists. Its policy orientation alienated the newly elected provincial government of the Parti Québécois which, in any event, was not anxious to tangle with Drapeau and was quite prepared to stay out of city politics if Drapeau would keep his influential voice out of the sovereignty-association debate. A new party, the Municipal Action Group (essentially a front for federal Liberals) emerged in time for the election, but Drapeau was re-elected easily and his Civic Party won fifty-two of the fifty-four seats on council.[47]

According to Milner, the resurrection of the MCM in the early 1980s was largely due to its new leader, Jean Doré. While Drapeau was re-

---

[45]*Ibid.*, p. 73.

[46]*Ibid.*

[47]*Ibid.*, p. 76.

turned in 1982 and his Civic Party captured 39 of the 57 council seats, popular support was down — almost 18% less with respect to Drapeau. The 1986 election saw a massive victory for the MCM, with only one Civic Party councillor and two independents elected to council. In Milner's view, the Doré-led MCM "appeared reasonable and approachable, especially when contrasted with Drapeau's Gaullist style; its hammering at everyday bread and butter issues corresponded more closely to the emerging public mood than Drapeau's seeming preoccupation with grand projects."[48]

In contrast to the autocratic, secretive style long followed by Drapeau, the new administration was characterized by a cautious and consensual approach. Consultation was the watchword. The fact that little of substance appeared to change in Montreal during the MCM's first term was, in Milner's view, due less to the style of the new administration than to the nature of power at the municipal level. He points out that even a very activist administration is powerless to act in many spheres of local concern and cites the powers allocated to separate local boards and to the upper tier government of the Montreal Urban Community.

However, Milner also noted that grass roots involvement in the MCM had apparently diminished. Developers and businessmen were not long in courting the new administration and party activists soon found little scope for their activities. Their best leaders had become city councillors or political advisors. Milner's assessment of what happened bears repeating:

> The syndrome is a classic one: the reformist movement takes power and effectively moves toward the centre of the spectrum, attempting to rule in the name of the electorate as a whole, not merely the party activists, who find their activities largely confined to vindicating such limited actions, raising money and recruiting new members. And with no opposition left in City Hall, the external enemy is gone: there's no one, out there, to fight.[49]

Four MCM councillors defected before the first term was up. They complained of overwhelming pressure to follow the party line and the silencing of debate within the party. Ironically, these were charges that one would have expected to hear (and did) about the previous regime. The MCM dissidents set up their own party, the Democratic Coalition of

---

[48]Henry Milner, "The Montreal Citizens' Movement, Then and Now," in *Quebec Studies*, No. 6, 1988, p.5.

[49]*Ibid.*, p. 8.

Montreal (DCM) which they claimed was closer to the original ideals of the MCM.[50]

The MCM was easily reelected in 1990, although with only 37 of the 51 seats on council. Critics still found little real change in operating style from the days of Drapeau. The executive committee was still all-powerful, and it was made up exclusively of MCM councillors who were expected to display party solidarity.[51] Rumblings within the party, and some defections, led to some changes in September 1992 — including a commitment to increase councillor power through local district advisory committees (discussed below) and to improve civil service efficiency and service delivery.

In addition, the MCM did initiate a number of steps designed to increase citizen access to city hall. One notable feature was the establishment of Access Montreal, a storefront, neighbourhood based network of public information offices. These offices encompass a broad range of functions, acting as consultation centres, information relay points, and outlets for direct transactions with the city.[52] Citizens with questions or concerns can make contact with their municipal government at one of these offices, at a meeting of their local district advisory council, at a meeting of one of the city's five standing committees or, on major issues, by presenting a brief to the public consultation office. In spite of all of these opportunities for public input, however, critics charge that nothing happens unless it finds its way to, and receives the approval of, the executive committee. That body is composed of the mayor and six other councillors named by the mayor and approved by council, usually within a week after an election. The executive committee holds weekly, closed meetings. Other councillors are not allowed to attend. Nearly every motion presented to council is prepared by the executive committee.[53]

Further evidence of the closed-door, top-down approach to decision making is found in the operation of the city's five council committees. These were established after the 1986 election to allow elected represen-

---

[50]Karen Herland, *People, Potholes and City Politics*, Montreal, Black Rose Books, 1992, p. 14.

[51]*Ibid.*, p. 15.

[52]Pierre Niedlispacher, "Access Montreal: Customer-Driven Municipal Services," in James McDavid and Brian Marson (eds.), *The Well-Performing Government Organization*, Toronto, Institute of Public Administration, 1991, pp. 65-67.

[53]Herland, *op. cit.*, p. 37.

tatives to examine important issues carefully before city hall made decisions. But, one observer points out that Mayor Doré made sure to exclude members of opposition parties from almost all positions on these committees. "By naming MCM councillors to 26 of the 27 committee positions, he got lapdogs instead of watchdogs."[54] It is also charged that Doré steered controversial issues away from these committees, leaving them to spin their wheels discussing secondary matters.[55]

Indicative of the gap between rhetoric and action is the MCM creation of district advisory councils.[56] When it was first established as an opposition party, MCM made much of the importance of neighbourhood councils, which would involve the decentralization of city government. These councils would deal with specific political and economic concerns from a grassroots perspective. In the party platform for the 1986 municipal election, MCM referred to decentralizing municipal services to ten neighbourhoods directed by decision-making councils. What was established in 1987 after the MCM came to power, however, were district (not neighbourhood) advisory (not decision making) councils. Moreover, the city defined the districts without consultation, sometimes dividing the jurisdictions of particular community centres. With populations of up to 150 000 each, the districts were also too large for effective grassroots representation. In practice, district advisory councils have become "a place where local and individual concerns can be raised, but are then easily lost in the subsequent paper-shuffle."[57]

Quesnel offers a somewhat more positive assessment of the MCM performance.[58] She notes that it took office at a time of economic downturn, closing of offices and loss of jobs in Montreal, conditions which constrained its scope for action. She acknowledges that MCM handled some issues awkwardly — notably the case of Overdale in which residents of 100 housing units in the Overdale area were displaced to make room for a 100 million dollar condo project, which has yet to be built. She also describes the criticism of MCM for giving too much consideration to

[54]Henry Aubin, "Promises Not To Keep," *Montreal Gazette*, November 8, 1994.

[55]*Ibid.*

[56]The analysis which follows is based on *ibid.*, p. 57.

[57]*Ibid.*, p. 48.

[58]Louise Quesnel, "Party Politics in the Metropolis," in Frisken, *op. cit.*, pp. 581-612.

developers, and for being too slow in establishing parks and green areas in the city. Overall, Quesnel rates the MCM's achievements as impressive, and cites such initiatives as reorganization of the administrative structure, establishment of a neighbourhood information network (Access Montreal), creation of consultative committees on planning issues, and creation of a new program for waste recycling.[59] She argues, however, that the city lacks the resources to tackle the social and environmental issues it faces unless it receives greater support from the provincial and federal governments.

In the November 1994 municipal election, the MCM was reduced to six seats on council. Doré was among the MCM candidates not re-elected and he announced his intention to leave municipal politics — while not ruling out the possibility of running for mayor again in four years time.[60] Pierre Bourque was elected mayor, and the Vision Montreal party which he heads captured 38 other seats on the 51 member city council. Bourque has promised to cut spending by $100 million in 1995 and to abolish half of the very controversial $108 million surtax on commercial and industrial properties this year. He has also talked about abolishing some of the consultative structures which has been established by the MCM, including the district advisory councils and the standing committees of council. In light of the preceding discussions, it is ironic that one of the main concerns of Doré in the aftermath of his defeat was to "keep the precious heritage of opening city hall to a democratization process."[61]

IV Toronto

Citizen activism became prominent in Toronto during the 1960s. A well documented example concerned an urban renewal scheme for the Treffann Court area of the city, which proposed the usual demolition of buildings.[62] Citizen opposition led, as in Vancouver, to a new approach in which the affected citizens became involved in the development of the urban renewal plans. More generally, the extent of high-rise commercial

---

[59]*Ibid.*, pp. 600-601.

[60]Michelle Lalonde, "Doré Quits City Politics," *Montreal Gazette*, November 8, 1994.

[61]Quoted in the *Montreal Gazette*, November 8, 1994.

[62]An excellent analysis of this episode is found in Graham Fraser, *Fighting Back*, Toronto, Hakkert, 1972.

redevelopment and apartment construction was threatening middle and upper class neighbourhoods. Opposition to such projects prompted the establishment or revival of ratepayers' and residents' groups, which became increasingly aggressive in their opposition. "In 1968, a Confederation of Residents' and Ratepayers' Associations (CORRA) was established as a co-ordinating agency; it not only linked the middle-class organizations with one another, but brought them into contact with community groups being formed in poorer neighbourhoods."[63] Equally significant was the creation of the Stop Spadina, Save Our City, Coordinating Committee (SSSOCCC).[64]

Both inner-city poor who felt ignored and middle class urban conservatives who felt their neighbourhoods threatened agreed that city council had sold out to development interests. In addition to opposing specific development projects, the citizens' movement became influential in the municipal election process. The 1969 election brought a minority of reformers onto city council, and they were quite effective in defining their issues and concerns. The 1972 election appeared to be a breakthrough (just as it had appeared to be in Vancouver) with the election of a majority of reformers on council and a self-proclaimed member of the reform group — in the person of David Crombie — as mayor.

Once elected, however, David Crombie operated as a moderate and, in fact, voted against the reform councillors on many of the major issues facing council.[65] While he was genuinely concerned about the threat to neighbourhoods posed by the excessively pro-growth mentality of previous councils, Crombie was no less committed to private property and private enterprise. Rather, he wanted to find a way of providing continued development without the disruption and dislocation which had accompanied it in the recent past.[66] The Crombie-led council was not radical enough for some and the reform majority soon splintered (as discussed below). But it did establish for the first time a concept that is now taken for granted as common sense — that major development decisions are a legitimate matter of public concern, to be made only after extensive consultation and debate.

---

[63]Warren Magnusson, "Toronto," in Magnusson and Sancton, *op. cit.*, p. 115.

[64]See Higgins, *op. cit.*, pp. 282-287, and Leo, *The Politics of Urban Development*.

[65]See Jon Caulfield, *The Tiny Perfect Mayor*, Toronto, James Lorimer and Company, 1974.

[66]Magnusson in Magnusson and Sancton, *op. cit.*, p. 119.

The reform group which had appeared to capture control of council in 1972 soon split into moderates and more militant reformers, with the latter becoming increasingly critical of Crombie's moderate policies. Ironically, while reform councillors continued to be elected throughout the 1970s, one of them — Michael Goldrick — persuasively argues that the election of 1972 was not the beginning but "the zenith of the reform movement."[67] As he explains, the moderates were satisfied that the reform movement would now ensure that neighbourhoods were protected, the automobile would be treated with common sense, and the style of development would be modified — all objectives of the middle class. The hard line reformers elected from working class wards, however, believed that the objective was one of redistributing wealth and power.

They wanted real, not token, decision-making power shifted to neighbourhoods, not only the style of development controlled but its pace, location and ownership subject to public decision; they challenged private property rights exercised by financial institutions and development corporations and attacked the fortresses of civil service power.[68]

After the 1974 election, six of the more radical reformers established the reform caucus, a disciplined group which attempted to develop alternative policies to those proposed by the moderates and the "Old Guard." While it was successful in expressing the interests of working class people, the reform caucus suffered from a negative, obstructionist image in the eyes of the media and from internal differences, partly based on personality conflicts.

A key figure was John Sewell, undoubtedly the most conspicuous and widely identified member of the reform group, and a community activist who had been earlier associated with a number of the citizen confrontations with city hall.[69] Sewell was a very independent minded politician and while he had made some unsuccessful attempts to build a reform party around himself, when he ran for mayor in 1978 it was as an independent.[70] After one very controversial term, especially in relation to

---

[67]Michael Goldrick, "The Anatomy of Urban Reform in Toronto," in *City Magazine*, May-June 1978, p. 36, an article which provides an excellent analysis of the reform group to that point in time.

[68]*Ibid.*

[69]For his personal reflections on these experiences, see John Sewell, *Up Against City Hall*, Toronto, James Lewis and Samuel, 1972.

[70]Magnusson in Magnusson and Sancton, *op. cit.*, p. 123.

Sewell's defence of various inner-city minorities and his demands for police reform, he was defeated by Arthur Eggleton, a Liberal with strong ties to the business community. Eggleton was re-elected throughout the 1980s.

In the meantime, however, reform councillors continued to be elected to council, although increasingly identified with the NDP. By 1980 they had nine of the twenty-three seats on council, with all but one of the victorious candidates having run with official party endorsation.[71] The differences between reformers and old guard seemed more muted by the early 1980s, partly as a result of the policies which had been adopted by the councils of the time and partly because the economic decline in the country had reduced the growth pressures.

It was this economic downturn, Frisken claims, which most influenced the rapid decline in Toronto city council's commitment to restricting the height and density of downtown buildings.[72] Even John Sewell, during his one term as mayor, gave high priority to keeping industrial jobs in the city and attracting new ones. By the mid-1980s, critics referred to a "let's make a deal" mode of decision-making to signify the city's willingness to allow developers building heights and densities that greatly exceeded the limits specified in its Central Area Plan.[73] By this time, as well, a building boom was underway in Toronto, highlighted by such major projects as the new domed stadium and the development of Harbourfront and railway lands at the south end of the city. Indeed, one observer described the air at city hall as full of "echoes of the 1960s," the heyday of the developers and their lobbyists.[74] He claimed that city hall was once again firmly under the control of the development industry which had simply acquired a new level of sophistication in its dealings with the council — a council which was more pro-development than any since the end of the 1960s.

If the developers were back, so were the citizens' groups - although perhaps not to the same degree. Frisken states that citizen group activity has been both limited and fragmented since the mid-1970s, posing little threat to incumbent aldermen or the conservative make-up of council as

---

[71]*Ibid.*, p. 122.

[72]Frances Frisken, *City Policy-Making in Theory and Practice: The Case of Toronto's Downtown Plan*, Local Government Case Study No. 3, London, University of Western Ontario, 1988, pp. 98-99.

[73]*The Globe and Mail*, May 23, 1984, as quoted in Frisken, p. 81.

[74]Geoffrey York, "The Politics of Influence," *Toronto*, November 1986, p. 50.

a whole.[75] Part of the problem, she notes, is that citizens' groups have become very issue-specific, lacking the tendency toward coalition building that characterized political pressure groups in the early 1970s — such as the previously cited examples of CORRA and SSSOCCC. Nonetheless, such groups as the Federation of North York Resident Associations and resident associations in Markham and Vaughan have been quite conspicuous.

Given this background, the results of the 1988 municipal elections in Toronto were quite striking. The voters defeated two pro-development aldermen, voted in a majority of designated reform candidates, and elected reform candidates to fill six of the eight city positions on the Metropolitan Toronto council.[76] More specifically, nine of the seventeen members of Toronto City Council are considered to be the reform group, of which six are NDP members. One of the nine was acclaimed to office, but all others were endorsed by Reform Toronto, a citizens' coalition which was established out of opposition to the pro-development old guard at city hall.

It is noteworthy that a number of other Ontario municipal election results in 1988 appeared to reflect a victory for citizens' groups over pro-development forces. For example, the heads of council in both Richmond Hill and Markham, very rapidly growing areas just north of Toronto, were both defeated after a series of reports about the allegedly excessive influence of the development industry in their municipalities. Cottage owners also used their voting power to elect councillors concerned with the environment and committed to slowing the pace of growth in a number of Ontario's resort areas.[77]

The 1991 municipal election in Toronto featured two candidates for mayor who represented quite contrasting positions on the political spectrum. A former chief commissioner of police and former councillor, June Rowlands, ran against a well known NDP member and former councillor, Jack Layton. The election victory for Rowlands was strongly influenced by what had been happening to the economy of the Toronto area. The boom which had lasted until the late 1980s had disappeared! Increased unemployment, empty office towers, more homeless roaming the streets,

---

[75]Frisken, *City Policy Making*, p. 93.

[76]Michael Valpy, "Voters Demonstrate Power of Ballot Box," *Globe and Mail*, November 16, 1988, p. A8.

[77]"Cottagers Pick Slow-Growth Councillors," *Globe and Mail*, November 16, 1988, p. A24.

food banks needed for thousands, mounting racial tension and crime — these were now the defining characteristics of the "world-class city" Toronto had sought to become. Such conditions clearly favoured the conservative, pro-development, and "law and order" platform of Rowlands. Moreover, Layton also had to contend with growing voter uncertainty about their wisdom in electing an NDP provincial government the previous year.

There was little real change in the make-up of the council itself. All incumbents who ran were returned and three new councillors were elected. City council remained split with 6 NDP members, two moderate or swing councillors and 8 right wingers.[78]

Rowlands ran for mayor of Toronto again in November 1994, but this time was defeated by an NDP councillor, Barbara Hall. However, the result was less a victory for the NDP than voter disillusionment with Rowlands, who stumbled in the final couple of weeks of her campaign, and growing respect for the personal qualities of Hall, as she became better known during the campaign. Indeed, although Hall was seen as the leader of the NDP caucus on Toronto city council during the 1991-94 term, she often voted with council's so-called old guard pro-development minority. For example, she broke with the NDP caucus to support the controversial Bay-Adelaide office tower and was the only NDP councillor who supported Toronto's failed 1996 Olympic bid from the outset.[79]

Hall campaigned on a social justice agenda, including more support for environmental projects and more public housing,[80] and six other NDP councillors were elected — the same number as in the previous council. But the pragmatism Hall has displayed in the past will be needed again, because the Toronto area has still not recovered from the severe recession which has been battering Ontario, and city tax revenues have fallen by $110 million over the past two years.[81] While the NDP has 7 of the 17 seats on Toronto's council, it remains to be seen how much room to maneuvre the party will have in light of the economic realities facing Toronto. If the past is any indication, business interests will face a receptive hearing when they approach city council with growth plans.

---

[78]This at least was the assessment by Kent Gerecke shortly after the election in "City Beat," *City Magazine*, Winter '91/92, p. 5.

[79]Article by Laurie Monsebraaten, *Toronto Star*, November 15, 1994.

[80]Tom Fennell, "Caught in the Middle," *Maclean's*, November 28, 1994, p. 38.

[81]*Ibid.*

Observations about the Local Political Process

Drawing from this admittedly brief overview of experiences in four large Canadian cities, and from the insights of other writings on this topic, what observations can be made about the local political process in practice? For ease of reference, the seven observations which follow are numbered accordingly.

1. There is continuing resistance to overt political party activity at the local level. The word overt should be stressed, since many local elected members are widely known to be associated with one of the provincial or national political party organizations. This type of association is apparently quite acceptable to the voters, but a more negative reaction could be expected if the same individuals were to run locally with a specific party affiliation.

An interesting example of this mind-set is provided by the results of the 1969 municipal elections for the City of Toronto. The Liberal Party, fresh from its 1968 national election victory, was interested in establishing a stronger base in Toronto, partly as a necessary prerequisite to the overthrow of the long-entrenched Progressive Conservative provincial government. The decision to enter a slate of candidates for municipal office was hotly debated, however, and the internal split in the party on this issue resulted in a less than wholehearted effort in the ensuing election.[82] Whatever the reasons, the election results were not heartening for the national parties. The Liberal Party's candidate for mayor, Stephen Clarkson, finished third with fewer than half as many votes as the victorious William Dennison. Significantly, Dennison had refused to run as an NDP candidate even though he was closely associated with the party. Only three candidates of the NDP and two of the Liberal candidates were elected as aldermen.[83]

2. Our second observation is that where we find political parties at the local level, they are not usually branches of the long-established provincial and federal parties but are purely local creations — often in the guise of

---

[82]For an examination of this election campaign by one of the key participants, see Stephen Clarkson, *City Lib*, Toronto, Hakkert, 1972. See also the exchange of views between Clarkson and J. L. Granatstein in Jack K. Masson and James Anderson (eds.), *Emerging Party Politics in Urban Canada*, Toronto, McClelland and Stewart, 1972, pp. 60-67.

[83]Donald J. H. Higgins, *Urban Canada: Its Government and Politics*, Toronto, Macmillan, 1977, p. 239.

a non-partisan group whose primary objective is to keep party politics out of local government, especially if it comes in the form of the NDP. This pattern has already been noted in connection with the rise of the Civic Election Committee in Winnipeg in 1919 and the Non-Partisan Association (NPA) in Vancouver in 1936. In addition, for over two decades after 1934, elections for Edmonton's council "revolved around the slate-making activities of the Citizens' Committee...."[84] This group splintered in 1959 when its leader, William Hawrelak, resigned as mayor after conflict of interest irregularities. While the number of new factions reached the point where local parties really no longer existed, "aldermen sharing a business orientation retained total domination of council."[85]

One further example is provided by the experience of Brandon, Manitoba, in which the local establishment successfully resisted an effort by the municipal NDP to elect members to city council.[86] The NDP challenge was mounted after the provincial NDP government elected in 1969 implemented recommendations which introduced a ward system in Brandon. In September 1971 plans were announced for a nominating meeting to choose a slate of NDP candidates in order to "break the domination of council by Conservatives and Liberals."[87] The meeting led to the nomination of a candidate for mayor and candidates for seven of the ten aldermanic positions on council.

The response of the local establishment took a rather familiar form. A Citizens Independent Voters Election Committee (CIVEC) was set up, to encourage and support candidates who would be independent of party politics. All of those elected to the executive of CIVEC were active in the Conservative and Liberal parties.[88] By early October CIVEC had endorsed candidates in all 10 wards (seven of whom were incumbents) as well as the incumbent mayor. The election saw a 55% voter turnout, the largest since the Second World War — and it is apparent that many of them turned out to support CIVEC. No NDP candidates were elected, and most received far fewer votes than the victorious CIVEC candidates.

---

[84]James Lightbody, "Edmonton," in Magnusson and Sancton, *op. cit.*, p. 261.

[85]*Ibid.*, p. 264.

[86]See Errol Black, "Small City Politics: The Brandon Experience," in *City Magazine*, Summer 1984, pp. 28-35, on which the following outline is based.

[87]*Ibid.*, p. 29.

[88]*Ibid.*, p. 31.

In the aftermath of the defeat, a number of explanations were offered for the poor showing of the NDP. These included the rather hurried preparations for entering the municipal election campaign, the overly comprehensive and detailed nature of the election platform, and the lack of credible candidates. Most of all, however, the results were attributed to the effectiveness of CIVEC's campaign against party politics at the local level.

3. A third observation, which follows closely from this second one, is that the NDP — of all the national parties — has shown by far the most persistence and commitment to the introduction of party politics at the local level. As a result, "if other national parties are not to be outflanked in the organization of the core metropolitan areas, the necessary response has to be an electoral challenge."[89]

It is unclear, however, how quickly municipal elections in our major urban areas will become party contests. Even the NDP contests municipal elections only sporadically and selectively. Experience has shown that there is still strong voter resistance to the overt introduction of party politics at the local level. Moreover, the other two national parties have continued to devote their energies to working behind the scenes supporting, and sometimes organizing, local groups of candidates who would oppose the NDP. About the only certainty is that the increase in partisan activity will continue to generate controversy and debate as to its appropriateness.

It is Sancton's view that we are farther away from municipal party politics in Canada than we were in the 1970s.[90] He notes that apart from cities in Quebec, Vancouver is the only major Canadian city whose council is in any way controlled by a political party. The continuing prominence of the Non Partisan Association (NPA) may be partly attributed to the at large elections in that city, which require extensive campaign finances of the sort more easily obtained by right-wing business candidates.

4. A fourth observation is that the relative influence of citizens' groups versus development interests seems to wax and wane, acting almost like a self-correcting pendulum swing. In admittedly over-simplified terms, the experience of the past couple of decades suggests that pro-development forces can prevail for some considerable period until their perceived

---

[89]Lightbody in Masson and Anderson, *op. cit.*, p. 199.

[90]Andrew Sancton, "The Municipal Role in the Governance of Canadian Cities," in Trudi Bunting and Pierre Filion (eds.), *Canadian Cities in Transition*, Toronto, Oxford University Press, 1991, pp. 473-476.

excesses prompt renewed citizen activism, leading to changes on city council. However, the citizen activism is difficult to sustain — partly for reasons discussed in the fifth observation, below — and pro-development forces again begin to assert themselves.

Thus, for example, the so-called citizens' movement of the 1960s appeared largely to disappear during the 1970s. Much of the progress in reducing the influence of the property industry and the business community generally over council operations seemed to have dissipated. Whether in Vancouver, Toronto, Winnipeg or even Montreal, the "gains" of citizens' groups and the election successes of "reform councillors" were not consolidated. Instead, the traditional pro-business councillors regained some of the ascendancy in the first three of these cities, and quickly came to terms with the MCM in Montreal.

The municipal election results in Toronto in 1988 and 1991 serve to illustrate this pattern. The first election occurred toward the end of a boom period in which a "let's make a deal" attitude had returned to city hall. Voters responded by electing a majority of reform candidates, all endorsed by a Reform Toronto coalition opposed to the pro-development stance of the previous council. Just three years later, however, Toronto found itself in a serious economic downturn. Regaining lost jobs and dealing with the perception of increased violence in the streets and neighbourhoods were suddenly more important, and the reform and NDP candidate for mayor, Jack Layton, was soundly defeated.

5. Part of the explanation for this waxing and waning of citizen influence can be found in a fifth observation, that reformers upon gaining power tend to moderate their positions and objectives. As Lorimer has pointed out, "the thrust for democratic reforms has been blunted by citizen-oriented politicians once in office. They are inclined to take their own election as an indication that the present political system can work reasonably well...."[91] This pattern was previously noted with respect to the experience of Toronto's city council after the election of reformers in 1972. It is also apparent in Milner's comments, quoted earlier, about MCM's move toward the centre in Montreal.

Citizen influence is also limited by the fact that the various citizens' groups which emerge are far from unanimous in what they hope to accomplish. According to Sancton, some are genuinely committed to various forms of neighbourhood self-government, others want to use local

---

[91]James Lorimer, "Introduction: The Post-developer Era for Canada's Cities Begins," in *City Magazine Annual 1981*, Toronto, James Lorimer and Company, 1981, p. 9.

issues mainly as a way of mobilizing the working class for larger battles to be fought in the national political arena, and most are concerned only with the particular issue at hand.[92] Magnusson refers to the fragile political alliances between working-class and middle-class neighbourhoods.[93] As he explains, middle-class neighbourhoods only need to be protected against adverse changes, as they see them. Such changes might well include "half-way" houses and public housing developments, as well as tax increases to support public services. Neighbourhood improvement often took the form of rehabilitation and in-fill construction oriented toward the profitable middle-class market, a process usually referred to as "gentrification." The result, of course, was to displace more of the poor into an inflated housing market.[94]

Sancton is critical of the narrow and limited views and approaches of those who are part of what he terms the "urban reform movement." He contends that none of them have expressed a vision of a stronger, multi-functional municipal government, one endowed with final decision-making power. To the contrary, he claims, most of the reformers are "suspicious of any political institutions, including municipal governments and local political parties, that would have the potential to overrule the expressed preferences of local neighbourhoods and their leaders..."[95]

Frisken points out that citizen activism may be strongly biased against city government initiatives that are sensitive to social needs.[96] It may be aimed at preventing the provision of housing for low income families, keeping public transit out of residential areas, or otherwise discouraging any municipal initiative that disturbs the status quo.

Sewell is even more critical of neighbourhood groups and their resistance to change.[97] In his view, the neighbourhood focus that was the building block behind the reform movement in the 1960s and 1970s will

---

[92]Sancton, *The Municipal Role*, p. 473.

[93]Warren Magnusson, "Metropolitan Change and Political Disruption," in Frisken, *op. cit.*, p. 551-552.

[94]*Ibid.*, p. 552.

[95]Sancton, *The Municipal Role*, p. 473.

[96]Frisken, *The Changing Canadian Metropolis*, p. 30.

[97]John Sewell, *Prospects for Reform*, Research Paper 180 (The City in the 1990s series), Toronto, University of Toronto, Centre for Urban and Community Studies, January 1991.

be the stumbling block of the next such movement. He argues that the NIMBY (Not in My Backyard) syndrome has hijacked the neighbourhood concept. It seized on the idea that local decision making is best and converted it to a justification for blocking any change which would alter the exclusivity of a neighbourhood.[98] As a result, Sewell contends, councillors are wary of addressing the major problems and issues of the day because they may upset constituents and trigger the NIMBY outcry. He cites lack of action on the severe housing crisis in many Canadian cities and on solid waste disposal as two examples of this shortcoming.

6. A sixth point concerns the influence on local political developments of the provincial party in power and its prevailing attitude and philosophy. This point is obvious in one sense, given the all-pervasive nature of provincial controls over local governments. But, over and above that fundamental relationship, local political actors may be reinforced or undermined in their efforts depending on the position taken by the provincial governing party.

Three examples should suffice. Frisken, in discussing the increasingly pro-growth mentality of Toronto's council during the 1970s and 1980s, stated that "in following this course of action the council majority acted consistently with, and sometimes directly in response to, signals or directives from other governments. Ontario Municipal Board and Ontario Cabinet decisions favoured a more rapid pace of downtown development than was provided for in the Plan...."[99]

Mention has also been made of the constraints under which Vancouver operated in relation to the provincial Social Credit government after it elected an NDP mayor. More generally, Magnusson and others warned of the threat to local autonomy in British Columbia in the mid-1980s because of the provincial government's apparent viewpoint that it should curb local initiatives contrary to its governing philosophy.[100]

Problems can also arise even where provincial and local parties share the same philosophy, according to Gerecke's description, above, of the provincial NDP's interference with the election efforts of the local NDP in Winnipeg.

All of these Canadian examples pale by comparison to the situation in British local government during the 1980s, when Margaret Thatcher

---

[98]*Ibid.*, p. 13.

[99]Frisken, *City Policy Making,* p. 90.

[100]Magnusson et al., *The New Reality.*

took a number of very strong actions to impose her conservative views about the appropriate scale of municipal government spending and activity on resistant municipal councils composed of Labour Party members.

7. A seventh, and final, observation relates to the effect of the underlying economic conditions on the local political patterns which unfold. Lorimer, for example, contends that it was the downturn in economic activity toward the end of the 1970s, and the resultant reduction in urban growth pressures, which led to more moderation in city hall — not the citizens' movement or the election of reform councils.[101] According to this school of thought, the prominence of developers and the pro-growth mentality only abated because these features were not compatible with the changed economic conditions.

A decade later, Toronto entered another and even more severe economic downturn, and Fowler describes the impact of the changed circumstances on Cityplan 1991.[102] He documents a number of examples of provisions which were dropped from the plan or modified. To cite one instance, a proposal that new development *must conform* to environmental standards became a proposal to *encourage* development to meet environmental objectives.

To a considerable extent, then, one can expect local political activity and council positions on the desirability of growth to increase and decrease in response to underlying economic performance and growth and development pressure. In good economic times, councils feel they can afford the luxury of tighter controls, but such controls tend to be relaxed or abandoned when an economic downturn makes it essential to attract any growth possible. While Barbara Hall may want to bring social justice to Toronto and Pierre Bourque may want to plant flowers, build parks and improve libraries in Montreal,[103] both may find that they will first have to come to terms with the business community. Without an economic revival in these urban centres, their mayors will have little hope of financing their other objectives.

The suggestion that politics is influenced and constrained by economics is hardly a new one. We will have more to say about the links between economic forces and municipal decision making in the next chapter.

---

[101]Lorimer, *op. cit.*, p. 9.

[102]Edmund P. Fowler, "Decision Time for Cityplan '91," in *City Magazine*, Winter '93, pp. 10-11.

[103]Peggy Curran, "Mayor's Agenda," *Montreal Gazette*, November 9, 1994.

Political Parties in Local Government: A Closer Look

Much of the preceding discussion about local political activity in our cities has concerned political parties. It has been shown that only the NDP has made a concerted effort to run candidates in municipal elections, and with limited success. The Liberals and Conservatives have been more inclined to throw their support behind like-minded candidates running as independents or as members of some local coalition — ostensibly opposed to party politics, but in reality opposed to the philosophical stance of the NDP.

These local coalitions vary considerably in their structure and cohesion, but a number have shown sufficient durability to be considered a form of local party, usually called a "civic" party. Over the years, these civic parties have appeared in most of Canada's major centres. Indeed, twenty-four of twenty-eight cities examined in 1969 had at least one such party.[104] Several examples of this type of party were outlined in the preceding section.

In addition to their more or less covert activities in municipal politics, political parties were also cited in Chapter 6 as a potentially key element of a strengthened political executive. It is time to consider, therefore, what it is about organized political parties that allegedly makes them such an important, and yet strongly resisted, addition to the municipal organization.

Examining the Arguments for Parties

Basically, parties perform the same task locally as they do at the senior levels: they organize the council into a governing group and an opposition group. The creation of a governing majority is significant because it provides the basis for concerted action. If heads of council are chosen by council, they would presumably be leading members of the majority party or group on council and thus would have a power base to support their leadership. If they in turn choose their executive committee from this ruling group then the committee has cohesiveness because of the common party affiliation and is somewhat analagous to a federal or provincial cabinet. The creation of a strong executive centred on the mayor is felt to be necessary for decisive action on the increasingly complex issues facing the municipality, especially in large urban areas.

[104]J. G. Joyce and H. A. Hosse, *Civic Parties in Canada*, Ottawa, Canadian Federation of Mayors and Municipalities, 1970.

Organized political parties provide the potential for not only strong leadership but also more effective scrutiny of the municipality's activities through an organized opposition or alternative governing group. As a result there is a group within council pledged to scrutinize and criticize municipal activities, an important role which is normally left to everybody — and nobody. The mayor and executive committee members need to retain the confidence of council since they owe their positions to council, not the electorate. Those who find this situation somehow less democratic might reflect on the fact that this is the same process followed in choosing our heads of government at the senior levels. If it is felt that the head of council must be elected at large, then why do we not choose Premiers and Prime Ministers that way?

In addition, with political parties the operations of council become more understandable and accountable to the public. Since councillors run as a group on the basis of specific programs, there is a greater likelihood that citizens will vote on the basis of substantive issues and policies instead of on the usual basis of selection among personalities. It is also argued that an election campaign organized around opposing parties and alternative approaches generates greater public interest and a higher voting turnout. In part this is because parties can be expected to play their usual roles of aggregating interests, mobilizing public support, and attempting to draw more citizens into the political arena. More importantly, at the end of a term the public can attach responsibility for performance to the governing party since this group had the means to effect change. It is not possible for a ruling party to evade responsibility for action or inaction as individual councillors can and do.

Examining the Arguments Against Parties

Critics of political parties at the local level would question the validity of a number of the advantages cited above.[105] For example, evidence from the senior levels of government hardly supports the claim that parties provide clear platforms and alternatives for the voter, or stick to their platforms after elected! Nor is it apparent that parties at the senior levels provide strong leadership — at least according to the complaints often heard from both those within the system and from the public. Accountability at the municipal level arises from the small scale of operations and ready accessibility of the decision makers (in most municipalities) and

---

[105]See, for example, David Siegel, "City Hall Doesn't Need Parties," in *Policy Options*, June 1987, pp. 26-27, on which the following points are based.

does not need parties to ensure it. As for the likelihood of increased voter turnout with parties, how beneficial this would be depends on the reason for the turnout. If municipal electors had gone to the polls in record numbers in municipal elections in the early 1990s to defeat Conservative candidates because of their dislike of Brian Mulroney and the GST, this would hardly be striking a blow for local democracy.[106]

There are, of course, a number of other arguments against the introduction of organized political parties at the local level. Chief among these is the assertion that parties would introduce division where none exists or should exist. "There is no political way to build a road," claim proponents of this viewpoint which reflects the lingering notion that local government activities are administrative not political in nature. Yet if the actual construction of a road is a matter of engineering not politics, the decision on where to locate a particular road is certainly political. The decision on whether the traffic problem in question should be solved through building a road or providing an alternative form of public transit is also clearly political. The decision on whether the scarce financial resources of the municipality should be used on transportation or some other pressing need is again political.

Indeed, if the municipal council is concerned with establishing priorities in relation to conflicting public needs and demands, its role must be political. If the council is not to be charged with this task, one may well question the value of a separate level of municipal government. Since political decisions are an essential element of municipal operations then, they are not brought into the local arena by parties. Rather, parties — for reasons already advanced — may help to make these unavoidable political decisions more systematic and also more accountable to the public.

At the same time, it must be acknowledged that parties tend to exaggerate differences and to criticize excessively for purely partisan purposes. These traits have been all too evident in the actions of the parties operating at the senior levels of government. Kaplan provides a good example of this excessive polarization in the operation of party politics in the City of Montreal in the postwar period.[107] He notes that the Ligue d'Action Civique (LAC), the first local party with which Drapeau was involved, found itself opposing a 1956 public housing project which it would otherwise have supported because the project was associated with Quebec

---

[106]*Ibid.*, p. 27.

[107]Harold Kaplan, *Reform, Planning and City Politics: Montreal, Winnipeg, Toronto*, Toronto, University of Toronto Press, p. 380.

Premier Duplessis and the anti-LAC element of council. Similarly, urban renewal reports in 1959 and 1960 were judged by their source rather than their contents, and there were frequent deadlocks which at times paralyzed the administration of the city. Opponents of party politics in local government decry this type of division.

A second major objection to parties is the feeling that they bring corruption and unsavoury practices into local government. This feeling was undoubtedly strongly influenced by the excesses of party politics and the spoils system in the United States in the period leading up to the turn of the century reform era. Nor were such practices entirely absent from Canadian local government, as illustrated by discussions in Chapter 3. However, it should be remembered that it is people who are potentially corruptible, not that specialized subgroup known as politicians. If there are opportunities for dishonesty and abuse, some people may succumb to the temptation, but they will presumably do so whether they are individual councillors or members of an organized political party.

One advantage of a non-partisan system is that it fosters a direct accountability relationship between individual councillors and their electors. In contrast, where disciplined parties exist, councillors can only promise voters that they will present their views in a party caucus.[108] It is also argued that the absence of overt party labelling allows councillors to work together more effectively. Even though many councillors are known to be active in particular political parties, they can overlook any such political differences when at council as long as they are allowed to leave the party labels "at the door."

An important qualification in all of this discussion is the nature of the political parties involved. In particular, the discussion of potential advantages presumes a balanced situation with two or more parties which would alternate in power. If one party is very dominant and controls council for many years, then there is undoubtedly more likelihood of insensitivity to public opinion and other abuses — traits exhibited by the provincial and federal governments in the same situation. Here again, Montreal provides an example from the lengthy regime of Jean Drapeau and his Civic Party. Higgins observes that:[109]

> Indicative of how unprogressive is the City of Montreal is the fact that in the whole month that I was there conducting research, the city council

---

[108]*Ibid.*

[109]Donald J. H. Higgins, "Progressive City Politics and the Citizen Movement: A Status Report," in *City Magazine*, Winnipeg, Annual 1981, p. 93.

did not meet at all - and there are no real committees of council which could have met, aside from the powerful executive committee, which met only in camera.

Another key consideration is whether the parties involved are local or are branches of the existing provincial and federal parties. In the latter case, the concern is that the parties would likely neglect local issues and become essentially a grass roots organization for the senior level party. There is also the danger that local election results will reflect the popularity or unpopularity of the "parent" parties rather than the positions taken by the parties on local matters. This pattern has been noted in Britain, where many municipal council elections are contested by the national Labour and Conservative parties.

On the other hand, local parties are often short-lived coalitions of local interests which display very little ongoing discipline or concerted action once elected. Indeed, they may more properly be described as "factions" which reappear under a variety of names at election time and attempt to ensure the election of certain types of candidate, but do not exercise disciplined party voting in council.[110] As we have seen, Canada's limited experience with political parties in local government has been very much of the latter category involving factions. In such instances, few of the alleged benefits of parties are gained.

Summary

This chapter began by exploring the links between municipal government and democracy, an exploration which soon found closer links between municipalities and property — and the property development industry as well. It noted the combined impact of the depression, World War II and rapid post-war urbanization in squeezing municipal government out of the limited social services responsibilities it had begun to assume and returning it to a preoccupation with property.

Through profiles of four large cities, the chapter has examined Canada's experience with political party and citizen group activity at the local level. While organized political parties offer a number of potential advantages, Canadian voters have shown much more inclination to elect candidates who claimed to be nonpartisan or opposed to the introduction of party politics at the local level. The result has been that the councils

---

[110]See Harold Kaplan, "Electoral Politics in the Metro Area," in Masson and Anderson, *op. cit.*, p. 147.

of major cities have been dominated by like-minded, pro-business representatives, often active in the Conservative and Liberal parties nationally.
While these councillors have had the numerical strength to accomplish
many of their objectives of accommodating rapid growth and development, they have managed to avoid responsibility for their actions because
of their supposedly independent status.

Citizen activism has tended to wax and wane in response to the growth
pressures being experienced and the extent to which particular councils
were successful in "managing" this growth in a way which did not threaten
established neighbourhoods or values. There is some indication of a cy-
clical pattern in which citizens mobilize against developers and their
council allies, achieve some electoral success, moderate their actions in
light of their apparent victory, find themselves facing renewed developer
"excesses," and start a new cycle of vigorous action again. There is also
a concern that the citizen activism of recent years has been less focused
on bringing about genuine change and more preoccupied with "NIMBY-
ism" and the protection of the status quo.

The political activities of municipal government and the factors
influencing municipal decisions will receive further attention in the next
chapter which explores municipal policy making — in theory and in practice.

CHAPTER 9

The Municipal Policy-Making Process

OBJECTIVES:

1. To describe the key players in the municipal policy-making process.

2. To contrast the rational model of decision making with the way municipal decisions are made in practice.

3. To examine and compare the main theories advanced to explain municipal policy output.

4. To illustrate the nature of municipal policy making through examination of particular policy issues.

Introduction

Most of this text thus far has been concerned with describing and analyzing the existing structure and internal organization of municipal government and how it evolved and adapted to various pressures. The last chapter broadened the focus somewhat by examining the local political process and illustrating the political activity by citizens' groups and political parties in a number of Canada's urban centres. Ultimately, however, the measure of municipal government, at least for its citizens, is what policy decisions it makes. This chapter seeks to explain the municipal policy making process: how policy decisions get made, why municipalities produce the kinds of policy outputs that they do, and what happens to these policies in practice, when they are implemented.

Nature of Policy Making

A necessary first step is to clarify the meaning of the term policy. One of the simplest definitions is provided by Morgan,[1] who suggests that public

---

[1]David R. Morgan, *Managing Urban America*, Belmont, Wadsworth Publishing Company Inc., 1979, p. 69.

policy is "whatever governments choose to do or not to do." This definition is useful in recognizing that a failure to take action may represent
government policy, although such inaction is sometimes the result of
omission or oversight rather than a deliberate decision. To distinguish
policy making from decision making, Morgan goes on to suggest that a
policy can be viewed as a potential series of decisions which create a
more comprehensive set of standards or guidelines dealing with a subject.[2]

It is in this fashion that municipal governments often make policy,
sometimes not even consciously. Over time a council makes a series of
decisions about purchasing or personnel matters which may gradually
evolve into something approaching a general policy on the subject. One
danger, of course, is that such isolated decisions may not be consistent —
especially if made over a number of years with a changing representation
on council. The preferred alternative is for council to make a conscious
decision to establish its position and approach to a particular subject and
to adopt this position formally as a council policy. Examples would include a purchasing by-law setting out the purchasing policies and procedures to be followed or a council policy on development charges to be imposed in connection with subdivision developments. Similarly, the adoption of an official plan provides policies on a wide range of planning
matters which hitherto had to be decided by council on an ad hoc basis.

Traditionally, the policy making role of municipal government has
received very little attention. In large part, this is because of the almost
total preoccupation with the service delivery role of local government.
Municipalities existed to administer services as efficiently as possible; they
weren't expected to become involved in debating issues or resolving conflict. Such activities smacked of politics and, as Chapter 3 has made clear,
the turn of the century reform era had been largely successful in establishing the notion that politics had no place in local government.

In any event, with the extent of provincial supervision and control over
municipal governments and the strict legal and financial constraints within
which they operated, there was a widespread feeling that municipal councils didn't have sufficient autonomy and discretion to undertake any significant policy making. Municipalities were creatures of the province and,
as Chapter 7 pointed out, they were strongly and often adversely influenced by ill-considered actions by both the provincial and federal governments. In such circumstances, was it not presumptuous to speak of a
policy making role for local government? As discussed in the next section,
several factors combined to alter this perception and to direct increased

---

[2]*Ibid.*

attention to municipal policy making — although they produced diverse and contradictory views about the nature of that policy making. There are also differing views on the focus of any study of municipal policy making.

Conflicting Perspectives on Municipal Policy Making

As described in Chapter 4, the urbanization of the post-war period had a major impact on perceptions of the role of municipal government. The resulting pressures undermined, and revealed the inappropriateness of, the nonpolitical tradition inherited from the turn of the century reform era. Increasingly activist citizens and citizen groups demanded to know how municipalities made decisions and also insisted that the views and concerns of the affected public must become an integral part of the decision making process. The general support for such concepts as participatory democracy, the public's right to information and the desirability of more openness in government all conspired to direct attention to the "democratic nature" of the municipal decision making process and the extent to which council policies reflected the apparent wishes and needs of the local populace. As already discussed, a major issue was the perceived power of the property industry and resultant narrow focus of many council decisions.

Interest in policy making in the post-war period also arose from another completely different set of influences. Faced with ever-growing demands and needs and yet very limited financial and personnel resources, municipalities have become increasingly concerned with methods and techniques for improving their efficiency and effectiveness. There has been greater recognition of the need for improved planning and priority setting, for more rigorous research and analysis, and for the measurement of performance or results to ensure value for the dollar spent. During this same time period, approaches to research, analysis and policy making were being refined as a result of the advances in science and technology spurred by the space and defence programs of the United States government. More rational, systematic approaches to policy making were developed, often described by the term policy analysis.[3] Thus, just when local governments were interested in a more rigorous policy making process, a variety of new techniques and approaches appeared to be available.

---

[3]See Kenneth L. Kraemer, *Policy Analysis in Local Government*, Washington, International City Management Association, 1973. A brief outline of the main quantitative and non-quantitative techniques of policy analysis is found in Association of Municipal Clerks and Treasurers of Ontario, *Municipal Administration Program*, Unit Two, Lesson 5.

It is important to recognize that these two sets of influences directing attention to municipal policy making are not easily reconciled and, indeed, even appear to conflict. While they want the policy making process "improved" and made more rational, most citizens also want it to be open and responsive to their particular views and concerns. They believe that the views of the populace affected by a potential decision are just as valid in the decision making process as the testimony of technical experts. In addition, while people believe that governments need more research and analysis in relation to policy problems, they also believe that the elected representatives should remain in charge. Representatives should call on the services of experts and analysts but should not abdicate their political functions to them. To use some over-worked terms, there is a widespread feeling that experts should be "on tap, not on top," and a fairly strong attitude of fear and mistrust of "the bureaucracy."

The result as Lindblom points out, is that a deep conflict runs through common attitudes toward policy making.

> On the one hand, people want policy to be informed and well analyzed. On the other hand, they want policy making to be democratic, hence necessarily political .... On the one hand they want policy making to be scientific; on the other they want it to remain in the world of politics.[4]

For municipal governments, this conflict represents the tension between their two basic administrative and political roles, to which frequent reference has been made. But the conflict is made more complex by the fact that even those who want local governments to be more democratic, to pay more attention to their representative role, often think that they don't want local governments to be political — thanks again to the distorted legacy of the reform movement. As has been argued in earlier chapters, however, one must recognize that municipal councils make (and should make) political decisions. They don't necessarily follow the recommendations made by their staff; nor do they necessarily follow the apparent wishes of local interests. Instead, councillors consider these factors as well as their own beliefs, values and judgment, and make what they feel are appropriate decisions in the circumstances.

Conflicting perspectives are also evident in how one approaches the study of municipal policy making. The traditional public administration approach is to focus on the formal machinery of municipal government, to the relative neglect of the broader context within which this machinery operates. Officially, policy decisions are made by municipal councils,

---

[4]Charles E. Lindblom, *The Policy Making Process*, Englewood Cliffs, Prentice-Hall Inc., 1980, p. 12.

usually on the basis of advice and recommendations from municipal staff, and always within the limits of authority delegated to the municipality by provincial legislation. To understand municipal policy making, therefore, it is necessary to study the roles and relationships of municipal councillors and staff, and also the relationship between the municipality and the senior levels of government.

A contrasting perspective is provided by Cockburn who argues that we need to step out of our conventional frame of reference and see "local government, our old red-brick town hall, for what it really is: a key part of the state in capitalist society."[5] She coined the term "local state" as an alternative to local government, in an attempt to avoid the narrowness of the latter term — although what should be included in the local state is a matter of some dispute. Magnusson suggests that the local state should be seen "as encompassing only those agencies that are physically present in the local community and specifically concerned with its affairs."[6] However the term is defined, this perspective directs attention beyond the machinery of government to the external forces shaping municipal policy decisions.

The discussion in the remainder of this chapter begins with a traditional approach which describes the official actors and other key players involved in municipal policy making. It quickly extends, however, to an examination of broader socio-economic factors — by summarizing and comparing a number of widely held theories about the nature of municipal policy making.

Key Players in Municipal Policy Making

Any attempt to list the "key players" in municipal policy making is bound to invite differences of opinion and dispute. A safe starting point is the official players — the municipal councillors and staff. Other key players who will be described below include the local electorate, local groups, political parties, and the mass media. A number of provincial bodies, such as departments of municipal affairs and municipal boards, could be included, but they have already been examined in Chapter 7. The citizen appointees who are found on the governing bodies of local special pur-

---

[5]Cynthia Cockburn, *The Local State*, London, Pluto, 1977, p. 41, quoted in Gerry Stoker, *The Politics of Local Government*, London, Macmillan, 1988, p. 219.

[6]Warren Magnusson, "Urban Politics and the Local State," in *Studies in Political Economy*, 16, 1985, p. 123.

ρυse bodies could also be included — but they will not be, since the focus of this chapter is on *municipal* policy making, not policy making by local government more broadly defined.

Municipal Councillors

The powers given to any incorporated municipality are exercised, on behalf of the inhabitants, by the elected councillors — making them the most important players officially (if not always in practice). It is very difficult for individual councillors to exert significant influence over the policy output of a municipality. It is even difficult for a municipal council to pursue policy objectives over time with any consistency, given that members — with very limited exceptions — are not formed into voting blocs. Voting patterns change from issue to issue and there is usually little cohesion and common purpose within a municipal council.

Heads of council, however, can carry through a policy agenda — if they have the personality and leadership style which allows them to overcome the lack of formal powers attached to their position. Some colourful and long-serving mayors have certainly "put their stamp" on their cities, with names like Elsie Wayne of Saint John, Stephan Juba of Winnipeg, Jean Drapeau of Montreal and Hazel McCallion of Mississauga coming readily to mind.[7] Observers of rural Canadian political life will have no difficulty identifying examples of reeves and other rural heads of council who have served for 20 years or more, often operating rather like "benevolent despots," but also providing indispensable leadership to their particular communities.

Municipal Staff

While municipal councillors constitute the official decision-making body at the local level, municipal staff are considered by many to be at least as important players in that decision-making process.

First and foremost, senior staff provide technical expertise, research and analytical capability, and policy advice. Since councillors serve, in most instances, on only a part-time basis, they come to rely very heavily on the recommendations given by their staff. Indeed, there is a widespread concern that senior staff are too dominant in the policy process, with elected bodies being reduced to rubber-stamping decisions which are essentially made by appointed personnel.

---

[7]For a highly readable profile of eight Canadian mayors (including Juba and Drapeau) see Allan Levine (ed.), *Your Worship*, James Lorimer & Company, 1989.

Second, municipal staff are key players in the local policy process because they often have their own objectives and priorities which they want to see achieved. In other words, far from playing an essentially passive role responding to policy initiatives of councillors, municipal staff may attempt to control the policy agenda themselves — determining what gets attention and (equally important) what doesn't get attention.

Municipal staff are also key players because of the extent to which they are in contact with the local public. As much as or more than councillors, they are likely to be aware of the public view on a variety of local issues — especially concerning existing policies and programs. Increasingly, staff find themselves acting as brokers or arbiters of conflicting local interests, seeking to find common ground and to build a basis for action. Staff with good negotiating and human relations skills can make a major contribution in this area, but in so doing they are also helping to define the issue and to determine the limits of possible action on the issue — critical elements of the local policy process.

A fourth and final example concerns the role of staff in implementing council decisions. As will be discussed later in this chapter, this implementation stage can be far from smooth, and staff actions can be the major determinant of how effectively or ineffectively the objectives of a policy decision are realized.

The Electorate

The local electors *ought to be* key players in the local political process — if the oft-repeated statement about local government as the foundation of democracy is to have any meaning. The policy decisions which are made are supposed to reflect the views and concerns of the local citizens. By what means is this accomplished? In theory, at least, this desirable objective is achieved by allowing the public to vote for the candidates of their choice at regularly scheduled elections.

The first problem with this concept is that a disappointingly low proportion of voters take advantage of their democratic opportunities every municipal election year. The factors influencing this voting turnout were examined in the previous chapter.

In addition to the problem of low voting turnout, there is a second, and more fundamental, problem with the concept that regular elections help to ensure that municipal decisions reflect the views and concerns of the local citizens. The reality is that voters are not able to enforce any sort of accountability for actions through the mechanism of periodic elections. There is no clear focus of accountability and responsibility within virtually any of our municipal councils. Without organized political parties, there is no "Government" and no "Official Opposition." The result, as described in Chapter 8, is that everyone is responsible for everything but no one is really responsible for anything.

The fact that municipal governments have become narrowly equated with the provision of various services to the neglect of their political role also undermines the significance of the act of voting in municipal elections. If municipalities were viewed, as they should be, as a political mechanism for a community to express its collective concerns, the election process would have much more meaning.

Local Groups

Those who do exercise their franchise tend to find voting a passive and all too infrequent activity. Many citizens want more continuous, direct involvement as decisions are being made. For such citizens, forming or joining local groups is often seen as the answer.

Such groups have existed for over a century, but they became particularly prominent as part of the citizens' movement in Canadian cities after World War Two. The preceding chapter provides numerous examples of such group activity and of the widely varying objectives of these groups. While many groups in the 1960s and 1970s appeared to want to open up the municipal decision-making process, some municipal observers contend that the increasing influence of "NIMBYism" is making groups more narrowly focused and negative.

The previous chapter also describes the activities of business groups which ran and elected slates of candidates in several of our largest cities. While ostensibly committed to keeping party politics out of local government, these groups were, in fact, a means of ensuring that middle-of-the-road business "parties" retained power at city hall and kept out left-wing candidates from the CCF and NDP. These "non-party parties" have been aided in their objectives by the strong voter antipathy toward candidates who run as official representatives of any of our national parties. As a result, except for the NDP, political parties have not been directly or officially represented on municipal councils; rather, they have exercised their influence for the most part covertly, by supporting like-minded candidates, or by using their links with council to push for decisions consistent with their viewpoints.

The Mass Media

The mass media are key players in the local policy process in a number of ways. The most direct and obvious way is through the coverage which they give (or don't give) to local government activities and issues. In addition, however, they are also influential because of the sheer size of some of the major corporations in the media field. Media outlets representing the Thomson and Irving empires or Power Corporation are part of major, diversified business interests which have considerable economic influence in their own right.

Local issues usually receive very little coverage in the national electronic media. Yet studies suggest that the general public is particularly interested in local and regional news,[8] and it is coverage of these issues which is most pertinent from the point of view of municipal governments. The adequacy of local news coverage depends on the local radio and television stations (where they exist) and on local newspapers — with the latter being regarded by most citizens as their primary source of information.

It can be argued, however, that the media have contributed to the limited public participation in local government by their generally poor performance in providing information about, and promoting understanding of, local government. News stories tend to concentrate on the supposedly more important and glamorous activities of the senior levels of government. The municipal beat is often assigned to junior reporters and is seen as an unavoidable stepping stone to bigger and better things. Moreover, while local weekly newspapers may devote considerable space to municipal coverage, even printing the council minutes, the dailies are much more limited and selective in their coverage. As with all news items, there is a tendency to emphasize controversial or sensational matters. The bulk of the council's deliberations is regarded as routine, preoccupied with administrative details and not especially newsworthy. While there may be some truth in this assessment, the fact remains that without some media coverage of these ongoing municipal activities the public is ill-informed and lacks the background necessary to the understanding of local issues. Municipal councils and staff often become disillusioned with the media because occasional controversies are highlighted while the vast majority of municipal government activities appear to be largely ignored.

One conspicuous example of media influence relates to the coverage of municipal tax increases. Such increases receive very prominent, and

---

[8]See Canada, Royal Commission on Newspapers, *Report* and *Research Studies*, Ottawa, Supply and Services, 1981, and P. Audley, *Canada's Cultural Industries*, Toronto, James Lorimer and the Canadian Institute for Economic Policy, 1983. These studies are briefly discussed in Donald Higgins, *Local and Urban Politics in Canada*, Toronto, Gage, 1986, p. 300.

negative, attention in the media. Paradoxically, while the media may criticize inadequate municipal services throughout the year, at budget time
councils are somehow expected to hold the line on taxes. Council budget
deliberations conducted in this atmosphere focus almost entirely on mill
rate considerations and ignore the basic priority setting exercise which
should be undertaken. Once again, the result is to reduce what should be
a very fundamental political and policy making process into an administrative exercise, preoccupied with juggling and cutting expenditure figures
until the resulting mill rate increases stay below some predetermined
acceptable level.

The influence of the media is also felt in the positions they take on
local issues and the editorial views presented. It is probably fair to say
that the growth mentality which infected most municipalities, at least until
recent years, has been encouraged or reinforced by the media. Lightbody,
for example, describes the *Edmonton Journal* as "unashamedly a booster
press," and notes that it normally endorsed the Citizens' Committee or
its Civic Government successors, and the business pro-growth interests
which they represented. He observes that "While the evidence is insufficient to prove that the Journal was able to structure electoral choice,
judging by results we can conclude with some certainty that the environment was scarcely conducive to the emergence of an effective challenge
to the Citizens' Committee."[9]

Whittle offers some interesting insights into the part played by a city
newspaper in influencing the outcome of a municipal election, although
in assessing his observations one should bear in mind that he is writing
about his own unsuccessful candidacy in Hamilton, Ontario in 1991.[10] He
ran in Ward 3, which had long been held by Brian Hinkley, a member of
the NDP. Hinkley moved up to challenge incumbent mayor, Bob
Morrow, and Whittle, also an NDPer, was drafted to run in his place.
Whittle's candidacy was endorsed by Hinkley.

From early in the campaign, columnists in the *Hamilton Spectator*
characterized the election in Ward 3 as a party contest between Whittle
of the NDP and Morelli, a candidate of the Liberal party.[11] While the
party focus attracted attention to the Ward 3 election campaign, it also

---

[9]James Lightbody, "Edmonton," in Warren Magnusson and Andrew Sancton
(eds.), *City Politics in Canada*, Toronto, University of Toronto Press, 1983, p. 266.

[10]Alan Whittle, "Running for City Council: Lessons from a first time candidate,"
in *City Magazine*, Spring 1992, pp. 15-22.

[11]*Ibid.*, p. 19.

served to link Whittle's fortunes with those of Hinkley, running for mayor, and with the provincial NDP — whose popularity was continuing to slide. At the beginning of the last week of the campaign, the *Hamilton Spectator* released a poll of its own which showed Morrow, the incumbent mayor, decisively defeating Hinkley of the NDP. At that point, Whittle knew that he was finished; being identified with Brian Hinkley was not going to help this time. In its final editorial on the ward races, the newspaper endorsed Whittle's chief opponent, Morelli (of the Liberal Party), while questioning whether Whittle could be independent because of his connection to the NDP.

Whittle concedes that being associated with the NDP and being endorsed by Hinkley provided him with organizational support and public profile without which he might have done even more poorly in the election. What is pertinent for our purposes, however, is the tactics used by the one daily newspaper in the city to exert its influence over the election outcome.

A Bureau of Municipal Research study documented several instances where press coverage appeared to have an influence on the outcome of issues.[12] One analyst suggested that the media influence was even greater — actually setting the agenda of public discussion. After studying three small Ontario cities, he concluded that there was a fairly close parallel between the ranking of items in the agendas of the press and of the local political community, and that the daily newspapers had influenced politicians to make particular policy decisions that they might not otherwise have made if left on their own.[13]

Dealing still with newspapers, the degree of concentration of ownership is seen by many as a concern. One worry is that newspapers may be hesitant to provide news coverage and editorial comment which appears critical of any of the varied business interests of their corporate owners. There is also a fear that newspapers will be similarly constrained from critical commentary which might offend major advertisers, notably the property industry.

Whatever their faults, it must be acknowledged that the media often receive very little support from municipalities in attempting to carry out their responsibilities. There are too many examples of municipal govern-

---

[12]Bureau of Municipal Research, "The News Media and Local Government," in *Civic Affairs*, Toronto, August 1976.

[13]E. R. Black, *Politics and the News: The Political Functions of the Mass Media*, Toronto, Butterworths, 1982.

ments which at best exhibit no concern for public relations and at worst maintain as much secrecy as possible about their deliberations. While the desire to shield discussions from "sensationalized media coverage" is understandable, attempts to conceal information almost always result in even worse media coverage. Municipal councillors and staff need to take a more positive approach and to use more imagination and sensitivity in developing effective relations with the media.[14]

This criticism is equally true of the local boards and commissions which are part of local government, with school boards traditionally being among the most secretive.[15]

Theories of Policy Making

There are many ways to examine municipal policy making. The preceding section outlined some of the key players involved in the policy-making process. Another approach is to explore municipal policy making by examining the kinds of policies which are made (or not made) by councils. This approach helps to remind us that many of the important public policy issues of the day fall — at least partly — within the domain of municipal government. On any given day, one can find "front page stories" dealing with such matters as:

1. the construction of a multi-storey office or residential complex.
2. the search for a new waste management site.
3. proposals to limit the number of "strip clubs" or adult video stores allowed within a community.
4. the introduction of one-way streets, or the return to two-way traffic on formerly one-way streets.
5. the introduction of, or increase in, fees for the use of municipal recreational facilities.

Both of these approaches to studying policy making are important. We need to know who is formally responsible for enacting municipal policies and the process through which policies are enacted. In addition, we are

---

[14]For a good discussion of the media, its influence, and ways of dealing with it, see W. T. Stanbury, *Business-Government Relations in Canada: Influencing Public Policy*, Scarborough, Nelson Canada, 1993, Chapter 10.

[15]For a wide-ranging indictment of school boards in Ontario, see the four part series by Paul Bennett, "What's Wrong With the Present School Board System" in *Municipal World*, August-November 1994.

obviously interested in the kinds of policies made by municipal governments.

The most common approach used to explain public policy making, however, is on the basis of theoretical models. To the practitioner, theories sound like abstract and probably jargon-filled musings which bear little relation to reality. But theories have great practical value. They provide "an explanation of why things happen the way they do."[16] The economics theoretician who had arguably the greatest influence over the policy decisions of Western nations in the mid-20th century, John Maynard Keynes, offered this colourful observation on the practical impact of theories:

> Practical men, who believe themselves to be quite exempt from any intellectual influences, are usually the slave of some defunct economist. Madmen in authority, who hear voices in the air, are distilling their frenzy from some academic scribbler of a few years back.[17]

As will be seen, theories of policy making vary widely in their assumptions, their primary focus and their scope. Some take the individual as their starting point, some see groups as the essential mobilizing force, others look at the broader context within which policy decisions are made, and still others concentrate on particular features of that external context, especially the external economic forces.

Theories can be distinguished as *normative* and *descriptive*. Normative theories deal with how things *should be*, while descriptive theories depict how things *are*. A further distinction relates to whether theories focus on the micro level or the macro level. The micro level is concerned with how an individual policy decision gets made. The macro level is concerned with the policy output of a government over an extended period of time.

Explaining Individual Decisions

Using the micro level as our starting point, we find some markedly contrasting explanations of how individual policy decisions are made. This contrast can be illustrated by comparing three theories of decision making. The rational model, described first, represents a normative theory.

---

[16]Stephen Brooks, *Public Policy in Canada: An Introduction*, Toronto, McClelland & Stewart, 2nd edition, 1993, p. 26.

[17]J. M. Keynes, *The General Theory of Employment, Interest and Money*, London, Macmillan, 1936, p. 383, quoted in Brooks, *op. cit.*

The incremental model and the "penny arcade" model are both descriptive theories, depicting how things *are*.

The Rational Model

Much has been written about what is termed the rational-comprehensive or classical approach to policy making. This approach is the way management textbooks say that decisions should be made. It presumes that the official actors are the ones who actually make the decisions. In the case of municipal government, then, the rational model accepts that municipal decisions are made by municipal councils, on the basis of research and recommendations provided by municipal staff.

According to this rational model, municipal policy decisions are made on the basis of a logical series of interrelated steps which might be summarized as follows:[18]

1. The issues requiring a response from the municipal council are correctly identified and are dealt with in the proper sequence. This task is facilitated by the existence of overall (corporate) objectives which provide a framework for the consideration of more specific issues. These objectives, in turn, may have been developed following a strategic planning exercise in which the municipality has "scanned its external environment" and identified those strategic issues which it must address.

2. Each issue is subjected to thorough policy analysis. As Kraemer describes this step, the process of analysis involves three interrelated activities — perception, design, and evaluation.[19] The perception stage is concerned with the clarification of the issue, the determination of the limits of the inquiry, and the identification of objectives in a way which helps to highlight alternatives. The design stage identifies existing alternatives, develops new alternatives and gathers information for the comparison of these alternatives. The final, evaluation stage examines the alternatives for feasibility and compares them in terms of their benefit and cost.

3. After careful consideration of all of this information, the "best" alternative is selected and a decision is made by the municipal council.

4. The decision is communicated to the appropriate personnel within the organization who proceed to implement it accordingly.

---

[18]What follows is partly based on Association of Municipal Clerks and Treasurers, *op. cit.*, Unit Two, Lesson Five.

[19]Kraemer, *op. cit.*, p. 30.

5. The implementation stage is subjected to careful evaluation and analysis to determine the effectiveness of the decision, policy or program in practice and, where necessary, to introduce modifications.

In the idealistic municipality being depicted in the rational model, councillors and staff have quite clearly defined roles which are distinct and yet complementary. The task of issue identification is primarily carried out by councillors, who, as elected, responsible representatives, possess a clear understanding of the "public interest" and are able to determine how best to serve it. The staff of the municipality have both the time and the expertise to undertake in-depth research and analysis into all of the alternative courses of action which must be considered. The councillors are then responsible for weighing the alternatives studied and are able to determine the one which is "best" from both a technical viewpoint and in terms of the perceived public interest.

Council's decision is then communicated clearly to an administrative structure that is organized in a manner which provides for prompt, thorough implementation of the decision. Since the decision was "rational," it will have the support of staff who will accept it uncritically and devote themselves to carrying it out. Mechanisms exist to ensure that council's decision is implemented as intended and to monitor and assess the consequences of that implementation. Various forms of performance measurement and analysis provide councillors with information which can be used to refine the decision and the implementing process where necessary.

The idealized policy process described above is attractive in many ways. Most people have an understandable tendency to believe that policy decisions should be based on this kind of rigorous, scientific approach. There is a widely held view that for every issue or problem there is a "correct" answer to be found — if only all of the pertinent information is assembled and analyzed sufficiently.

It is difficult to argue against the apparent logic of this viewpoint. One would hardly suggest that policy decisions be made after only half-hearted or incomplete research. Nor would one gain much support for the notion that, in making policy decisions, municipal councillors should give more weight to political considerations of their own than to facts, research and analysis — especially given the narrow and negative meaning long ascribed to the term politics.

Whatever the apparent logic and appeal of the rational model, however, in practice decisions are not made in such a neat, sequential order. The policy-making process is more fluid, the internal stages are less distinct, and the whole process is definitely not as tidy and rational as suggested above. The two descriptive theories outlined below offer a critique of the rational model and an alternative view of the real nature of municipal decision making.

The Incremental Model

Charles Lindblom argues that our problem-solving capacity is too limited to encompass all of the options and potential outcomes which might arise, that there is usually insufficient information to assess accurately all options, and that comprehensive analysis is both too time-consuming and too expensive.[20] These observations certainly ring true for most municipalities in Canada, which are small and rural and which have very limited research and analytical capacity.

Lindblom also points out that facts and values cannot be neatly separated as required by the rational approach. There is no such thing as a decision based on "just the facts," since these facts are assembled, analyzed and presented by people — individuals with their own backgrounds, experiences, values, biases and judgments. This human dimension inevitably colours what is presented and how it is presented. Sometimes, the staff influence is deliberate and manipulative. Other times, staff biases may be completely unconscious and unknown to those presenting reports and recommendations. It doesn't really matter which is the case. The point is that the completely neutral, value-free, objective, "pure" policy advice presumed by the rational model does not exist in real life.

Ironically, efforts to shield decision making from the influence of "politics" as sometimes arise with extreme versions of the rational model, may only serve to expose decision making to the influence of "bureaucratic politics" instead. In this connection, it is almost amusing to read of the near-hysterical reaction of the school board bureaucracy in Ontario to a report which dared to call for a reaffirmation of "the basic democratic principle that local control over education is centred in the elected trustees."[21] A leadership letter[22] to the directors of education throughout Ontario and across Canada warned that "a new wave of the worst kind of politicization" was sweeping through the pristine world of education.

---

[20]Charles E. Lindblom, *The Intelligence of Democracy*, New York, The Free Press, 1965, pp. 138-143. The discussion of Lindblom which follows is largely based on Morgan, *op. cit.*, pp. 100-102.

[21]*Third Report of the Select Committee on Education*, Queen's Park, January 1990, p. 44, quoted in Bennett, Part 2, *op. cit.*, p. 12.

[22]*Ibid.*

Once again, the dreaded "P" word is used as a rallying cry to block the legitimate role of elected representatives and to reduce an elected local government (the school board in this instance) to a service agency which needs only the expertise provided by staff.

Two American observers provide some valuable insights into the limitations of analysis and the fallacy inherent in the notion of objective policy advice. They note that:

> The definition of issues and the data needed to develop rational policy choices are produced by organizational units whose goals, history, and inner workings colour their outputs. Analysis is not something apart from these organizational processes; it is intertwined with and affected by them.[23]

They further note that it is widely recognized that "the resourcefulness and influence of particular advocates carry weight beyond the measure of the objective merits of the arguments which they advance."[24] It must be appreciated then, that a decision made on the basis of internal analysis and recommendations is not necessarily shielded from politics and therefore purer and more objective. Instead it may simply reflect the outcome of bureaucratic politics.

Lindblom's view of policy making is that decision makers recognize the realities and limitations of their world. As a result, they look for simpler approaches to problem solving. Rather than attempting to identify every possible course of action, they consider those few alternatives which represent only small or incremental changes from existing policies. Lindblom has therefore developed an alternative policy making approach which he calls incrementalism or the science of muddling through.

However inglorious this approach may sound, Lindblom's observations are certainly closer to reality than those of the rational model. He points out that there is little evidence to suggest that organizations which utilize a rational comprehensive approach to policy making produce consistently better decisions (however one might measure "better"). Canadians who have been following the performance of their federal government since the 1960s can make their own assessment by comparing two quite contrasting regimes. The Liberal government of Lester Pearson seemed to operate without any overall plan, and often appeared to lurch from one crisis to another. Yet it produced significant policy changes in areas such

---

[23]Richard S. Rosenblom and John R. Russell, *New Tools for Urban Management*, Boston, Harvard University Press, 1971, p. 229.

[24]*Ibid.*, p. 230.

as pensions and medicare even while operating without a majority government in either of Pearson's two terms. In contrast, the early Trudeau years were marked by a strong emphasis on the rational model of decision making. Existing policies were questioned and reviewed. New initiatives, large or small, were subjected to a rigorous process of analysis and reporting. The prevailing viewpoint was reflected in a remark supposedly made by Michael Pitfield, Trudeau's chief of staff, to the effect "that's all right in practice, but will it work in theory?" Whether true or not, the quote typifies the extremes to which proponents of a rational model can go. In spite of all of the analysis and "number-crunching," however, it is hard to demonstrate that the early Trudeau years generated a superior policy output to the Pearson era.

One of the biggest and most obvious advantages of Lindblom's incrementalism is the reduction in the workload for those involved in policy analysis. There are also several other alleged advantages. Decisions which are a major departure from existing policy may be quite unpredictable in their consequences, and errors which may result are easier to correct when decisions are successive and limited. Also, incremental decisions are likely to be more acceptable politically than are the far-reaching changes that might result from the rational model of policy making. To his critics, Lindblom asserts that "the piecemealing, remedial incrementalist ... may not look like an heroic figure. He is nevertheless a shrewd, resourceful problem-solver who is wrestling bravely with a universe that he is wise enough to know is too big for him."[25]

Lindblom's views are criticized as offering a theoretical justification for defence of the status quo. They are rejected as reinforcing the "resistance to change" attitude already too prevalent in people and as being a conservative recipe for standing pat. These limitations are evident in the writings of Wildavsky,[26] who has examined incrementalism in relation to the annual budget process. While this process should involve a comprehensive assessment of the relative merits of all the conflicting claims on a municipality's scarce resources, its focus is much narrower in practice. It does not "reconsider the value of all existing programmes as compared to all possible alternatives." Instead, this year's budget takes as its starting point last year's budget, "with special attention given to a narrow range

[25]Charles E. Lindblom, *The Policy Making Process*, Englewood Cliffs, Prentice-Hall Inc., 1968, p. 27.

[26]A. H. Wildavsky, *The Politics of the Budgetary Process*, Boston, Little Brown, 1974.

of increases or decreases." As a result, those involved in the budget process "are concerned with relatively small increments to an existing base."[27]

The Penny Arcade Model

The second descriptive theory we offer as a contrast to the rational model is one provided by Yates, who uses a metaphor based on three familiar games found in most penny arcades.[28]

First, Yates points out that the process of determining the problems which require the attention of the policy maker is like being in a shooting gallery. "Like the urban policy maker the shooting gallery player has far more targets than he can possibly hit, and they keep popping up in different places or revolving around and around in front of him."[29] The player is continually reacting to a new target (problem) and is conscious of the fact that firing at any one target (dealing with any one problem) means letting most of the others go by until the next time. Given the need to react quickly and to deal with such a variety of targets, the player is likely to rely on reflexes more than any considered plan of action.

Second, Yates compares the municipal policy maker's ability to predict and control the kinds of decisions he must make with that of someone operating a slot machine. By this he means that the policy making characteristics of a particular problem can vary just as randomly as the apples, oranges and cherries which appear in various combinations on a slot machine. "Urban policy making variables include the nature of the problem, the issue context, the stage of decision, the configuration of participants, the institutional setting, and the government function involved."[30] The policy maker does not know what kind of problem he will be dealing with from one moment to the next, or which of his available policy responses or procedures is likely to be relevant or useful. He may need to negotiate, appeal to the senior levels of government, enforce an existing policy more thoroughly, set up an interdepartmental task force, provide new channels for citizen input — or a wide variety of other pos-

---

[27]*Ibid.*, p. 15.

[28]Douglas Yates, *The Ungovernable City*, Cambridge, M.I.T. Press, 1977. (Presumably an enterprising academic will update this metaphor in line with our brave new world of video games and give rise to a new school of policy making.)

[29]*Ibid.*, p. 91.

[30]*Ibid.*, pp. 91-92.

sible approaches. The policy maker who relies on one or two standard responses or develops a standard approach to decision making will be responding inappropriately much of the time.

Finally, Yates views the process of policy implementation as similar to the operations of a pinball machine.

> Given the central policy maker's weak control over his own administration, street-level bureaucrats, and higher level governments, decisions once taken are likely to bounce around from decision point to decision point.[31]

In other words, even when a policy decision is made by the municipality, it may be knocked off course by both predictable and unforeseen obstacles by the time it reaches the street level. If this happens, the implemented policy may well give rise to a new set of problems which enter the shooting gallery of agenda setting all over again.

> To that extent urban policy making will become a continuous process in which a particular problem receives brief, often frantic, attention; some kind of decision is made, which bounces around in the implementation process; and then the problem pops up again in a new or altered form.[32]

Examples of such a pattern are fairly common. A stricter enforcement of property standards may lead to housing abandonment and/or rent increases which create new problems of housing shortages for low income residents. A police department moves to car patrols to increase coverage and then faces demands that the police officers go back on the beat to provide greater visibility and responsiveness. Planning policies call for the infilling of existing hamlets so as to prevent strip development in rural areas and then the concentration of septic tanks and wells bring health problems which necessitate the provision of expensive water and sewer systems. The policy making process is rarely simple and straightforward.

Obviously, Yates' portrayal of policy making in the penny arcade provides a marked contrast with the rational model outlined as a starting point for discussion. It may exaggerate somewhat the random, unpredictable nature of policy making, and it is based on the experiences of large urban areas. But it does highlight the idealistic nature of the rational model which assumes that answers can be found for any policy problems if enough intelligence is brought to bear on them.

---

[31]*Ibid.*, p. 93.

[32]*Ibid.*

The real world of policy making doesn't work that way.[33] Policy makers cannot carefully select their problems and then analyze them with great thoroughness and detachment. They face a constant barrage of new and changing problems and service demands. It is not possible to stop the policy making process, "freeze" a particular problem, and then dissect it in clinical fashion. In addition, municipal policy makers deal with problems which may not be clearly understood or which generate conflicting political pressures. Rather than undertaking thorough research and analysis, as suggested by the rational model, the response may be to grope for a plausible remedy and hope that it works better than previous ones.

In any event, often the issues involved do not call for analytical solutions as much as subjective assessments and political bargaining. The rational model also ignores the rapidity with which municipal policy problems may change. "To abstract and analyze a problem in a meticulous, detached way may be to lose track of the problem and wind up fighting yesterday's battles."[34] Finally, even if the "right" decision is made, implementing it is often not easy because of the fragmentation of the local government structure and because of resistance or modifications which may be introduced by what Yates terms "street-level bureaucrats." Given all of these considerations, Yates dismisses the rational model of policy making as "a greenhouse conception that cannot thrive in the harsh climate of urban politics."[35]

Explaining General Policy Output

The preceding discussion of how individual decisions are made, ideally and in practice, was largely focused inside the municipality. This section turns our attention from individual decisions to general policy outputs over time. Why do municipalities exhibit a certain approach or emphasis in their policy making over a period of years? Are there theories or models which help to explain why, for example, municipal policies appear to be preoccupied with facilitating the activities of the property development industry or appear to be very limited and restrictive when it comes to action on various social issues? These questions relate to the macro

---

[33]See Yates, *op. cit.*, pp. 94-97.

[34]*Ibid.*, pp. 96-97.

[35]*Ibid.*, p. 96.

level of decision making and attempting to answer them will direct our attention to the external forces which exert influence over municipalities.

The Socio-Economic Context

It is important to remember that policy making does not take place in a vacuum but in the real world, where it is subject to numerous external influences. The very significant impact of urbanization and industrialization, for example, has been discussed in Chapter 4. As economic and social conditions change, so too does the emphasis of municipal policy making. A very simple example of this point is provided by Masson's description of Spruce Grove, a community on the outskirts of Edmonton.[36] During the 1970s it became a dormitory suburb, with many young families attracted by its cheaper housing. Its population doubled between 1966 and 1970 and its per capita expenditure for recreation and community services went from $2.47 to $13.43. This substantial policy shift occurred because the younger population increased the demand for recreation.

Another common example is provided by various rural municipalities within commuting distance of cities. The public's desire for open space, and especially for waterfront properties, has led to very strong development pressures on those rural municipalities with attractive land for residential development and has posed major policy challenges for those municipalities in attempting to reconcile this growth with the preservation of the beauty of their natural features.

The aging of Canada's population presents quite a different challenge for municipal policy makers, especially for some places which have become attractive as retirement communities. In these municipalities, other policy initiatives and shifts will be necessary — and not just in the direction of health care. Growing numbers of "healthy elderly" will cause a demand for varied recreational and cultural facilities.

A major policy issue affecting both urban and rural municipalities concerns the development of waste management guidelines and the selection of future waste management sites. While debate rages about the relative merits of various waste disposal alternatives, and while studies and public hearings drag on interminably, our ability to dispose of the waste which we create moves closer and closer to a crisis situation. There is no better example of the NIMBY (not in my back yard) syndrome, and yet

---

[36]Jack Masson, *Alberta's Local Governments and Their Politics*, Edmonton, University of Alberta Press, 1985, p. 137.

with little land available in Canada's major urban centres, the search for sites inevitably involves the surrounding less developed areas.

The shift from an industrial to an information economy poses a number of challenges for municipal policy making. According to one analysis, "the old methods of local economic development are gone, along with the old economy. The new economy is based on service jobs which must be found and developed locally instead of trying to attract a branch plant to locate in your community."[37] As a result, new policies will be needed: "supporting local entrepreneurs by providing information and assistance, networking, providing capital and creating an entrepreneurial mentality."[38]

Who Wields Power?

Any examination of the external economic environment quickly raises questions about the alleged domination over policy making exerted by the business class. This is hardly a new theme. Chapter 3 provided numerous examples of the influence of business people during the turn of the century reform era and Chapter 8 described the efforts of business groups in several large Canadian cities to secure the election of slates of candidates who would be sympathetic to the business community in their policies. Efforts to document the actual influence of business on municipal policy output have produced conflicting evidence, however.

Elite versus Pluralist Models

There have been numerous studies designed to measure who actually wields power in a particular community. American studies of this nature have traditionally revealed two main viewpoints. One is the power elite concept originally propounded in Floyd Hunter's study of Atlanta.[39] Largely on the basis of interviews with people holding formal positions of power and with those reputedly influential, he concluded that policy making in Atlanta was the preserve of a fairly small group of people. These people were prominent in the business community and/or socially

---

[37]Marcel Cote, "Local Development in the New Economy," in *Municipal Monitor*, Richmond Hill, Kenilworth Publishing, October 1994, p. 8.

[38]*Ibid.*, p. 10.

[39]Floyd Hunter, *Community Power Structure*, New York, Anchor Books, 1953.

prestigious, and were on close personal terms with those public officials nominally in charge.

Hunter's findings were unsettling to those who preferred to see municipal political processes (and political processes at all levels of government) as participatory and incorporating the public interest rather than private, business interests. In response, there were more studies of community power which led to a competing model known as pluralism.

The groundbreaking study in this regard was centred on New Haven, Connecticut.[40] In this study, Robert Dahl examined a number of specific issues to determine who exercised influence, but concluded that no single elite dominated. Decision makers in one issue area, like education, were not influential in another, like urban redevelopment. Instead, numerous individuals and groups had some influence, which they might exert depending on the issue involved.

It is perhaps surprising that two trained social scientists would come to such completely opposite findings about who wields power in two American cities. One possible explanation might have been that the two cities in question were quite different in their make-up and in the actual exercise of power within them. That possibility, however, must be discarded in light of further research which has been done on these cities. This research found, in direct contrast to the earlier studies, that New Haven was controlled by a business elite and Atlanta was influenced by a series of competing coalitions.[41] A more likely explanation is that Hunter and Dahl got different findings because they used different approaches — "what you see depends on how you look at it."[42]

Since Hunter asked those reputed to be influential who it was that wielded power in Atlanta, it is perhaps not too surprising that they answered "we do!" Since he focused on informal social networks, he gave less weight to the formal machinery of government in the decision-making process. Dahl, on the other hand, emphasized the importance of the formal government structure. But his approach has also been criticized as flawed. By focusing on a number of decisions which had taken place,

[40]Robert Dahl, *Who Governs?* New Haven, Yale University Press, 1961.

[41]Kent Jennings, *Community Influentials: The Elites of Atlanta*, Glencoe, Free Press, 1964 and William Domhoff, *Who Really Rules? New Haven and Community Power Reexamined*, New Brunswick, Transaction, 1977.

[42]The discussion of this explanation which follows is based on E. Barbara Phillips and Richard T. LeGates (eds.), *City Lights: An Introduction to Urban Studies*, New York, Oxford University Press, 1981, Chapter 12.

Dahl overlooked another whole dimension of power — the ability to keep issues out of the decision making arena altogether.[43]

Flawed approach or not, Dahl's work has been very influential, and pluralist theory has been widely cited as an explanation of the policy outputs of governments. Essentially, pluralists see government action as the outcome of a competition among organized groups that seek to protect or promote the interests of their members.[44] Government is a rather passive arbiter and policy decisions emerge from the clash and interaction of these various groups.

Critics of the pluralist model point out that many citizens don't belong to groups, that groups vary greatly in their resources and effectiveness, and that not all groups have equal access to government. Too often, the apparently diversified influences implied in the pluralist model serve to conceal or distract attention from the fact that one type of group — the business group — is by far the most dominant. This issue has been memorably summarized by Schattsneider in the comment that "the flaw in the pluralist heaven is that the heavenly chorus sings with a strong upperclass accent."[45]

Pluralists insist that economic factors are not the only important determinants of public policy. They point to such other factors as language, religion, gender, region, ethnicity and ideology. They also claim that governments can't cater to business interests and neglect popular demands without running the risk of being replaced at the next election. However, if one governing group controlled by business is replaced by another governing group controlled by business, what has really changed in terms of who wields power?

The strong influence of the business community can be expected to continue, especially since the business ideology about the sanctity of private property, the benefits of free enterprise, and the energizing power of the profit motive seem to be well inculcated into North American values. The basis for business domination is persuasively explained by Lindblom, with his description of "the market as a prison."[46] He argues

---

[43]*Ibid.*, pp. 320-323.

[44]Brooks, *op. cit.*, p. 33.

[45]E. E. Schattsneider, *The Semi-Sovereign People*, New York, Holt, Rinehart and Winston, 1960, p. 35.

[46]Charles Lindblom, "The Market as Prison," in Thomas Ferguson and Joel Rogers (eds.), *The Political Economy*, New York, M. E. Sharpe, 1984, pp. 3-11.

that government actions which are seen as harmful to business prompt punitive responses from the business community — from cutbacks in production to the shifting of production to other jurisdictions. Public policies, therefore, are greatly constrained by the automatic punishment that the market system imposes on governments that trespass beyond the line of business tolerance.[47] The increasing globalization of the economy and the attendant increased mobility of firms has made this market punishment even more likely — a point central to Peterson's views on the limits of municipal policy making, discussed in a later section.

Perhaps surprisingly, the first major study of community power in Canada concluded that if there was a dominant elite it was composed of the elected and appointed municipal officials. Harold Kaplan, studying the operations of Metropolitan Toronto, found that "The creation, agitation and resolution of issues occurred within the formal institutions of government. Interaction among public officials was far more significant for the outcome of issues than interaction between officials and private actors."[48]

However, Kaplan was examining an upper tier government while many of the issues which would directly affect community groups were handled by constituent lower tier municipalities. If his study were expanded to include these lower tier units or repeated since the reorganization of January 1, 1967, gave Metropolitan Toronto more powers, much more outside involvement would likely be evident. As Chapter 8 pointed out, citizens' groups and reform councillors became much more prominent in Toronto in the 1970s. To a large extent, the citizen and reform activism was in response to the perceived threat to existing communities from pro-growth councils too closely allied to the property industry.

One of the reform councillors of this period, subsequently Mayor of Toronto, was John Sewell, who assessed the decision making process quite differently. Admittedly, he was writing about the City of Toronto not Metro, and his political autobiography was hardly a scholarly analysis of the Kaplan variety.[49] Sewell emphasized the intimate links between councillors and the development industry. From his experience, councillors did represent and speak for outside interests — those of the developer — and power was concentrated outside the formal institutions. A

---

[47]Brooks, *op. cit.*, p. 35.

[48]Harold Kaplan, *Urban Political Systems: A Functional Analysis of Metro Toronto*, New York, Columbia University Press, 1967, p. 157.

[49]John Sewell, *Up Against City Hall*, Toronto, James Lewis and Samuel, 1972.

similar viewpoint was echoed by a number of other writers during this period.[50]

Extensive studies of city politics in seven major Canadian cities at the beginning of the 1980s generally confirmed the prominence of business interests and the extent to which debates over development versus the quality of life have dominated the urban political scene. Whether expressed as boosters versus cutters or production interests versus consumption interests, these forces have remained the focal point of debate and political differences.[51] At the same time, however, these studies also suggested that the business domination was moderating. Sancton concluded that "the political representatives of the property industry no longer control the municipal councils of the country's major cities" and that "in most Canadian cities local politics is now genuinely competitive."[52] The property industry has regained at least some influence in the past few years, however, partly because the prolonged economic downturn has made municipal governments loath to antagonize the business community.

The Public Choice Model

Another model of policy making is the political economy or public choice approach. This has a long history, finding expression in such writings as the essays by Alexander Hamilton and James Madison in *The Federalists* and Alexis de Tocqueville's *Democracy in America*. After being ignored for much of the 20th century, public choice theory has made a strong comeback in recent decades — particularly as part of the swing to the right exhibited by governments since the late 1970s.

Public choice theory incorporates the concepts of classical economics about "economic man," motivated by self-interest, making choices which are reflected through the laws of supply and demand in the operations of the marketplace. It finds that these basic economic forces don't work as well when applied to public goods and services. Private goods and ser-

---

[50]See James Lorimer, *The Real World of City Politics*, and *A Citizen's Guide to City Politics*, Toronto, James Lewis and Samuel, 1970 and 1972, and *The Developers*, Toronto, James Lorimer and Co., 1980. See also Donald Gutstein, *Vancouver Ltd.*, Toronto, James Lorimer and Co., 1975.

[51]See Warren Magnusson and Andrew Sancton (eds.), *City Politics in Canada*, Toronto, University of Toronto Press, 1983, especially the concluding chapter.

[52]*Ibid.*, p. 297.

vices are normally available in the marketplace, and individuals are able to obtain these readily if they are willing to pay the price. Consumer demand (or lack thereof) influences the supply of a private good made available and the price that will apply to it.[53]

Public goods, such as police services, fire protection, or control of contagious diseases, present quite a contrast to private goods. Public goods are enjoyed or consumed by all members of a community. Individuals cannot be excluded from enjoying a public good once it is provided for someone else. By their nature, such goods and services can not be provided on a long term basis through voluntary efforts and financing. If they were, each citizen would find it in his or her interest to forgo payment, as long as enough others were paying to keep the good or service available. Governments levy taxes as a way of forcing everyone to pay a share of the cost of public goods and services.

Consumers express their preferences for, and their evaluation of, private goods by buying them or not. That choice is not available for public goods, for reasons already indicated. Instead, preferences for public goods and services are expressed through a variety of other means. These include voting, lobbying, public opinion polls, petitions, public hearings, demonstrations, court proceedings, political party organizations, and other indirect means including "taxpayer revolts" and resorts to violence when things are desperate.[54]

Public choice theorists contend that public bureaucracies and representative democracy are both seriously flawed in comparison to the operation of the marketplace.[55] Private companies, it is argued, must stay lean and efficient because of the existence of competition and alternative sources of goods and services. Not only is government a monopoly (for almost all goods and services), but also the way government operates serves to generate excess growth and spending. This happens, explain public choice theorists, because of the natural instinct of politicians and bureaucrats to pursue their own self-interest. For politicians, this means retaining voter support by promising more and better services to the electorate — although a long-suffering electorate may finally be running

---

[53]This discussion is based on Robert L. Bish and Vincent Ostram, *Understanding Urban Government: Metropolitan Reform Reconsidered*, Washington, American Enterprise Institute for Public Policy Research, 1973, Chapter 3.

[54]*Ibid.*, pp. 22-23.

[55]The analysis which follows is largely based on Gerry Stoker, *The Politics of Local Government*, London, Macmillan Education Ltd., 1988, Chapter 10.

out of patience with the idea of being bribed with its own money! Civil servants also pursue expanded programs and services, since the bigger their empires and budgets, the higher their status in the hierarchy. Both politicians and bureaucrats may make common cause with the constituencies which receive goods and services, as a way of developing pressure for their retention and expansion. Interest groups spring up to protect established programs and to advocate their expansion. Pirie claims that municipal governments, in particular, suffer from the excessive influence of pressure groups.

> Each service provided creates its class of beneficiaries which sees itself as a distinct interest group and will campaign for its privileges. The taxpayer and ratepayer, by contrast, are a more amorphous mass, not acting as a self-conscious interest group.[56]

Public choice theorists also find deficiencies in the arrangements for expressing consumer preferences concerning public goods and services. The votes cast in an election every few years are not a good or clear indication of citizen preferences concerning public goods and services. Voters are responding to a wide range of issues and are not able to signal their response to the provision of a particular good or service. This shortcoming has been referred to as the "all-or-nothing blue-plate menu problem," where à la carte purchasing is not permitted.[57] Citizens also express their preferences in other ways, as listed above, but access to these alternatives varies for different citizens. There are also costs to participating and citizens will only be motivated to express their preferences, therefore, when they feel the benefits of such activity will exceed the costs.

The smaller the political unit and the fewer the services provided, the easier it is for citizen preferences to be indicated precisely. For this reason, public choice theorists reject the creation of large, multi-purpose "regional governments" which have been the objective of most local government reformers. Such structures are held to be too large and bureaucratic and to work against citizen participation. Public choice proponents find the much-maligned fragmentation of local government to be a virtue. They support the retention of separate special purpose bodies. For them, the best structure is to have a large number of small local governments so that the diverse preferences of many different citizens can be satisfac-

---

[56]M. Pirie, "Economy and Local Government," in E. Butler and M. Pirie (eds.), *Economy and Local Government*, London, Adam Smith Institute, 1981, p. 11, quoted in Stoker, p. 226.

[57]Bish and Ostram, *op. cit.*, p. 23.

torily accommodated.[58] This approach reflects the contribution of Tiebout, who put forth the view that for each unit of local government there is a natural "optimum community size" based on the mixture of taxes levied and services provided toward which all local governments should strive.[59] This size is achieved as a result of individual consumers "searching around" to find that community which suits their needs best. If taxes increase too much or desired services are not provided, the argument goes, then consumers will respond by expressing their discontent or by "voting with their feet" and moving to another jurisdiction.

Critics of public choice dispute the notion of well-informed consumers making careful assessments of the package of services and tax levels available to them in their own and neighbouring municipalities.[60] They also point out that most consumers are not that mobile, and can't readily shift locations even if they have information which might suggest more attractive options. This lack of mobility particularly applies to the poor and disadvantaged. As a result, one of the strongest criticisms of public choice theory is that it can serve to justify the establishment or preservation of separate jurisdictions which house the rich and privileged and keep out the poor and undesirable and their expensive servicing needs. This practice is more evident in the multiple servicing districts and separate jurisdictions found in American urban areas.

City Limits: Pluralism Plus?

If consumers aren't especially mobile, businesses certainly are. The trend towards the globalization of the economy has given rise to "hypermobile" capital, which Smart describes as a force that cities require but cannot command.[61] As a result, the bargaining power of capitalists is increased and the socio-economic autonomy of cities declines. Cities are forced to compete more intensively for investment, and their policies and programs are shaped according to their attractiveness to investors. This is not a new

---

[58]Stoker, *op. cit.*, p. 228.

[59]Charles Tiebout, "A Pure Theory of Local Expenditures," *Journal of Political Economy*, Vol. 64, pp. 416-424.

[60]For a good discussion of the dubious assumptions underlying the Tiebout hypothesis, see L. J. Sharpe and K. Newton, *Does Politics Matter?* Oxford, Clarendon Press, 1984, pp. 61-68.

[61]Alan Smart, "Recent Developments in the Theory of the State," in Frisken, *op. cit.*, p. 569.

idea and earlier reference has been made to the fact that ultimately city politics has always been about "boosterism."

But this idea has been taken to its limits, one might say, by the writings of Paul Peterson.[62] Peterson begins by placing the city in the larger socio-economic and political context. He argues that the place of the city within the larger political economy of the nation affects in a very fundamental way the policy choices that cities make. It is the city's interpretation of its interests in this broader context that limits city policies, not the internal struggles for power within the city. According to Peterson, the "community power" studies already described above — whether identifying a dominant elite or a power-sharing pluralistic society — all assumed that cities had few, if any, limits on their powers. Yet many issues never become the subject of local debate or dispute because they are outside the limited sphere of local politics.

Peterson points to the fact that cities constantly seek to upgrade their economic standing. They attempt to improve their attractiveness as a location for economic activity. This is hardly surprising. Such an emphasis is almost inevitable, given that the municipality's primary source of local revenues is a tax on real property. Economic growth means an expanded tax base and increased revenue sources (although it also means increased costs, something which pro-growth politicians sometimes overlook or underestimate). Economic growth also means more jobs for the local community, something which generates widespread community support. In that regard, pursuit of economic growth by politicians could be explained in public choice terms as being in the politician's self-interest. What makes Peterson's analysis distinctive is his argument that the policies adopted by a city will be constrained and shaped by how the policies affect the overriding objective of promoting economic growth.

Peterson describes three types of public policy for consideration.[63] Developmental policies enhance the economic position of the city. Examples would be initiatives to attract industry, to extend the transportation system or to revitalize economically depressed areas. Developmental policies strengthen the local economy, generate employment, and add to the local tax base. They are widely supported as providing a net financial gain to the municipality. Development policies are largely formed in behind-the-scenes discussions between public and private elites who share a common view of what is needed to promote economic growth.

---

[62]Paul Peterson, *City Limits*, Chicago, University of Chicago Press, 1981.

[63]*Ibid.*, Chapter 3.

Redistributive policies, as defined by Peterson, are those which involve income transfers from higher to lower income segments of the population. They benefit low income residents but at the same time usually have a negative effect on the local economy. They can be economically beneficial in particular circumstances, and Peterson gives the example of a city supplying workers with such redistributive services as low-cost housing or free medical care when it needs additional low income workers to help staff its service industries or work in manufacturing. In most cases, however, he argues that such policies have negative economic effects. They supply benefits to those least needed by the local economy by taxing those who are most needed.[64] Whatever limited support exists for these policies is largely based on humanitarian feelings that helping the needy is "the right thing to do." Local governments avoid such policies as much as possible; they are excluded from the local political agenda.

Allocational policies are fairly neutral in their economic effects. Many local government services fall into this middle ground, with the housekeeping services being the best example. Police and fire protection and garbage and waste disposal are provided throughout the city to all residents. They do not particularly benefit a needy segment of the community at the expense of the average taxpayer.

Because they are open systems (and increasingly so with the globalization of the economy), municipal governments are very sensitive to external changes. To preserve their economic health, they must maintain a local efficiency that leaves very little scope for concerns about equality. They must pursue developmental but not redistributive policies.[65]

The implications of the arguments of Peterson and the public choice theorists is that it is in the shared interests of members of municipalities to maximize their tax base. For both residents and local business firms, a stronger tax base means a better benefit/cost ratio between services received and taxes paid. For politicians, a stronger tax base allows them to take credit for more services without tax increases. For local bureaucrats, a stronger tax base allows them to build their budgets and departmental empires without the kind of resistance which would come if taxes were increased accordingly. Overall then, various interests combine in the pursuit of economic expansion, making the city a "growth machine."[66]

---

[64]*Ibid.*, p 43.

[65]*Ibid.*, p. 69.

[66]These points are made by Mark Schneider, *The Competitive City*, Pittsburgh, University of Pittsburgh Press, 1989, p. 21.

Peterson's views have generated much debate but, like every other attempt to theorize about municipal policy making, they have their share of critics. Schneider studies the local market for public goods through an examination of the interaction of suburban governments within any given metropolitan region. He finds evidence to support the public choice claims that increased competition from multiple service providers serves to limit the growth of government and the costs of its services.[67] But his findings do not support key parts of Peterson's arguments. Schneider observes that competition as measured by the number of nearby local competitors and by variations in the taxes paid for local services "consistently restrains expenditures in all policy domains."[68] Therefore, competition has a broader impact than Peterson predicts and restrains all expenditures, even the developmental ones which Peterson suggested would always find support.

After studying planning in Vancouver and Edmonton, Leo finds — like Peterson — that a city's economic situation does set limits upon its freedom of action. But he also concludes, contrary to Peterson, that these limits are not all-encompassing. They leave "substantial space for community action and for the forging of unique community identities through political action."[69] Leo illustrates this point by contrasting Edmonton's willingness to accommodate business interests in the redevelopment of the city with Vancouver's determination to maintain strict controls over development. He suggests that the approach followed by Edmonton was less a result of objective economic circumstances than "a panicky misreading of its economic situation"[70] which led it to conclude that it had to give in to the demands of the business community to bring about an economic revival. While the global economic context is important, Leo contends that attempts to explain any city's performance must also take into account the particular circumstances of that city, "including local political cultures and the political forces that comprise the local state and control the direction it takes."[71]

---

[67]*Ibid.*, pp. 68-69.

[68]*Ibid.*, p. 88.

[69]Christopher Leo, *The Urban Economy and the Power of the Local State*, in Frisken, *op. cit.*, p. 663.

[70]*Ibid.*, p. 693.

[71]*Ibid.*, p. 694.

Stone and Sanders are also critical of Peterson and his assumptions about the nature of developmental policies — that they are free of conflict, are based on a widespread consensus of what needs to be done, and are formulated from specialized information known to experienced actors. They find Peterson guilty of excessive faith in the rational model of decision making, discussed earlier in this chapter.[72] They also find that Peterson ignores or overlooks much case study evidence that conflict, not consensus, is characteristic of redevelopment and expressway issues — a point clearly borne out by Canadian experiences. Stone and Sanders reexamine the experience of New Haven under Mayor Richard Lee, one cited by Peterson in support of his views. They find the opposite of Peterson's contention that development is a process in which any initial resistance gives way as the general benefits of development become known. Instead, their examination of New Haven suggests that resistance grows as plans give way to concrete actions.[73] While acknowledging that *City Limits* is a very ambitious book which attempts to synthesize the findings of both pluralists and elitists, Stone and Sanders conclude that "when all of his cards are put on the table, Peterson is very much the pluralist, largely reiterating the argument of Robert Dahl in *Who Governs?*"[74]

Marxist Theory

Most of the theories discussed above emphasize the influence of economic factors in shaping policy outputs. The ultimate theory of economic determinism is, of course, Marxism. It sees society as divided into classes, with class being the basis for political and economic conflict. The state or government is biased in favour of the dominant class, the capitalists or those who own the means of production. Government policies reflect this bias. They are either accumulative policies which are directly supportive of profit-oriented business activity or legitimation policies which reduce class conflict by providing subordinate classes with benefits (like housing, education and health services) that reduce their dissatisfaction with the inequalities produced by the capitalist economy.[75]

---

[72]Clarence N. Stone and Heywood T. Sanders (eds.), *The Politics of Urban Development*, Lawrence, University Press of Kansas, 1987, p. 164.

[73]*Ibid.*, p. 179.

[74]*Ibid.*, p. 165.

[75]Brooks, *op. cit.*, p. 41.

Marxists and neo-Marxists reject pluralist, public choice and elite theories as being too narrowly focused. Writers like Harvey and Castells have attempted to broaden the focus by examining the relationship between the city, its politics and the dominant mode of production.[76] For Castells, the "urban" was to provide collective consumption in order to reproduce labour power for the capitalist mode of production. As Magnusson explains this viewpoint:

> The need for reliable, energetic and skilled workers became more apparent; the workers themselves demanded better conditions; and everyone found that many of the goods and services workers demanded could be provided more economically on a collective basis. Hence, the development of capitalism as a system of production involved considerable socialization of consumption, in the form of health, education and welfare services, cultural and recreational facilities, public housing and so on.[77]

Much of the responsibility for providing these collective consumption goods fell to local governing bodies and, it is claimed, gave local politics its particular character.

Magnusson comments on the similarity between the neo-Marxist and public choice viewpoints. Both see local authorities as agencies for collective consumption. Both reduce the local community to "a set of economic relations between individuals or a struggle between classes formed by the mode of production."[78]

On the surface, attempts to explain political activity at the local level as a class struggle may seem curious in a North American society which likes to believe it is classless, or one in which the vast majority see themselves as middle class. Certainly, this explanation fits more obviously in the British context, where most analyses of city politics emphasize the importance of social class.[79] But we have noted many examples of the dominance of the business class in getting its pro-development agenda adopted by municipal councils. It has been shown that the push for such

---

[76]D. Harvey, *Social Justice and the City*, Baltimore, John Hopkins University Press, 1973, and M. Castells, *City, Class and Power*, London, Macmillan, 1978 — both of whom are discussed in Smart, *op. cit.*, pp. 562-563.

[77]Warren Magnusson, "The Local State in Canada: Theoretical Perspectives," in *Canadian Public Administration*, Winter 1985, p. 594.

[78]*Ibid.*, p. 595.

[79]Magnusson and Sancton, *op. cit.*, p. 305.

features as at large elections and the introduction of a board of control system during the turn of the century reform movement was at least partly motivated by the desire of members of the middle class to arrest the growing influence of ward politicians representing working class and ethnic neighbourhoods. Early zoning by-laws often featured building standards and sizes designed to protect the exclusive nature of established middle and upper class neighbourhoods — not just from the intrusion of inappropriate types of commercial or industrial use, but also from the possibility of residential development which might house those from lower classes. Class issues have been more muted in Canada, and often expressed in other than class language, but they have still been there.

The Conservative Influence

Limits on municipal policy making and increased emphasis on the virtues of the market can both be traced to the upswing of conservatism in the 1970s.[80] This developed out of the perceived fiscal crisis of the welfare state — the growing feeling that extending, or even preserving, the existing welfare services could not be achieved without unacceptable levels of taxation or borrowing. The development of international capital markets made it easier for international investors to play off one state against another in demanding concessions, a tactic long employed with success among municipalities as well.

From Magnusson's perspective, the rhetoric of neo-conservatism is now being used to dress up and legitimize a drift back to traditional municipal politics. Thus boosterism is now called entrepreneurship, and deals with developers become "public-private partnerships."[81] Magnusson also finds the new conservatism behind the growing resistance to developments which are seen as having any adverse local effects and the growth of NIMBYism.

Much of the impact on local government of the new conservatism has resulted from actions taken by the senior levels of government. Growing federal government restraint has, in turn, caused provinces to reduce transfer payments to municipalities, schools, hospitals and other local agencies. One of the more dramatic interventions came from — surprising as it may seem — an NDP government in Ontario which introduced a social contract under which expenditure cutbacks were imposed on local

---

[80]The discussion which follows is largely based on Warren Magnusson, *Metropolitan Change and Political Disruption*, in Frisken *op. cit.*, pp. 553-556.

[81]*Ibid.*, p. 555.

governments. The Reagan administration slashed federal transfers to municipalities, resulting in the abandonment of many programs which attempted to address the more serious social ills of the day. In Britain, the Thatcher government waged war on Labour-controlled municipal councils. Its tactics included transfer cuts, the imposition of limits on how much municipalities can increase their tax rates, even the abolition of upper tier municipal governments (notably the London County Council) which were not sufficiently responsive to the conservative dictates being imposed.

As a result of these various developments, local governments are being squeezed, in Magnusson's words, "between the state and the market."[82] They are legally subordinate to the provincial level and their actions are controlled and influenced by policies and decisions of the provincial (and federal) government. Local governments are also influenced and constrained by the demands of the marketplace and the pressure to enhance the property tax base. Moreover, the prevailing philosophy of senior level governments has been to respect and to protect the market and, as discussed earlier, to view local governments as providing the physical infrastructure supportive of continued private sector land development.

Concluding Observations

What do the foregoing admittedly brief theoretical summaries tell us about municipal policy making? That depends. The conflicting views of Hunter and Dahl about community power were explained above on the basis that "what you see depends on how you look at it." The answer to the question posed in this section could be expressed as "what you see depends on where you look." If the municipal government is the focus, policy decisions will be related to the adequacy of the structure in place, and the motivations of the personnel who operate that structure. If, however, the focus is on the local community, then activities of local interest groups and media may be cited to explain policy outcomes. If the focus is broadened further, to recognize the larger economic and technological forces affecting the community, still other explanations will be found.

To illustrate, consider the not untypical municipal issue outlined below, and how its resolution might be explained by the theories discussed above.

---

[82]Magnusson in Frisken, *op. cit.*, p. 546.

A rapidly urbanizing township adjacent to a medium-sized city continues to experience strong growth pressures. There is little undeveloped land left within the city. The other nearby municipalities are small and rural, and lack the infrastructure necessary to support any large scale development. The urbanizing township has an abundance of serviced land and its council has been actively pursuing new growth for several years, believing that the increased assessment is the key to financial survival. A prominent local developer applies for a zoning amendment to allow a higher density mixed-use project. This application is referred to the township's Planning Advisory Committee, consisting mainly of citizen appointees — most with ties to the business community. The application is supported by the Committee. There is some lobbying from a couple of local citizens' groups opposed to the rezoning — one being a hastily formed coalition of neighbours living adjacent to the proposed project. Another group expressing opposition is a rural-based coalition of long-time residents who feel that the township is neglecting its rural and farm interests in its obsession with growth and development. However, the rezoning is subsequently approved by council and upheld on appeal to the provincial tribunal responsible for such matters.

On the surface, this is a straightforward exercise of decision making power by the appropriately authorized bodies. Under provincial legislation, municipal councils have the authority to amend their zoning by-laws. They can establish planning advisory committees to provide assistance in the planning process. Objections to a rezoning usually result in a hearing by a provincial tribunal, which then makes the final decision.

But what explanations might be provided for the policy decision which was made by the municipality in this instance? Traditionally, the first explanation would look for answers in the formal machinery of municipal government. What we have here is a typically fragmented structure, with several different municipalities operating within one urban area (the city and its surrounding hinterland). Instead of a coordinated approach to planning and development, there are separate municipalities pursuing their own agendas. Thus, the "pro-growth" township is able to attract the bulk of the new development in the area — whether or not that might be the best location for development if viewed from an area-wide perspective.

Further fragmentation can be found within the structure of the township itself. While it is only advisory in nature, the planning advisory committee does divide consideration of planning issues between council and this separate body. Moreover, the fact that the advisory committee consists mainly of citizen appointees increases the likelihood of a different point of view than that of the council. The internal governing structure of the township may also be fragmented, depending on the specifics of its organization. Since it has been growing rapidly, it has almost certainly been adding new staff and departments in a rather ad hoc fashion. There may be a series of standing committees, each focusing on the activities of their department(s) and perpetuating or even reinforcing these specialized viewpoints. If there isn't any Chief Administrative Officer, then the various department heads are officially equals. They will respond to development proposals such as the one outlined above largely on the basis of how such proposals might affect their departments. But what about the impact on the overall municipality? Where is that perspective found?

A second explanation for the planning decision outlined above is that it reflects the self-interest of the politicians and bureaucrats involved. From this point of view, politicians seek to be elected and then to maintain themselves in power, while staff seek to expand their empires and therefore their own importance. This *public choice* perspective suggests that politicians would support the rezoning application because they see the resulting development and increased assessment as enhancing or at least maintaining their political support base. To the township staff, continued growth means an almost certain increase in their operations, responsibilities, staff complements and budgets — in short, expanded empires which would, in turn, enhance their stature.

The specific reaction of politicians and bureaucrats to an issue of this sort would also be influenced by such factors as the perceived capacity of the media to influence public opinion and the ability of interest groups to mobilize supporters. Given the outcome of the scenario outlined above, it can be concluded that the media did not "run" with this issue for any length of time, and that the citizens' groups lined up against the rezoning were not considered to carry much weight.

The significance and influence of the local groups within this municipality is at the heart of the third explanation of the planning decision. It sees decisions as the result of the interaction of groups, all seeking to influence policy outcomes. This *pluralist* perspective views the government as an essentially passive force and government decisions as the outcome of a competition between organized groups that seek to protect or promote the interests of their members. Given the planning decision which resulted above, we must assume that, in addition to the citizens' groups opposed to the rezoning, there were other influential groups at work. These might include ratepayer groups and "fair tax coalitions" pressuring the township council to hold the line on taxes. To most councillors, this goal can only be achieved by increasing assessment and, therefore, by supporting the rezoning. They would certainly include business groups such as a local chamber of commerce, construction association and home builders' association. Pluralists would presumably explain the planning decision above by conceding the stronger influence (and superior lobbying resources and tactics) usually exhibited by business groups.

Given the prominence of business groups, one might explain the planning decision above from yet a different perspective of *economic determinism*. Supporters of this political economy approach would point to the pervasiveness of capitalist values within Canadian society. The virtues of private enterprise and pursuit of profit are seldom questioned. The upswing of conservatism since the 1970s has reinforced the positive view of the operation of the market. The role of local government is seen as providing the physical services needed to support growth and development. Government decisions are seen as the outcome of the lines of cleavage in Canadian society which, in turn, result from the way wealth is distributed. Thus, the economic power of the property development industry prevails.

In the case of the planning decision above, the prevalence on the planning advisory committee of citizens with ties to the business community is of note. There might also be a similar pattern of close linkages between many of the councillors and the business community — perhaps reinforced by financial support from the development industry for the election campaigns of these councillors.

Economic determinists would also point out that if the township did not respond to the developer's proposal, this development would likely end up somewhere else within the area (or beyond) — taking its attractive assessment and tax yield to a different municipality. This, of course, reflects Peterson's viewpoint in *City Limits* that municipalities must pursue policies favourable to development and Lindblom's argument that the market is a prison.

As a final observation, the planning issue under discussion can also be seen as reflecting Magnusson's point about municipalities being caught between the state and the market. It is the provincial level which is cutting transfer payments to municipalities and forcing them to finance more of their expenditures from the property tax — even as the same provincial level tightens environmental and other controls designed to prevent municipalities from allowing "inappropriate" development. As each municipality seeks increased assessment to finance its expenditures, it finds itself at the mercy of firms which are becoming increasingly mobile in response to the globalization of the economy.

Most of the theories summarized herein direct our attention to the way municipal decision making is constrained by economic and social conditions. This provides a marked contrast to the traditional emphasis (reflected in the discussion in Chapter 7), which focuses on the constraints on municipal decision making imposed by the senior levels of government. As Smart points out, it is that latter set of relationships which has received most of the attention in writings on Canadian local government. Yet the degree of "socioeconomic autonomy" enjoyed by a municipality is equally important. The power of local elites or the demands of competition in a rapidly changing economy may severely limit the freedom and discretion of local decision makers.[83]

---

[83]Smart, *op. cit.*, p. 567.

CHAPTER 10

Reinventing Municipal Government for the 21st Century

OBJECTIVES:

1. To review why municipal government was invented and why it now needs reinventing.

2. To present the essential elements in a new turn of the century reform movement which will position municipal governments to meet the challenges of the 21st century.

Introduction

When the first edition of this text was being written in the late 1970s, it seemed safe to include in the final chapter some musings about "Prospects for the Future: Local Government in the Year 2000." With each successive edition, however, that once far away threshold loomed closer. It is a sobering thought to realize that this new edition will probably still be in use when we reach the year 2000.

That reality was one of the factors which prompted a new approach to this final chapter in this edition. Another factor is the timeliness of the theme of "reinventing" municipal government. We are in a period of flux and change. Governments at all levels face severe challenges, and since "adversity is the mother of invention," this period is also producing a reconsideration of what governments do and how they carry out their roles. Municipal governments are in the forefront of the exciting new approaches being considered. A third factor, and the most influential in shaping this final chapter, is the fascinating historical parallel which presents itself. One hundred years ago, municipal governments faced a crisis with features very similar to those affecting the system today. The "solution" 100 years ago was a turn of the century reform movement which introduced a number of changes in structure and operating philosophy. It is now time for another such turn of the century reform initiative but, as will be seen, one with quite different ingredients.

First, however, let us remind ourselves why municipal government was invented and why it now needs to be reinvented. With this background, we can then describe the central elements in its reinvention.

Why Municipal Government Was Invented

The answer to this question varies somewhat from province to province. As discussed in Chapter 2, in several instances the main impetus for change appeared to be the desire of the colonial or provincial administrations of the time to shift their own growing expenditure burden to a new level of government and a new tax source — real property. (How's that for another fascinating historical parallel!)

In a few provinces, notably Ontario, there was a very pronounced demand for municipal government on the part of the citizens, led by the United Empire Loyalists. Chapter 2 described how continued agitation, highlighted by the 1837 Rebellion, persuaded the British authorities to introduce elected municipal governments throughout Upper and Lower Canada (Ontario and Quebec). These took over local government responsibilities from the Courts of Quarter Sessions, fully 50 years before this form of local administration was abandoned in Britain itself.

The system of municipal institutions established in the 1840s was unquestionably intended to serve two key purposes:

1. to continue to provide a variety of local services (as had been done by the Courts of Quarter Sessions which they replaced) and
2. to provide for elected councils to represent and make decisions on behalf of the local inhabitants within each municipality.

From the outset, municipal governments were invented to serve two key purposes — administrative or service delivery and representative or political. Of these two purposes or roles, the second one must be paramount. It incorporates the notion that municipal governments represent the views and concerns of their local communities and take action to deal with these concerns. The service delivery role is (or at least should be) subservient to the political role; services are provided in accordance with the needs and wishes of the local inhabitants. If the settlers in Central Canada in the 1840s had only been interested in receiving services, there would have been no reason for them to push for elected municipal governments. They were already receiving local services, from the Courts of Quarter Sessions. What they wanted, clearly, was something more — a say in those servicing decisions, a vehicle through which they could express collective concerns about their communities. No matter how many or what services are provided by municipalities, their primary importance is as an expression of local choice. As Clarke and Stewart explain it, there would be no point, other than administrative convenience, in local governments providing services in which there was no significant local choice.[1]

Why Municipal Government Needs Reinventing

The single most important reason why municipal government needs to be reinvented is that it has never fulfilled its two primary roles. In particular, it has never been able to carry out the political role which is the ultimate reason for its existence. The reasons for this failure have been explained in the preceding chapters, but will be briefly summarized herein as a refresher and as a basis for the recommendations to follow.

The Neglected Political Role

From the outset, municipal governments were never created as an extension of the community. Instead, they were established as the creations of colonial and provincial administrations — and their legal subordination to that level of government was enshrined in the Canadian constitution in 1867. As a result, municipal governments have been increasingly regarded as the provider of a series of separate services mandated by provincial legislation, not as the political voice of their local communities.

The second setback came with the turn of the century reform movement. It is ironic that barely 50 years after the establishment of a system of elected municipal governments its representative features should be so severely attacked and undermined by the misguided zeal of the reformers. Reacting to the apparent inability of municipal governments to handle the increased service demands of the rapidly urbanizing population of the late 1800s, and to the perceived excesses of party politics at the local level in the United States, the reformers hit upon what they saw as the ideal solution. *Politics must be removed from municipal government.* They agitated for various structural changes including:

1. the introduction of the city manager (CAO) system, to provide a clear separation between policy and administration and to ensure professional, competent municipal leadership — free of political interference.
2. the establishment of a number of separate boards and commissions, to handle functions considered to be too complex or too sen-

---

[1]Michael Clarke and John Stewart, *Choices for Local Government for the 1990s and Beyond*, Harlow, Longman, 1991, p. 2.

sitive to be entrusted to politicians, and to attract the contributions of knowledgeable citizens.

3. the introduction of the board of control system, as part of efforts to reduce the influence of ward politicians and their perceived narrow representation of neighbourhoods.

Most of all, however, the reformers sought to instill the notion that politics had no place in municipal government. Their rallying cry was *"there's no political way to build a road."* This statement is true, as far as the technical requirements of paving materials and building standards. But the decision on where to build a road is certainly political. The decision on whether to build a road or to respond to transportation needs by spending money on public transit is political. The decision on whether to allocate limited funds to roads (or transportation) versus such other competing needs as waste management, fire protection or public housing is also political.

By the term "political" we do not mean corrupt, partisan, sleazy, self-motivated or any of the other negative and value-laden meanings usually added to this word. Politics refers to the process of making decisions in a democratic society. It refers to the process of making choices, an inevitable requirement since human wants and needs are always greater than the resources available to satisfy them. As a result, competition and conflict arise, especially about how equitably scarce resources are distributed. The central purpose of all governments — their political role — is to resolve such disputes by deciding who gets what resources.

In spite of the widespread negative public perception of the term "politics" or "political," most scholarly works on government acknowledge both the inevitability and desirability of political decisions. Makuch[2] argues that municipalities must have a wide policy-making role in the delivery of services so that they can make local decisions respecting local political matters. He grants the need for some province-wide or nation-wide standards to protect minority rights and to ensure that all citizens have certain minimum rights, but feels that this must be balanced against the desirability of local control.

Gyford[3] notes that much of the literature about local government has lacked any political dimension, but that in the past couple of decades the public has shown "an increasing awareness that the decisions which issue

---

[2]Stanley M. Makuch, *Canadian Municipal and Planning Law*, Toronto, Carswell, 1983, pp. 5-6.

[3]John Gyford, *Local Politics in Britain*, London, Croom Helm Ltd., 1976, p. 9.

from their local council are not immaculately conceived." He goes on to explain that it is as true locally as it is nationally that "politics arises in the first instance when one realizes that there is no such thing as the people — that no single decision can please all people. There are only peoples, with contradictory and conflicting ideas and interests."[4] Higgins makes much the same point when he refers to politics as "competition among diverse interests to achieve goals that may not all be mutually compatible. According to that conception, it is impossible to have government without politics."[5]

As the 20th century unfolded, however, municipal governments were increasingly associated with administration and service delivery, not with being political institutions designed to provide a forum for the discussion and resolution of local issues. As discussed in earlier chapters, this narrowed perspective was evident in a number of developments, four of which were:

1. the adaptations of the system during the first half of the 20th century to the pressures of industrialization and urbanization.
2. the local government reform initiatives of the mid-20th century.
3. the disentanglement exercises of recent years.
4. the provincial treatment of municipal governments as just another expenditure category, to be cut at will to meet provincial fiscal objectives.

Let us review briefly these four developments.

Adaptations of the System

As part of these adaptations, responsibility for many traditionally municipal services was shifted to a higher level of government or hived off to special purpose boards or commissions. Financing of the remaining services was increasingly paid for out of provincial grants, with the overwhelming majority of these being conditional in nature. Through these grants, and through a wide variety of approval, inquiry and supervisory powers, provincial governments exercised fairly detailed control over most aspects of municipal operations. To those only interested in the administrative role of municipal government, everything seemed to be in order. A growing range of services were provided and yet property tax increases

---

[4]*Ibid.*, p. 11, quoting D. Bell and V. Held, "The Community Revolution," in *Public Interest*, No. 16, 1969, p. 177.

[5]Donald Higgins, *Local and Urban Politics in Canada*, Toronto, Gage, 1986, p. 254.

were kept in check. The reality, however, was less positive. People continued to elect municipal councils, but these elected bodies had less and less discretion to respond to the varying needs and wishes of their local inhabitants — less and less scope to carry out a political role.

Local Government Reform Initiatives

The impetus for these reforms came mainly from servicing crises associated with the most urbanized areas of the country, with some of the earliest reforms being introduced for Canada's two largest cities — Toronto and Montreal. Most of the reforms which were implemented also focused on improving service delivery.

One of the main reforms was to create or strengthen upper tier levels of municipal government, as with Ontario's regional governments, British Columbia's regional districts and Quebec's urban communities and regional county municipalities. But boundaries drawn for administrative needs are not necessarily appropriate for political needs. Indeed, many of the upper tier governments have been criticized as aloof, bureaucratic and unresponsive — especially those which are elected indirectly and have little direct contact with the electorate. Ironically, many of the upper tier governments have also turned out to be too small for fulfilling their service delivery requirements. As a result, we have such additional creations as the GTA (Greater Toronto Area) to provide the broader jurisdiction deemed necessary for planning and major service decisions in the Toronto area and the proposal that a Montreal Metropolitan Region be established to deal with similar region-wide issues in the Montreal area. The result is a "worst of both worlds" scenario, with upper tier governments too small for effective service delivery and too large for effective political representation.

Local government reforms also involved increased use of inter-municipal boards, in areas such as Fredericton, Saint John and Moncton in New Brunswick, in Halifax, in St. John's and in 14 regional service boards in Alberta — all discussed in Chapter 5. Whatever their service delivery potential, these boards and their composition tended to blur the lines of responsibility and accountability.

One local government reform did give particular attention to the representative and political role of municipal government. But, as has been seen, many of the innovations which made the Winnipeg Unicity reform seem so promising did not work all that well in practice and/or have been gradually undermined or abandoned over the years. The large (51 member) municipal council has been reduced to only 15, the number of community councils has been reduced from 12 to 5 and the resident advisory groups have been abolished.

The Disentanglement Process

There was some consideration of the realignment of local and provincial responsibilities as part of the local government reform initiatives discussed in the previous section, notably in the comprehensive studies of New Brunswick and Manitoba in the early 1960s and of Nova Scotia in the early 1970s. More recently, Ontario and Nova Scotia embarked on major disentanglement exercises — although the Ontario initiative has been abandoned, at least for the moment.

The general concept of disentanglement is superficially attractive. By reducing overlap and clarifying the lines of responsibility it suggests an improvement in accountability and political control. But, as discussed in Chapter 7, disentanglement holds dangers for the municipal level. If municipalities are to end up with only those functions which are local, they will have greatly diminished responsibilities and — ultimately — a reduced political role. They can hardly be the political mechanism through which a community expresses its collective objectives if most of the policies of interest to the community are decided by higher levels of government. The flaw in the disentanglement concept is the preoccupation with service delivery and administrative tidiness.

Municipalities as Provincial Expenditure Category

This is perhaps the ultimate example of the danger which arises when municipal governments are viewed as little more than agents for service delivery. Instead of being seen as an extension of the community, a mechanism for the community to govern itself, municipalities have been increasingly viewed as a kind of sub-category of provincial administration, existing to meet provincial not local needs. Plunkett and Graham, for example, refer to municipal governments as "the administrative peons of provincial policy-makers." They observe that "local governments are adhering to their role as agents of provincial interest to the detriment of their role as interpretors of the local scene."[6] Bird and Slack are at least as pessimistic, concluding that municipalities have been virtually downgraded to field offices of the provincial governments and that they have insufficient control over their own fate to mount any real opposition to this development.[7]

---

[6]T. J. Plunkett and Katherine A. Graham, "Whither Municipal Government," in *Canadian Public Administration*, Winter 1982, pp. 616 and 614.

[7]Richard M. Bird and N. Enid Slack, *Urban Public Finance in Canada*, Toronto, Butterworth, 1983, p. 116.

If municipalities are seen as little more than an extension of provincial operations, then it doesn't take much of a leap to treat them as just one more provincial expenditure category. If that is all municipalities are, then transfers to municipalities can be treated just like any other provincial expenditure when fiscal restraint calls for cutbacks. This, in fact, has been the approach taken by a number of the provinces in recent years. Probably the most dramatic and arbitrary example is Ontario's "social contract" initiative in 1993. It involved the imposition of sizeable transfer cutbacks when the municipal fiscal year was already one-third over, and when many municipalities had already finalized their budgets.[8]

This narrow view of municipal government as merely a provincial expenditure category must be rejected. An excellent rebuttal was provided by New Brunswick municipalities when faced with a similar situation in 1988, and their words bear repeating.

> The reality is, however, that municipal government is much more than just another program or interest group demanding its share of a shrinking pie. Notwithstanding its constitutional position as a creature of the Province, municipal government is precisely what the name suggests: *another distinct and legitimate level of government.* Comprised of representatives directly elected by the people, funded to a greater and greater extent by direct taxation, empowered to independently legislate within a defined mandate, and directly accountable to those who are taxed and serviced, municipal governments exist as a legitimate co-equal of the other two levels of government in Canada. Thus the unilateral decision by the Province not to honour the full financial transfer agreement made with municipalities is more than merely another program cut; it is nothing less than the abrogation of a genuine intergovernmental commitment.[9] [emphasis added]

These four developments — the adaptations of the system in the first half of the 20th century, the local government reform initiatives of recent decades, the disentanglement exercises, and the increasing tendency to view municipal governments as a provincial expenditure category — should provide sufficient evidence of the neglect of the political role of

---

[8]The combined effect of the reduction in transfers under the social contract and the accompanying expenditure control program was estimated to be about $475 million for the province's 1993-94 fiscal year, according to Association of Municipal Clerks and Treasurers of Ontario, *Municipal Monitor*, June 1993, p. 8.

[9]Brief to the Policy and Priorities Committee of the Government of New Brunswick, *Re The Unconditional Grant to Municipalities and Related Matters*, Provincial-Municipal Council, Inc., October 11, 1988, pp. 2-3.

municipal government throughout this century, and of the dangers of that neglect.

Municipalities Undermine Themselves

It would be wrong, however, to blame the province alone for the present state of affairs. Those in municipal government must accept a share of the blame. Too many of them have accepted uncritically the turn of the century notion that politics has no place in municipal government. Too many have distorted the meaning of the word "politics," turning it into a kind of "boo word" to use whenever they don't like a government decision. We have created a phony distinction between good decisions and political decisions. In fact, we should recognize that government decisions are inherently political — and that these decisions can be good, bad or indifferent.

Municipalities have also contributed to their problems because of their penchant for secrecy, for the "non-meeting meeting," the meeting before the meeting, the agreements obtained through discussions during shared car rides on the way to the meeting — in short, through any and every possible means of avoiding the chance of a heated debate on some issue during the meeting.

In their defence, councillors claim that public discussions about controversial local issues result in sensationalized coverage by the media. Yes, this is quite true. Newspapers don't exist to provide informed commentary and analysis; they are private business interests concerned with making a profit — which they can do better by playing up conflict and clashes, not by giving coverage to routine administrative matters. But this reality of media coverage does not justify secrecy in the discussion of what should be public business.

Councillors also claim that a closed discussion is needed so that everyone will feel free to speak frankly. What this also means is that members won't express their true feelings when facing a meeting hall filled with concerned or angry citizens. Such hesitancy is understandable. But if municipal government is stoutly defended as the level closest to the people — and it always is, especially when there is any suggestion of boundary changes or amalgamations — then shouldn't municipal councillors be prepared to enter into honest debate in front of the local people?

Perhaps most of all, and particularly in smaller municipalities, councillors behave the way they do out of a feeling that having public arguments is somehow unseemly. Bruised feelings may result, making later cooperation more difficult. It is better, goes the argument, to sort out the differences in private, and then to present a united front, or at least a minimum of divisions, in the public meeting. But in "managing debate" in this fashion, councillors rob municipal government of much of its vitality. They rob citizens of an opportunity to see that their councils do debate issues of importance to the community, that they do care passionately about these issues, that there are a number of points of view on most subjects, and that difficult choices have to be made. Worst of all, they rob municipal governments of an opportunity to demonstrate their relevance and value. Once again, the end result is to portray municipal governments as bodies concerned with administering services because the messy stuff of politics is handled elsewhere and out of the public eye.

The Servicing-Financing "Crunch"

Municipal government also needs to be reinvented because it faces an impossible combination of severe servicing challenges and decreased financial resources. The current "pass-the-buck" behaviour of the senior levels of government can be expected to last indefinitely. Given the extent of the federal debt, federal governments will continue to cut transfer payments to provinces, which — in turn — will cut back on transfers to municipalities. While special financial assistance may be offered from time to time for particular purposes (as is happening at present with the "infrastructure program" introduced by the federal government after the 1993 election), it is conceivable that there won't be any general, universal transfer payments to municipalities within a decade.

This financing "crunch" is made more severe by the fact that municipalities are facing increasingly serious servicing challenges. Consider the following issues.[10]

The water supply of most cities is of doubtful quality, often contaminated with industrial discharges and other toxic wastes. Few of the water bodies on which Canadian cities sit are even fit for simple recreational uses like swimming or windsurfing. Fish caught in many of our lakes cannot be safely eaten. Disposal of human wastes is proving to be unmanageable. Sewage treatment plants often discharge effluent which is dangerous to human health. There is an increasing disparity in our cities between rich and poor. Welfare systems make recipients more rather than less dependent. Food banks are increasingly relied upon to feed the poor. Some bus shelters are gaining permanent inhabitants. Successive waves of post-war immigration have created ethnic ghettos in a number of our largest cities, racial tensions have increased, and policing, in particular,

---

[10]Largely based on John Sewell, *Prospects for Reform*, Research Paper 180, University of Toronto, January 1991, pp. 17-18.

has been plagued by charges of racial discrimination. The increase in population has contributed to severe traffic congestion in Canadian cities, along with continuing disputes over the relative merits of further expressways versus improved public transit.

Sanitation, traffic congestion, concern about the poor and homeless, racial tensions — does anything sound familiar? This list of problems, of course, is strikingly similar to those found at the beginning of this century and described in Chapter 3. The solution then was a turn of the century reform movement and it is contended that the time is ripe for another such reform movement, but one with rather different aims and elements. To outline the central ingredients in a new turn of the century reform movement to reinvent municipal government is the purpose of the remainder of this concluding chapter.

Ingredients in a Reinvented Municipal Government

A number of the suggestions which follow are interrelated or build one upon another. This will become clearer as the various proposals are outlined and will also be evident from the summary section at the end of the chapter. The large number of specific examples which are included are intended to demonstrate that these suggestions for reinventing municipal government are not abstract or idealistic; most are already being practised by progressive municipalities. The fact that most of the municipal examples are drawn from the province of Ontario simply reflects the sphere of operation of the authors. No doubt similar examples can be found for municipalities in other parts of Canada.

Reviving the Political Role

It will be obvious from references throughout this book that one of the central elements of a new turn of the century reform movement should be to undo the damage of the last turn of the century reform movement — to put politics back into municipal government, or at least to acknowledge the inherently political nature of municipal government. As has been amply illustrated above, it is only by acknowledging and practising their political role that municipal governments can escape the limiting trap of being viewed as mere vehicles for service delivery, acting only under instructions from a higher authority.

This point is self-evident and easy to state, but it is more difficult to visualize how it can be achieved in practice. Much could be done by municipal politicians themselves, by refusing to accept (much less to perpetuate) the notion that politics is a dirty word and that political decisions must mean bad decisions.

In addition, a different conception of municipal government is needed, one which sees the municipality as an extension of the community, as the community governing itself. The municipal council must be recognized as a political mechanism for expressing and responding to the collective concerns of members of the community. There are several important implications of this different conception of municipal government.

1. If the municipality is an extension of the community, its identity and its purpose derives from that community, not from the particular services it provides.[11]

2. The municipality has a legitimate right to take actions that are needed by the community. This right derives from the nature of the municipality as an extension of the community, and does not depend on what specific powers have been assigned to the municipality by some higher level of government.

3. The municipality's primary role is concern for the problems and issues faced by its community. The interests and values of the community are expressed and resolved through the municipality. It is "a political institution for the authoritative determination of community values."[12]

4. It follows that the municipality should broaden its focus to encompass all government issues of interest or concern to its community. The objective should not be to concentrate on a limited range of responsibilities over which the municipality has total or primary control. That approach mistakenly defines the municipality in relation to what services it provides. If the municipality is defined by the community it serves, then it should stay (or become) involved in areas in which it has no expectation of local control if those are areas of concern to the community.

5. If the municipality is to function as an extension of the community, one must reexamine the proliferation of separate local boards, and their relationship to the municipal council. The more boards there are, and the more independently of council they operate, the less possible it is for the municipal council to be the political mechanism for the expression of the collective concerns of the community.

---

[11]The points which follow are largely based on John Stewart, "A Future for Local Authorities as Community Government," in John Stewart and Gerry Stoker (eds.), *The Future of Local Government*, London, Macmillan Education Ltd., 1989, Chapter 12.

[12]*Ibid.*, p. 241.

Providing a More Flexible Legal Framework

How, specifically, can such a concept of municipal government be introduced for Canadian municipalities? A partial answer may lie in a different approach to provincial authorization for municipal actions. As discussed above, the standard approach in Canada has been for provinces to provide quite specific guidelines on what powers municipalities can exercise and how they can be used. In contrast, most Western European countries give their local authorities the power of general competence — "the right to take any action on behalf of its local community, that is not specifically barred to it."[13] No power of general competence can be unlimited, and the Western Europe arrangements include limits to prevent local authorities from infringing on individual rights or from carrying out functions given to other agencies of government.[14] But, the real value of the power of general competence is not the specific provisions underlying it but the concept of municipal government which it represents.

> It bolsters the conception of the municipality as a general political authority which acts in its own right to foster the welfare of its inhabitants and confront whatever problem may arise in the local community. It encourages the citizen to see in the local authority not one agency among many for carrying out administrative tasks, but the corporate manifestation of the local community ... which is the first resort in the case of difficulty.[15]

Alberta passed a new Municipal Government Act (Bill 31) in June 1994 which provides the closest thing to a power of general competence so far in Canadian legislation respecting municipal governments. In addition to the specific powers provided to municipalities in this and other statutes, Bill 31 states that municipalities have "natural person powers," except to the extent that they are limited by this or any other enactment. In addition, the new legislation introduces the concept of "spheres of jurisdiction." Instead of detailing specifically those matters on which a municipality is authorized to pass by-laws, Bill 31 provides broad authority within general subject areas. For example, section 7 contains a blanket

---

[13]*Ibid.*, p. 238.

[14]*Ibid.*, p. 246.

[15]Philip Blair, "Trends in Local Autonomy and Democracy," in R. Batley and G. Stoker (eds.), *Local Government in Europe: Trends and Developments*, London, Macmillan, 1991, quoted in Michael Clarke and John Stewart, *Choices for the 1990s and Beyond*, Harlow, Longman, 1991, p. 17.

power for municipalities to pass by-laws for the safety, health and welfare of people and the protection of people and property. Section 9 goes on to state that the power to pass by-laws under this section is stated in general terms to:

(a) give broad authority to councils and to respect their right to govern municipalities in whatever way the councils consider appropriate, within the jurisdiction given to them under this or any other enactment, and

(b) enhance the ability of councils to respond to present and future issues in their municipalities.

It is too soon to know how much greater discretion Alberta municipalities will actually be able to exercise in practice, or how the courts will respond to this attempt by the legislature to delegate spheres of law-making authority rather than specific provisions. What is known is that the advance in this regard has been at least partly cancelled out by other actions taken by the Alberta government on the financial front. As discussed in Chapter 7, transfer payments will be cut almost in half between 1994/95 and 1996/97. As a result, Alberta municipalities may find themselves with greater scope for legislative initiatives but without the resources to launch them!

The Alberta experience suggests that, to be effective, delegation of a power of general competence needs to be accompanied by a corresponding financial commitment on the part of the provincial government — an unlikely prospect given the financial realities facing all levels of government. The best bet, because of the degree of financial stability it would provide, is some form of revenue-sharing agreement. It need not be especially generous (and, these days, it certainly won't be!). The important thing is to have a provincial government commit to a specified level of transfer payment on an ongoing basis so that municipalities can undertake long term financial planning with some degree of certainty.

Constitutional Recognition of Municipal Government

In the past it has frequently been suggested that one way of reinforcing the general position and importance of municipal government is to give it some form of constitutional recognition. Such a step seems unlikely, however, not least because of the widespread public feeling that the country has "wasted" much of the past decade in divisive and ultimately futile attempts to bring about constitutional change. Constitutional recognition for the municipal level of government was totally ignored in both the Charlottetown and Meech accords and was also left out of the 1982

Constitution Act which repatriated the constitution. There would doubtless be strong provincial resistance to any new attempt to introduce such recognition. In any event, L'Heureux has argued persuasively against any constitutional amendment that would provide a guarantee of municipal institutions. He claims that protection of municipalities by the constitution would achieve the very opposite.

> It would favour direct federal intervention and direct dealings between the federal government and the municipalities. The resulting division of powers would be even more complicated and a matter of contention. Given the difficulties the federal government and our ten provinces have now in reaching agreement, it is easy to imagine what would happen if the more than 4,600 Canadian municipalities were added![16]

Instead, L'Heureux suggests that it would be more realistic to protect municipal interests by way of provincial constitutions. Cameron agrees, arguing that since the division of powers between provincial and local government promotes such values as liberty and equality, this division should be recognized and protected, but within provincial constitutions.

> Municipalities have no place in a federal constitution, at least not beyond the present references which consign them to provincial jurisdiction. Any further reference could only serve to remove decisions about the provincial-municipal division of power to extra-provincial constitutional processes. Any direct participation by municipalities in the federal-provincial constitutional process could only occur at the price of their becoming special interest groups.[17]

To protect municipalities, L'Heureux suggests including in the provincial constitutions such principles as the existence of autonomous municipalities governing local affairs, the election of municipal councillors, and the possession by municipalities of independent sources of revenue sufficient to allow them to perform their obligations. The right of a municipality to act by itself in the absence of legislation to the contrary, as well as its right to delegate its powers, might also be included, along with a limitation on the review of municipal by-laws by the courts.[18]

---

[16]Jacques L'Heureux, "Municipalities and the Division of Power," in Richard Simeon, Research Coordinator, *Intergovernmental Relations*, Vol. 63, Royal Commission on the Economic Union and Development Prospects for Canada, Toronto, University of Toronto Press, 1985, pp. 200-201.

[17]David M. Cameron, "Provincial Responsibilities for Municipal Government," in *Canadian Public Administration*, Summer 1980, pp. 222-235.

[18]L'Heureux, *op. cit.*, p. 202.

In recent years, municipal associations in several provinces have been pushing for some form of provincial charter recognizing the existence of a separate level of municipal government.[19] Since 1991, the Union of British Columbia Municipalities (UBCM) has proposed the creation of a local government Charter of Rights or Bill of Rights to establish that the province recognizes local government as an order of government and is committed to maintaining a legislative framework which allows local governments full authority to meet community needs. Under such a charter the province would provide to local government in legislation responsibility to manage all areas except those occupied or reserved by it or the federal government. The charter would also recognize the province and local governments as partners in providing essential services to the public and would include a commitment to consultation and cooperation. This commitment would extend to such things as the right of local governments to have guaranteed access to provincial decision making, consultation on all matters affecting local government, joint decision making in areas of shared responsibility and negotiation of conflicts.

The Union of Nova Scotia Municipalities (UNSM) is pursuing the development of a municipal charter. The concept was first broached during the May 1993 provincial election and the Union has since presented a paper outlining options which could be followed and the possible content of the charter. The Premier of Nova Scotia has offered his support in principle to the concept of a municipal charter.

The Association of Municipalities of Ontario (AMO) has also proposed a charter or bill of rights within which the principles, values and rights of local governments would be enshrined. The AMO position is that:

> Municipalities are more than agents of service provision, they are essential to meet the needs, concerns and aspirations of the diversity of citizens who live in our communities. In terms of the lives that citizens lead and the concerns they have, local government is, to many, the most important level of government, dealing with matters of direct and immediate concern, and providing the most accessible and directly accountable political institution.[20]

AMO calls for a municipal charter that will grant greater discretionary authority to local governments, as opposed to the "creatures of the prov-

---

[19]The examples which follow are based on Association of Municipalities of Ontario, *Local Governance in the Future: Issues and Trends*, 1994, pp. 56-66.

[20]Association of Municipalities of Ontario, *Ontario Charter: A Proposed Bill of Rights for Local Government*, Toronto, 1994, p. 3.

ince" concept of strict limits on local discretionary authority. It asks for a commitment that municipal government will be guaranteed access to provincial decision making and consultation on all matters affecting municipal government. It also calls for recognition of the principle of local self-government, that municipalities have a right and duty to regulate and manage public affairs under their own responsibility and in the interests of the local population. The AMO paper also proposes new municipal legislation which is more permissive in nature and which authorizes municipalities to act on their own initiative with regard to any matter which is not exclusively assigned to any other authority nor specifically excluded from the competence of municipal government.

These three examples provide sufficient indication of what might be encompassed by a municipal charter. Provincial initiatives in this regard could do much to help reinforce a new concept of municipal government, one which recognizes the inherent right of municipalities to take actions needed by their communities. There is little reason to be very hopeful of a positive provincial response to these requests for a municipal charter. Even so, the possibilities of some type of provincial recognition seem more likely of success than the efforts to obtain municipal recognition in the constitution of Canada.

In the meantime, however, there are a variety of other actions which can be taken by municipalities on their own initiative — all of which are part of our ingredients for reinventing municipal government.

Don't Get Trapped in the Service Delivery Box

One of the most important things municipalities can do is to take a long and critical look at "what business they are in." Most municipalities have grown in a haphazard fashion, in response to outside pressures such as the servicing demands brought on by urbanization or new regulations and requirements imposed by the province. They have also operated on the basis of a model of self-sufficiency, by which is meant that they have assumed that if something needed to be done then the municipality must do it. As a result, municipalities have become busier and busier with the day-to-day demands of service delivery. They have felt constant upward pressure on scarce resources, financial and personnel, and have often been unable to respond to perceived local needs and desires because of these limited resources. What is needed, it is suggested, is for municipalities to distinguish between the role of governance and the role of providing services. Governance involves making decisions about what services and programs should be provided to the community — but it does not mean that the municipality will provide these services and programs.

This different perspective has been described as the "enabling author-ity."[21] It relates back to the concept of the municipality as the community governing itself. The community involves many different individuals and organizations. In its role as the community governing itself, the munici-pality will find it natural to work with and through other organizations. Since the municipality is defined by the needs and problems facing its community, it obviously cannot and should not always act directly. It has to work with others. An enabling municipality is one "which takes a broad responsibility for the social and economic issues confronting its area and uses all the means at its disposal to meet the needs of those living in the area.[22] It may provide services directly, having no preconceived notion of the superiority of the market or of private administration. Rather, the enabling municipality uses the most efficient means at its disposal.

This distinction between governance and service delivery has recently been popularized as steering versus rowing.[23] It means separating policy decisions about what needs to be done (steering) from the provision of services (rowing). Steering organizations are able to define an issue or problem comprehensively because they are not limited to the resources and services that they can allocate to the matter. Having defined the issue broadly, steering organizations "shop around" for the resources needed to deal with it. They may regulate, license or otherwise monitor some activity, they may stimulate action through seed money, they may enter into a variety of partnership arrangements — the options are almost endless.[24] Because their approaches vary, steering organizations can ex-periment, try various methods and learn from their experiences.

Given the new financial reality, the increased conservatism over the past ten or fifteen years, and the emphasis on such concepts as privati-zation, it appears that the role of government is shrinking. But this assess-

---

[21]This term is used by a number of British authors on local government, including John Stewart in *The Future of Local Government, op. cit.*, Chapter 12 and in *Choices for Local Government, op. cit.*, Chapter 2, on which this discussion is based.

[22]Gerry Stoker, "Creating a Local Government for a Post-Fordist Society," in Stewart and Stoker, *op. cit.*, p. 167.

[23]These terms are probably best known from their use in David Osborne and Ted Gaebler, *Reinventing Government*, New York, Penguin, 1993.

[24]Osborne and Gaebler identify 36 alternatives to standard service delivery. See *ibid.*, p. 31 and pp. 332-348.

ment must be qualified. There is less demand and less support for government as a bureaucratic machine that provides services and increases taxes to pay for them. There is more demand and need for *governance* — for leading society and convincing its various interest groups to embrace common goals and strategies.[25]

Recognizing and adhering to this distinction is particularly difficult for municipal councillors. Given the small scale of operations of most municipalities and the immediacy of the impact of their decisions within the community, most councillors become quite involved in the details of day-to-day administration. They devote a great deal of their time and energy to supervising municipal staff, often through a standing committee system, and to following up on citizen complaints about servicing issues and problems. They spent far too little time on steering, on determining the direction in which the municipality should move and the key issues it must confront and in developing strategies for confronting those issues.

These fundamental matters are receiving more attention in recent years through increased use by municipalities of strategic planning. By means of this process, municipalities attempt to increase their awareness of the key issues and challenges which they will face and to position their organizations accordingly. They follow the approach of hockey legend Wayne Gretzky, who has said: "I skate to where I think the puck will be." While the specific process used will vary among organizations, it usually includes the following steps:[26]

1. *Clarifying the mandate and the mission of the organization.* For municipalities, this means determining what they must do according to provincial requirements and also what is not ruled out by their mandates — in other words, what things can they do which they are not doing at present. Through this exercise, a municipality can identify its "room to maneuver," however limited that may be. A mission statement is a declaration of the organization's purpose. What is this municipality? What basic social and political needs does it exist to fulfil? What makes it distinctive or unique?

2. *Conducting a SWOT analysis.* This involves an examination of the internal strengths and weaknesses of the organization in relation to the

---

[25]*Ibid.*, p. 34.

[26]This discussion is based on Association of Municipal Clerks and Treasurers of Ontario, *Municipal Administration Program*, Unit Four, Lesson 7, which is in turn largely drawn from John Bryson, *Strategic Planning for Public and NonProfit Organizations*, San Francisco, Jossey-Bass Inc., 1988.

external opportunities and threats it faces. The external examination, normally called an environmental scan, is carried out first. It usually includes a stakeholder analysis, that is, a survey of the customers and clients of the organization, all those who have a stake in the organization's future, those who have an interest in the issues facing the organization.

3. *Identifying strategic issues.* This is the central step in the exercise, and it involves identifying the fundamental policy choices facing the organization. It selects from among the many issues on the horizon those which are of strategic importance and must be addressed by the organization.

4. *Developing strategies and action plans.* The preceding steps will come to nothing unless the organization develops goals and objectives in relation to each strategic issue, develops an action plan with clear time lines, and assigns responsibilities for achieving the objectives.

This brief four point summary is hardly an adequate description of a strategic planning exercise. But it should be enough to illustrate the relevance of this concept to the new view of municipal government we have been discussing. Municipalities which want to increase their emphasis on steering rather than rowing will benefit from the heightened awareness of their external environment and the challenges awaiting them which can come from a well run strategic planning exercise.

The city of Burlington, Ontario, has been one of the pioneers in this area, with its first strategic plan, "Future Focus," adopted in 1988, updated in 1991, and undergoing a further update at the time of writing. Consistent with the above-noted theme of deciding what kind of business we are in, Burlington has also launched, in April 1994, a study of its existing services to determine:

a) Which services are seen as essential and justify continuation at a high level.
b) Of those to be continued, which could be restructured or re-engineered to run more efficiently.
c) Which services could be examined for a number of alternative options including reduction, elimination or transfer.[27]

Encouraging More Community Involvement

One of the biggest challenges we face is the prevailing public attitude which, in response to most issues and problems, is expressed in the complaint: "Why doesn't the government do something about this?" There

---

[27]City of Burlington, *Restructuring Task Force*, 1994, p. 1.

appears to be little appreciation that calling for government solutions almost always means higher taxes, or that accepting responsibility for solving the problem — or for not causing it in the first place — may be much more effective than government action. It is ironic that people used to undertake self-help and community-initiated ventures almost as a matter of course. But, as the scope of government activity has expanded throughout the 20th century, these tendencies have disappeared. Somehow, the notion has developed that once the government gets involved with some subject then it is the government's problem, not ours. Governments have contributed to this unfortunate development by appearing to exclude the public, by acting as if only professionals and experts could have the answers.

Gradually this trend is being reversed. Progressive governments are finding ways to involve their communities in dealing with problems. In many instances, they are working with communities to reduce the likelihood that problems will arise in the first place. A few examples will illustrate the wide range of initiatives which are possible.

1. Concerted efforts by municipalities and public health agencies can increase public awareness of the importance of healthy communities and healthy lifestyles as primary methods of avoiding sickness and associated treatment costs.

2. Many municipalities are opening "storefront operations" in various parts of their community as part of a shift to community policing. The basic idea is to make public safety a community responsibility rather than just the job of professionals. Neighbourhood watch programs have long incorporated this concept, but community policing attempts to carry it much farther. For example, working with the community may lead police to the realization that crime and associated costs can be reduced if more youth-related recreational facilities are provided in a particular area.

3. A similar change in emphasis is also evident with respect to municipal fire departments. A traditional approach would be based on the notion that their role was to fight fires, and their involvement with the community would come if and when they had to intervene in response to a fire. Increasingly, however, attention is shifting to fire prevention. This involves fire departments in working with the community and through the community to reduce the possibility of fires. An excellent example is provided by the efforts of the Laval, Quebec, fire department which gave away smoke detectors to every household in the city and then returned for the next three years to hand out fire prevention booklets and to inspect the smoke detectors to ensure that they were installed and working.[28]

4. New approaches to environmental issues, highlighted by the growing emphasis on the three Rs (reduce, reuse and recycle) clearly illustrate the involvement of the community in minimizing a problem — that is, the amount of garbage being generated, and the costs associated with its collection and disposal. Indeed, community members have led the way in this regard, pushing their municipalities into recycling programs and other initiatives designed to minimize environmental problems. The Kingston Area Recycling Corporation in Ontario and Pittsburgh Township, one of the members of this corporation, both use volunteers to run household hazardous waste days. This direct involvement of the community not only cuts costs, it also develops a neighbourly feeling on the part of volunteers and participants.

5. Many municipalities have recognized their own financial limits and the importance of community involvement by setting up mechanisms which encourage local groups, organizations or businesses to accept responsibility for providing or maintaining particular facilities or services. A common example is an arrangement under which the municipality provides the site and the boards, but a neighbourhood accepts responsibility for maintaining an outdoor ice rink in its area. Schemes to "adopt a park" or "adopt a flower bed" are also widespread. The organization which takes on "ownership" is recognized with its name on a plaque at the site.

Besides the obvious advantage of defraying the municipality's costs for services, this type of program encourages community involvement and a sense of community responsibility. A secondary benefit can be reduced vandalism and general abuse of municipal facilities. If members of the community have volunteered their time and energy to maintain a park or a flower bed, they view it quite differently; it is "their" park, not just a municipal park. They are not going to damage or neglect "their" park; nor are they likely to tolerate others being similarly inconsiderate.

6. A simple but effective way of emphasizing the concept of community involvement is demonstrated by St. Paul, Minnesota, using a technique that Canadian municipalities could easily follow (and perhaps some have?). St. Paul publishes a booklet listing all municipal departments and services — in itself not an unusual step. But the important difference is that St. Paul's booklet is entitled "Owner's Manual."

---

[28]Mark Stevenson, "Canada's Best-Run Cities," in *Financial Times of Canada*, November 7, 1992, p. 13.

Developing Partnerships — Public and Private

If municipalities emphasize governance, if they accept the concept of an enabling authority rather than a self-sufficient one, it must follow that such municipalities will recognize the need to get things done through others. One of the biggest stumbling blocks with many Canadian municipalities has been a strong streak of parochialism, and an unwillingness to share information and to look outward at possible allies who could help in serving the public. Somehow, collaborating with another municipality or with a local board was seen as a sign of weakness, an indication that the municipality could not stand on its own. Joint servicing arrangements might be the "thin edge of the wedge" that would eventually lead to the takeover of the municipality through annexation or amalgamation. Such false pride and misguided fear can no longer be tolerated — and won't be, by a public increasingly concerned about duplication and inefficiency in government. Happily, as the following examples indicate, many Canadian municipalities are now in the forefront in recognizing the benefits of wider collaboration, with private as well as public organizations.

1. Cooperative purchasing ventures have been particularly common. An early example from Ontario is the Peterborough Public Buyers Association, which since 1968 has tendered for commonly used goods and services for five municipalities, five educational institutions or school boards and two hospitals.[29] Beginning in 1981, a number of municipalities and other public bodies in Wellington County in Ontario began cooperative purchasing ventures, which expanded in the spring of 1992 into the Wellington County Public Sector Consortium, which will look into other joint ventures such as sharing school busing, engineering services, equipment and ground crews.

2. Simcoe County in Ontario is involved in developing a Geographic Information System called LINC for use by public and private partners — including Bell Canada, municipalities, the Ministry of Revenue, school boards and Ontario Hydro. All will benefit from access to such information, but none of these organizations could easily have developed the information base acting on its own.

3. The city of Markham, Ontario, took an innovative approach to the need to provide concession services for the new community centre it was developing for its Milliken Mills community. It negotiated a 20 year lease with McDonald's for land on which McDonald's built its restaurant (with

---

[29]Details on this Association are found in Ministry of Municipal Affairs, *Joint Services in Municipalities: Five Case Studies*, Toronto, April 1983.

compatible architectural design), a parking lot, and a connection to the community centre. Besides the money from the lease, Markham will receive a share of the gross revenue from the restaurant once it reaches a certain level.[30]

4. Successful public-private partnerships need not involve a large municipality nor a multi-national corporation, as the experience of Cobden, Ontario, indicates.[31] This village of fewer than 1 000 people received a request from one of the local service clubs to air condition the municipal hall. This club used the hall for its regular meetings and for a weekly bingo. The cost for such a step was excessive for a municipality of this size; it would have meant increasing the rate to users of the hall to prohibitive levels. The service club included a member who was a plumbing and heating contractor. The club offered to install the air conditioning for the municipality in return for a preferred rental rate for the use of the hall. Everyone benefited from the new arrangements, with the club enjoying increased attendance at its bingo nights and the municipality being able to offer an air conditioned hall for community events and for its municipal employees.

5. Selective use of the private sector has proven to be a cost-effective approach to meeting transportation needs in a number of Canadian municipalities. In 1988 Winnipeg began contracting out half of its rides for the disabled to taxi and van companies. Edmonton does the same. While rides in Winnipeg increased from 97 000 in 1987 to 282 000 in 1991, costs per trip fell from $21 to $14 over the same period.[32] Beginning in 1989, Markham, Ontario, has been using taxis to cover outlying bus routes during slow evening hours.[33] Customers contact the transit office, which dispatches a taxi to the nearest bus stop. The customer pays the regular bus fare to the cab driver, and the taxi company bills the municipality for the fare run up on the meter less the amount of the bus fare. Markham has been saving more than $150 000 a year since introducing this scheme.

---

[30]This joint venture is described in *Innovative Financing: A Collection of Stories from Ontario Municipalities*, Toronto, Municipal Finance Officers Association of Ontario and Association of Municipal Clerks and Treasurers of Ontario, 1993, pp. 24-25.

[31]*Ibid.*, p. 35.

[32]Stevenson, *op. cit.*, p. 13.

[33]Information from Paul Schliesmann, "Bus-taxi Swap Could Help City Save Dollars," Kingston, *Whig Standard*, July 26, 1994.

6. An example from Kitchener-Waterloo, Ontario, illustrates both the public-private partnership theme of this section and the previous section's theme of involving the community in preventing or minimizing problems. The area's police department had been emphasizing community policing, with a gradual increase in "beat cops." But when a downtown Kitchener neighbourhood wanted a storefront police office, the expense appeared prohibitive. This problem was overcome when the downtown business association put up the money to rent space for the police operation.[34]

Becoming More Entrepreneurial

Most municipalities have responded to the new financial reality by focusing on expenditure cuts. Councillors commit to a target of zero or very limited increase in the tax rates, and then staff prune and slash until the "magic" figure is reached. Entrepreneurial governments take a different approach. They are not unmindful of costs, but they devote much more of their energy and creativity to generating revenues. Traditionally, governments undertook projects and then figured out what the costs would be. Enterprising governments undertake projects and figure out how much money they will make.[35]

Often this involves joint ventures with the private sector, several examples of which have already been noted in previous sections of this chapter. More fundamentally, it requires a change in outlook on the part of municipal personnel, and a commitment to the concept of revenue generation. A good starting point is for municipalities to identify which public services do not/should not generate any revenue and which ones do/can generate revenue. The latter category can be further divided into those activities which can partially subsidize themselves, those which can operate at break-even, and those which can generate a profit (subject to any provincial limits or restrictions on such profit-generation).[36]

One area, for example, that usually could benefit from careful review involves municipal provision of such facilities as golf courses, tennis courts and marinas. Typically, user charges for these facilities are minimal or non-existent, with the result that taxpayers are subsidizing facilities enjoyed mainly by the more affluent in the community. The introduction

---

[34]Stevenson, *op. cit.*, p. 12.

[35]Osborne and Gaebler, *op. cit.*, p. 198.

[36]This distinction is drawn from *ibid.*, p. 214.

of, or increase in, user fees is often opposed on the grounds that it will deny access to the facility for poorer members of the community. But as one tax expert has argued, "it defies logic to give services free to high-income folk because you're worried about low-income folk. That gives welfare to the rich."[37] In any event, there are various ways that municipalities can waive user fees for those unable to pay.

Entrepreneurial governments do not fear competition from the private sector, or the possibility of losing services or jobs through contracting-out. On the contrary, they aggressively seek out opportunities for expanding their services into the community. Some municipalities perform services on private property for a fee, such as cutting trees or unclogging a drain. Some sell souvenirs, publications, municipal crests or insignia, and various other items. Some "hire out" specialized equipment for use by other municipalities or organizations. Some "hire out" specialized services such as engineering or planning expertise.

Consider the ambitious initiative by the city of Azusa, California.[38] All city departments were asked to reduce their budgets by three percent without a decrease in services. A typical strategy would have been to look at contracting out services to private companies, and reducing municipal staff through attrition. The city's response was the exact opposite. It implemented "Services Marketing," an initiative under which the city sells its labour and services to outside companies. As a result, it has contracts to look after such things as: tree trimming for a local golf course, street sweeping for two neighbouring cities, landscape management for a cable television company, and highway maintenance for the state. The work is done during regular city hours by the existing staff, and it brings in an additional $100 000 annually.

The city of Thunder Bay, Ontario, demonstrated imagination with respect to revenue generation and effective community involvement in the way it handled the challenge it faced in giving about $600 000 in grants each year to a number of local charitable, non-profit, recreation and arts groups. The city provided staff time, legal advice and a start-up loan of $50 000 toward the establishment of the Thunder Bay Lottery Corporation, which runs weekly lotteries on behalf of 78 charitable, non-profit

---

[37]John Mikesell, quoted in *ibid.*, p. 204.

[38]The description which follows is based on a report in *Public Innovations Abroad*, published by the International City Management Association, and summarized in Ontario Municipal Administrators' Association, *Management Information Exchange Newsletter*, Summer 1994.

local organizations.[39] The Corporation is owned by the member organizations and run by a board elected by them. The city loan was repaid within a few weeks of start-up, and the Corporation's profits in its first full year of operation were expected to be between $600 000 and $1 million. As a result of this initiative, the city has been spared the annual cost and public pressure from community groups seeking financial assistance, while the groups are almost certain to end up with greater funding from their own efforts than would be available from the city. The entrepreneurial spirit surrounding this venture is also evident from the fact that an information package is offered to other municipalities interested in setting up a similar lottery corporation — for a fee of $100.

Probably the biggest hurdle to overcome in making municipal governments more entrepreneurial is the lack of any incentive for municipal employees to incur savings or to generate profits. Under the existing arrangements found in most municipalities, any such excess funds at year end go into general funds and become part of the revenue base for the subsequent year. The department which has generated this surplus does not benefit from it; indeed, it may even be penalized by being told that it must have asked for more money than it needed and should, therefore, receive less money the following year. Meanwhile, a department which has overspent its budget apparently demonstrates its need for more and is rewarded with increased funds. Under these ludicrous arrangements, municipal staff could actually see savings generated by their efforts going the following year to other employees who "earned" this reward by being less efficient! Such incentives stimulate exactly the opposite kind of behaviour from what is needed. As a result, we need a new approach to the way performance of municipal employees is measured and rewarded.

Measuring Results and Rewarding Success

Traditionally, governments funded inputs. Schools got money based on how many students were enrolled, not what they learned. Welfare agencies got money based on how many people needed welfare, not how many people were helped to get off the welfare rolls and into employment. Police and fire departments got money based on how much crime there was or how many fires had to be fought, not on how much crime or fires were reduced because of efforts directed at underlying causes. Fortunate-

---

[39]The description which follows is based on Evelyn Dodds, "A Funding Innovation That Worked: The Thunder Bay Experience," in *Municipal World*, St. Thomas, January 1994, pp. 10-11.

ly, the emphasis is gradually changing. More and more governments, including municipal governments, are introducing performance measurements or standards which allow the organization to quantify what output is gained from the expenditure of funds, what level of service is being provided to the community.

Central to the new approach is the extension of cost accounting techniques to the municipal sector, with the objective of identifying the total cost for providing a particular program or service at a specified level — regardless of how many departments might be involved in aspects of this operation. It involves determining not only direct costs but also indirect costs such as administrative support and overhead. This is not the place for a detailed discussion of such a technical matter, but it is increasingly realized that there is virtually no limit to the unit service output costs that can be generated for municipal operations. Consider these examples:[40]

*   cost per response for fire service
*   cost per building for fire safety inspection
*   cost per passenger mile for bus service
*   cost per acre or hectare maintained for park service
*   cost per participant for recreational services
*   cost per million litres of water treated
*   cost per tax bill issued (or tax dollar collected)
*   cost per license issued for animal control
*   cost per ton of garbage for waste collection

If municipalities can identify the total, actual cost of providing the services and levels of service that they do, then they can shift their attention from expenditure cuts to cost reduction. Expenditure cuts are made for the purpose of getting total expenditures below some predetermined level. These cuts are often arbitrary and capricious in nature. The ultimate impact of such cuts is frequently not known at the time the decision is made. The result of such cuts is often the elimination of a program or a reduced level of service. In contrast, cost reductions are based on identifying ways in which a municipality can continue to provide a program or service, but less expensively. Programs are not eliminated or reduced; instead, they are provided more cost-effectively through a review of all stages and costs involved in their delivery. The currently fashionable concept of "re-engineering" is essentially a variation of this approach.

Pittsburgh Township in Ontario introduced a very effective cost management program in 1993, in which it challenged employees to generate

---

[40]From Dalhousie University, *Municipal Services*, Lesson 3, Halifax, 1991.

savings of 10 percent of its operating budget or over $500 000. It also pledged to share 10 percent of any such savings with the employees. All employees were asked for at least five suggestions. The municipality, wisely, did not emphasize "big savings" items, realizing that many staff could only achieve small savings. Each municipal department was audited to review the job specifications and operations and to help identify areas for improvement. A monthly newsletter updated staff on progress with the initiative. In addition, bi-monthly meetings were held to explain cost components so that employees had a better basis for finding savings. The effort was successful, the savings target was met, and the Pittsburgh Township employees also took home a Christmas bonus of about $700 each. Pittsburgh Township's efforts placed it among the finalists for the 1994 IPAC Award for Innovative Management.[41]

The Pittsburgh Township initiative with cost management is continuing. Its 1994 target was to save 5% of its budget, or $250 000. Once again, the effort was successful, and more than $300 000 was saved.[42]

Being able to identify the full costs for municipal services can also be very helpful when municipalities are asked to explain servicing decisions to a concerned public. Still with the Pittsburgh Township example of cost management, the Township decided that the Madoma outdoor skating rink should be closed due to lack of use. When residents complained to council, it was able to itemize the fact that this facility was costing $7 000 a year to maintain. The residents responded by proposing a compromise in which the Township agreed to repair the boards and provide the lights for the facility and the residents accepted responsibility for flooding the rink and maintaining the ice surface. The result was another example of the community involvement theme discussed above. But the municipality was in a stronger position in discussing the proposed closure of the rink because it knew and was able to document the actual costs of operation.[43]

With solid information about the full cost of individual services, it is possible for councillors and staff to take a completely different approach

---

[41]Winners and finalists for these annual awards are described in *Public Sector Management*, a quarterly publication of the Institute of Public Administration of Canada, and a good source of examples of innovative practices by Canadian public sector bodies.

[42]Murray Hogden, "Hard-nosed staff beat cost-cutting goal," *Kingston Whig-Standard*, November 30, 1994.

[43]Information provided by Leonore Foster, Pittsburgh Township Councillor, May 6th, 1994.

to municipal budgeting.[44] Instead of considering expenditures by department (based on last year's budget plus X percent), council can relate expenditures to defined levels of service. Staff requests for funds have to be explained in relation to the specified level of service to be provided, not on the grounds that "this was the amount in the budget last year." If council decides to cut the budget, members will be aware of the reduced service standard which will result. For example, "if we cut X percent from parks maintenance, the result will be that Y percent fewer acres of parkland will be maintained."

This information base changes the nature of the discussion between councillors and staff and the nature of the budget document itself. It is no longer necessary for councillors to dig through hundreds of pages of specific figures in line-item budgets, attempting to find "padding," duplication or waste. Instead, council controls the budget process by telling staff what results, what service level, it wants to have. Staff then tell council how much that service level will cost. Whatever service level is agreed upon, that is council's budget control. Staff are free to organize their resources and use whatever approach they feel is appropriate — so long as they provide the service to the defined level and within cost.

Both councillors and staff gain from such an arrangement. Municipal staff gain the freedom to apply their expertise in administration and service delivery. They gain a sense of clear direction from council. They know what is expected of them; they know what they have to do to meet council's objectives. Council gains true policy control over the operations of the municipality; council decides what services will be provided at what level. This is a far cry from the illusory control which councillors have in the traditional budget process when all they really decide is how much each department can spend.[45]

One of the greatest potential benefits of a results-based budget is that it can allow council the opportunity to escape the existing trap of year end fiscal extravagance. It can allow council to reward staff who meet agreed-upon standards at less cost by letting them keep some portion of any such "savings" and invest them within their department or section. Such an approach unleashes the creativity found in all of us. Under the old

---

[44]The discussion which follows is based on C. Richard Tindal, *The Municipal Councillor's Course*, Kingston, Centre for Government Education & Training, St. Lawrence College, Lesson 4.

[45]These distinctions about the gains by both councillors and staff are largely drawn from Osborne and Gaebler, *op. cit.*, Chapter 5.

arrangements there was really no incentive for staff to find better and more cost-efficient ways of doing things (except the incentive of holding on to their jobs, some might respond). The new approach being proposed leads to gains for both the municipality (and its taxpayers) and for the municipal staff.[46] The whole community benefits from the savings which are generated and the staff benefit by sharing in some of those savings. Staff also benefit, perhaps even more than they do financially, by being given a reason to work *up* to their full potential — instead of being held *down* by rules, regulations, detailed budget appropriations and a general atmosphere that tells them to stay in line, within budget, and out of trouble.

Introducing a Competitive Atmosphere

The concept of competition has already been raised by at least two of the earlier suggestions in this chapter. Obviously, efforts to involve the community and to seek out new public-private partnerships introduce a competitive element into traditional municipal operations. Similarly, generating detailed information on the total real cost of providing services invites comparison and the associated competitive atmosphere. There is overwhelming evidence to support the notion that competition increases cost-consciousness and stimulates superior service and products. This section explores some of the ways in which greater competition can be introduced into municipal operations.

1. One approach is to invite competitive tendering for particular services. Yes, unions will resist fiercely, but this concept may be "sellable" if jobs are guaranteed. The usual arrangement in the United States has been that if a private company wins the contract from municipal staff, those staff have to be offered jobs with that private company or, if they prefer, are assured of jobs somewhere within the municipality—although not necessarily at the same level or pay. Natural attrition, which runs as high as 10% a year, can also allow a municipality to make significant staffing adjustments without layoffs. Armstrong describes his experiences in St. Catharines and Hamilton-Wentworth in Ontario and in the city of Edmonton in expanding the tendering for, and contracting out of, previously municipal operations.[47] The main areas affected by this approach

---

[46]This discussion is based on Tindal, *op. cit.*, Lesson 4, p. 37.

[47]Cy Armstrong, *Thoughts on Canadian Municipal Management*, Local Government Case Studies #5, London, University of Western Ontario, 1993.

were in construction, grass cutting, garbage collection, custodial care, and transit.

It should be emphasized that the primary reason for advocating competitive tendering should be to stimulate greater efficiency and productivity among municipal personnel, not to shift jobs to the private sector. Unfortunately, the latter appears to be the motivation behind many of the tendering initiatives which are launched. The superiority of the private market place is assumed from the outset. Such a conservative viewpoint, for example, was behind the action of the Thatcher government in Britain when it passed legislation in 1988 introducing compulsory competitive tendering for a full range of municipal government services.[48] In contrast, some of the American experiences detailed by Osborne and Gaebler demonstrate the ability of municipalities to compete with the private sector if they persevere. Particularly heartening is the story of Phoenix which really did "rise from the ashes" of its garbage collection tendering experiences.[49] After losing out on several bids for collection activities in various areas of the city, the Public Works department finally won a contract in its sixth year of trying. After 10 years, the department had won back contracts for all of the areas of the city. But employees can never rest on their laurels, because there are always contracts coming up for renewal. The most important lesson of the Phoenix story is the impact on employee morale. When the department finally won back that first contract, morale soared. Management held a dinner for all employees and handed out new hats with the city logo and the words "Sanitation #1." Employees knew that they had the job because they were the best and had demonstrated that in open competition.

2. Competition can also be introduced among public organizations. Some examples of this approach were cited in an earlier section dealing with entrepreneurial governments. One aspect of this involves municipal governments offering to supply services, equipment or expertise to other municipalities or public bodies. More fundamentally, competition is provided when citizens within an area have the option of obtaining services from a variety of different local governing bodies. It is for this reason that public choice theorists, as discussed in Chapter 9, are opposed to the municipal consolidations and centralized regimes favoured by most local

---

[48]Kieron Walsh, "Competition and Service in Local Government," in Stewart and Stoker, *op. cit.*, Chapter 2.

[49]The description which follows is based on Osborne and Gaebler, *op. cit.*, pp. 76-78.

government reform efforts in Canada. It is curious that most people accept the virtues of competition in the private sector, but regard competition in government (as exemplified by the existence of a number of separate local government jurisdictions) as wasteful duplication.

3. A form of competition can be introduced by compiling and publicizing comparative statistics about performance — assuming, of course, that municipalities have solid information about costs and service levels, as discussed above. Such statistics might compare a department's performance from one year to the next, or its performance with other departments in the same municipality, or its performance with departments in other municipalities. It is human nature for people to respond to the challenge of being measured against their peers. Pride comes to the fore, and all staff want to do their best and to be the best.

4. A form of friendly competition can come from arranging week long staff exchanges between a municipality and another governing body, or even private company, with the exchange used for "creative swiping" — that is, for taking the best ideas the other organization has to offer.

Developing a Stronger Focus on the Customer

How well municipalities measure up against the competition, how well they demonstrate value for the dollar spent, how wisely they set their priorities, how effectively they serve their communities — in short, how well they fulfill almost all of the desirable objectives we have been describing above, will depend on how well they take care of their customers.

The literature tells us that one of the defining characteristics of successful organizations is that they take exceptional care of their customers.[50] In contrast, many organizations still treat their customers with T.D.C. (thinly disguised contempt). They tend to dismiss customer complaints as a problem of perception, that the public just doesn't understand what they are doing or why they must do it this way. This attitude ignores the fact that perception is all there is.

> There is no reality as such. There is only perceived reality, the way each of us chooses to perceive a communication, the value of a service, the

---

[50]This theme has been popularized by the "In Search of Excellence" writings. In particular, see Tom Peters and Robert Waterman Jr., *In Search of Excellence*, New York, Warner Books, 1982; Peters and Nancy Austin, *A Passion for Excellence*, New York, Random House, 1985; and Peters, *Thriving on Chaos*, New York, HarperCollins Publishers, 1988. Much of the discussion which follows is drawn from these three sources.

value of a particular product feature, the quality of a product. The real is what we perceive.[51]

Traditionally, those in government — including municipal government — would question the relevance of customer service for them. "We aren't trying to increase sales or market share. Our customers can't shop elsewhere." This was often the typical response or mind-set. It should be readily apparent from the preceding discussions that this viewpoint is not valid, especially for those in municipal government. No competition, you say. What about public transit systems trying to attract customers from the comfort and convenience of their private motor cars? What about recreational programs and facilities competing with private fitness centres and other recreation-type facilities? What about customer competition provided by neighbouring municipalities seen as providing a better combination of price (taxes) and service?

Municipal governments should be just as concerned as private sector organizations about their customer service and the quality of their products. Indeed, it is contended that an increased emphasis on the customer may represent the only real option for municipal governments, faced as they are with cost pressures, scarce resources, and a disillusioned public — strongly opposed to tax increases and critical of what services they do get for their money.[52] In response to these pressures, many municipalities have reacted in the same short-sighted way as many private organizations have; they have focused on cutting expenditures, on holding the line on prices (taxes). Whatever short term gains there may be from such a strategy, it is doomed in the longer term. In fact, municipal governments today face a servicing crisis with respect to their basic infrastructure, partly as a result of the failure to maintain and upgrade such basic services as roads and water and sewer systems over the years.

A downward spiral is evident in the present relationship between municipal personnel and the public which they serve. Faced with almost constant criticism, hampered by scarce resources, worn down by years of cutback management, many municipal staff are understandably dispirited and demoralized. As a result, their commitment to productivity, to quality, to customer service, is likely to erode. As performance declines, public criticism increases, which in turn encourages a further decline in performance — and the downward spiral continues.

---

[51]Peters and Austin, *op. cit.*, p. 112.

[52]This discussion is based on Municipal Administration Program, *op. cit.*, Lesson 4, pp. 58-60.

What happens, however, when the preoccupation with cutbacks is replaced with a focus on providing top-quality service for the customer? There is substantial documented evidence to suggest that the following benefits result.

1. The public perception of municipal government improves — and remember that perception is reality. As a result, the widespread disillusionment with government is eased, and the critical and often hostile atmosphere in which municipal personnel have to function becomes less unpleasant and stressful.

2. The tolerance for current taxation levels improves, because people are willing to pay for a quality product. They respond positively when shown that they are receiving value for the tax dollar spent.

3. Not immediately, but over time, the emphasis on providing quality for the customer actually results in cost savings.

4. The morale of municipal personnel improves. In part, of course, this improvement comes about from the less hostile and critical working environment. Even more so, however, it results from staff (and councillors) energized by the pursuit of the positive objective of top quality and customer service. It is certainly far easier to generate enthusiasm and commitment to such positives than to the largely negative achievement of "holding the line."

5. The improved morale, commitment and enthusiasm results in increased productivity and additional cost-savings.

The net effect is an upward spiral of mutually reinforcing positive results, rather than the downward spiral which has been too often in evidence.

Enhancing Links with the Community

Ultimately, of course, municipal governments must go beyond customer service, no matter how excellent. They have an even more fundamental relationship with their citizens in that they exist to represent and act upon their wishes as part of a democratic and accountable process. This point brings us back to the first theme introduced in this chapter, that of the municipality as a political mechanism for expressing the collective concerns of the community. All of the intervening suggestions about improving management and productivity must not allow us to neglect the equally important need to strengthen the political role of municipal government.

As has been seen, this role has received little attention because of the preoccupation with the service delivery role of municipal government. As a result, there have been far fewer innovations directed toward making municipal government more accessible and accountable to the community it supposedly serves. Suggestions in this regard usually deal with such matters as more openness in meetings, more advance consultation with the public before municipal decisions are made, and more efforts in reporting back to the public and explaining the basis for decisions. These are all important in their own right and can make a difference, but they all accept the conventional arrangements for representative democracy and the relatively passive role that it allows for citizens.

In contrast, consider the dramatically different arrangements currently in place in Rossland, British Columbia.[53] Concerned about the growing rift between citizens and their governments in the aftermath of the collapse of the Meech Lake accord, the councillors of Rossland and their city administrator searched for new approaches which would allow members of the community to exercise more control over their own affairs. The result was a paper entitled "A Constitution for Local Government," which gave local citizens three avenues to participate more directly in the city government. First, there would have to be a referendum for any change to be made to the new constitution by-law of Rossland. Second, either council or the citizens (providing that 20 percent of them signed a petition) could subject a council decision to public confirmation by initiating a referendum within 30 days after the third reading of a by-law. Third, members of the community (again with 20 percent backing) could initiate a referendum to force council to take action on an issue.

Interestingly, the initial reaction of the provincial Ministry of Municipal Affairs was guarded and resistant. The Ministry expressed concern that council would not be able to take actions which, while limited in popularity, were needed to address fiscal, health, safety or other concerns. In effect, this amounted to an argument that ordinary citizens don't know what is best for them, and it is up to council to show the way. Rossland's constitutional paper had taken the opposite view, claiming that "electors are as qualified as members of council to make reasonable and rational decisions. Council members are drawn at random from the electorate; election is not dependent on a test of skills, knowledge or ability."[54] Another concern expressed by politicians from other municipalities was that the new system was ripe for exploitation by pressure groups.

---

[53]The discussion which follows is based on an article by Susan Delacourt, *The Globe and Mail*, May 21, 1994, and an information package provided by André Carrel, Administrator of Rossland.

[54]City of Rossland, *A Constitution for Local Government*, p. 6.

Based on the limited experience to date, neither of these concerns has been borne out. Of the first six referendums initiated after Rossland passed its constitution by-law, three were put forward by the public and three by council. The most notable involved a proposed $100 tax increase to finance an improvement in the municipality's drinking water. It was approved by the public. On the other hand, efforts by anti-logging protestors to reverse council's decision to allow limited logging on an 11 hectare parcel of land in the municipality were abandoned when 20 percent of the local citizens could not be persuaded to sign the petition needed to initiate a referendum — suggesting that the new system is not easily swayed by at least one pressure group.

The possibility that special interest groups could abuse the system led the Rossland council to propose a change to the constitution by-law, raising the petition threshold from 20% of registered voters to 33%. When this referendum was overwhelmingly defeated, the mayor of Rossland declared that: "With this vote, the people of Rossland have assumed ownership of their municipal constitution; it is no longer council's experiment to play with."[55]

Perhaps the most important aspect of the Rossland approach is not the number of referendums or their outcome, but the changed atmosphere in the community. Instead of just complaining about council action or inaction, more people are discussing policy issues. Because they have been given some say in municipal decisions, they feel a greater responsibility to be informed and to exercise their new power thoughtfully. They are also gaining a sense of ownership of city policy. Such changes suggest that in Rossland the municipality is becoming increasingly an extension of the community, a vehicle for the community to govern itself. Forging such a link can give a municipality much greater relevance and legitimacy in the eyes of its citizens than any provincial statute or constitutional declaration.

Any final assessment of the Rossland experiment is premature. In addition, the ability of municipalities to institute changes such as these varies depending on the powers they have been accorded by their provincial governments. Moreover, it cannot be assumed that arrangements which may work in this small Western Canadian municipality could be successfully transplanted to large cities. For these areas, such changes as the introduction of ward systems for stronger neighbourhood representation and the organization of council along party lines to provide a focus

---

[55]Quoted in André Carrel, "Direct Democracy," October 22, 1994 presentation, p. 8.

for stronger leadership and accountability may be more appropriate. Rossland is cited simply to illustrate that innovative changes are also possible with respect to the political role of municipal government.

Concluding Comments

Given all of the above suggestions, what are the prospects for municipal government as it approaches the 21st century? Let us first remind ourselves of the observations offered by the last edition of this text, as outlined in the summary below.[56]

The third edition of *Local Government in Canada* concluded that many of the prognostications about municipal government exaggerated its problems and overlooked its long record of survival and adaptability. But while municipal government was unlikely to collapse before the end of this century, neither was it expected to undergo a radical restructuring and to emerge as a new and stronger system. The barriers to this fundamental reform were described as including:

1.   Provincial government hesitance to introduce fundamental reforms that would significantly strengthen municipal government — lest such a stronger local level might pursue different priorities and provide an overly forceful challenge to the authority of the provincial level.

2.   The unwillingness of municipal governments to accept the changes which are needed. Just as a chain is only as strong as its weakest link, so the systems of municipal government in the various provinces are only as strong as the weakest municipalities among them.

3.   The attitude of the general public, which is characterized by widespread apathy tempered by occasional outbursts of vigorous resistance when changes are proposed. There is a strong tendency for citizens to regard reforms as undesirable and somehow destructive of local autonomy, even though precious little autonomy is to be found in the present system.

The overall conclusion of the third edition was that the municipal government system was likely to continue to the year 2000 and beyond as it had in the past — wracked by recurring crises, never completely collapsing but never becoming much stronger or more independent either. It would adapt as much as it needed to survive or, perhaps more accurately, provincial governments would shore it up enough to keep it functioning.

The concluding observations in this edition of the text are more positive and optimistic. This may seem surprising, since the pressures, problems and financial restraints facing municipal governments are even more

---

[56]The comments which follow are based on C. Richard Tindal and Susan Nobes Tindal, *Local Government in Canada*, Third Edition, Toronto, 1990, pp. 350-351.

severe now. The difference is that the solutions which can transform municipal government are more within their grasp than those advocated previously — in other texts as well as this one. It is striking when we look back over the various suggestions in this chapter how few of them require action by the province. Most of the suggestions for reinventing municipal government can be introduced now, by municipalities acting on their own. Let us review that list of suggestions before going further.

1. Emphasize the political role of municipal government. Promote the municipality as an extension of the community, as the community governing itself.
2. Provide a more flexible legal framework. Authorize municipalities to operate within broad spheres of authority, not specific provisions. Allow municipalities to take actions on behalf of their communities except where prohibited.
3. Provide basic stability to municipal operations with some form of provincial-municipal revenue-sharing scheme.
4. Have provincial declarations or charters which recognize the existence and rights of the municipal level of government.
5. Don't get trapped in the service delivery box. Recognize the importance of governance, of deciding what things need to be done. Recognize that the actual provision of services can be done through a variety of agencies.
6. Zero in on what business you are in/should be in. Be sensitive to the external environment and to the strategic issues which must be faced.
7. Encourage more community involvement. Engage the community to help prevent or reduce problems in the first place.
8. Develop partnerships, public and private.
9. Become more entrepreneurial. Don't just focus on expenditure cuts. Give at least equal attention to ways of increasing revenue.
10. Know the real, total cost for providing services. Measure performance and results.
11. Introduce new approaches to budgeting focused on service commitments not historical spending patterns. Free staff to achieve the servicing targets. Reward superior performance.
12. Introduce a competitive atmosphere within municipal operations.
13. Develop a stronger focus on the customer.
14. Enhance links with the community, and strengthen the political role.

These fourteen points, and the more than forty specific examples provided above to illustrate and elaborate upon them, represent the key ingredients we are proposing to reinvent municipal government for the 21st century. They are not idealistic or impractical suggestions; they are increasingly being followed by municipalities in Canada and elsewhere. For the most part, they do not depend on or require prior action by the provincial level. In fact, the more that they are pursued, the more the municipality can become self-sufficient, anchored in its community, and less vulnerable to the future arbitrary actions of provincial and federal governments that will doubtless occur.

One final note of caution is in order. There is a currency, a trendy "fashionableness" about many of the themes discussed in this last chapter, in large part because of the great popularity of the book *Reinventing Government*,[57] and the promotion of many of its ideas by the current U.S. administration in Washington. The danger is that when ideas become fashionable they are embraced all too uncritically by those eager for a "quick fix." Siegel rightly points out, for example, that the appeal and apparent success of entrepreneurship should not lead us to abandon proper controls and accountability, least we create private fiefdoms presided over by benevolent or not-so-benevolent entrepreneurs.[58] He cites the well-documented example of Robert Moses,[59] who built much of the infrastructure of New York state, but did so with increasing disregard for any form of public accountability. Siegel also expresses concern that an enabling authority could become a captive of its environment. He cautions that municipalities considering the contracting out of a service must keep some internal capacity to perform the service as well — without which they will lack the expertise to monitor and hold accountable the outside service providers.[60]

Inevitably, there will soon be a reaction against many of the ideas proposed in this chapter. The "reinventing government prophets" will over-sell the virtues of their approach. Too many organizations will embrace only the terminology and the trappings of the new approaches, without making the fundamental changes "in the trenches" where things really happen. Lip-service will be paid to the new approaches, but employees will grow increasingly cynical as no real change occurs. This pat-

---

[57]Osborne and Gaebler, *op. cit.*

[58]David Siegel, "Reinventing Local Government: The Promise and the Problems," in Leslie Seidle (ed.), *Rethinking Government: Reform or Revolution*, Montreal, Institute for Research on Public Policy, 1993, p. 196.

[59]See especially Robert A. Caro, *The Power Broker: Robert Moses and the Fall of New York*, New York, Alfred A. Knopf, 1974.

[60]Siegel, *op. cit.*, p. 197.

tern has been witnessed over and over again with respect to such innovations as program budgeting, management by objectives, theory Z, MBWA (Management by Wandering Around), and TQM (Total Quality Management). There is no reason to expect the reinventing government ideas to be immune to this process.

The unfortunate thing is that when this cycle runs its course, organizations throw out whatever approach they have been attempting and embrace instead some new panacea. In so doing, they throw out many excellent and common sense ways of operating effectively. The jargon changes, new initials are shaped into catchy acronyms, and a newly packaged theory of good government or good management starts to make its rounds. No matter what they are called, however, some things never lose their relevance and importance. If municipalities are to meet the challenges of the 21st century, they must resist the temptation to hop from one panacea to another and must stick to the basics which are inherent in the ideas presented above. Those basics boil down to these brief prescriptions:

1. Municipalities should build their strength upward from the communities they represent, not downward from the specific provincial authority they have been given.

2. Municipalities should recognize that their primary role is to act as a political mechanism for expressing the collective concerns of their communities. They may provide services in support of this role, or they may work through other agencies to ensure their provision.

3. Municipalities should focus on identifying strategic issues and priorities, determining the real costs of the services they provide, measuring performance in relation to results achieved, and rewarding desired performance.

Bibliography

Advisory Commission on Intergovernmental Relations, *A Look to the North: Canadian Regional Experience*, Washington, D. C., 1974.

Allen, Edwin G., *Municipal Organization in New Brunswick*, Ministry of Municipal Affairs, Fredericton, 1968.

Anderson, Wayne, Chester A. Newland and Richard J. Stillman, *The Effective Local Government Manager*, Washington, International City Management Association, 1983.

Antoft, Kell (ed.), *A Guide to Local Government in Nova Scotia*, Halifax, Centre for Public Management, Dalhousie University, 1992

Armstrong, Cy, *Thoughts on Canadian Municipal Management*, Local Government Case Studies #5, London, University of Western Ontario, 1992.

Armstrong C. and H. V. Nelles, *The Revenge of the Methodist Bicycle Company: Sunday Streetcars and Municipal Reform in Toronto, 1888-1897*, Toronto, Peter Martin, 1977.

Armstrong, J. L., "Retrenchment at City Hall," in *Canadian Public Administration*, Winter 1986.

Association of Municipalities of Ontario, *Local Governance in the Future: Issues and Trends*, Toronto, 1994.

_____, *Ontario Charter: A Proposed Bill of Rights for Local Government*, Toronto, 1994.

Axworthy, T., "Winnipeg Unicity," in Advisory Committee on Intergovernmental Relations, *A Look to the North: Canadian Regional Experience*, Washington, D.C., 1974.

Baker, M., "William Gilbert Gosling and the Establishment of Commission Government in St. John's, Newfoundland, 1914," *Urban History Review*, Vol. IX, No. 3, February 1981.

Banfield, Edward C., *The Unheavenly City*, Boston, Little, Brown and Company, 1968.

_____ and James Q. Wilson, *City Politics*, New York, Random House, 1963.

Barbour, George et al, *Excellence in Local Government Management*, Washington, International City Management Association, 1985.

Beck, J. M., *The Government of Nova Scotia*, Toronto, University of Toronto Press, 1957.

Bennett, Paul, "What's Wrong With the Present School Board System," *Municipal World*, St. Thomas, August-November 1994.

Bernard, Andre, Jacques Leveille, and Guy Lord, *Profile: Calgary, The Political and Administrative Structures of the Metropolitan Region of Calgary*, Ottawa, Ministry of State for Urban Affairs (MSUA), 1975.

_____, *Profile: Edmonton, The Political and Administrative Structures of the Metropolitan Region of Edmonton*, Ottawa, MSUA, 1974.

_____, *Profile: Halifax-Dartmouth, The Political and Administrative Structures of the Metropolitan Region of Halifax-Dartmouth*, Ottawa, MSUA, 1974.

_____, *Profile: Hamilton-Wentworth, The Political and Administrative Structures of the Metropolitan Region of Hamilton-Wentworth*, Ottawa, MSUA, 1975.

_____, *Profile: Montreal, The Political and Administrative Structures of the Metropolitan Region of Montreal*, Ottawa, MSUA, 1974.

_____, *Profile: Ottawa-Hull, The Political and Administrative Structures of the Metropolitan Region of Ottawa-Hull*, Ottawa, MSUA, 1974.

_____, *Profile: Quebec, The Political and Administrative Structures of the Metropolitan Region of Quebec*, Ottawa, MSUA, 1975.

_____, *Profile: Toronto, The Political and Administrative Structures of the Metropolitan Region of Toronto*, Ottawa, MSUA, 1975.

_____,*Profile: Vancouver, The Political and Administrative Structures of the Metropolitan Region of Vancouver*, Ottawa, MSUA, 1975.

_____,*Profile: Winnipeg, The Political and Administrative Structures of the Metropolitan Region of Winnipeg*, Ottawa, MSUA, 1975.

Bettison, David G., J. Kenward and L. Taylor, *Urban Affairs in Alberta*, Edmonton, University of Alberta Press, 1975.

Bird, R. M. and N. E. Slack, *Residential Property Tax Relief in Ontario*, Toronto, Ontario Economic Council and University of Toronto Press, 1978.

_____, *Urban Public Finance in Canada*, Toronto, Butterworths, 1983 and Toronto, John Wiley & Sons, 1993.

Bish, Robert L., *Local Government in British Columbia*, Richmond, Union of British Columbia Municipalities in cooperation with the University of Victoria, 1987.

_____, *The Public Economy of Metropolitan Areas*, Chicago, Markham Publishing Company, 1971.

_____, and Vincent Ostrom, *Understanding Urban Government: Metropolitan Reform Reconsidered*, Washington, American Enterprise Institute for Public Policy Research, 1973.

Black, Errol, "Small City Politics: The Brandon Experience," *City Magazine*, Summer 1984.

Black, E. R., *Politics and the News: The Political Functions of the Mass Media*, Toronto, Butterworths, 1982.

Boswell, Peter G., "Regional Government for St. John's?" in *Urban Focus*, Institute of Local Government, Queen's University, January-February 1979.

Bourne, Larry S. (ed.), *Internal Structure of the City*, Toronto, Oxford University Press, 1971.

Boyer, J. Patrick, *Lawmaking by the People, Referendums and Plebiscites in Canada*, Toronto, Butterworths, 1982.

Brief to the Policy and Priorities Committee of the Government of New Brunswick, *Re The Unconditional Grant to Municipalities and Related Matters*, Provincial-Municipal Council, Inc., October 11, 1988.

British Columbia, Government of, *Financing Local Government*, Ministry of Municipal Affairs, Recreation and Culture and the Union of B.C. Municipalities, September 1988.

Brittain, Horace L., *Local Government in Canada*, Toronto, Ryerson Press, 1951.

Brooks, Stephen, *Public Policy in Canada: An Introduction*, Toronto, McClelland & Stewart, 2nd edition, 1993.

Bryant, Christopher and Daniel Lemire, *Population Distribution and the Management of Urban Growth in Six Selected Urban Regions in Canada*, Toronto, Intergovernmental Committee on Urban and Regional Research, 1993.

Bryson, John, *Strategic Planning for Public and NonProfit Organizations*, San Francisco, Jossey-Bass Inc., 1988.

Bunting, Trudi and Pierre Filion (eds.), *Canadian Cities in Transition*, Toronto, Oxford University Press, 1991.

Bureau of Municipal Research, *Citizen Participation in Metro Toronto: Climate for Cooperation*, Toronto, 1975.

_____, *Reorganizing Local Government: A Brief Look at Four Provinces*, Toronto, 1972.

_____, *The Metro Politician: A Profile*, Toronto, June 1963.

_____, "The News Media and Local Government," *Civic Affairs*, Toronto, August 1976.

_____, "Cost Saving Innovations in Canadian Local Government," *Civic Affairs*, September 1979.

_____, *Providing Municipal Services: Methods, Costs and Trade-offs*, 1981.

Busson, Terry and Philip Coulter (eds.), *Policy Evaluation for Local Government*, Westport, Greenwood Press, 1988.

Butler, E. and M. Pirie (eds.), *Economy and Local Government*, London, Adam Smith Institute, 1981.

Cameron, David M., "Provincial responsibilities for municipal government," *Canadian Public Administration*, Summer 1980.

_____, "Urban Policy," in G. Bruce Doern and V. Seymour Wilson (eds.), *Issues in Canadian Public Policy*, Toronto, Macmillan, 1974.

Cameron, John R., *Provincial-Municipal Relations in the Maritime Provinces*, Fredericton, Maritime Union Study, 1970.

Canadian Federation of Mayors and Municipalities, *Puppets on a Shoestring*, Ottawa, April 28, 1976.

Canadian Tax Foundation, *Provincial and Municipal Finances*, Toronto, biennial.

_____, *Provincial and Municipal Finances 1991*, Toronto, 1992.

Canadian Urban Institute, *The Future of Greater Montreal: Lessons for the Greater Toronto Area?*, Conference Proceedings, Toronto, 1994

_____, *Disentangling Local Government Responsibilities — International Comparisons*, Toronto, 1993.

Caro, Robert A., *The Power Broker: Robert Moses and the Fall of New York*, New York, Alfred A. Knopf, 1974.

Carver, H., *Cities in the Suburbs*, Toronto, University of Toronto Press, 1962.

_____, *Compassionate Landscape*, Toronto, University of Toronto Press, 1975.

Caulfield, Jon, "Reform as a Chaotic Concept: The Case of Toronto," in *Urban History Review*, October 1988.

_____, *The Tiny Perfect Mayor*, Toronto, James Lorimer and Co., 1974.

Chandler, J. A., *Local Government Today*, Manchester, Manchester University Press, 1991.

Chekki, Dan and Roger T. Towes, *Organized Interest Groups and The Urban Policy Process*, Report no. 9, Winnipeg, Institute of Urban Studies, University of Winnipeg, 1985.

City Magazine Annual 1981, Toronto, James Lorimer and Company, 1981.

Clarke, Michael and John Stewart, *The Choices for Local Government*, Harlow, Longman, 1991.

Clarkson, Stephen, *City Lib*, Toronto, Hakkert, 1972.

Cochrane, Allan, *Whatever Happened to Local Government?*, Buckingham, Open University Press, 1993.

Cote, Marcel, "Local Development in the New Economy," *Municipal Monitor*, Richmond Hill, Association of Municipal Clerks and Treasurers of Ontario, Kenilworth Publishing, October 1994.

Connerty, Ian, "Disentanglement: Changing the Provincial-Municipal Balance," in *Municipal Monitor*, Association of Municipal Clerks and Treasurers, Richmond Hill, Kenilworth Publishing, October, 1992.

Cook, Gail C. A., and Lionel D. Feldman, "Approaches to Local Government Reform in Canada: The Case of Winnipeg," *Canadian Tax Journal*, May-June 1971.

Colton, Timothy J., *Big Daddy*, Toronto, University of Toronto Press, 1980.

Cox, A. William, "Development of Municipal-Provincial Relations," *Task Force on Local Government*, Report to the Government of Nova Scotia, April 1992.

Craig, Gerald M. (ed.), *Lord Durham's Report*, Toronto, McClelland and Stewart Limited, 1963.

Crawford, K. G., *Canadian Municipal Government*, Toronto, University of Toronto Press, 1954.

Cullingworth, J. Barry, *Urban and Regional Planning in Canada*, New Brunswick, Transaction Books, 1987.

Dahl, R. A., *Who Governs? Democracy and Power in an American City*, New Haven, Yale University Press, 1961.

Decore, Laurence, (an interview with Mayor), "A Better Deal for Cities," *City Magazine*, Vol. 8, No. 3 & 4, Fall 1986.

Dente, Bruno and Francesco Kjellberg (eds.), *The Dynamics of Institutional Change: Local Government Reorganization in Western Democracies*, Newbury Park, Sage Publications, Inc., 1988.

Department of Municipal Affairs and Environment, *Review of New Brunswick's Unconditional Grant to Municipalities*, Fredericton, 1986.

Dickerson, M.O, S. Brabek and J. T. Woods (eds.), *Problems of Change in Urban Government*, Waterloo, Wilfred Laurier Press, 1980.

Dodds, Evelyn, "A Funding Innovation That Worked: The Thunder Bay Experience," *Municipal World*, St. Thomas, January 1994.

Doerr, Audrey, "Public Administration: Federalism and Intergovernmental Relations," in *Canadian Public Administration*, Winter 1982.

Domhoff, William, *Who Really Rules? New Haven and Community Power Reexamined*, New Brunswick, Transaction, 1977.

Downs, Bryan T., "The Management of Fiscal Stress by Municipal Governments in British Columbia," in Michael Fitzgerald and William Lyons (eds.), *Research in Urban Policy*, Greenwich, Jai Press, 1987.

Duce, Norm and Associates Ltd., *Final Report: Review of Organization - Council and Commission Board in the City of Edmonton*, Edmonton, July 8, 1982.

Dunn, Christopher (ed.), *Saskatoon Local Government and Politics*, Saskatoon, University of Saskatchewan, 1987.

Dupre, J. Stefan, *Intergovernmental Finance in Ontario: A Provincial-Local Perspective*, Toronto, Queen's Printer, 1968.

Economic Council of Canada, *Fourth Annual Review*, Ottawa, Queen's Printer, 1967.

d'Entremont, Harley and Patrick Robardet, "More reform in New Brunswick: rural municipalities," *Canadian Public Administration*, Fall, 1977.

Eden, Lorraine, "Provincial-Municipal Equalization in the Maritime Provinces," in *Canadian Public Administration*, Winter 1987.

Federation of Canadian Municipalities, *Municipal Government in a new Canadian Federal System, Report of the Task Force on Constitutional Reform*, Ottawa, F.C.M., 1980.

_____, *Management and Planning Capabilities in Small Communities*, Ottawa, 1982.

_____, *Brief to the Royal Commission on the Economic Union and Development Prospects for Canada*, October 1983.

Feldman, Lionel D., *Ontario 1945-1973: The Municipal Dynamic*, Toronto, Ontario Economic Council, 1974.

_____, "Tribunals, Politics and the Public Interest: The Edmonton Annexation Case, A Response," in *Canadian Public Policy*, Spring 1982.

_____ (ed.), *Politics and Government of Urban Canada*, Toronto, Methuen, 1981.

_____ and Katherine Graham, *Bargaining for Cities*, Toronto, Butterworths, 1979.

Ferguson, Thomas and Joel Rogers (eds.), *The Political Economy*, New York, M. E. Sharpe, 1984.

Finnis, Frederick, *Property Assessment in Canada*, Toronto, Canadian Tax Foundation, 1979.

Fowler, Edmund P., *Building Cities That Work*, Kingston, McGill-Queen's University Press, 1992.

_____, "Decision Time for Cityplan '91," *City Magazine*, Winter 1993.

Fraser, Graham, *Fighting Back*, Toronto, Hakkert, 1972.

Frisken, Frances (ed.), *The Changing Canadian Metropolis: A Public Policy Perspective*, 2 Vol., Toronto, Canadian Urban Institute, 1994.

_____, *City Policy-Making in Theory and Practice: The Case of Toronto's Downtown Plan*, Local Government Case Study No. 3, London, University of Western Ontario, 1988.

_____, "Canadian Cities and the American Example: A Prologue to Urban Policy Analysis," in *Canadian Public Administration*, Fall 1986.

Gerecke, Kent, "Winnipeg Hits Bottom," *City Magazine*, Winter 1986-87.

_____, "City Beat," *City Magazine*, Winter 1991/1992.

Gertler, L. O. and R. W. Crowley, *Changing Canadian Cities: The Next 25 Years*, Toronto, McClelland and Stewart Limited, 1977.

Goldenberg, H. Carl, "Municipal Finance and Taxation: Problems and Prospects," in *Forecast of Urban Growth Problems and Requirements 1956-1980*, Montreal, Canadian Federation of Mayors and Municipalities, 1955.

Goldrick, Michael, "The anatomy of urban reform in Toronto," in Dimitrios Roussopoulos (ed.), *The City and Radical Social Change*, Montreal, Black Rose Books, 1982.

Goldsmith, Michael, *Politics, Planning and the City*, London, Hutchinson, 1980.

Goodman, J. S., *The Dynamics of Urban Government and Politics*, New York, Macmillan, 1980.

Gottdiener, M., *The Decline of Urban Politics: Political Theory and the Crisis of the Local State*, Newbury Park, Sage Publications, 1987.

Granatstein, J. L., *Marlborough Marathon*, Toronto, Hakkert and James Lewis and Samuel, 1971.

Gunlicks, Arthur B. (ed.), *Local Government Reform and Reorganization: An International Perspective*, London, Kennikat Press, 1981.

Gutstein, Donald, "The Developers' TEAM: Vancouver's 'reform' party in power," *City Magazine*, December 1974-January 1975.

_____, *Vancouver Ltd.*, Toronto, James Lorimer and Co., 1975.

_____, "Vancouver: Progressive Majority Impotent," *City Magazine*, vol. vi, no. 1.

_____, "Civic Election Wars," *City Magazine*, Summer 1985.

_____, "Vancouver Voters Swing Right," *City Magazine*, Winter 1986-87.

Gyford, John, *Local Politics in Britain*, London, Croom Helm Ltd., 1976.

_____, Steve Leach and Chris Game, *The Changing Politics of Local Government*, London, Unwin Hyman, 1989.

Halifax Commission on City Government, *Report on the Structure and Processes of Halifax City Government 1982*, Halifax, Institute of Public Affairs, Dalhousie University, 1982.

Hall, Dave, "Twisted Tale of Intentions," *City Magazine*, Winnipeg, April 1984.

Hanson, Eric, *Local Government in Alberta*, Toronto, McClelland and Stewart Limited, 1956.

Hardy, Cynthia, "Fighting Cutbacks: Some Issues for Public Sector Administrators," in *Canadian Public Administration*, Winter 1985.

Herland, Karen, *People, Potholes and City Politics*, Montreal, Black Rose Books, 1992.

Hickey, Paul, *Decision Making Processes in Ontario's Local Governments*, Toronto, Ministry of Treasury, Economics and Intergovernmental Affairs, 1973.

Higgins, Donald J. H., *Urban Canada: Its Government and Politics*, Toronto, Macmillan, 1977.

_____, "Nova Scotia's 'New Directions in Municipal Government'" in *Urban Focus*, Institute of Local Government, Queen's University, March-April 1979.

_____, "Progressive City Politics and the Citizen Movement: A Status Report," *City Magazine*, Winnipeg, Annual 1981.

_____, *Local and Urban Politics in Canada*, Toronto, Gage, 1986.

Higgins, Benjamin, *The Rise and Fall of Montreal: A Case Study of Urban Growth, Regional Expansion and National Development*, Moncton, Canadian Institute for Research on Regional Development, 1986.

Hobson, Paul A. R., *The Economic Effects of the Property Tax: A Survey*, Ottawa, Economic Council of Canada, 1987.

Hodge, Gerald, *Planning Canadian Communities*, Toronto, Methuen, 1986 and Scarborough, Nelson Canada, 1991.

Hunter, Floyd, *Community Power Structure*, New York, Anchor Books, 1953.

Institute of Local Government, *Urban Population Growth and Municipal Organization*, Kingston, Queen's University, 1973.

Ircha, Michael C., "The Crisis of Central-Local Government Relations: The British Experience," in *Canadian Public Administration*, Spring 1986.

Isin, Engin F., *Cities without Citizens*, Montreal, Black Rose Books, 1992.

Jacobs, Jane, *The Death and Life of Great American Cities*, New York, Random House, 1961.

Jacek, Henry J., "Regional Government and Development: Administrative Efficiency versus Local Democracy," in Donald C. MacDonald (ed.), *The Government and Politics of Ontario*, Toronto, Nelson, 1985.

Jennings, Kent, *Community Influentials: The Elites of Atlanta*, Glencoe, Free Press, 1964.

Jones, George and John Stewart, *The Case for Local Government*, London, Allen & Unwin Inc., 1985.

Joyce, J. G. and H. A. Hosse, *Civic Parties in Canada*, Ottawa, Canadian Federation of Mayors and Municipalities, 1970.

Kaplan, Harold, *The Regional City*, Toronto, Canadian Broadcasting Corporation, 1965.

_____, *Urban Political Systems: A Functional Analysis of Metro Toronto*, New York, Columbia University Press, 1967.

_____, *Reform, Planning and City Politics: Montreal, Winnipeg, Toronto*, Toronto, University of Toronto Press, 1982.

Kay, B.J., "Voting Patterns in a Non-partisan Legislature: A Study of Toronto City Council," *Canadian Journal of Political Science*, June 1971.

_____, "Urban Decision-Making and the Legislative Environment: Toronto City Council Re-examined," *Canadian Journal of Political Science*, September 1982.

Keating, Michael, *Comparative Urban Politics*, Aldershot, Edward Elgar, 1991.

Kellar, Elizabeth K. (ed.), *Managing with Less: A Book of Readings*, Washington, International City Management Association, 1979.

Kitchen, Harry M., *Local Government Finance in Canada*, Toronto, Canadian Tax Foundation, 1985.

_____, *Local Government Enterprise in Canada*, Ottawa, Economic Council of Canada, 1986.

_____, *The Role for Local Governments in Economic Development*, Toronto, Ontario Economic Council, 1986.

_____, and Melville McMillan, "Local Government and Canadian Federalism," in Richard Simeon, Research Coordinator, *Intergovernmental Relations, Vol. 63*, Royal Commission on the Economic Union and Development Prospects for Canada, Toronto, University of Toronto Press, 1985.

Kraemer, Kenneth L., *Policy Analysis in Local Government*, Washington, International City Management Association, 1973.

Krause, Robert and Trevor Price, "The Impact of Financial Restraint on the Provision of Municipal Services in Canada," in *Planning and Administration*, 23, 1980.

Krueger, Ralph R., "The Provincial-Municipal Revolution in New Brunswick," *Canadian Public Administration*, Spring 1970.

L'Heureux, Jacques, "Municipalities and the Division of Power," in Richard Simeon, Research Coordinator, *Intergovernmental Relations, Vol. 63*, Royal Commission on the Economic Union and Development Prospects for Canada, Toronto, University of Toronto Press, 1985.

Landon, Fred, *Western Ontario and the American Frontier*, Toronto, McClelland and Stewart Limited, 1967.

Lang, Vernon, *The Service State Emerges in Ontario*, Toronto, Ontario Economic Council, 1974.

Lapointe, Jean-Louis, "La Reforme de la Fiscalité Municipale au Quebec," *Canadian Public Administration*, Summer 1980.

Leach, Richard, *Whatever Happened to Urban Policy? A Comparative Study of Urban Policy in Australia, Canada and the United States*,

Research Monograph no. 40, Canberra, Australian National University, 1985.

Leo, Christopher, "The Urban Economy and the Power of the Local State," in Frances Frisken (ed.), *The Changing Canadian Metropolis: A Public Policy Perspective*, Vol. 2, Toronto, Canadian Urban Institute, 1994.

_____, "The Erosion of Unicity and the 1992 Civic Election," in *Institute of Urban Studies Newsletter*, Winnipeg, University of Winnipeg, Autumn 1992.

_____, *Strong Government, Weak Government: Classifying Municipal Structural Change*, Research and Working Paper no. 23, Winnipeg, Institute of Urban Studies, University of Winnipeg, 1986.

_____, *The Politics of Urban Development: Canadian Urban Expressway Disputes*, Monographs on Canadian Urban Government, no. 3, Toronto, Institute of Public Administration, 1977.

Leonard, Jean-Francois and Jacques Leveillee, *Montreal After Drapeau*, Montreal, Black Rose Books, 1987.

Levine, Allan, (ed.) *Your Worship: The Lives of Eight of Canada's Most Unforgettable Mayors*, Toronto, James Lorimer, 1989.

Lightbody, James, "With Whom the Tolls Dwell: The Great Edmonton Telephone Dispute, 1984-1987," in *Canadian Public Administration*, Spring 1989.

_____, "The Reform of a Metropolitan Government: The Case of Winnipeg," in *Canadian Public Policy*, Autumn 1978.

_____, "The Rise of Party Politics in Canadian Local Elections," *Journal of Canadian Studies*, February 1971.

Lindblom, Charles E., *The Policy Making Process*, Englewood Cliffs, Prentice-Hall Inc., 1980.

_____, *The Intelligence of Democracy*, New York, The Free Press, 1965.

Lithwick, N. H., *Urban Canada, Problems and Prospects*, Ottawa, Central Mortgage and Housing Corporation, 1970.

----------, and Gilles Paquet (eds.) *Urban Studies: A Canadian Perspective*, Toronto, Methuen, 1968.

Loreto, Richard and Trevor Price, *Urban Policy Issues: Canadian Perspectives*, Toronto, McClelland & Stewart, 1990.

Lorimer, James, "Introduction: The Post-developer Era for Canada's Cities Begins," *City Magazine Annual 1981*, Toronto, James Lorimer and Company, 1981.

_____, *The Developers*, Toronto, James Lewis and Samuel, 1978.

_____, *A Citizen's Guide to City Politics*, Toronto, James Lewis and Samuel, 1972.

_____, *The Real World of City Politics*, Toronto, James Lewis and Samuel, 1970.

_____ and Carolyn MacGregor (eds.), *After the Developers*, Toronto, James Lorimer and Company, 1981.

_____ and E. Ross (eds.), *The City Book: The Planning and Politics of Canada's Cities*, Toronto, James Lorimer and Company, 1976.

Loughlin, Martin, David Gelfand et al, *Half a Century of Municipal Decline, 1935-1985*, London, George Allen & Unwin, 1986.

Lowe, Jeff, "Winnipeg: User-Unfriendly," *City Magazine*, Spring 1988.

Lowi, Theodore, *The End of Liberalism*, 2nd Edition, New York, W. W. Norton, 1979.

Lustiger-Thaler, Henry (ed.), *Political Arrangements: Power and the City*, Montreal, Black Rose Books, 1992.

_____, "On Thin Ice: Urban Politics in Montreal," *City Magazine*, Spring 1993.

Makuch, Stanley M., *Canadian Municipal and Planning Law*, Toronto, Carswell, 1983.

Magnusson, Warren, "The Local State in Canada: Theoretical Perspectives," *Canadian Public Administration*, Winter 1985.

_____, "Urban Politics and the Local State," *Studies in Political Economy*, 16, 1985.

_____, "Community Organization and Local Self Government" in Lionel D. Feldman (ed.), *Politics and Government of Urban Canada: Selected Readings*, Toronto, Methuen, 1981.

_____, "Metropolitan Reform in the Capitalist City," in *Canadian Journal of Political Science*, September 1981.

_____, "The New Neighbourhood Democracy: Anglo-American Experience in Historical Perspective," in L. J. Sharpe (ed.), *Decentralist Trends in Western Democracies*, London, Sage Publications, 1979.

_____ and William K Carroll, Charles Doyle, Monika Langer and R. B. J. Walker (eds.) *The New Reality: The Politics of Restraint in British Columbia*, Vancouver, NewStar Books, 1984.

_____ and Andrew Sancton (eds.), *City Politics in Canada*, Toronto, University of Toronto Press, 1983.

Manitoba, Government of, *Proposals for Urban Reorganization in the Greater Winnipeg Area (White Paper)*, Winnipeg, Queen's Printer, 1970.

Manitoba Royal Commission on Local Government Organization and Finance, Winnipeg, Queen's Printer, 1964.

Masson, Jack, *Alberta's Local Governments and Their Politics*, Edmonton, University of Alberta Press, 1985.

_____, "Decision-Making Patterns and Floating Coalitions in an Urban City Council," *Canadian Journal of Political Science*, March 1975.

_____ and James D. Anderson (eds.), *Emerging Party Politics in Canada*, Toronto, McClelland and Stewart Limited, 1972.

McDavid, James and Brian Marson (eds.), *The Well-Performing Government Organization*, Toronto, Institute of Public Administration, 1991.

_____ and Gregory K. Schlick, "Privatization Versus Union-Management Cooperation: The Effects of Competition on Service Efficiency in Municipalities," in *Canadian Public Administration*, Fall 1987.

McEvoy, John M., *The Ontario Township*, University of Toronto, Political Studies, 1st series no. 1, 1889.

McIver, J. M., "Survey of the City Manager Plan in Canada," *Canadian Public Administration*, Fall, 1960.

Mellon, Hugh, "Reforming the Electoral System of Metropolitan Toronto," in *Canadian Public Administration*, Toronto, Spring 1993.

Miles, Simon R.(ed.), *Metropolitan Problems*, Toronto, Methuen, 1970.

Milner, Henry, "The Montreal Citizens' Movement: Then and Now," Hanover, Quebec Studies, No. 6, 1988.

_____, *The Long Road to Reform: Restructuring Public Education in Quebec*, Kingston and Montreal, McGill-Queen's University Press, 1986.

Minister of Urban Affairs, *Strengthening Local Government in Winnipeg: Proposals for Changes to the City of Winnipeg Act, Discussion Paper*, Winnipeg, February 27, 1987.

Ministry of Municipal Affairs (Ont), *Toward an Ideal County*, January, 1990.

_____, *Report of the Consultative Committee to the Minister of Municipal Affairs, County Government in Ontario*, Toronto, January 1989.

_____, *Report of the Advisory Committee on County Government, Patterns for the Future*, Toronto, 1987.

_____, *Joint Services in Municipalities*, Toronto, April 1983.

_____, *Performance Measurement for Municipalities*, Toronto, 1981.

Montgomery, Byron, *Annexation and Restructuring in Sarnia-Lambton*, Local Government Case Studies #4, London, University of Western Ontario, 1991.

Morgan, David R., *Managing Urban America*, Belmont, Wadsworth Publishing Company Inc., 1979.

Municipal Finance Officers Association of Ontario and Association of Municipal Clerks and Treasurers of Ontario, *Innovative Financing: A Collection of Stories from Ontario Municipalities*, Toronto, 1993.

Municipal Submission to the first National Tri-Level Conference, Policies, Programs, and Finance, Ottawa, 1972.

Municipality of Metropolitan Toronto, *The Crumbling Financial Partnership*, Toronto, March 1989.

Munro, W. B., *American Influences on Canadian Government*, Toronto, Macmillan, 1929.

Naisbitt, John, *Megatrends*, New York, Warner Books, 1982.

New Brunswick, Government of, *Local Government Review Panel, Miramichi City: Our Future - Strength Through Unicity*, and *Greater Moncton Urban Community: Strength Through Cooperation*, April 1994.

_____, *The Commission on Land Use and the Rural Environment: Summary Report*, Fredericton, April 1993.

_____, *Strengthening Municipal Government in New Brunswick's Urban Centres*, Ministry of Municipalities, Culture and Housing, December 1992.

Niagara Region Study Review Commission, 1975-1977, Report (W. L. Archer, Commissioner), Toronto, Ministry of Treasury, Economics and Intergovernmental Affairs, March, 1977.

Niagara Region Review Commission, Report (Harry Kitchen, Commissioner), Toronto, Ministry of Municipal Affairs, 1989.

Nova Scotia, Government of, *Interim Report of the Municipal Reform Commissioner, Cape Breton County*, Department of Municipal Affairs, July 8, 1993.

_____, *Task Force on Local Government*, April 1992.

Nowlan, David and Nadine Nowlan, *The Bad Trip*, Toronto, New Press/House of Anansi, 1970.

O'Brien, Allan, *Municipal Consolidation in Canada and its Alternatives*, Toronto, Intergovernmental Committee on Urban and Regional Research, May 1993.

_____, "Holding Pattern: A Look at the Provincial-Municipal Relationship," in Donald C. MacDonald (ed.), *Government and Politics of Ontario*, Toronto, Nelson, 1985.

_____, "The Ministry of State for Urban Affairs: A Municipal Perspective," in *The Canadian Journal of Regional Science*, Halifax, Spring 1982.

_____, "Local Government Priorities for the Eighties," in *Canadian Public Administration*, Spring 1976.

Ontario Economic Council, Government Reform in Ontario, Toronto, 1969.

_____, *Municipal Reform: A Proposal for the Future*, Toronto, 1971.

_____, *Municipal Fiscal Reform in Ontario: Property Taxes and Provincial Grants* (by John Bossons et al) Toronto, 1981.

Osborne, David and Ted Gaebler, *Reinventing Government*, New York, Penguin Books, 1993.

Ottawa-Carleton Regional Review, (David Bartlett, Chairman), Phase I Report: Accountability and Representation and Phase II Report: Functions and Finances, Toronto, Ministry of Municipal Affairs, 1989.

Ouellet, Lionel, "La Privatisation: Un Instrument de Management Public?" in *Canadian Public Administration*, Winter 1987.

Peckham, Donald, "Amalgamation Program Undertaken in the Province of Newfoundland and Labrador," in *The Boardroom Files*, Halifax, Maritime Municipal Training and Development Board, Spring-Summer 1993.

Persky, S., *The House That Jack Built: Mayor Jack Volrich and Vancouver City Politics*, Vancouver, Newstar Books, 1980.

Peters, Evelyn J., *Aboriginal Self-Government Arrangements in Canada, Background Paper 15*, Kingston, Institute of Intergovernmental Affairs, Queen's University, 1987.

Peters, Thomas J., *Thriving on Chaos*, New York, HarperCollins Publishers, 1988.

_____ and Robert H. Waterman Jr., *In Search of Excellence*, New York, Warner Books, 1982.

_____ and Nancy Austin, *A Passion for Excellence*, New York, Random House, 1985.

Peterson, Paul E., *City Limits*, Chicago, University of Chicago Press, 1981.

Phillips, E. Barbara and Richard T. LeGates (eds.), *City Lights: An Introduction to Urban Studies*, New York, Oxford University Press, 1981.

Plunkett, T. J., *City Management in Canada: The Role of the Chief Administrative Officer*, Toronto, Institute of Public Administration of Canada, 1992.

_____, "Municipal Collective Bargaining," in *Collective Bargaining in the Public Service*, Toronto, Institute of Public Administration, 1973.

_____, *The Financial Structure and the Decision Making Process of Canadian Municipal Government*, Ottawa, Central Mortgage and Housing Corporation, 1972.

_____, *Urban Canada and its Government*, Toronto, Macmillan, 1968.

_____ and Meyer Brownstone, *Metropolitan Winnipeg: Politics and Reform of Local Government*, Berkeley, University of California Press, 1983.

_____ and Katherine Graham, "Whither Municipal Government," *Canadian Public Administration*, Winter 1982.

_____ and James Lightbody, "Tribunals, Politics and the Public Interest: The Edmonton Annexation Case," in *Canadian Public Policy*, Spring 1982.

_____ and G. M. Betts, *The Management of Canadian Urban Government*, Kingston, Queen's University, 1978.

_____ and W. Hooson, "Municipal Structure and Services: Graham Commission," *Canadian Public Policy*, Summer 1975.

Poole, Robert W. Jr., *Cutting Back City Hall*, New York, University Books, 1980.

Price, Trevor (ed.), *Regional Government in Ontario*, Windsor, University of Windsor Press, 1971.

Provincial-Municipal Council, Inc., *Brief to the Policy and Priorities Committee of the Government of New Brunswick, Re The Unconditional Grant to Municipalities and Related Matters*, Fredericton, October 11, 1988.

Regional District Survey Committee, *Summary Report of the Regional District Survey Committee*, Victoria, Queen's Printer, 1986.

Reid, Barton, "City Beat," *City Magazine*, Winter 1992/1993.

Report of the Advisory Committee to the Minister of Municipal Affairs, on the Provincial-Municipal Relationship (Hopcroft Report), Toronto, January 1991.

Report and Recommendations, Committee of Review, City of Winnipeg Act, Winnipeg, Queen's Printer, October 1976.

Report by the Task Force on Representation and Accountability in Metropolitan Toronto, *Analysis and Options for the Government of Metropolitan Toronto*, November 1986.

Report of the Task Force on Nonincorporated Areas in New Brunswick, Fredericton, Queen's Printer, 1976.

Report of the Municipal Study Commission (Parizeau Report), Montreal, Union of Quebec Municipalities, December 1986.

Report of the Special Representative (Drury Report), *Constitutional Development in the Northwest Territories*, Ottawa, 1980.

Report prepared by the British Columbia Ministry of Municipal Affairs, Recreation and Culture and the Union of B.C. Municipalities, *Financing Local Government*, September 1988.

Richardson, Boyce, *The Future of Canadian Cities*, Toronto, New Press, 1972.

Richmond, Dale, "Provincial-Municipal Transfer Systems," in *Canadian Public Administration*, Summer 1980.

_____ and David Siegel (eds.) *Agencies, Boards and Commissions in Canadian Local Government*, Toronto, Institute of Public Administration, 1994.

Neil Ridler, "Fiscal Constraints and the Growth of User Fees Among Canadian Municipalities," *Canadian Public Administration*, Fall 1984.

Robinson, Ivan, "Managing Retrenchment in a Public Service Organization," in *Canadian Public Administration*, Winter 1985.

Rosenblom, Richard S. and John R. Russell, *New Tools for Urban Management*, Boston, Harvard University Press, 1971.

Roussopoulos, Dimitri (ed.), *The City and Radical Social Change*, Montreal, Black Rose Books Ltd., 1982.

Rowat, Donald, *International Handbook on Local Government Reorganization*, Westport, Greenwood Press, 1980.

_____, *Your Local Government*, Toronto, Macmillan, 1975.

_____, *The Canadian Municipal System*, Toronto, McClelland and Stewart Limited, 1969.

Rothblatt, Donald N. and Andrew Sancton (eds.), *Metropolitan Governance: American/Canadian Intergovernmental Perspectives*, Berkeley, Institute of Governmental Studies Press, 1993.

Royal Commission on Education, Public Services, and Provincial-Municipal Relations in Nova Scotia. Report (John Graham, Commissioner), Halifax, Queen's Printer, 1974.

Royal Commission on Metropolitan Toronto. Report (H. Carl Goldenberg, Commissioner), Toronto, Queen's Printer, 1965.

Royal Commission on Metropolitan Toronto. Report (John Robarts, Commissioner), Toronto, Queen's Printer, June 1977.

Royal Commission on the Future of Toronto Waterfront, *Regeneration: Toronto's Waterfront and the Sustainable City*, Toronto, 1992.

Royal Commission on Municipal Government in Newfoundland and Labrador. Report (H. Whalen, Commissioner), St. John's, Queen's Printer, 1974.

Rutherford, Paul (ed.), *Saving the Canadian City: The First Phase 1880-1920*, Toronto, University of Toronto Press, 1974.

Rutter, Laurence, *The Essential Community: Local Government in the Year 2000*, Washington, International City Management Association, 1980.

Ryan, Claude, Minister of Municipal Affairs, *Quebec, The Sharing of Responsibilities Between The Government and Municipalities: Some Needed Adjustments*, 1990.

Sancton, Andrew, *Governing Canada's City Regions: Adapting Form to Function*, Montreal, Institute for Research on Public Policy, 1994.

_____, "Canada as a Highly Urbanized Nation," in *Canadian Public Administration*, Fall 1992.

_____, "Provincial-Municipal Disentanglement in Ontario: A Dissent," in *Municipal World*, July 1992.

_____, *Local Government Reorganization in Canada Since 1975*, Toronto, ICURR Press, April 1991.

_____, "Montreal's Metropolitan Government," Hanover, Quebec Studies, No. 6, 1988.

Scanlon, J., "Board of Control: Its Merits and Defects," *Canadian Public Administration*, Fall, 1960.

Schneider, Mark, *The Competitive City*, Pittsburgh, University of Pittsburgh Press, 1989.

Seidle, Leslie (ed.), *Rethinking Government: Reform or Revolution*, Montreal, Institute for Research on Public Policy, 1993.

Sewell, John, *The Shape of the City*, Toronto, University of Toronto Press, 1993.

_____, *Prospects for Reform*, Research Paper 180, Toronto, Centre for Urban and Community Studies, University of Toronto, January 1991.

_____, *Up Against City Hall*, Toronto, James Lewis and Samuel, 1972.

Sharpe, L. J. (ed.), *The Local Fiscal Crisis in Western Europe, Myths and Realities*, London, Sage Publications, 1981.

_____, "Failure of Local Government Modernization in Britain," *Canadian Public Administration*, Spring 1981.

_____ and K. Newton, *Does Politics Matter?*, Oxford, Clarendon Press, 1984.

Shortt, Adam, *Municipal Government in Ontario, An Historical Sketch*, Toronto, University of Toronto Studies, History and Economics, vol. II, no. 2, undated.

_____, and Arthur G. Doughty (eds.), *Canada and its Provinces: A History of the Canadian People and Their Institutions*, Toronto, Glasgow, Brook and Company, 1914.

Siegel, David, "Reinventing Local Government: The Promise and the Problems," in Leslie Seidle (ed.), *Rethinking Government: Reform or Revolution?*, Montreal, Institute for Research on Public Policy, 1993.

_____, "Disentangling Provincial-Municipal Relations in Ontario," in *Management*, Toronto, Institute of Public Administration, Fall 1992.

_____, "City Hall Doesn't Need Parties," *Policy Options*, June 1987.

_____, "Provincial-municipal relations in Canada: An Overview," *Canadian Public Administration*, Summer 1980.

Smith, Patrick J., "Regional Governance in British Columbia," in *Planning and Administration*, 13, 1986.

_____, "Open Government: Recent Policy Options and Applications in Canada," in *Planning and Administration*, 11, 1984.

Stanbury, W.T., *Business-Government Relations in Canada: Influencing Public Policy*, Scarborough, Nelson Canada, 1993.

Stein, David Lewis, *Toronto for Sale: The Destruction of a City*, Toronto, New Press, 1972.

Stelter, Gilbert A. and Alan F. Artibise (eds.), *Power and Place: Canadian Urban Development in the North American City*, Vancouver, University of British Columbia Press, 1986.

_____, *Shaping the Urban Landscape*, Ottawa, Carleton University Press, 1982.

_____, *The Canadian City: Essays in Urban History*, Toronto, Mc-Clelland and Stewart Limited, 1977.

_____, "Urban History Comes of Age: A Review of Current Research," *City Magazine*, vol. 3 no. 1, September/October 1977.

Stewart, John, *The Responsive Local Authority*, London, Charles Knight and Co. Ltd, 1974.

_____ and Gerry Stoker, *The Future of Local Government*, London, Macmillan Education Ltd., 1989.

Stoker, Gerry, *The Politics of Local Government*, London, Macmillan Education Ltd., 1988.

_____ and Stephen Young, *Cities in the 1990s*, Harlow, Longman, 1993.

Stone, Clarence N. and Heywood T. Sanders (eds.), *The Politics of Urban Development*, Lawrence, University Press of Kansas, 1987.

Task Force on Housing and Urban Development. Report, Ottawa, Queen's Printer, 1969.

Task on Local Government, *Report to the Government of Nova Scotia*, April 1992.

Task Force on Nonincorporated Areas in New Brunswick. Report, Fredericton, Queen's Printer, 1976.

Tennant, Paul, "Vancouver Civic Politics, 1929-1980," in *B. C. Studies*, no. 46, 1980.

_____ and David Zirnhelt, "Metropolitan Government in Vancouver: the strategy of gentle imposition," *Canadian Public Administration*, Spring 1973.

Tiebout, Charles, "A Pure Theory of Local Expenditures," *Journal of Political Economy*, vol. 64.

Tindal, C. R., *Municipal Councillor's Course*, Kingston, St. Lawrence College, 1994.

_____, *You and Your Local Government*, Whitby, Ontario Municipal Management Institute, 1988.

_____, *Structural Changes in Local Government: Government for Urban Regions*, Monographs on Canadian Urban Government, no. 2, Toronto, Institute of Public Administration of Canada, 1977.

Tri-Level Task Force on Public Finance. Report (3 volumes), Toronto, Queen's Printer, 1976.

Vaillancourt, F., "Financing Local Governments in Quebec: New Arrangements for the 1990s," in *Canadian Tax Journal*, vol. 40, No. 5, 1992.

Walisser, Brian, *Understanding Regional District Planning: A Primer*, Victoria, Ministry of Municipal Affairs, June 1987.

Weaver, John C., *Shaping the Canadian City: Essays on Urban Politics and Policy, 1890-1920*, Monographs on Canadian Urban Government, no. 1, Toronto, Institute of Public Administration of Canada, 1977.

Weller, G. R., "Local Government in the Canadian provincial north," *Canadian Public Administration*, Spring 1981.

Whalen, H. J., *The Development of Local Government in New Brunswick*, Fredericton, 1963.

Whittington, Michael S. and Glen Williams (eds.), *Canadian Politics in the 1990s*, Third Edition, Scarborough, Nelson Canada.

Whittle, Alan, "Running for City Council: Lessons from a first time candidate," *City Magazine*, Spring 1992.

Wichern, Phil H., *Evaluating Winnipeg's Unicity: Citizen Participation and Resident Advisory Groups, Research and Working Paper no. 11*, Winnipeg, Institute of Urban Studies, University of Winnipeg, 1984.

_____, *Evaluating Winnipeg's Unicity: The City of Winnipeg Act Review Committee, 1984-1986, Research and Working Paper no. 26,* Winnipeg, Institute of Urban Studies, University of Winnipeg, 1986.

Wildavsky, A. H. *The Politics of the Budgetary Process,* Boston, Little Brown, 1974.

Yates, Douglas, *The Ungovernable City,* Cambridge, M.I.T. Press, 1977.

Index

Urban Development, 223-24
Federation of Canadian Munici-
palities, 223, 225, 228, 229-31,
236
Federation of Prince Edward Island
Municipalities, 233. *See also*
Municipal associations
Feldman, Lionel, 122, 143, 234-35
Fiebig, Rick, 219
Finance. *See* Provincial-local finan-
cial relations
Fowler, 7, 69, 84, 85, 250, 273
Fredericton, 31, 55, 115
Frisken, 70, 222, 264, 271-72
Front d'action politique (FRAP),
257
Gaebler, Ted, n340, 362
Gardiner, Fred, 92, 103, 107, 128
General vote elections. *See* At large
elections
Global economy, 10, 66
Godfrey, Paul, 158
Goldenberg, H. Carl, 78
Goldrick, Michael, 263
Governance, 339, 341
Graham Commission (NS), 135-36
Graham, Katherine, 82, 122, 234-35,
329
Grants, 10, 78-80, 209-10, 215-16
Greater Toronto Area (GTA), 94,
98, 100, 134, 328
Gretzky, Wayne, 341
Guelph, 57
Gutstein, Donald, 221, 250, 254-55
Gyford, John, 326

Halifax, 28, 136, 138, 242, 290
Hall, Barbara, 266, 273
Hamilton, 181, 353
Harcourt, Michael, 254, 256
Hawrelak, William, 268
Head of council, 161-62, 178
Hellyer, Paul, 223, 224
Henley Commission Nfld), 140
Hickey Report (Ont), 130, 183, 187

Higgins, Donald J. H., 28, 30, 32,
108, 242, 250, 277, 327
Hodgetts, Dr. Charles, 50
Hopcroft Report (Ont), 202
Hudson's Bay Company, 33, 34, 37
Hull. *See* Outaouais
Hunter, Floyd, 303-04

Illingworth, Dick, 155
Immigration, 13, 16, 17, 20, 45, 46,
222. *See also* United Empire
Loyalists
Incrementalism, in policy making,
296-99
Independent Citizens Election
Committee (ICEC), 251
Information age, 10, 63, 98, 303
Infrastructure, 228-29, 332
Intergovernmental relationships. *See*
Federal Government and also
Tri-Level Relations
Isin, 5, 25

Jacobs, 7, 84
Juba, Stephen, 75, 104, 286
Justices of the peace. *See* Courts of
Quarter Sessions
Kaplan, Harold, 42-43, 60, 81, 92-
93, 103, 276, 306
Keating, Michael, 60
Kelso, J.J., 49
Keynes, John Maynard, 293
Kingston, 20, 154, 168-69, 193, 218-
19
Kitchen, Harry, 198
Kitchener-Waterloo, 347
Kraemer, Kenneth L., n283, 294
Laval, 343
Layton, 2, 265-66, 270
Leo, 111, 254, 313
Lethbridge, 36
L'Heureux, Jacques, 337
Liberal party, in municipal elec-
tions, 267, 290
Lightbody, James, 154, 175, 290